The Incredibly
Strange Features
of Ray Dennis Steckler

ALSO BY CHRISTOPHER WAYNE CURRY

*Film Alchemy: The Independent Cinema
of Ted V. Mikels* (McFarland, 2013 [2008])

The Incredibly Strange Features of Ray Dennis Steckler

Christopher Wayne Curry

McFarland & Company, Inc., Publishers
Jefferson, North Carolina

ISBN (print) 978-1-4766-8936-4
ISBN (ebook) 978-1-4766-4768-5

LIBRARY OF CONGRESS AND BRITISH LIBRARY
CATALOGUING DATA ARE AVAILABLE

Library of Congress Control Number 2022046360

© 2023 Christopher Wayne Curry. All rights reserved

*No part of this book may be reproduced or transmitted in any form
or by any means, electronic or mechanical, including photocopying
or recording, or by any information storage and retrieval system,
without permission in writing from the publisher.*

Front and back cover artwork by Tom Bagley

Printed in the United States of America

*McFarland & Company, Inc., Publishers
Box 611, Jefferson, North Carolina 28640
www.mcfarlandpub.com*

Acknowledgments

Julie Marie Curry (for her near-unwavering patience and support, especially during the writing of the Ray Dennis Steckler adult films), John W. Curry (R.I.P.), Carolyn Brandt (this book would not be near as fetching without your gracious input), Laura H. Steckler (for giving me the time of day when I was certain she wouldn't), Gary Kent, Raleigh Bronkowski (for his expertise in the world of movie ads), Tom Bagley (for, at the least, his bad-to-the-bone artwork), Boyd Rice (for graciously allowing the use of Ray's words in his *Incredibly Strange Films* book interview), Jim Morton, Michael Weldon, Rob and Cathy Tharp, Joe O'Connell, David Dent, Jean Coffinberry, James Elliot Singer, Buddy Barnett, Michael Copner, Rob Spay, xhamster.com (for providing me with free streams of movies that I did not have to buy), Jonathan Ross and *The Incredibly Strange Film Show*, Joe Bob Briggs.

A very special thank you to Patrick M. Leer for his invaluable knowledge and guidance in the editing of this work.

Unless otherwise noted, photos and illustrations have been culled from the personal collections of the author, Carolyn Brandt, Laura Steckler and Raleigh Bronkowski.

I'm recording history and this is how it happened
and what happened.
—David F. Friedman, from the documentary
Sex & Buttered Popcorn (1989)

The falcon has molted. The fat man bowls alone.
But the drive-in will never die.
—Joe Bob Briggs' sign-off in the video series
The Sleaziest Movies in the History of the World (1990)

Table of Contents

Acknowledgments   v
Preface   1
Introduction   6

Part One: The Films of Ray Dennis Steckler   13
   Wild Guitar (1962)   13
   Goof on the Loose (1963)   22
   The Incredibly Strange Creatures Who Stopped Living and Became Mixed-Up Zombies!!? (1963)   24
   The Thrill Killers (1964)   45
   Rat Pfink a Boo Boo (1966)   65
   The Lemon Grove Kids Meet the Monsters (1967)   79
   Body Fever (1969)   96
   Sinthia: The Devil's Doll (1970)   110
   Blood Shack (1971)   120
   The Hollywood Strangler Meets the Skid Row Slasher (1979)   134
   Las Vegas Serial Killer (1986)   144

Part Two: The Adult Films of Ray Dennis Steckler   153
   Introduction   153
   The Films   154

Part Three: Unfinished Films, Unreleased Films and Compilations   191

Part Four: Homage and Memorabilia   198

Part Five: The Interviews   207
   High Hopes to Hard Knocks: Carolyn Brandt on Living and Working with Ray Dennis Steckler   207
   Growing Up Steckler: A Conversation with Laura H. Steckler   218

Gary Kent: The Danger God Speaks   225

Have Talent, Will Travel: A Conversation wwith Cult Movie Star
Ron Jason   230

Conclusion   239

Bibliography   243

Index   245

Preface

Ray Dennis Steckler, a staple among independent moviemakers (H.G. Lewis, Ted V. Mikels, Ed Wood, Al Adamson *et al.*) deserves more than his "footnote" in the cinematic history books. The forementioned have compendiums and documentaries dedicated to their craft, but none until now on Steckler. So here it is, bound and in print for the world to see, should they indeed want to see it.

Maybe the world is not even aware a book on Steckler and his work is in order. In truth, why would they? He did not create the nudie-cutie like Russ Meyer.

Ray Dennis Steckler in 2004 (courtesy Media Blasters).

He did not create the gore genre like H.G. Lewis and he did not bother running amok with those tried-and-true ingredients like Al Adamson. The only thing Steckler was guilty of was creating a Steckler movie, and that is where pinning down this low-budget auteur can get tricky.

Steckler's declaration to interviewer Boyd Rice in the book *The Incredibly Strange Films* (p. 36) says all that really needs to be said: "I'm not saying I'm a great filmmaker or anything; I try to just be different. It's so easy to copy someone else and I just don't do that."

An examination of Steckler's film work reveals a singular voice that pushes his films into unique territories. Furthermore, scenarios unfold that belong solely to the mind and cinematic world of Steckler's making. This voice pervades Steckler's films, influencing them visually and stylistically, giving a tactile quality and gravity to an otherwise wholly exploitative body of work.

Now, getting straight on with it, no matter how likable, none of Steckler's films are remotely perfect. All of them were made with cripplingly low budgets. Heck, early on, Steckler could not even get the title card correct to his 1965 Batman and Robin spoof. He opted instead to stand behind the largely confusing (and inane) title *Rat Pfink a Boo Boo*.

Most of Steckler's movies are at least entertaining, but a few, frankly, border on tedium. Still, Steckler had an unbridled passion for his craft that tended to skew even the simplest of traditional moviemaking parameters. His work resided within an idiom that attracted as many viewers as it repelled. Like his old friend Ted V. Mikels, he was a man seemingly gone mad with a movie camera.

Make no mistake about it. Steckler's films harbor no hidden subtexts, social or political undertones. Their existence is merely testament to the passion of the human spirit. Steckler is a unique man with unique visions made all the more so by his, ostensibly, self-imposed disorganization. A script (if there even was one) and the shooting schedule were completely arbitrary and was seen as only a loosey-goosey guideline.

Judging from his cinematic output, Steckler clearly had no desire to operate within the expected norms of filmmaking. It was the Wild West as far as he was concerned; shoot first and ask questions later (and, more times than not, that meant questioning himself). Steckler never thought his films were anything other than what they were; warts and all, he accepted them. "Gooble gobble."

Steckler aims his camera and shoots without permission. He shoots without permits. Legend has it for one film he hijacked a parade without permission or permits. Was it the element of surprise that allowed him to get away with it? Almost nothing could stop this renegade and his guerrilla style of moviemaking. Damned and determined to a fault, whatever the show was, it would go on.

Sometimes these films move along at a pace only Steckler understood. With interviewer John Roberts on the video *Steckler Interviews Volume #1*, he argued the merits of "Real" time vs. "Reel" time, with the director preferring the former. He may have favored "Real" to "Reel" but he was still working with film. Despite his predilections, "Reel" time is assured.

With Steckler's admitted affection for filming in "Real" time, it is curious he did not apply that shooting method more often to the documentary. Furthermore, the 1960s and '70s were chock full of those cinematic oddities called mondo movies. These films were made quickly and cheaply, and for decades they were wildly popular. Surely there was room for *Mondo Steckler* or at least a Steckler tourist travelogue.

Within the frames of Steckler's films, anything can happen, and that can include nothing happening. Sometimes the on-screen action is mind-boggling, while at other times it is mind-numbing. It is all a part of the director's sleight of hand, erratic style and allure. Moreover, his films possess interesting storylines with interesting characters played by actors with interesting faces. Arch Hall Jr., Atlas King, Carolyn Brandt and Steckler himself all sported unforgettable mugs.

The notion that these types of films see completion and ultimately screentime is fascinating. In fact, their mere existence is oft-times more intriguing than the films themselves. It is a head-scratcher for the uninitiated. But for the seasoned viewer of ultra-low budget cinema, there is a complicity with the filmmaker's intentions, no matter how misguided or mishandled they might appear to be.

Furthering this notion, director Frank Henenlotter (*Basket Case, Brain Damage*) offered this to Andrea Juno in *Incredibly Strange Films* (p. 10):

> Often through bad direction, misdirection, inept direction, a film starts assuming surrealistic overtones. This takes a dreadfully

clichéd story into new frontiers—you're sitting there shaking your head, totally excited, totally unable to guess where this is going to head next, or what the next looney line out of someone's mouth is going to be. Just as long as it isn't stuff you regularly see. I'll never be satisfied until I see every sleazy film ever made—as long as it's different, as long as it's breaking a taboo, whether deliberately or by misdirection. There's a thousand reasons to like these films.

Henenlotter's comment may not have been leveled at Steckler's films directly, but there is little doubt his films are unpredictable, surreal and downright looney. Steckler would have it no other way. The filmic phenomenon "paracinema" might come to mind, but it is unlikely to have ever crossed Steckler's.

French moviemaker Michel Lemoine stated during an interview on the Mondo Macabro DVD release of his 1974 film *Seven Women for Satan*, "So what if they're just B-films? These guys, with their shoestring budgets, have created incredible films just because they loved cinema. They were mad for it. They didn't care about being rich. They just loved what they did."

There is a good chance Lemoine has not heard of Steckler, but in five short sentences he is spot-on in regards to his cinematic ethos. Steckler was "mad" about making movies. He "loved" making movies and even on "shoestring" budgets some of them were incredible. In retrospect, Lemoine's next-to-last sentiment might have been a wee off target. Steckler may have not known for certain he *wanted* to be rich, but there is no way he would not have given it a shot.

When it came to making movies, Steckler accepted the medium, but otherwise threw all conventions to the cosmos. He rooted around for odd angles and emerged with something resembling a marketable piece. He managed to stay just enough off the mark to confound even the more hardened of filmgoers and critics. Armed with a movie camera rather than an electric guitar, Steckler was constantly in search of the cinematic riff no one had seen or heard.

Case in point; Steckler shot *Bloody Jack the Ripper* in 1972 and purportedly sat on it for ten years. The idea was to complete the picture a decade later, giving it an "authentic" "passage of time" look which in actuality would be "real." He incorporated a unique way to break away from film's norms and possibly generate a new film form. Steckler claims that no one else has ever done this on purpose. He may be right.

Then what of Steckler's roadshowmanship? His ballyhoo and promotional gimmicks were rivaled by few. Hallucinogenic Hypno-Vision: simply glorious. By the thousands, people lined up around the blocks to experience the latest "Terrifying New Screen Innovation." This *innovation* consisted of teenage theater employees in rubber monster masks rushing the audience with rubber axes. Sometimes the film's creator would also be in costume. Steckler hammered and nailed this curious gimmick time and time again with great success.

Also, prepare to marvel at a time when a few thousand dollars and a few friends could put a feature-length film in theaters. Additionally, a snappy ad campaign and a goofy gimmick could not hurt either. The aforementioned, along with the desire and drive to transport these films from town to town and strike up theatrical engagement deals, helped as well. Unquestionably, Steckler's mindset was the cornerstone by which he saw his films to completion, compromises and all.

Another intriguing aspect to these films: Steckler rarely had the time or funds to create a set on a stage. Generally, he scouted locations that required very little in the way of modifications or dressing. These locations perfectly echoed their time and place in history. The architecture, furniture, decor and various accoutrements all reflected the very moment the films were shot. All of those seldom-noticed nuances help elevate the director's work from mere pop culture or entertainment to archival cinematic time capsules.

What will not be on display is a pseudo-analytical dissection of Steckler's work. If some film scholar wishes to address the social and political climate of 1964 and insist that Steckler was observing those ills within the frames of *The Thrill Killers,* then more power to them. That is not happening here. Move along, folks, nothing subversive to see here. Steckler's films were made for fun and meant to be fun. It is only entertainment. It is only a movie.

Many secondary sources have been utilized since Steckler passed away in 2009. Several direct quotes were sourced from the audio commentaries provided on the eight Media Blasters DVDs of his films. These and all other quotes have been credited within the body of this work.

Steckler's films, like so many others of their ilk, existed outside of the Hollywood norm. They were promoted and exhibited apart from the accepted confines of cinematic convention. Therefore, he was allowing these works to live and breathe without the moviemaking machine's death grip. Additionally, Steckler's films thrived merely by word of mouth and midnight screenings. Ultimately, without Hollywood's input, these types of films managed not only to exist, but also declare and sustain an almost legendary status.

Steckler's "adult" titles will not be discussed at great length. They are here, however, represented with as much praise as they deserve. Not Steckler's proudest moments, but they are part of his movie making canon. Their inclusion was deemed significant enough to endure.

Almost in closing, Steckler dug into his filmmaking projects like a one-man dynamo. He tore the accepted technique to ribbons, then processed and released the finished product. Almost without fail, he presented the public with something wholly unique. This was something they had never quite imagined experiencing. Oftentimes he was financing his own projects, so his imagination was allowed to run amok. There was no need to fence in that unhinged thought-processing. Rather, he would allow it to creep, ooze and smear itself across the screen.

This is not so much a critical study of Steckler's work, but an attempt to view these films in a different light. There are many books on this type of cinema and trashing Steckler's work seems to be the norm. That is entirely too easy. But finding ways to re-evaluate these films is the goal. Having said that, it is important to note that Steckler's "classic" era films (1963–1970) are expressive in similar ways such as: camerawork, lighting, sound design, editing and/or pacing. However, as the '70s rolled on into the '80s, Steckler seemed to have given up on any kind of artistic style or he simply stopped caring what his films looked like or how they played to an audience.

Also, the hope is that there is something within these pages to help arm the reader when encountering someone like the character of actress Honey Whitlock (Melanie Griffith) from John Waters' *Cecil B. Demented*. She states,

"Hollywood makes the best films in the world and I am proud to be a part of that system." Cecil's exasperated and frustrated response is at once hilarious and telling: This statement causes the guerrilla-style filmmaker to seethe. It is certainly worth mentioning that Cecil is also a real-to-reel kind of director.

Anyone reading this has most likely experienced that sort of cinematic stand-off and has caught themselves passionately defending their favorite low-rent director and/or movie. An immediate retaliation to Ms. Whitlock's assertion could be, "Oh yeah? Got any idea where the awarding winning cinematographer Laszlo Kovacs cut his teeth?" It is unlikely the answer will be forthcoming and the first round is won, providing the answer has been committed to the memory banks.

In closing, Steckler considered his cinematic exercises more adventures than moneymaking enterprises. By the director's own admission, he should have cared more about the process of making movies. But the experiences while making them seemingly outweighed the need to create art. Some may consider them silver screen pollution, but for other viewers they are a breath of filmic fresh air. There are no other movies like Steckler's and there are no two Steckler movies alike.

Introduction

Raymond Dennis Steckler was born January 25, 1938. From the hospital, he was taken to 242 South 10th Street in Reading, Pennsylvania. Growing up, Ray loved his neighborhood, but years later his mother reminded him that it was a slum. Reading was known as "The Pretzel City." Steckler frequented the pretzel manufacturers who gave the youngster their damaged goods. The enterprising Steckler slipped into local bars and sold the defective snacks to the tipsy ones for pocket money.

Soon "The Pretzel Kid" expanded his business to mangled cigars. His grandmother worked for Yocum Brothers Cigars and happily collected the floor sweepings for her grandson to peddle. Steckler figured that half a cigar was better than no cigar at all. Busted pretzels and broken cigars hawked by some street kid certainly aided in coloring the picture of Steckler's poor neighborhood. It also demonstrated a never-say-die work ethic that Steckler carried with him into adulthood.

Steckler was primarily raised by his grandparents as a result of a broken home. The grandparents were also responsible for nurturing young Ray's love of photography and the movies. Before Ray was ten years old, his grandparents presented him with a Donald Duck camera. The small fry's obsession with photography began at that early age.

Approximately six years later, his stepfather made him a gift of an 8mm home movie camera. In an act that would help define his moviemaking approach, Steckler went about shooting amateur pirate and Western films with his friends. This cocktail of cohorts and cameras would serve Steckler well as a template for his future cinematic endeavors. Steckler relayed this to interviewer Boyd Rice in *Incredibly Strange Films* (p. 37): "They were just fun things. Today, kids 14 or 15 are out there making epics, but in those days an 8mm camera was very expensive—just to shoot film was expensive. At that time, it was all fun and games for me."

After graduating from Reading High School in 1955, Steckler served in the Army from 1956 to 1959. It should come as no surprise that he was an Army photographer. He served in Korea and spent a year in the Army Pictorial Service of the Signal Corps. Shortly after the soldier's stint at Kaufman Astoria Studios, he was discharged as a sergeant.

Wasting little time after receiving his release papers, Steckler headed out to the highway with a friend to Hollywood. The goal was to break into the motion picture industry. The soon-to-be cult movie legend would find work rather quickly.

Ray Dennis Steckler's Army photograph, from the late 1950s (courtesy Laura H. Steckler).

An exasperated Cassavetes presented the film at the Cannes Film Festival, and it won the Critics' Award. After this achievement, Lion International (based in England) distributed the film throughout Europe, where it was quite successful. Eventually, to the dismay of Hollywood, the film was reasonably well-received in America. Actor-stuntman Gary Kent wrote in *Shadows & Light: Journeys with Outlaws in Revolutionary Hollywood* (p. 53), "John Cassavetes and his small band of banditos had started a genuine revolution, not only in story content, but in the way a film is filmed, from finance to distribution. The crisp honesty of their work spawned an important new visionary force in American cinema, the *truly independent* motion picture."

This is not to suggest that indie filmmakers did not exist before 1958. On the contrary, Kroger (*Mom and Dad*) Babb, Dwain (*Maniac*) Esper and Dan (*A Night at the Follies*) Sonney had all been making small fortunes roadshowing their features in tents and drive-ins across America.

Not long after landing in Hollywood, Steckler found himself working as a prop man on arguably the most ambitious effort in low-budget cinema, *The World's Greatest Sinner*. This almost mythical tale of a disenfranchised insurance salesman turned rockabilly god has baffled cinephiles for decades with its hardlined push and pull between atheism and Christianity. The film was written, produced and directed by its star, the equally mythical Timothy Carey. Carey was a favorite of Stanley Kubrick's; decades later, Quentin Tarantino wrote the part of Joe Cabot in *Reservoir Dogs* specifically for him. (A snafu involving Carey and co-producer Harvey Keitel ended the short-lived

What also helped was that, in 1948, the Supreme Court ruled that five major Hollywood studios (and three smaller ones) were running an illegal monopoly by casting, producing, distributing and exhibiting their films when and where they decided. These studios had exclusive contracts with the actors, writers and directors and they also owned the theaters where their films played. Now, all of a sudden, a theater was free to exhibit a non–Hollywood feature (i.e., a foreign film), and this gave way to the independent moviemaker. A decade later, Ray Dennis Steckler would cash in on that golden ticket.

Couple the above with John Cassavetes' 1958 film *Shadows,* about interracial relationships in New York City. It was a powder keg of a topic that Hollywood was not ready to touch. Cassavetes was forced to fund his cinematic yarn with money that he had raised from various investors. Still distributors turned him and his project away.

union and the part wound up in Lawrence Tierney's lap.)

Regarding *The World's Greatest Sinner*, Steckler told interviewer Boyd Rice in *Incredibly Strange Films* (p. 43), "[I]t was not a great movie by any means. Timothy Carey had some great ideas but he lacked technique—he didn't know how to put them together."

A newspaper ad for *The World's Greatest Sinner* when it played at Hollywood's Vista Theater, circa 1960. The Vista opened in 1923 presenting vaudeville productions as well as films; in the '60s, it began showing softcore sex movies before later moving onto hardcore and eventually gay porn. The theater can be seen in the Ed Wood documentary *Flying Saucers Over Hollywood* (1992). In July 2021, director Quentin Tarantino purchased the theater (image and commentary courtesy film historian and archivist Raleigh Bronkowski).

In a 1966 interview with Alex de Laszlo for *Uno Mas* magazine in 1966, Steckler recalled,

> I was living in Tim's garage with two dogs, a boxer named Caesar and some poor old German shepherd. He did run out of money and I stayed with him for as long as I could. We'd shoot a little here and there, and then all of a sudden it became years. He was always good at buying a lot of lunches. He would always pick up the tab. I think he was kinda hurt that I didn't finish the movie.
>
> ... Tim Carey was having an adventure—whatever happened—he thought it was great. As far as the script goes, it never made sense at the beginning when I read it. He didn't care about that 'cause he just threw the pages away anyway.

Steckler was given the job of assistant cameraman when the initial director of photography was fired. This was quite a step up from props. It is noteworthy that *The World's Greatest Sinner* featured plenty of gut-bucket garage rock music throughout (the title track was penned and performed by Frank Zappa). Steckler had to have picked up a thing or two from Carey in that department, as many of his upcoming films heavily emphasized the use of music.

As pointed out, *The World's Greatest Sinner* took years to complete, and before Carey could settle on a final cut, Steckler was on to other projects. Steckler's hometown friend Rick Dennis had been Carey's lighting technician. One day Steckler took a ride with his friend over to the set of *Wild Ones on Wheels* and things changed. Originally, the film was entitled *Drivers to Hell* and began production in 1959. It did not see a silver screen until half a decade later. Dennis snagged a bit part while Steckler took on the role of jive-talking thug Preacher Man in front of the camera and the job of cinematographer behind.

While visiting the soundstage of the

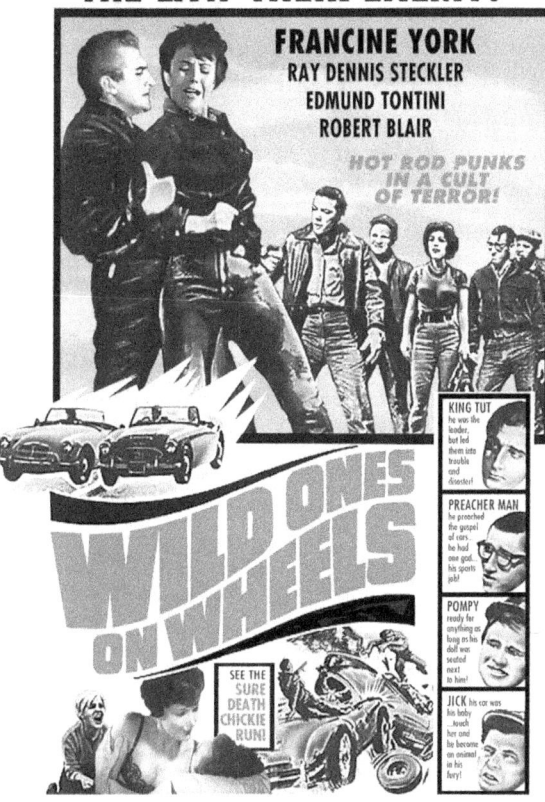

Poster art for *Wild Ones on Wheels* (1962) (author's collection).

in San Francisco. She later finished her high school tenure at the Immaculate Heart in Hollywood. At both institutes, she was at the top of her class, earning her the nickname "The Brain."

In 1954, Carol's stepfather enrolled her in the Elizabeth Holloway School of the Theater, 1511 Gough Street, San Francisco. There she studied diction and drama and continued to nurture her love of the theater (musicals in particular) and movies. A couple of years later, the family made the move to Hollywood where Carol soon found herself working with a small theater group headed by David Bond. She was active in this group when she answered the call to audition for *The Magic of Sinbad*.

Still in the throes of their brand-new love huddle, Steckler was living in his car. His dwelling was an early 1950s television series pilot *The Magic of Sinbad*, Steckler spotted a hottie. Shooting out of his league, he pursued the raving beauty relentlessly for months. She gave in to his amiable but persistent pressures and agreed to a date. She was and still is the inimitable Carolyn Brandt. Supposedly, Steckler's catch visited her astrologer, who informed her, "There's a definite link between the two of you."

Carolyn Brandt was born Carol Glenn on the twentieth of November 1940 at the New York City Physicians Hospital in Queens, New York, at 5:15 in the afternoon. The family later relocated to the West Coast where Carol would attend the Convent of the Sacred Heart

Carolyn Brandt and Steckler as Carrie Erskine and Charlie Smith on the set of *Body Fever* (1969) (courtesy Carolyn Brandt).

Nash Rambler which he parked on Santa Monica Boulevard. The Rambler is considered America's first successful compact car, so Steckler was low on square-footage. However, Brandt stopped by daily to deliver her brand spanking new beau breakfast. They married in 1961 (and divorced in 1980) and worked together in films for more than two decades.

During this time, Steckler was doing some grunt work at Universal Studios. Attempting to impress his employers, he hurried along rolling a wooden A-frame lighting rig through the backstage area to its next destination. En route, the overzealous newbie nearly ran it onto Alfred Hitchcock. Later in the day, Steckler was given his "walking papers" and shown the door.

In 1961, Steckler took yet another cinematography job on a cheapie entitled *Secret File: Hollywood*. As Michael Weldon describes it in his *Psychotronic Video Guide* (p. 490), "This absurd b/w movie looks like it was made in the '40s at PRC. I don't remember *ever* seeing a movie with so many shots of painfully visible boom microphones (the cameraman was Ray Dennis Steckler!)."

The "PRC" Weldon wrote of was Producers Releasing Corporation. PRC was one of Hollywood's less distinguished studios. It made low-budget (or "Poverty Row") movies. It is unlikely that Steckler included this low-rent job on his résumé as his name was not even listed in the credits. *Secret File: Hollywood* also featured Carolyn in an uncredited role as a gal getting her groove on to some beatniks with bongos. Steckler also got the ball rolling with Arch Hall, Sr., who played the TV Director.

About the time of *Secret File: Hollywood*, Steckler and Brandt toiled as ushers at the Ivar Theater on Hollywood Boulevard. The Ivar, built by restaurateur Yegishe Harout, presented stage plays for its first two decades. In its heyday, the upper crust of L.A.'s society could catch *Cat on a Hot Tin Roof* and other productions on that level. By the early '70s,

Poster art for *Secret File: Hollywood* (1961) (author's collection).

the 350-seater had a very different clientele as it began exhibiting porno films in and around burlesque performances. The irony here is that by the early '70s, Steckler would be creating "adults only" fare that perhaps played at the Ivar.

Nineteen sixty-two would prove to be an even busier 12 months for young Steckler. His upcoming career choices would help characterize his work ethic for years to come. Rekindling his working relationship with Arch Hall, Sr., Steckler stepped in to do some second unit photography on the horror-comedy potboiler *Eegah*. Steckler also turned in an acting performance as Mr. Fishman and, no great surprise, Carolyn Brandt played his kissy-face girlfriend.

Eegah was Arch Sr.'s second production to star his handsome teenage son Arch Hall, Jr., and his electric guitar.

Newspaper ad for the Ivar Theater in Hollywood. Adult film star René Bond would have performed there in the mid–1970s. The theater opened in 1951 featuring legit live stage productions and this continued on into the '60s. But by the next decade, the Ivar was a burlesque theater. It has had facelifts and various owners and is still in operation today (image and commentary courtesy film historian and archivist Raleigh Bronkowski).

Their first feature together was the 1961 hot rod movie *The Choppers*. Both were made under Arch Sr.'s Fairway International banner, and in the coming years four more such projects reached the silver screen.

Before Fairway was even a glimmer in Sr.'s eye, he left the comfort of his hometown in South Dakota and got himself some work in Hollywood as a stuntman. These stuntman stints earned him some acting roles but mostly just bit parts in Westerns from 1938 to 1945. After that, everything seemed to come to a grinding halt. For 16 years, Arch Sr. amassed no more screen credits. But by then, his son was a teenager and a good-looking one at that.

Hall Sr. saw great potential in his son's looks and talents and set about turning him into an Elvis Presley type.

The institutionalizing of Fairway International was the first order of business and from there *The Choppers* was given its life. Hall turned a profit and wagered it against the success of *Eegah*. Now, Hall had two hot tickets in his hands and decided to go for the third.

As far as Arch Jr.'s involvement went, Steckler laid it out for Boyd Rice in *Incredibly Strange Films* (p. 55):

Arch Jr. is a nice kid, and he was a good singer, but he didn't seem to have his heart in it; he never seemed to really care. It was all just handed to him on a silver platter. And I always felt, to be honest, that Arch was just attempting to re-live his youth through his son. It was a big disappointment that his son didn't want to continue in the business.

The minute his son stopped making movies, Arch stopped making movies. He didn't have the desire to go out and tackle the industry without his kid in the picture.

Steckler may have nailed the Halls' sentiments, but he failed to mention two quasi-important facts. One was that Arch Sr. had been an Air Force pilot (his tenure was satirized in the 1961 film *The Last Time I Saw Archie*). Junior followed in the footsteps laid by his father and became a commercial airline pilot. The other note of interest is that Senior wrote the screenplay for Ted V. Mikels' 1971 cult classic *The Corpse Grinders*. So the old man *did* plunge his hands into the movie industry fire without the driving catalyst of his son, at least once.

In any event, fate brought this trio together and their next project was a doozie which entertains audiences to this day. Arch Sr. would write and produce, Arch Jr. would star and compose the music (incidental cues included) and Steckler would act and direct. It may have not been the elusive trifecta, but for the most part it was a harmonious union that would give us *Wild Guitar*.

August 6, 1965, the Jet Drive In in Montgomery, Alabama, focused on the types of movies that defined the ozoner scene with many of its ads classics of the era—perfect for Steckler's 1960s movies. This ad depicts two Steckler-related films starring Arch Hall, Jr., *The Choppers* (1961) and *Eegah* (1961) (image and commentary courtesy film historian and archivist Raleigh Bronkowski).

Part One

The Films of Ray Dennis Steckler

Wild Guitar (1962)

Synopsis from Pressbook

Guitar-playing country boy singer Bud Eagle (Arch Hall, Jr.) motorcycles from Spearfish, South Dakota, to Hollywood to crash show business. He wants to make money to put his brother through college. After aimless wanderings around famed Hollywood landmarks, he finds he has 15 cents left. This he spends for coffee and a doughnut in the Coffee Cup Cafe and meets Vickie Wills (Olympic skating star Nancy Czar) and goes with her to a TV Talent Search Show.

Vickie persuades Hal Kenton to put Bud on the show when a contestant gets stage fright and Bud captures the audience with one of his "homemade" songs. Seen by the big recording company promoter, Mike McCauley (Arch Hall, Sr.), Bud is signed and "imprisoned" in a swank Sunset Strip apartment where he turns out one smash hit after another, amassing a fortune for Mike McCauley (his manager) but gaining only a new suit and a gilded guitar for himself. He is the victim of Mike's "racket"—promoted with phony fan clubs and fads whereby the wild teenage rage is to wear "eagle feathers" and buy Bud's records like popcorn. Mike makes nothing but money while Bud works night and day. Mike even employs his bodyguard, Steak (Cash Flagg), to keep Bud's nose to the grindstone, never have a date, never see Vickie.

Bud learns, finally, what makes Mike tick and he returns disgustedly to the Coffee Cup Cafe to work as a dishwasher. He wants no more "phony business" and he wants to renew his acquaintance with Vickie Wills who he has not been allowed to see. While he temporarily gives Mike the slip, it is not without problems. He is kidnapped, bamboozled and brainwashed repeatedly. His honesty and integrity remain unshaken (as does his love for Vickie Wills) and when Mike McCauley tries to frame him, Bud fights back and wins the final round.

Then a miracle happens. Mike and Steak, the phony fan clubs and the kidnappers are converted to Bud's good, sound philosophy and the refreshing finale witnesses Bud and Vickie co-starring in a motion picture directed by (who else) Mike McCauley himself. *Wild Guitar* is full of action and hit songs.

Exploitation
(taken from pressbook)

1. "GUITARS: As a giveaway prize! Bud Eagle Guitars!"
2. "MUSIC: Sponsor a Guitar Festival!"
3. "MOTORCYCLES: Club Participation!"
4. "RADIO STATIONS: Tie in a contest with many avenues to pursue!"
5. "RECORD STORES: Hook-up with a record promotion!"
6. "HOLLYWOOD: Circuit financed trip to Hollywood, etc.!"
7. "FEATHERS: Offer free colored feathers to all girls to wear in their hair per fad shown."

Credits

Cast: Arch Hall, Jr. (Bud Eagle); Nancy Czar (Vickie Wills); Arch Hall, Sr. [as William Watters] (Mike McCauley); Cash Flagg [Ray Dennis Steckler] (Steak); Marie Denn (Marge); Robert Crumb (Don Proctor); Virginia Broderick (Daisy); Al Scott (Ted Eagle); William Lloyd, Jonathan Karle, Mike Treibor (Kidnappers); Paul Voorhees (Hal Kenton); Rick Dennis (Stage Manager); Carol Flynn [Carolyn Brandt] (Dancer); Raeme Patterson, Danny Silvers (Fan Club Leaders)

Production: Producer: Nicholas Merriweather [Arch Hall, Sr.]. Screenplay: Nicholas Merriweather [Arch Hall, Sr.], Robert O. Wehling. Additional Dialogue: Joe Thomas. Photographer: Joseph Mascelli. Second Unit Photographer: William Zsigmond [Vilmos Zsigmond]. Editor: Anthony Lanza. Art Director: Patrick S. Kirkwood. Production Manager: Don Russell. Music Director: Alan O'Day. Music Editor: Rod Moss. Sound Engineer: Samuel Kopetzky II. Director: Ray Dennis Steckler. 89 minutes. Black and White.

Featured Songs

"Theme from *Wild Guitar*," "Organ Twist," "Yes, I Will," "Judy Poody," "I'm Growin' Taller," "Money and Records," "Vickie, Run Vickie Run," "Daisy Dance," "Stairfall," "Steak's Theme," "The Kidnappers," "Bud and Steak Square Off," "Twist Fever" by Arch Hall, Jr.

Note: A promotional-only seven-inch single was given out to radio stations and theaters. The A-side sizzled with the "Theme from *Wild Guitar*" while the grooves of the B-side featured "Yes, I Will."

The Film

> We're gonna hit this town like a bomb!
> —Bud Eagle from *Wild Guitar*

Hot on the (w)heels of *Drivers in Hell*, Ray Dennis Steckler seamlessly throttled from adept cinematographer to driving and directing motion pictures. He did this alongside upstart B-movie mogul and producer Arch Hall, Sr. According to Steckler, Arch Sr., mover-and-shaker extraordinaire, decided to live out his musical and acting dreams through his son Arch Jr. The producer scraped together 30 grand (Steckler reported 12) to finance *Wild Guitar*. This was twice as much as his previous outing, which was his third in a string of six vicarious vanity pieces that were created to feature his son.

Hall Sr. was determined to make his son the star *he* never was. Whether it was though rock'n'roll or becoming a Hollywood leading man, Arch Jr. was going to get there one way or another. Previously,

Poster art for *Wild Guitar* (1962) (author's collection).

in 1961 and '62, Arch Sr. produced the campy drive-in features *The Choppers* and *Eegah* on the cheap. Knowing Arch Sr.'s predilections towards his son, it should come as no surprise these were, most definitely, cinematic vehicles for Arch Jr. Arch's charismatic offspring rocked out and acted out in them both.

Wild Guitar, Steckler's directorial debut, opens with some fantastic shots of Arch Jr. tooling through the desert on his motorcycle. These shots give way to highway shots that eventually give way to shots of early 1960s Los Angeles. Along the way, Steckler allows the viewer glimpses of Revue Studios, the Capital Records tower, the Pantages, Grauman's Chinese and Egyptian theaters and finally Dino's Lodge.

Arch Jr. is playing burgeoning rock star and fish-out-of-water hayseed Bud Eagle. Having motored straight from Spearfish ("Beerfish"?), South Dakota, he finds himself virtually busted, broke, thirsty and hungry. With a mere 15 cents to his cool-school name, Bud saunters into the dining area of Marge's Koffee Kup Cafe.

Once inside, Bud is eyed by three unnamed goobers (they think *he's* a hick), cafe owner Marge and the cute-as-a-button Vickie Wills. Upon closer inspection, a young boy can be seen sitting behind the goobers in a cowboy costume. It is unclear why he is there or what his relationship could possibly be to anyone in the restaurant. Steckler is an odd director and his placement of this youngster amongst these slacks is proof positive of his oddness.

The walls of the Koffee Kup Cafe sport one-sheets for *The Choppers*, *Eegah* and *Drivers in Hell* (aka *Wild Ones on Wheels*). This type of self-promotion is something Steckler would return to time and time again. It is as though the director was branding his films. (Note: If you are watching a movie and spot a Ray Dennis Steckler poster, then you are probably watching a Ray Dennis Steckler movie.)

After the off-putting glances and eye contacts, Bud drops his bags and pops a

Alternate poster art for *Wild Guitar* (1962) (author's collection).

squat on the counter stool nearest Vickie. Vickie is visibly taken aback by Bud's boyish charms and good looks. Bud is visibly nervous and awkward. Vickie, noticing that Bud has ordered the cheapest items on the menu, offers her plate of untouched food. Bud, hungry and embarrassed, sheepishly accepts.

Vickie bids him farewell, stands and nearly trips over Bud's guitar case. After a round of apologies and some additional conversation, it is revealed that Vickie is a dancer and Bud is a guitar player. Vickie has a gig on the Hal Kenton TV program and asks Bud to join her. Within seven minutes, these two have become friends. Forty-five minutes later, during their second date, they will fall in love. Even in 1962, Los Angeles was a fast town and Steckler was determined his characters would keep up.

The two soon-to-be love birds race off to the TV studio where Vickie is to do her swinging shimmy. She gyrates accordingly to the lo-fi garage rock, but the scene begins to breathe a visual life very different from the audio. While Vickie's dance moves are applicable to the music, the stark yet ominous backlighting gives the scene an artistic texture. It is an experimental technique that Steckler's lighting people and cinematographers would employ more than once throughout the film.

In real life, actress Nancy Czar's other foot-savvy moves included ice skating. Whether or not Steckler previously knew the extent of her skating talents is not known, but had it not been for an inexplicable turn of events it would not have mattered. As it happened, on February 15, 1961, 18 of the 19-member U.S. figure skating team were killed in a plane crash in Berg-Kampenhout, Belgium. The team was on its way to the 1961 World Figure Skating Championships in Prague, Czechoslovakia. The nineteenth member, Nancy Jean Czarnecki (aka Nancy Czar), missed the flight.

Originally the Vickie character was not in Arch Hall, Sr.'s script. Steckler explains her late-in-the-game placement to Boyd Rice in RE/Search's *Incredibly Strange Films* (p. 40): "I wanted to find a little extra kicker because I felt that Arch Hall, Jr., wasn't strong enough to carry the movie. I [thought] it would be nice if we had a girl who had a talent we could use in the movie—something entertaining. I remembered that she had come in for an ice-skating interview, so I said let's use her."

On with the film: Vickie returns backstage to a fawning Bud. The next act gets cold feet from nerves and vomits into a saxophone. Vickie insists that Bud take his place. Producer Hal Kenton concedes and after a messy entrance (tripping over a guitar cable and crashing to the stage floor on live television), Bud rocks the house with "Yes, I Will." Spearfish, South Dakota's finest, has been in Los Angeles no more than four hours and is already a star on the rise.

Fairway Records executive Mike McCauley trolls the Hal Kenton TV program for new talent. He is impressed with Bud and sends his goon Steak to fetch him. Steckler portrays Steak in a very heavy-handed manner ("slimy" as Steckler put it in numerous interviews) under the nom de screen Cash Flagg.

Originally a black actor was fitted for the role of Steak: Steckler's LACC classmate Eddie Rowan (or Roland; it has been printed both ways). Arch Sr. worried about audiences in the South, requested the role be recast. Thus, the legend that is Cash Flagg was born. Still, what is with this name that is clearly a fake? A few years later, actor-stuntman Gary Kent asked Steckler essentially the same question. He wrote in *Shadows & Light* (p. 72), "Because," he replied, with his lopsided Steckler grin, "I've been cheated out of my salary so many times, I want producers to know it's cash up front if they want me!"

Fairway Records lifts its name from Fairway International Films. In the "reel" world, Mike McCauley, played by Arch Hall, Sr. (credited as William Watters), heads Fairway Records. In the "real" world, Hall Sr. heads Fairway International Films. The organization appears to have exclusively represented the projects between Hall Sr. and his son.

As Arch Hall, Jr., recounted to Miriam Linna for her bio notes on the 2005 Norton Records release of *Wild Guitar: Arch Hall, Jr., and the Archers* (p. 9), "Fairway International was a pretty unique place. My dad bought the property at 2221 West Olive Avenue at Lincoln in Burbank in the late 1940s." Junior went on to tell how his father built a two-story office rental where they all more or less lived. "All" included actors, musicians, film crew members, his parents, his dog, Richard Kiel and a myriad of girlfriends. Apparently, the arrangement resembled something between a volunteer fire department and a brothel. The Archers recorded there and rooms were converted into sets for the movies filmed there. Junior summarized that Fairway International was more a form of "lifestyle" than merely a physical locale.

Bud and McCauley meet, and a record deal is promised along with some custom suits, a swanky pad and a new Fender Jazzmaster. This new guitar replaces his old ("It's probably got termites") Dan Electro. Bud falls over himself accepting the offer. The trap has been laid and McCauley is calling the shots ... for now. Still, there is more to come: a portable recording studio ("A midget tape recorder"), a backing band, a fan club and a groupie, all to sweeten the pot. For Bud, it is the deal of a lifetime. It is his dream come true.

McCauley launches a publicity campaign to squeeze maximum mileage out of his new "star." Gimmicks are employed and deployed; decoys are hired to tear Bud's clothes off in public. Some of these same plants will sport "eagle" feathers in their hair while giving lip service to Bud and his records. McCauley, pumping his fists, blurts out to his snide sycophants, "All right, gang, let's see you blast off with some smash success. Action means dollars!"

McCauley books nationwide

TV appearances at exorbitant dollar amounts. The shady manager even tells the media of the numerous record companies vying for Bud's attention, of which there are actually none … yet. In short order, compounding his control of Bud and his career, McCauley signs the fledgling rocker to Fairway Records. A deal of "eight sides" (four 7" singles) is struck without Bud's consultation or knowledge. His elation supersedes any rational thought.

Bud's new manager demands his complete devotion and undivided attention. The young guitarist is not necessarily thrilled with the rigid arrangement

On August 27, 1965, the Jet Drive In in Montgomery, Alabama, teamed with WHHY (1440 on the AM dial) for this great rock'n'roll show featuring Steckler's classic *Wild Guitar* (1962) starring Arch Hall, Jr., in one of his best performances. It's easy to wonder if the Fairway-International release of "Wild Guitar" backed with "Yes, I Will" was one of the records that were in its promotion. The Jet Drive In's most exciting, eye-catching ads were published in the '60s and early '70s (image and commentary courtesy film historian and archivist Raleigh Bronkowski).

but with stars in his eyes he complies. Loose ends must be sewn shut and the shifty Steak is sent to dispose of Vickie. Bud's brother Ted (who's only been mentioned in passing) is next on the short list to get the figurative ax. McCauley will focus Bud's efforts at any cost as he asserts, "It takes a lot of money to put a personality before the public."

McCauley wastes little time manipulating Bud with the simplest reverse psychology. Bud is so wide-eyed and naive that he is at once hilarious and pitiful. Still, as the press materials insist, "At the age of 18 [Hall Jr.] ranks with the top blues guitar players in the nation." In 1962 that may have been a stretch, but the statement transcends reality with non-reality. It sends up the very type of "phony" promo the character Bud Eagle will rail against.

Bud's star rises. He is on the ride of his life, but still he is methodically isolated from his former life and contacts. He is virtually being held hostage. His brother is kept at a distance, as is Vickie. The forlorn love interest even attends her suitor's shows in hopes of catching his attention. The desperate girl's efforts seem in vain as Bud is swept away in a sea of riotous and zealous fans.

Later, with an eagle feather tucked into the headstock of his Jazzmaster, Bud croons his current song "Vickie" before a live TV audience. Bud's "new" haunting sci-fi-surf-rock-love-song really is not all that new as it was performed a year earlier in *Eegah*. A reasonable deduction is that Steckler wanted to use the song and thus Nancy Czar's character became "Vickie." From there, the scene practically writes itself. Vickie is at home watching and has a hunch he is serenading her from the elaborate stage with the ornate sweeping ramp.

Carolyn Brandt, in an uncredited role, executes a floating, almost ethereal dance to the otherworldly sounds coming from the stage. Once again, the camera lens tells no lies and in this scene Ms. Brandt is a real looker.

Vickie literally runs to the TV station to reunite with Bud. Steak is waiting in the wings but is not quick enough to prevent their get-together. Bud wants to go someplace. Vickie suggests skating. They are off to her uncle's rink. It is after hours, so the couple have the place to themselves. On the ice, Vickie is a natural. Bud, on the blades, is a complete disaster despite assuring Vickie he had skated all the time. "I thought you meant roller skating," Bud exclaims.

Much has been made of the backlighting during this largely unnecessary and innocuous scene. Seemingly, its only real purpose for inclusion was to utilize Nancy Czar's real-life skating talents. Steckler claims that his cinematographer learned these lighting tricks from him and went on to win an award. Dubious claim or not, Vilmos Zsigmond (aka William Zsigmond) did indeed go on to be an award-winning cinematographer.

Born in 1930 in Hungary, Zsigmond worked with Steckler twice: handling second unit camera photography for *Wild Guitar* and later *The Incredibly Strange Creatures Who Stopped Living and Became Mixed-Up Zombies!!?* As Steckler predicted, Zsigmond won an Oscar in 1978 for best cinematography on Steven Spielberg's *Close Encounters of the Third Kind*.

After Steckler, but before his award-winning photography, Zsigmond continued cutting his cinematic teeth on a few of Al Adamson's most notable titles: *Psycho a Go-Go* (1965–67) and *Satan's Sadists* (1969). He later worked with John Boorman on *Deliverance* (1972) and with Michael Cimino on

The Deer Hunter (1978). From Steckler to Adamson to Boorman to Cimino to the Academy, Zsigmond became a legend in cinematography who worked all the way up to his death in 2016.

Regarding his cameramen's talents, Steckler relayed this much to film historian John Roberts for the video *Steckler Interviews #1*: "When you have someone like Willie Zsigmond, someone that talented, and you don't take advantage of his talent, you're losing it. I know directors who are just afraid that the cameraman is going to upstage them. They don't understand that the cameraman is amplifying what you are doing."

The other secret weapon Steckler had on hand was cinematographer Joseph V. Mascelli. Mascelli worked tirelessly on three of Steckler's career-defining films: *Wild Guitar, Incredibly Strange Creatures* and *The Thrill Killers*. Steckler leaned heavily on the natural talents and expertise of Mascelli's camera and lighting prowess. Mascelli had directed the cult classic *Monstrosity* aka *The Atomic Brain* in 1960.

Mascelli's claim to fame came in 1965 with the publication of his book *The Five Cs of Cinematography*. It has gone through numerous printings and, decades after it was first published, it's regarded as one of the classic texts on the subject. Still, prior to '65, Mascelli was handling the editing chores of the *American Cinematographer Manual*. This book is also an invaluable tool for the working cameraman. Mascelli was born in 1917 and died in 1981.

Back at the McCauley ranch, Bud runs into has-been rock star Don Proctor. Proctor had been McCauley's previous flavor-of-the-week performer. Bud's obviously a fan and welcomes the down-and-outer to partake in the wares behind his wet bar. Proctor gets smashed in record time, while explaining the score of the crooked manager's veritable musical white slavery racket. McCauley's *modus operandi* is to "cook" his books, snare all the profits while exploiting his talent and creatively bleeding them dry. Realizing that Proctor's position reflects his own future, Bud is suitably concerned. Yet, before he can approach his employer-captor he is kidnapped … for real.

The kidnapping is another sequence that was not included in the script. The film's running time was clocking in short, so Steckler took some liberties and gave the Koffee Kup Cafe goobers a job. Steckler adored vintage slapstick comedy and his kidnappers are obviously a Three Stooges or Bowery Boys send-up. The director revealed Hall Sr.'s stance, on the subject, to Boyd Rice in *Incredibly Strange Films* (p. 55):

> [H]e asked me to direct a film for him with his son. *Wild Guitar*. And he said, "Now, you mustn't do anything to distract from the script. You must do exactly what the script says." But since I'd never directed a movie, I figured I'd better do the best that I could. When I added in the early Lemon Grove Kids to the movie, Arch didn't like them at all—he thought they detracted from the story. So he cut out all the scenes with them: the kidnapping, everything, and then the movie only ran for something like 63 minutes.

The Koffee Kup Cafe goobers have a problem: Bud hates his arrangement with McCauley so much that he *wants* to be held for ransom. ("Hey, we got a nut on our hands.") Bud even encourages these halfwits to up their asking from 5,000 to 15,000. One of them asks for his autograph.

McCauley receives the ransom note and "shells out for a change." Steak dumps the loot in the specified garbage can and hides in the shadows. The goobers show up, find the scratch and do goober things. Steak locates the goobers' hideout and hits them up at gunpoint. They all flee, including Bud, and Steak retrieves McCauley's 15 grand.

Scam artist McCauley exploits Bud's disappearance as a publicity stunt: "Record sales will go to the top!" Bud hides out and washes dishes at Marge's Cafe and unites, once again, with the love of his life Vickie. Finally touching base with his brother Ted, Bud employs his sibling to "rat" him out. A Bud-McCauley encounter looms.

The tables are turning; *Bud's* trap is laid. Bud, knowing his popularity, demands a new bookkeeper and the dissolution of his "phony" fan club. Soon enough he will be calling the shots, but not before a physical confrontation with Steak. The lengthy and violent altercation is a result of McCauley realizing he has been recorded while giving Bud an incriminating list of demands and threats.

Steak's butt is kicked and McCauley, realizing his pinch, concedes to Bud's requests. The film ends with the making of a music video for "Twist Fever." Where, in 1962, this video would play is anyone's guess. Still, Steckler made the video, and perhaps history, 22 years before the advent of MTV.

In addition to the exploitation tactics, Arch Sr. booked a promotional tour for Junior and the Archers with Nancy Czar in tow. The itinerary had the band swinging into action before and/or after local premieres of *Wild Guitar*. They stomped through songs from the film, popular covers and joked around. Nancy, giving her go-go boots a breather, briefly interviewed Arch.

Initially, the Archers were to go out as a four-piece ensemble with dancing Nancy. For whatever reasons, bassist Deke Lussler was unable to make the trek. So the shows were performed with a truncated group consisting of Arch Jr. on vocals and guitar, Alan O'Day noodling the keys and Dave Sullivan kicking around the skins.

Arch Jr.'s rock'n'roll cavalcade concentrated its invasion on the South, New Orleans, Mississippi, Alabama, Louisiana and Florida being the primary targets. Rain or shine, the band played atop snack bars, makeshift platforms and gravel pits. They rubbed elbows with heroin-addicted strippers at one club, breakfasted on raw oysters at another and successfully crashed a teenybopper high school sock hop.

Along the way, the Archers received telephone threats from the locals and came face to face with some vicious Southern racism. "Coloreds" were forced to use separate rest rooms, store front entrances and drinking fountains while shunned as second-class citizens. It would be 19 months before President

Nancy Czar and Arch Hall, Jr., as Vickie Wills and Budd Eagle at the beach in the finale of *Wild Guitar* (1962) (author's collection).

Lyndon B. Johnson attempted to stamp out segregation by signing the civil rights bill that addressed this American atrocity. Turns out Arch Sr. was correct in his assessment of his film's Jim Crow–polluted Southern market.

The tour ended on the seventh of December 1962 in Pensacola, Florida, at the Twin Drive-In. The Archers jammed out on the back of a flatbed truck as the magnetic tape rolled; this tour wrap-up was recorded for posterity's sake. If the studio recordings, for the film, seem sluggish and uninspired, these live recordings do a damn fine job righting that wrong.

While breaking from the music, Arch steps up to the mic and thanks the theater for allowing them to perform. However, it is a generic pleasantry as he never specifies just which theater they are playing. This makes the recording thrifty fodder for exploitation that could easily be piped through the loudspeakers of any drive-in or hardtop across the country. This type of marketing tactic is not at all uncommon among seasoned exploiters.

Wild Guitar, as a film, is a product of its time. It may have been made in 1962, but Americans, as a collective, were still operating within the social parameters of the late '50s. This is not to suggest that Steckler's film is in any way an artistic observation of American's behaviors or thought processes. Its pedestrian direction is simply a reflection of what the producer desired.

Arch Hall, Sr., wanted a clean-cut movie about a clean-cut kid. Steckler followed orders and delivered a competent and fun film, even if it is somewhat dopey in its directness. The pressbook said it best: "*Wild Guitar* is aimed at wholesome but exciting family entertainment." But the theatrical trailer howls, "It's a frenzy of musical action!" This is hardly the case as *Wild Guitar* (despite its title) is nowhere near as wild or zany as Steckler's later efforts. But it is certainly worthy of a view or two or ten.

Goof on the Loose (1963)

Synopsis

A goof (Bert Leu Van) inadvertently parallels the universe of a drunk (Rick Dennis) and both manage to make a mess of one another's afternoon. At least a dozen zany characters are encountered within a cavalcade of wacky and unpredictable situations. These comical scenarios range from the innocuous to the hilariously perilous. In the end, no goof, nor drunk, nor loony characters were harmed in the making of this motion picture, thus proving that all is well that ends well.

Credits

Cast: Rick Dennis (The Drunkard); Bert Leu Van (The Goof); James Bowie (Native); Carolyn Brandt (Woman in Bathing Suit); Pat Kirkwood (Fisherman); Gene Pollock (Angry Neighbor); Ray Dennis Steckler (Mrs. Baits and Man/Woman Reading the Paper)

Production: Producer-Screenwriter-Director: Ray Dennis Steckler. Executive Producer: George J. Morgan. Associate Producer: Rick Dennis [as Richard J. Kozlowski]. Associate Producer: Don Snyder. Music: Andre

Brummer [as Henry Price] and Libby Quinn. Photographer: Ron McManus. Editor: Don Snyder. Art Director: Pat Kirkwood. Second Unit Director: James Bowie. 8 minutes. Black and White.

The Film

> Dedicated to the laugh makers of long ago.—dedication placard from *Goof on the Loose*

The years 1963 and '64 would be incredibly busy (and strange) years for Steckler. One of his greatest achievements in that 24-month stretch was his eight-minute short film *Goof on the Loose*. One year earlier, on *Wild Guitar,* Steckler virtually forced his love of slapstick comedy upon producer Arch Hall, Sr., in the form of the three kidnappers. This "lost" short has his adoration of *Keystone Cops*, Buster Keaton, Charlie Chaplin and the Bowery Boys on full display.

Goof on the Loose possibly marks the first official pairing of Steckler and producer George J. Morgan. In addition to this oddball short, the union led to four feature films in the coming years. It is likely that this initial Morgan-Steckler production was just the two men feeling out one another's work ethics. Or they were simply bored.

Arch Hall, Sr., was still in the wings. Hall's Fairway-International Pictures landed the distribution rights to the short subject but when and where it could have ever been screened is not known. As it is, the piece seems more experimental than remotely marketable.

The film's focus is on a goofball played by Bert Leu Van and his stumbling, bumbling shadow, a drunkard. This character is played by Rick Dennis. Rick was born Richard J. Kozlowski and uses said handle as associate producer on *Goof on the Loose*. Rick lived two houses down from Steckler in their hometown of Reading, Pennsylvania, from grade school through high school. When Steckler talked of his trip from the East to the West Coast to follow his moviemaking dreams, he often mentioned a friend being with him. It is quite likely that Rick Dennis was *that* friend. After all, Steckler and Dennis *had* previously worked together, in one capacity or another, on the films *The World's Greatest Sinner, Wild Ones on Wheels* and *Wild Guitar*. Interestingly enough, Dennis was cast as a salesman in the 1964 Arch Hall, Sr.–penned comedy *What's Up Front?*. Other present and eventual Steckler co-workers included Nancy Czar, Joan Howard, Jill Carson, Don Schneider, Vilmos Zsigmond and Laszlo Kovacs. *What's Up Front?* was more or less an extended Steckler family reunion.

In two years, Rick Dennis had five cinematic credits under his belt and must have felt confident in his relocation from Pennsylvania to Tinsel Town. But he called it quits in 1968. Bert Leu Van, the goof, called off Hollywood for good in 1964. Of this trio, only Steckler persevered.

As the film races along, it seems the Goof and the drunkard are oblivious to one another and their actions, but the cause and effect is the crux of the picture. The film works almost like a game of Mousetrap where every response creates a chain reaction. This accidental duo manages to get into as much madcap mischief, as humanly possible, in the film's short running time.

Loose goof and the drunk are pursued by a few who are less than impressed with their antics. This unlikely couple are repeatedly knocked out, knocked down and knocked around. They make out with hot chicks and they are tossed into the trunks of cars. Goof is bullied by a young boy with a lawnmower, another with a football, then later by a hip dude with a saxophone. The drunkard finds himself in everyone's way and is constantly being shoved or tripped. To get up or to stay down is the question.

For more fun, *Goof on the Loose* also features Carolyn Brandt in a one-piece, neighborhood friends and children, lifelong chums, a motionless Frankenstein's Monster, a jungle warrior and even a transvestite. The jungle warrior was played by James Bowie, who stuck with Steckler for three more films; they remained friends for life. The transvestite was amusingly played by Steckler, who had already taken a turn as the Mrs. Bates (*Psycho*) stand-in Mrs. Baits.

Goof on the Loose was shot in black and white in and around Echo Park Lake in Echo Park, Los Angeles. In keeping with his obvious homage, *Goof* was lensed without sound; cartoonish audio effects were added in post-production. Within the frames of *Goof*, all of Steckler's cinematic strengths are clearly visible and exhibited even if they are within family-friendly parameters.

The purposefully over-the-top performances combined with Steckler's fine camerawork and timing make this

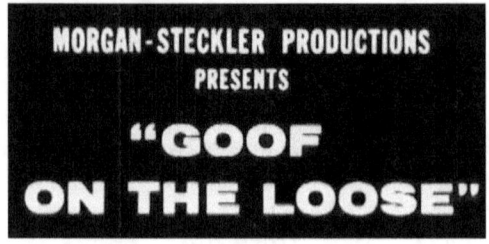

Title card for Steckler's early short film *Goof on the Loose* (author's collection).

breezy eight-minute movie an absolute delight. Judging from the results, it is easy to understand why Steckler continued to work with so many of the same cast and crew members. Easily, this film could have been paired with *The Lemon Grove Kids Meet the Monsters* which would pratfall its way through very similar territory.

The actual production dates and release dates of this film are not known. Steckler claimed in one interview that it was shot in 1958, in another interview '59. In 1974, Ron Haydock wrote for *The Monster Times* that the film came out in 1962. Many sources tag it with 1963 while the film itself says MCMLXIV—1964. In this book, it has been placed after *Wild Guitar* to highlight Steckler's eventual move from Fairway International to joining forces with producer George J. Morgan.

The Incredibly Strange Creatures Who Stopped Living and Became Mixed-Up Zombies!!? (1963)

Synopsis from Pressbook

The story revolves around a sinister gypsy fortune teller named Madame Estrella (Brett O'Hara) who with the help of her sister, Carmelita (Erina Enyo), a stripper, and a hunchback servant Ortega (Jack Brady) victimize people who come to the midway by hypnotizing them and throwing acid in their faces, disfiguring them so they look like monsters. She then locks them in cages like pets.

Marge (Carolyn Brandt), a dancer at a local nightclub, has a premonition of death and goes to see Estrella. Her suspicions are confirmed when Estrella turns up the death card. Marge becomes hysterical and starts to run out of the tent. In her excitement she discovers the caged monsters. Marge has discovered Estrella's secret—Marge must die.

With her sister Carmelita as bait, she lures Jerry (Cash Flagg) into the tent as he and his girlfriend Angie (Sharon Walsh) and his pal Harold (Atlas King) are walking down the midway. Angie becomes very annoyed because of the way Jerry is staring at Carmelita and leaves with Harold.

Later Jerry is hypnotized by Estrella with the aid of a Zodiac wheel. She commands him to kill Marge. He goes to the nightclub and during her dance number, he stabs her to death. Next morning Jerry can't remember what happened. He goes to see Angie to apologize and while talking to her by the pool, she starts to spin her umbrella. The spinning effect puts Jerry in a trance and he starts to strangle her thinking he is strangling Marge. He is stopped by her brother (Madison Clarke) and mother (Joan Howard) before he kills her.

Jerry runs away and hears on the radio about the death of Marge. He heads back to the midway. Before he arrives, Madame Estrella is visited by Stella (Toni Camel), a dancer in the girlie show. Stella had seen Marge run out of the tent and was curious to know what Estrella had predicted the future held for her. Estrella denies that Marge was there. Stella does not believe her—Stella must die.

When Jerry arrives at the midway, he is again hypnotized and sent to kill Stella. Returning to Estrella's tent still in a trance, she throws acid in his face and tells Ortega to put him in the cage. While doing this, the other monsters break loose and strangle Estrella, Ortega and Carmelita. They then terrorize the midway until they are shot by police.

In the meantime Angie, Harold and Madison are on their way to the midway to find Jerry. They arrive at Estrella's tent at the same time as the police. At this point Jerry comes out of the cage with his face all scarred and jumps out the window. He is chased by the police and his three friends. They plead with him to stop. He refuses and is shot.

Exploitation (taken from pressbook)

1. "Do not allow your patrons to miss the SHOCKING first three minutes of the film."
2. "Give away free records of the 'ZOMBIE STOMP' to the first 25 patrons each night."
3. "Sponsor a contest for the best MONSTER MASK made by your patrons."
4. "PERSONAL APPEARANCES by some of the young stars can be made available."
5. "Have the local disc jockey's play the 'ZOMBIE STOMP' on the air."
6. "Sponsor a ZOMBIE STOMP for the best ZOMBIE STOMPERS."

Lobby Promotion and Catch Lines (taken from the pressbook)

1. "This film is INHUMANELY SHOCKING!!"
2. "DANCING GIRLS MURDERED by the INCREDIBLE NIGHT CREATURES of the midway!"

3. "WEAK HEARTS—STAY AWAY!!"
4. "TWISTED MINDS MURDER FOR KICKS!"
5. "See CASH FLAGG, the HUMAN ZOMBIE, commit MURDER before your very eyes!"
6. "Meet face to face with the TORTURED and TWISTED EYES of CASH FLAGG!!"
7. "A picture you will want to forget before you go to sleep at night!"
8. "Don't miss the SHOCKING BEGINNING of this film!!"
9. "SEE THE 'ZOMBIE STOMP'!!!!"

Credits

Cast: Cash Flagg [Ray Dennis Steckler] (Jerry); Carolyn Brandt (Marge Neilson); Atlas King (Harold); Madison Clarke [Pat Kirkwood] (Madison); Brett O'Hara (Madame Estrella); Jack Brady aka Don Russell (Ortega); James Bowie (Emcee/Comedian); Toni Camel (Stella); Sharon Walsh (Angela); Joan Howard (Angela's Mother); Whitey Robinson (Drunkard); Neil Stillman (Barker); Erina Enyo (Carmelita); Bill Ward (Dancer); Gene Pollock (Night Club Manager); Son Hooker (Policeman); Steve Clarke (Second Policeman); Titus Moede (Hobo); Don Snyder (Don Snyder the Entertainer); Carol Kaye (Carol Kaye the Entertainer); Teri Randal (Teri Randal the Entertainer); Patrice Michaels, Pat Lynn, Betty Downing, Denise Lynn, Cindy Shea, Patti Crandall (Dancing Girls); Jill Carson (Girl in Dressing Room/Dancing Girl), Jeanette Briggs (Woman in Audience); Robert Silliphant (Second Barker); Laszlo Kovacs (Man at Carnival)

Production: Executive Producer: George J. Morgan. Photographers: Joseph Mascelli and William Zsigmond. Assistant Cameraman: Laszlo Kovacs. Original Story: E.M. Kevke. Screenplay: Gene Pollock. Script Supervisor: John McKenna. Music: Libby Quinn, Andre Brummer. Music Editor: Rod Moss. Choreographers: Bill Turner, Alan Smith. Makeup: Joan Howard. Special Makeup: Tom Scherman. Sound Recordists: Lee Strosnider, Ken Carlson. Art Directors: Mike Harrington, Patrick S. Kirkwood. Assistant Director: Don Russell. Editor: Don Snyder. Production Manager: Austin McKinney. Electrician: Pat Kirkwood. Gaffer: Jimmy Parks. Grip: Greg von Berblinger. Producer-Director: Ray Dennis Steckler. 80 minutes. Color.

Featured Songs

"It's Not You" by Carol Kaye

"How Do I Stand with Your Heart" by Don Snyder

"Shook Out of Shape" by Carol Kaye and the Stone Tones

"Choo Choo Cha-Bootchie" by Teri Randal

"Mixed-Up Zombie Stomp" by Libby Quinn

The Film

> It is a deep spinning hole. You feel yourself falling ... falling into that hole. Deeper ... deeper ... deeper into the spinning hole.—Madame Estrella from *The Incredibly Strange Creatures Who Stopped Living and Became Mixed-Up Zombies!!?*

Well, this is it, the jewel in Ray Dennis Steckler's cinematic crown. What a bizarre and deformed jewel it is, filmed entirely in Terrorama. In 1963, the director worked with the largest monetary budget he would ever have access to, 38 grand. The film was shot in 11 days with $5,000 spent on cast, $5,000 for crew, $6,000 for rentals (lights, cameras, sound equipment), $1,000 for music, $6,000 in editing and $15,000 printing the film.

At the age of 25, Steckler had left the Arch Hall, Sr., nest and teamed with producer George J. Morgan. Morgan, who had never even been in a film, simply wanted to work in the movies, behind the scenes and any other capacity. By Steckler's own admission, Morgan did not always understand the director's vision, but willingly went along with him just the same. So, with a new partner in crime (one less meddlesome than the previous), Steckler set about making the one film he would be best remembered for, *The Incredibly Strange Creatures Who Stopped Living and Became Mixed-Up Zombies!!?*

The theatrical trailer, radio spots and one-sheets all touted *Incredibly Strange Creatures* as "The World's First Monster Musical," as though the world had been waiting. The pressbook also declares the film some sort of "psychological warfare." That is some head-scratching overkill lurching towards the absurd. As it is, *Incredibly Strange Creatures* is at least a three-headed mutant—an odd collision of Grand Guignol theater, vaudeville and near family-friendly burlesque. Steckler often boasted of his Hollywood independence. Quite frankly, he loathed the Hollywood machine and its machinations, contrivances and attitudes.

Columbia caught wind of *The Incredibly Strange Creatures, Or Why I Stopped Living and Became a Mixed-Up Zombie.* Too similar in title was their current Stanley Kubrick production *Dr. Strangelove Or: How I Learned to Stop Worrying and Love the Bomb.* So Columbia set their legal dogs loose, five in all, and for months Steckler resisted. Exasperated by the ordeal, he called Columbia and asked to speak with Kubrick. Steckler offered *The Incredibly Strange Creatures Who Stopped Living and Became Mixed-Up Zombies* as an olive branch, with an alternate title. According to Steckler, Kubrick's reply was, "Fine, that's good. Okay. Wrap it up. Back to work."

As Steckler recounted in the audio commentary for Media Blasters' *Incredibly Strange Creatures* DVD release, "I

Poster art for *The Incredibly Strange Creatures Who Stopped Living and Became Mixed-Up Zombies!!?* (1963) (author's collection).

wanted something different. I wanted a long title because I had a small budget. In fact, I had such a small budget—well, anyway it was like a no-budget movie."

One has to wonder how a tiny $38,000 production piqued the interest of any executive at any major studio, but it did. It was not Steckler's last run-in with lawyers concerning his little movie. Nearly 45 years later, more litigators reared their heads.

Once Kubrick was appeased, the film was again underway. The opening scene consists of an incredible overview shot of the equally incredible Cyclone Racer roller coaster. This shot leads to spirited neon-drenched frames of amusement park thrill rides situated at the Pike in Long Beach, California. Then, within seconds, Steckler takes us to the carnival's midway.

The fully fabricated midway is easily the nerve center of the film. Its construction was on the seventh floor of a former Masonic Temple (owned by Rock Hudson) in Glendale. This period of the film's production was not without issues. Part of the Hollywood machination Steckler hated was the unions and he intended for his latest project to be free of their rigid parameters. He filled *Incredibly Strange Films* interviewer Boyd Rice in on some particularly pesky union reps (p. 42):

> There was this one union guy who chased me around for years. I'll never forget him. When we were shooting *Creatures* in Glendale, he somehow found out where we were. We were several floors up in this old temple. The place was loaded with people, extras, lights and sets—we had to hoist the sets up from the street and put them together in the temple. All these people driving by had been seeing these sets going up into the air. So, while we were filming, we put warning signs on the elevators, like "Danger." "Out of Order." The union people showed up looking for us and couldn't find us. They didn't think anyone could go up in the elevators, so they left.

As the film moves forward, Steckler's camera casually roams the midway and here the movie introduces its villain, Madame Estrella. The set is a darkened den draped in tapestries, mood-lit by colored lighting and a glowing crystal ball. Estrella is a gypsy fortune-teller-cum-disfigurement-queen played by Brett O'Hara.

Steckler had met O'Hara on the set of *Wild Ones on Wheels* where she and her boyfriend Mike Kannon had bit parts. O'Hara's claim to fame is that she was actress Susan Hayward's double and the resemblance is notable. Kannon's biggest claim to fame would be his multiple appearances in more Steckler movies.

Estrella is chatting it up with a hopeful suitor. The visibly drunken target is played by the film's producer George J. Morgan. According to Steckler, Morgan never touched the sauce, but here he does a fine turn as a slobbering drunk. Morgan slurs his way through his lines, telling Estrella that the only reason he comes around is to see her sister Carmelita. To Estrella's ears, those are fightin' words.

In a tizzy, Estrella calls for her assistant Ortega to take the insolent to the ground. When the boozehound is scuffled into submission, Estrella grabs a skull-and-crossbones–labeled bottle and spills its contents into the drunkard's face. The bottle contains sulfuric acid and the eating-away of the offender's face begins. Then he is whisked away to a cell, across the room, to be with Estrella's other "pets."

The film's set-up gives way to the animated title sequence, which was executed by Tom Scherman. It is as well done as any of its type. A grainy black and white picture of Cash Flagg (Steckler) is pushed to the forefront while creepy-crawly organs and synths make transcendental noises and sounds. Surely the audio creators were influenced by Bebe and Louis Barron and their spooky space-age electronic soundtrack for *Forbidden Planet* (1956).

Composer Libby Quinn's opening piece is less of a musical number and more of a ghostly (or better yet ghastly) soundscape. As the music and the credits move forward, the Cash Flagg image slowly deteriorates and rots before the viewer's eyes. It could easily be seen as Steckler's stab at Oscar Wilde's classic *The Picture of Dorian Gray*. Assumptions aside, the progression really is quite ghoulish, freaky and effective.

The remainder of the music was either provided or written by Henri Price (aka Andre Brummer). Price assisted Steckler in scoring his films for many years. Steckler had met Price while working on *Wild Ones on Wheels*. Price is probably best known for his work on Russ Meyer's flesh flick *Mudhoney*. Even though Meyer insisted that he hired a garage band to record hours of music from which he could pick and choose, the Henri Price connection is still assured.

Steckler's camera reveals a seedy part of town lined with neon advertising questionable theaters, cocktail lounges and dance halls. Steckler zooms in on the Four "O" Cafe sign. Curiously, the emcee–stand-up comedian calls the place The Hungry Mouth. The emcee was portrayed by James Bowie, who went on to bigger and badder things in one of Steckler's later films.

Inside, the first of many dance and musical routines is underway. A fetching young couple spin, twist and pose through two minutes of an undanceable tune. It is sort of ballet, but mostly not. The film's choreographer Bill Turner dances as the character Bill Ward alongside Steckler's wife Carolyn Brandt.

Brandt is playing Marge Neilson, who has an unquenchable thirst for hooch, similar to Madame Estrella's latest acid bath victim. Marge tosses some spirits back while the set reveals Arch Hall, Jr.'s, return to the Steckler screen. This time Arch can be found on a *Wild Guitar* pressbook tacked haphazardly to the tipsy dancer's dressing room wall.

Marge's dance partner Bill Ward (aka Bill Turner) was often seen on 1950s television. He concentrated his career on Westerns and had roles dating back to 1943 where he played an orphan in *The Amazing Mrs. Holliday*. By 1963, Turner's

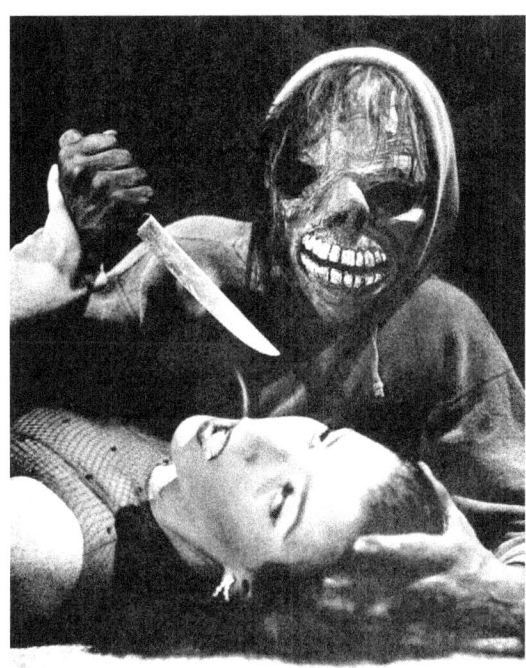

A mixed-up zombie (actor unidentified) attacks Marge Neilson (Carolyn Brandt) in a still promoting *The Incredibly Strange Creatures Who Stopped Living and Became Mixed-Up Zombies!!?* (1963). This scene was not actually in the film (author's collection).

acting days were mostly over but he and associate Alan Smith teamed to form a Hollywood dance troupe. Steckler culled the majority of this film's "talent" from their troupe.

Marge's boss is portrayed by Gene Pollock, who co-wrote the script. He was also responsible for the script for *Wild Ones on Wheels*. Pollock's character is concerned with his star's drinking habits and asks, "Why don't you lay off that stuff?" Marge snorts, "Why don't you lay off the father routine?"

Due to her incessant boozing, it is obvious that Marge is anxious and/or teetering on the verge of a breakdown. It is not revealed why. She is terrified of black cats and looks for answers within the pages of an astrology magazine. Soon she will seek the advice of a fortune teller. A fortune teller named Madame Estrella.

The film cuts to a modest room with one chair, a day bed, a ceramic zombie statue and a carved tiki head. Here Steckler reveals two of the film's stars, Jerry and Harold. Jerry, as critic Joe Bob Briggs describes him, is the "thrill-seeking slacker." He's played by none other than Cash Flagg (i.e., Steckler) and his nearly unintelligible friend Harold is played by Atlas King (aka Dennis Kesdekian, aka The Greek Fabian).

King had only recently immigrated to the States from Greece when he started making movies with Steckler. The fledgling U.S. citizen's English was not up to snuff, so he learned his lines phonetically. It is possible he knew what he was saying, but as commentator Joe Bob Briggs puts it on the audio commentary track of the Media Blasters DVD, "Atlas King was the actor who can't speak English, but he does anyway."

Before King's involvement, Steckler had agreed to a 50-50 split with George J. Morgan with the producer scraping his take straight off the top. King, sensing some monetary unrest, gave Steckler $300 to help finish the movie. Steckler had Carolyn and baby Linda to think of, and living expenses needed to be paid. Had King not extended his pal the scratch, *Incredibly Strange Creatures* may have not seen completion. The film's architect would have been forced to take a humdrum day job to support his new household. Something the new family man would have most assuredly done.

Thrill seekers Jerry and Harold lunge into a not-so-thrilling blue station wagon (then Steckler's only working car) and pop the clutch. The two pull away from the director's actual apartment building and barrel down a narrow alley. They land at Jerry's girlfriend's parents' house which in reality was George J. Morgan's abode.

Inside, on the phone and sitting on a gaudy floral print couch, is Jerry's flavor of the week, Angela. With her piled-high and fashionable beehive hairdo, she anxiously awaits Jerry while her mother fumes. Jerry is "fun, he's exciting and we go places I've never dreamed of before." Exactly how these two late-teens have found themselves in never-before-dreamed-of places is never explored. Angela's mother visibly hates her daughter's new boyfriend.

As Steckler legend has it, the part of Angela originally belonged to a semi-pro singer named Bonita Jaye. She had been introduced to Steckler by Caroline Graham, the actress playing Madame Estrella's sister Carmelita. Steckler felt that Graham had a Greek look about her, so a name change was in order and she was christened Erina Enyo.

The legend continues that Steckler had finished shooting all the elaborate dance routines (in one day) and still had time, money and film to continue into the night. It was decided that Bonita Jaye's scenes as Angela would be up next. Everyone was willing and able to go except for Steckler's female lead.

When informed of her upcoming duty, the actress resisted and fully expected Steckler to wait until the next day. Apparently, she had a boyfriend who drummed in a rock'n'roll band, and she never missed his shows. Steckler implored she miss the show just this once as he had the cast and crew at the ready. She emphatically declined. Steckler emphatically relieved her of her obligations.

George Morgan became apprehensive. Steckler assured his partner that the show would go on. As the dancers from the previous shoot began to dissipate, Steckler eyed the cute Sharon Walsh. He asked her if she would like to play the lead, and she reminded him that she had just finished a scene as a dancer. The girl's implication was that she could not be in one movie as two different characters. However, this was a Ray Dennis Steckler movie and such continuity concerns were, well … not really concerns at all.

Fact is, Walsh appears in every single dance number, though she is not easily recognizable. In post-production, at his editing bay, Steckler avoided using any close-ups of dancer Walsh's face, thus masking the fact that she played two roles. That was the hope and intention anyway.

In Angela's driveway, Jerry chats with his girlfriend's brother Madison. Angela's older sibling is played by Pat Kirkwood (credited here as Madison Clarke), who would go on to become a gaffer for Steven Spielberg. Madison washes his car and tells Jerry that he should try "college life." The gleefully unemployed Jerry sneers, "No thanks. The world's my college."

Jerry's sentiment sums up his world views if, indeed, he can even see past the small world of his own making. Jerry's sentiment also sums up Angela's mother's disdain for her daughter's latest beau. This very attitude, that Jerry wears smugly as a badge of honor, will do him no favors in his film future.

With Angela and Harold in tow, Jerry aims his nondescript station wagon directly towards the city's nearest carnival. Could this be the type of thing Angela had never dreamed of doing? If so, this "girl next door" is in for a *bad* dream. That afternoon will be bad, while tomorrow afternoon will be worse and the day after tomorrow will be indescribable. Angela is in for a hair-raising ride.

The three teens enter the carnival and ride a few dinky rides. They then head straight to the infamous Cyclone Racer. The POV shots were recorded by cinematographer Vilmos Zsigmond. Zsigmond sat in the front of the coaster handling a 16mm movie camera and collected the Cyclone Racer's greatest thrills and chills. Neither he nor Steckler were fond of rollercoasters and to the director's knowledge neither has been on one since.

The Cyclone Racer features so heavily in the film that a brief history is in order. Roller Coaster enthusiast Scott Rutherford noted in his book *Roller Coasters* (p. 47–48), "The Cyclone Racer opened in May 1930 to rave reviews. Standing almost 100 feet tall, the Cyclone Racer was an imposing structure." Rutherford's book goes on to inform readers that the Cyclone Racer was featured in an episode of *Leave It to Beaver* and also the 1953 sci-fi classic *The Beast from 20,000 Fathoms*. The "World's Greatest

Ride" was, despite much public outcry, demolished in September 1968.

Returning to the production: Steckler's right-hand man Vilmos Zsigmond shot *all* of the carnival sequences. The humble Zsigmond considered *Incredibly Strange Creatures* his "big break" as it allowed him to finally get a union card. Zsigmond felt that his career as a cameraman was well on its way after working with Steckler. He was absolutely correct.

By this point, the young Steckler was working with three award-winning cameramen. On *Wild Guitar* he had access to not only Vilmos Zsigmond but also Joseph Mascelli, and now Laszlo Kovacs becomes number three—and all of them in one $38,000 motion picture. The mind reels.

Early in the career of the Hungarian-born Kovacs (aka Leslie Kovacs, Lester Kovacks and Art Radford), he lent his cinematography skills to David F. Friedman's *The Notorious Daughter of Fanny Hill* (1966) and *A Smell of Honey, a Swallow of Brine* (1966). Around the same time, he also aimed and focused his camera for Al Adamson on *Blood of Dracula's Castle* (1969) and *Hell's Bloody Devils* (1970). Later he worked with Dennis Hopper on *Easy Rider* (1969) and *The Last Movie* (1971) and Martin Scorsese on *New York, New York* (1977).

The teens take more turns at the coaster and a sobering Marge finally visits the evil medium Estrella. The fortune teller notices a perplexed look on her face and plays her hokey role to the hilt. Estrella's inquiries produce Marge's vague response, "I'm not sure what it is. I only know that something evil lies ahead for me." Estrella consults the "cards" and turns up the ace of spades. As Marge's luck would have it, it is the "Death" card. Frenzied and barely able to contain herself, Marge leaps up from the table and unwittingly barges directly towards Estrella's "pets." The horrifying tarot-reading coupled with Estrella's horrible captives send Marge careening out of the gypsy's den and onto the midway. Marge has seen Estrella's caged creatures, and the proverbial cat is out of the bag. Something must be done.

The three teens see Marge's flight and decide that they, too, would like to be spooked. After Estrella's palm is greased with 50 cents, she informs Angela that she will become wealthy and that her mother does not approve of her future husband. Then she cautions Angela that someone very near to her will soon die on a beach. Was this foreshadowing or pure hokum?

The three teens head back to the midway and Jerry insists on seeing the "girlie show" which consists of Estrella's sexy sister Carmelita: "Twenty beautiful girls! Ten beautiful costumes!" Angela is not the least bit interested and lets Jerry know that if he goes, he goes alone. Jerry tosses Harold his car keys and instructs him to take Angela home. Jerry's going it alone. Jerry had the spell of Carmelita cast over him.

Before Carmelita's big entrance, an elaborate floor show is executed by nine dancing girls. Lots of high-stepping, side-stepping and hip-shaking going on here. Some of the girls were professional dancers while others were not dancers at all. The scene actually works far better than it should have considering the mixed bag of "talent."

Steckler never misses the opportunity to relay the story of how he asked the performers to chew gum in order to help them sync-up their dance moves. The fact it seemed to work to a degree is not the curious part of the story. The curious part is, what in the world made

A set of four lobby cards from *The Incredibly Strange Creatures Who Stopped Living and Became Mixed-Up Zombies!!?* (1963) (author's collection).

Steckler think sticks of gum would help anything?

This was the first of four dance numbers that were shot in one day with little to no rehearsal. Three cameras, manned by the best, were at the ready to capture the action all at once. These song-and-dance sequences were choreographed (such as they were) by the forementioned Bill Turner and Alan Smith.

From here, the film takes a brief detour backstage to introduce one of the dancers, Stella (Toni Camel): The midway barker is hitting up the cute-as-a-cupcake Stella for a date. She reluctantly accepts as he suggests a quiet evening at her place, assuring her he will do the dishes.

The barker is played by Neil Stillman, who did no acting before or since. He simply landed the role because Mike Kannon was a no-show. Stillman was actually a postman delivering the mail to the Masonic Temple when Steckler snagged him. For a guy with no training whatsoever, Stillman is surprisingly adept. The striking Toni Camel went on to play in *The Devil's Sisters* (1966) and an episode of *Flipper* (1967). A few years earlier, she was photographed by *A Taste of Blood* star Bill Rogers for her portfolio. Further, she and Atlas King were purportedly an "item" while shooting *Incredibly Strange Creatures*.

Next up is Carol Kaye singing the smoky ballad "It's Not You." However, the main attraction is about to begin. "Now, we give you our beautiful exotic gypsy dancer Carmelita!" While Carmelita dances, Estrella's henchman Ortega slips Jerry a handwritten note: "Meet me in my dressing room after the show. Carmelita." Jerry is about to crack the gypsy's inner sanctum.

Carmelita's "exotic dance" was not really a dance at all as there was literally zero music playing during the shoot. Erina Enyo fumbled about the stage while musical directors Turner and Smith merely yelled out, "One! Two! Three! Four!" *ad nauseam*. Enyo limped through the ordeal quasi-successfully, taking into account she did not have much to work with as far as inspiration goes. Perhaps Enyo could mambo, waltz, Watusi or even square dance but with no music whatsoever, what the hell could be expected of her?

With visions of Carmelita whisking about the stage to the wafting sounds of "The Pied Piper of Love" (added in post-production), Jerry makes his way backstage. Carmelita, dark and brooding, asks Jerry to follow her behind the curtains. She vanishes and a POV shot follows her behind the drapes to reveal the black-and-white spiraling Hypno-Wheel!

The Hypno-Wheel sports a glob of black electrical tape at its center. Steckler maintained that a hypnotist group visited the set and insisted that the Hypno-Wheel be modified thusly so as not to actually put theatergoers into a trance. How the group caught wind of this production on the seventh floor of a former Masonic temple is a mystery. Why Steckler cared what they thought is also a mystery.

Host of *The Incredibly Strange Film Show*, Jonathan Ross had a similar experience 25 years later as he recalled in his book *The Incredibly Strange Film Book* (p. 171):

> [T]he hokey moment in [*Incredibly Strange Creatures*] when Estrella the gypsy hypnotizes her victims [using] a spinning black wheel with a white spiral on it is briefly shown to the audience. Rather lame and unthreatening you might think, but when I showed that clip on a Channel 4 documentary about Steckler, I was told I had to blank out the centre of the wheel in case viewers at home fell under Estrella's control!

Gobbed-up Hypno-Wheel or not, Jerry is sure to be in a trance as all three gypsies have descended upon him. "Look at the wheel. Look at the beautiful spinning wheel." Along with their groovy gadget, they strike steely stares and Jerry blankly stares back. Estrella briefs him on his task: "You will do only that which I have commanded you to do."

Viewers do not know why this is happening to Jerry. It *is*, however, evident these three charlatans are up to no good. Judging by their activities, they appear as akin to a coven of satanic-occultists as they do gypsies. Also, a review of their names (Estrella, Carmelita, Ortega) indicates their European ancestors may have

Brett O'Hara as Madame Estrella in *The Incredibly Strange Creatures Who Stopped Living and Became Mixed-Up Zombies!!?* (1963) (author's collection).

made their trek to Long Beach by way of Mexico.

Jerry is deployed as the stars of The Hungry Mouth, Marge and Bill, await their time slot. Not to short-change his patrons, the club owner sends his emcee out to announce Don Snyder and his guitar. Snyder strums and warbles his way through "How Do I Stand with Your Heart." This performance was sure to help prop up the next. One could easily assume that this was Snyder's last go-round with a Steckler motion picture. It was not.

The dancing duo hardly get into their routine before a hood-cloaked, knife-wielding Jerry breaks onto the stage. The assailant immediately jabs his blade directly into Marge's face, putting her on the stage floor and bleeding. Jerry repeats the process numerous times, then turns to Bill and administers the same.

The midway gypsies have tweaked Jerry's thought processing for an indeterminate amount of time in order to murder Marge Neilson. Why? Because she knows of Madame Estrella's secret vault of "pets." Marge is removed from the equation and Jerry returns home to nightmare.

The dream sequence (arguably the film's pivot point) is chockfull of creepy, evil and downright satanic imagery superimposed over even more creepy, evil and satanic imagery. Women and men's faces are painted in garish reds, blues, whites and blacks while they howl and taunt the tortured mind of Jerry. Smoke billows from the bottom of the screen while flames enter from any direction, all bathed in swaths of multi-colored lighting.

The scene powers on for nearly four minutes by the spinning, pushing, jerking camera moves that (d)evolve into a series of disconcerting asymmetrical screen shots. The entire sequence lives and breathes with a disorienting otherworldliness. It is, after all, a nightmare.

Steckler's two young Hungarian cameramen, Kovacs and Zsigmond, were already testing the boundaries of what was acceptable within the norms of filmmaking. Still, no matter how unconventional their approach, Steckler was forever pushing them further to consider his less-than-time-honored methods. At times it ruffled some feathers, but as a cinematographer himself, Steckler knew a thing or two about camera movement and placements.

If Steckler had chosen to make this section a short film, he would have most assuredly found himself within the pages of a book focusing on experimental moviemaking. When it comes to bizarre, almost unexplainable outré cinema that packs so much visual punch (no one caring about its meaning), Steckler emerges a winner. Here, Steckler is in good company with José Mojica Marins (Coffin Joe) and/or Kenneth Anger.

Once Jerry awakens from this hellish ordeal, he stumbles through a doorway revealing an incredibly bright red bathroom framed in structured blacks. The sharp lines of black coupled with the garish red seem to indicate that Jerry may still be dreaming or hallucinating. With only Jerry in the frame, it is as if the bathroom exists in a parallel reality. The scene appears to continue the nightmare rather than conclude it.

In truth, Steckler found himself at the home of producer Aaron Spelling when he was married to actress Carolyn Jones of *Addams Family* fame. He excused himself to their washroom and found it red. He was so taken by the dramatic effect that he decorated his the same. Steckler's bathroom is the very one Jerry stumbles into.

With the nightmare in the can, Steckler returns the film to the real world which includes Harold toiling away under the hood of a late 1950s Nash Rambler. This is the very car in which Steckler had slept a few years earlier. Furthermore, had Atlas King not given Steckler the $300 for rent and food, he and his new family may have wound up living in that thing.

Historically speaking, as far as automobiles go, the Rambler was the first successful American-made compact car. Steckler's Rambler was dead on screen and remained sitting dormant in that parking lot long after filming had commenced. As Harold announces, "I won't be able to get this piece of junk running anyhow."

Jerry leaves Harold to continue with the impossible and makes his way over to Angela's. Madison is grilling burgers and his sister is sunbathing poolside. Once Angela is aware of Jerry's presence, she is still noticeably upset with her tomcattin' boyfriend. Jerry is not up to poring over his previous night's shenanigans, so Angela begins to spin an umbrella in his face.

There is no rational reason for Angela to twirl an umbrella in Jerry's direction, but without this activity Steckler would have been hard-pressed to reintroduce the Hypno-Wheel! As the umbrella rotates, Jerry hallucinates and suddenly, in his warped mind, Angela has become last night's quarry. He chokes Angela. Angela's mother screams. Madison grabs his sister's attacker and throws him to the ground.

Jerry is upset and embarrassed and takes to the streets to clear his unhinged head. He finds himself strolling about Los Angeles' infamous Angels' Flight cable cars (demolished four years later with Steckler capturing the only color footage of the unique transport). These cars (funiculars) connected Hill Street to Olive Street on 298 feet of cable in L.A.'s Bunker Hill district.

Author Howard Sounes paints a vivid picture of the Angels' Flight area in his biography on Charles Bukowski, *Locked in the Arms of a Crazy Life* (p. 19):

> Downtown bustled with garment makers, jewelers, street vendors, paperboys, cops, prostitutes, thieves and hawkers, all busy with some mysterious and important task. There were ethnic restaurants with crashing kitchens; back alleys where stock boys shared cigarettes; seedy bars; hotels both grand like the Biltmore and dives where the hookers worked. The funicular railway, Angels' Flight, climbed Bunker Hill and then racketed down again, spilling [Bukowski] across the street into Grand Central Market.

Returning to the film's hub, the midway, Carol Kaye and the Stone Tones tear through the raucous "Shook Out of Shape." This floor show, easily a contender for the best of the lot, features several shots of the adorable dancer Stella. Post-show goings-on consist of Stella reading about Marge's death and questioning Estrella about it. No good will come of this.

In the meantime, siren Teri Randal belts out "Choo Choo Cha-Bootchie" while Jerry questions the gypsies about their motives. The nomads deny any wrongdoing and within moments Jerry is once more eyeballing the Hypno-Wheel. It is quite clear that the nosy dancer Stella will be the crazed killer's casualty this evening.

On the other side of town, Angela's mother puts together a search party consisting of Harold, Angela and Madison. Despite the fact that Jerry attempted to murder her daughter, she

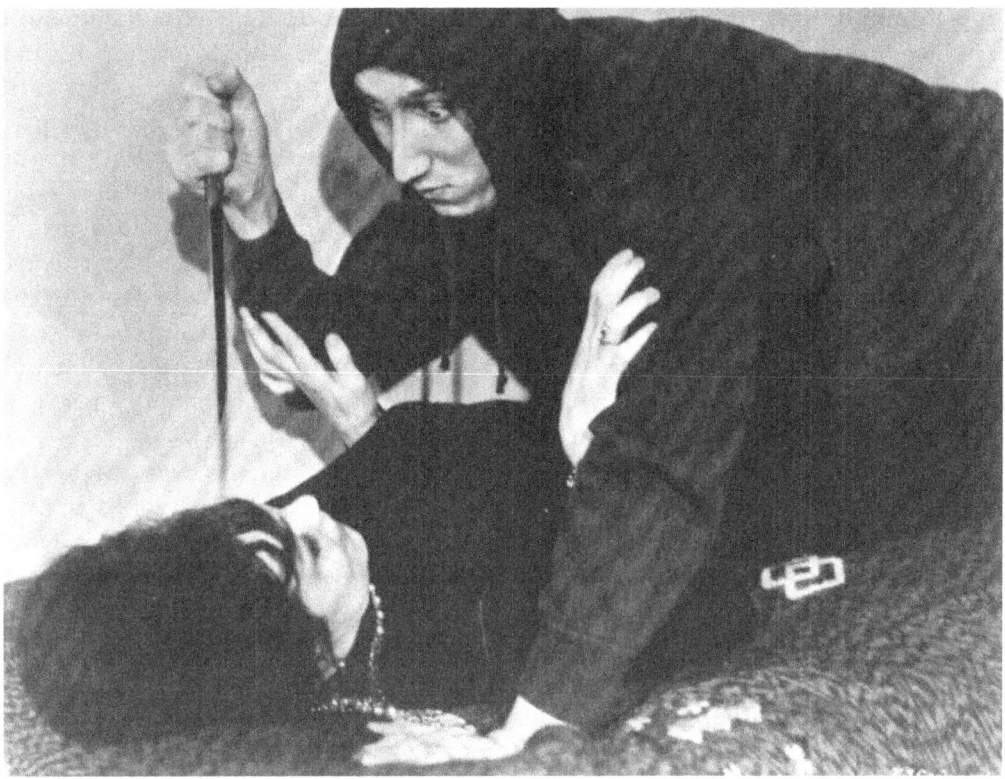

Jerry (Steckler) is about to stab Stella (Toni Camel) in *The Incredibly Strange Creatures Who Stopped Living and Became Mixed-Up Zombies!!?* (1963) (author's collection).

still agrees he should be located before the police apprehend him. The teenage sleuths deduce that Jerry is back at the carnival.

Stella is antsy to twist into the night alongside her date, the carnival barker, so she has left the gypsies' hideaway for home. In reality, cinematographer Vilmos Zigmond's apartment doubles for Stella's nifty crib. Stella's co-worker will eventually arrive at her place but not before Jerry. Jerry attacks, stabs and kills Stella, then executes the same business on the barker upon his later arrival.

In a daze, Jerry lumbers back to Madame Estrella's lair and is doused in acid. Apparently, the fortune teller is finished with Jerry as he is, and desires a new "pet." With the volatile liquid eating away Jerry's face, the ham-fisted Ortega leads him to the cage only to have the other creatures escape.

A fight, a struggle, a strangulation and three murders ensue. The gypsies are history. So, nearly 70 minutes into the film, Steckler finally has his mixed-up zombies emerge. Their faces are grotesquely misshapen, their attire is ripped to shreds. For zombies, they move about fairly quickly.

The creatures' masks were created by Tom Scherman, who went on to lead the makeup department on most of Steckler's films. He ran the project down to the wire as the masks were not completed until the very day Steckler needed them. Scherman was also responsible for Estrella's "wart of horror" (as the film's trailer described it).

The film's final musical piece is the

not-quite-a-hit-single "The Mixed-Up Zombie Stomp." The dancers barely get their performance off and running before the zombies crash the party and create all-out havoc in the theater. Police officers rush the stage while panicking theatergoers beeline for the exits. "See: The dancing girls of the carnival murdered by the incredible night creatures of the midway!"

No sooner have the mixed-up zombies graced the screen with their presence, Steckler has the cops kill them off. Those three meddling teenagers, Harold, Angela and Madison arrive in time to find the gypsies dead and one more zombie (George Morgan) hulking about. The police unceremoniously aim and pull the trigger on this one as well.

Jerry materializes, dives out a doorway and races from the midway to the beach. A few last parting shots of the Cyclone Racer are framed up before the film's crescendo. Jerry stumbles, flails and falls while pursued by his friends and the police. For reasons unknown, apprehending the crazed Jerry is apparently not an option as one of the policemen shoots and kills him. Madame Estrella's prediction becomes a reality. Angela lost someone very close to her on a beach.

If the ending seems pressed, it most likely was, as Steckler recounts in the Media Blasters audio commentary: "I didn't really know how the movie was going to end until we went out there on the beach. And even while I was doing all of this, I had no idea how the movie was going to end. I only knew that we were running out of film, and we'd run out of money—that it had to end soon."

If the storyline seems convoluted, it was what Steckler was shooting for, as he revealed on the audio commentary: "I just wanted to make a teenage-type movie that would be exploitable and I tried to think, with no money, I'll put music and dancers and monsters in it and teenagers and conflict with the parents. I tried to put everything in the movie and think I succeeded."

Steckler admittedly had a minor obsession with midways and carnivals. The film was inspired, in part, by the Reading (Pennsylvania) State Fair. Steckler never missed it. His attention was arrested by the carnies, the strippers and the sideshows.

Further, Steckler was infatuated with the gypsies. He was weaned on Universal monster movies, so Maria Ouspenskaya's portrayal of Maleva in *The Wolf Man* (1941) must have been lodged somewhere in his psyche. He also maintained that his movie was loosely inspired by the Universal picture *The Mad Ghoul* (1943). All of Steckler's carnival adorations are exhibited within the frames of his second film, augmented and anchored by his fondness for pop music.

The film originally went out under the Fairway International banner as the B-feature on a double bill with Arch Hall, Jr.'s *The Sadist*. It was not doing the business Steckler had envisioned, so he bought the distribution rights from Hall's father and sent the picture out again with the Coleman Francis vehicle *The Beast of Yucca Flats*. This is when the film began to sprout legs and really take off, albeit without any "real" gimmick.

All too much has been written about the connection between *Incredibly Strange Creatures* and Steckler's creation of Hallucinogenic Hypnovision. At this point in the film's history, no such gizmo had even occurred to Steckler. There is zero in the film's pressbook indicating that the film be promoted in this

E.M. Loews Center Theater in Boston, 1965: *The Incredibly Strange Creatures Who Stopped Living and Became Mixed-Up Zombies!!?* (1963) plays second fiddle to Christopher Lee's *Horror Castle* (1963) (author's collection).

manner. Still, the two were inexplicably linked.

Moreover, multiple distributors, ad campaigns, promoters and title changes have all helped convolute the history and lineage of Hallucinogenic Hypnovision. Upon closer examination of the one-sheets, pressbooks, radio spots and theatrical trailers, pieces of the mystery begin falling into place like a dealt hand of "stacked" cards. Hammering the point home best are these excerpts from the trailer for the film's re-release as *The Teenage Psycho Meets Bloody Mary*:

> He, more hideous than Jack the Ripper. She, bloodier than Bluebeard. No one is safe in *The Teenage Psycho Meets Bloody Mary*! Filmed in sensational Bloody Vision. Movie monsters come alive and go into the audience. You are suddenly surrounded by monsters. You become a party to the horror in *The Teenage Psycho Meets Bloody Mary*. Starring Cash Flagg in Bloody Color.

This later run is where Steckler fell face first into the idea of sending "live" monsters into the audience during the climax. The director inserted stock flashes of lightning before the monsters escape into the theater on screen, cuing the "real" monsters to stampede the "real" theater. There was also a female plant in the front row whom one of the creatures would snatch up and carry behind the screen. Steckler first researched and developed this technique at a Glendale theater and later it was given the brand

On May 26, 1967, the Lindsey Theater in Lubbock, Texas, showed *The Teenage Psycho Meets Bloody Mary* and the immortal *Rat Pfink a Boo Boo* (1966). The distinctive theater was closed circa the late '80s and demolished, reportedly to make room for a parking lot (image and commentary courtesy film historian and archivist Raleigh Bronkowski).

name Hallucinogenic Hypnovision. As producer George Morgan told Jonathan Ross of *The Incredibly Strange Film Show*, "It sold a lot of tickets."

These "live" shows were so successful that promoter Joe Karston (aka Joseph Price), known for his horror, spook and ghost show programs, decided to send the production out nationwide. As *The Incredibly Strange Creatures* made its way around the country, a name change was in order. These titles included *Incredibly Mixed-Up Zombies* and *Diabolical Dr. Voodoo* but the forementioned *The Teenage Psycho Meets Bloody Mary* was the most memorable. While Steckler's character Jerry could be chalked up as the Teenage Psycho, there simply was no "Mary" to be found, bloody or otherwise.

Forever the consummate promoter, Karston was the first roadshowman to initiate the unheard of "Two-for-One" ticket combo. He also obtained licenses from motion picture companies so he could produce a number of different monsters for his finale as opposed to a measly one or two. This is where Don Post Studios came into play and began constructing and manufacturing rubber masks of monsters. In 1949, Post had acquired a license from Universal and by 1955 his first version of the Frankenstein Monster mask was released. Other famous creatures followed and soon found their way into endless spook show programs, thereby releasing the ghost-masters from the pain-in-the-neck application of stage makeup and latex appliances.

Karston was considered a master of advertising when it came to his productions. His collage-work posters and advertisements were populated with ghouls, gals, skulls, disembodied heads and creepy-crawly creatures. The taglines were eye-catching as well, "We Dare You to See the World's Weirdest Movie" or "Monsters Come Out of the Screen and Invade the Audience!" All presented in something akin to "Horror Vision" or, in Steckler's case, "Bloody Vision"

Two posters display roadshowman extraordinaire Joe Karston's panache for the garish: "Horror Vision" vs. "Bloody Vision" (author's collection).

as the poster for *Teenage Psycho Meets Bloody Mary* announced. (Note: Joe Karston is not to be confused with magician Joe Karson from the 1940s and '50s, who performed illusions with names like "Zombie," "Voodoo" and "The Witch of the Pumpkin.")

Additionally, existing promo materials more than suggest that *Incredibly Strange Creatures* made some rounds in Spanish territories as *Infernales Extranas Criaturas* which translates to *Infernal Strange Creatures*. The promotional paper goods also were home to the tagline "Extanos Horripilantes Seres Movidos Por Una Orden Satanica ... I Matar!" This translates into "Creepy Strange Beings Moved by a Satanic Order ... to Kill!" This tagline seems to also infer that Estrella, Ortega and Carmelita are an evil witch-like coven rather than mere gypsies with a creepy pastime.

Mexican lobby card for *The Incredibly Strange Creatures Who Stopped Living and Became Mixed-Up Zombies!!?* (1963) (courtesy Carolyn Brandt).

At some special screenings, another "flash" of lightning would appear and cue Steckler himself to terrorize the audience as the psycho Jerry, wielding a plastic knife. When the show ran in out-of-town theaters where Steckler was unable to appear, a theater employee donned a custom Cash Flagg mask. These masks were made by Don Post Studios which, as stated before, was responsible for all of those collectable Universal monster masks in the '60s and '70s.

Even though Steckler was not in production cahoots with Arch Hall, Sr., he still found some work for his old friend. Steckler deemed Hall's inimitable voice the perfecto choice for the buzz-phrase babble (read: narration) of the film's initial trailer. Whether he is going by Arch Hall, Sr., William Watters or Nicholas Merriwether, it is undeniable who is reading the lines:

> Incredible is the word for the world's first monster musical. From the innocence of music and laughter comes the twilight of terror. See the dancing girls of the carnival murdered by the incredible night creatures of the midway. An unspeakable pit of dismal subhuman monsters who drool, gibber—moaning for the thrill for revenge. See the hunchback of the midway fight a duel of death with the mixed-up zombies. Turning men into monsters, twisted, tormented human vultures, yearning to kill. Incredible creatures clutching at the thin threads of their miserable lives. Human vultures, only the weird zombies remain.

As history has it, Steckler's film narrowly beat out director Del Tenney's *The*

Horror of Party Beach (1964) for "The First Monster Musical." Tenney's film had monsters, music, beach parties and even a song entitled "Zombie Stomp" by surf rockers The Del-Aires. It is fortunate that Steckler got his film to the finish line first because "The Second Monster Musical" just does not have the same ring to it.

Digging into the film's soundtrack, three versions of Libby Quinn's song "The Mixed-Up Zombie Stomp" can be found. The original version sung by Billy Gholston (as merely "Zombie Stomp" or "Graveyard Stomp") was recorded in 1963. One year later, Steckler had Gholston's (sometimes credited as Ghoulston) vocals removed and replaced with Danny Ware's. Ware's recording was released in conjunction with *Incredibly Strange Creatures* on REL Records as "The Mixed-Up Zombie Stomp." The confounding part is that while Steckler had the seven-inch single of "The Mixed-Up Zombie Stomp" pressed and distributed, he included an instrumental version in the film, thus offering up three interpretations of the same song that have almost zero in common with the Del-Aires song of the same name.

An odd and/or amusing observation is that 20 minutes of the film's 80-minute running time is spent on song-and-dance numbers. If these sequences were deleted, Steckler would have managed a mere 60-minute feature. Now, if this "padding" comes across as tedious or ineffective, just wait until the parades, rodeos and pedestrians get stuck in Steckler's cinematic quiver of arrows.

Incredibly Strange Creatures ran for nearly a decade before petering out in the early 1970s. Quite a run for a near no-budget horror movie made in 11 days. Still, Steckler's film just would not lie down and die. The movie was about to gain momentum again as magazine features, video cassette rentals and film retrospectives were on the haunted horizons.

Consider Lester Bangs' 1973 review for *Creem* magazine (reprinted in his book *Psychotic Reactions and Carburetor Dung*) proof of the film's initial longevity (p. 122):

> [T]his flick doesn't just rebel against, or even disregard, standards of taste and art. In the universe inhabited by *The Incredibly Strange Creatures...*, such things as standards and responsibility have never been heard of. It is this lunar purity which largely imparts to the film its classic stature. Like *Beyond the Valley of the Dolls* and a very few others, it will remain as an artifact in years to come to which scholars and searchers for truth can turn and say, "This was trash!"

Different REL records of 1963's "The Mixed-Up Zombie Stomp" (author's collection).

After *Incredibly Strange Creatures* had run its course, it became semi-legendary as a possible hoax. Even though it was no longer in theaters, it still wound up within the pages of *Fantastic Monsters of the Films*, *The Monster Times* and other magazines. The general consensus was that no one would use such a ridiculous (and ridiculously long) title for a movie. It was thought that one of the magazine's writers was simply having a spot of fun with its readers. In the mid–1980s, Camp Video put a knife through the heart of that mystery.

In 1989, MTV sponsored an *Incredibly Strange Creatures* screening at the historic York Theater, a 700-seat, single-screen movie house at 4949 York Boulevard in L.A.'s Highland Park district. The theater opened in 1923 and eventually became a Korean church.

Then the "so bad it's good" pundits showed up. Discovering unintentional humor within the frames of these low-budget movies is one thing, and it is an easy thing to do. Maliciously ripping them to shreds based on technical flaws is tacky and pointless. Viewers of this type of cinema should be able to look beyond the obvious, or simply resign themselves to the latest Hollywood potboiler.

This brings the narrative to the comedy series *Mystery Science Theater 3000* (*MST3K*). Joel Hodgson's creation began airing in 1988 and has continued to light up the small screen off and on for three decades with no signs of letting up. *MST3K* may have its focus, but it is not the only way to view this peculiar breed of film. Still, the show's place and point (to the positive) is that it helped expose millions of viewers to films that most likely they would not give a day in court.

Now, that leaves the not-so-positive part. *Mystery Science Theater 3000* could get pretty darned snarky and some directors and their fans were not at all amused. In the end, *MST3K* really is the ugly bastard child of Britain's *The Incredibly Strange Film Show*, which had a sense of humor about its subjects without the cruelty. Steckler loved the latter but had an entirely different take on the former. When daughter Laura Steckler was asked about her father's reaction to the show, she had this to say, "Wow! You've struck a nerve there. My dad was very upset by that. I've not seen all of it, but I can only assume I would be upset by the very same things that upset him. I just find it unfortunate that when you do an Internet search for that movie, their version is usually the one that pops up first."

MST3K's *Incredibly Strange Creatures* episode ran on June 14, 1997. Steckler's opinion of the show may have been colored by the fact he was once again embroiled in litigation regarding the film. By 1997, video cassette rentals were on the wane and DVD, introduced in 1995, was on the rise. It was time for Steckler to drag his catalogue into the digital age.

Around this time, Steckler was receiving a sizable amount of friction from the George Morgan Estate over the rights to *Incredibly Strange Creatures*. Morgan's four daughters assumed they owned the movie and that Steckler could lay no claim to it. Steckler, having given the film his all, felt quite differently about the matter.

According to Steckler, "George J. Morgan was the most honest person I ever knew." Still, Morgan's daughters railed on, propped up by their husbands, family members and a gaggle of attorneys. Once again, Steckler prevailed and his signature movie remained in his good hands. Those Morgan girls can just go away.

As it is, despite its outrageous ad campaign, *Incredibly Strange Creatures* is not necessarily a musical in the purest sense of the word. Musical films, by definition, are usually replete with songs and lyrics that advance the plot or develop characters, "but in some cases, they serve merely as breaks in the storyline, often as elaborate production numbers." So says Wikipedia.

Here, Steckler's use of music has less to do with the on-screen story and more to do with the story off-screen. Steckler is an affable guy. Affable guys tend to have lots of friends. Just so happens Steckler's friends were artists, performers, singers and songwriters. Steckler put his friends in his movie. End of *that* story.

From a working standpoint, the George J. Morgan–Ray Dennis Steckler fusion was far more successful than the previous pairing. *Wild Guitar* was a solid directorial launching pad for the young Steckler, but *Incredibly Strange Creatures*, for better or for worse, defined his career. And who really cares that the Passport Video documentary *The 50 Worst Movies Ever Made* actually gave Steckler the not-so-coveted #1 spot? Matters not what Passport Video thinks as the balance of Steckler's cinematic work would forever be held in comparison to *The Incredibly Strange Creatures Who Stopped Living and Became Mixed-Up Zombies!!?*

The Thrill Killers (1964)

Synopsis from Pressbook

Dennis Kesdakian (Atlas King), a traveling salesman, is en route to Los Angeles to close a business transaction when he hears over his car radio that three homicidal maniacs have escaped from a nearby insane asylum. He pays the broadcast little attention as he stops to pick up a hitchhiker, who turns out to be the notorious Mort "Mad Dog" Click (Cash Flagg), brother of Herbie, one of the asylum escapees. Mad Dog brutally slays Dennis, steals the salesman's car and drives into Los Angeles.

That night, at the Brentwood home of would-be movie star Joe Saxon (Brick Bardo) and his wife Liz (Liz Renay), a wild and riotous orgy is in full swing. Joe has thrown the girls-galore party to influence film producer George J. Morgan (himself) into giving him the lead role in Morgan's next picture.

Meanwhile, Mad Dog stalks the late-night streets of downtown Los Angeles and meets a shapely young brunette named Erina (Erina Enyo). They go up to her apartment. After making love to her, Mad Dog goes berserk, accusing Erina of being a shameless tramp. In his rage he seizes a pair of scissors and fiendishly murders her. He flees the bloody scene as neighbors react to Erina's screams and phone the police.

Joe and Liz Saxon have an argument the next day over all the money spent on the part—money they cannot afford—and Liz runs off to see her cousin Linda (Laura Benedict), who operates a roadside café in Topanga Canyon. At the café are Ron and Carol (Ron Burr and Carolyn Brandt), who plan to marry the next week. They go to look at an old house in the area which they are considering buying and fixing up.

At the house, while searching for

the owner, they meet up with the three escaped maniacs. Herbie, Keith and Gary (Herb Robins, Keith O'Brien and Gary Kent). The madmen maliciously assault Ron and Carol, finally lopping Ron's head off with an axe and dealing Carol a similar fate.

Joe Saxon and producer Morgan show up at the roadside café. Morgan tells Liz he's going to use Joe in his next production. The three maniacs burst into the café, assault Liz and Linda and terrorize Joe and Morgan. A free-swinging, axe-hurtling fight breaks out. Joe and Morgan subdue Keith as Linda poisons Herbie's coffee. Gary chases Liz up into the mountains, with Joe in pursuit.

Gary attacks Liz atop a mountain peak as Joe arrives on the scene. Joe and Gary engage in a hand-to-knife combat while Liz escapes, only to fall into the evil hands of Mad Dog Click, searching the area for his brother. Gary plunges a thousand feet to his death and Joe races off to rescue Liz from Mad Dog.

Mad Dog kills an innocent rancher and steals his horse. The police cut off Mad Dog's avenue of escape but the kill-crazy lunatic charges through the blockade. Motorcycle policeman Frank West (Titus Moede) is ordered to pursue the deranged Mad Dog. After a perilous, breathless chase between motorcycle and horse through treacherous Topanga mountain trails, Officer West captures Mad Dog. In a titanic kill-or-be-killed gun battle, Officer West is forced to shoot Mad Dog in the head, killing him and thereby bringing to a shock-charged ending the reign of terror incited by THE THRILL KILLERS and leaving producer Morgan free to cast Joe, Liz and Linda in his new movie.

Promotion

The Thrill Killers radio spot quotes:

1. "Shocking the screen with the confidential exposé of the Go-Go set."
2. "The lurid lives and loves. The wild and wanton all-night parties where anything goes."
3. "Its bestial backstreets where love and murder run amok."
4. "*The Thrill Killers* on a homicidal maniacs on a bloody rampage of horror!"
5. "Starring Cash Flagg as Mad Dog Click as the kill-crazy psychopathic maniac who would do anything for a kick!"
6. "*The Thrill Killers* with Liz Renay love star, nymphomaniac whose insatiable passions drove men to the very brink of Hell."
7. "Die with Mad Dog Click and the Head Choppers Three as they blaze a terror trail of manipulating evil in one the sin cities of the world."

The Maniacs Are Loose radio spot quotes:

1. "So scary, so terrifying, we dare you to see *The Maniacs Are Loose!*"
2. "The world's first horror movie made in Hallucinogenic Hypno-Vision!"
3. "Hallucinogenic horrors not only on the screen, but in the audience all around you!"
4. "It's a hallucinogenic nightmare!"
5. "You are put in the middle of the picture with bloodthirsty maniacs all around you, not only on the screen but 'live' maniacs in the

audience, all over the theater, looking for victims."
6. "Homicidal maniacs escape from an asylum. They terrorize a community. Gullible love-starved women become their prey, and you'll see these same bloodthirsty maniacs all around you ... ALIVE!"
7. "For the thrill of your life, see *The Maniacs Are Loose!*"

Credits

Cast: Cash Flagg [Ray Dennis Steckler] (Mort "Mad Dog" Click); Liz Renay (Liz Saxon); Brick Bardo [Joe Bardo] (Joe Saxon); Carolyn Brandt (Carol); Gary Kent (Gary Barcroft); Herb Robins (Herbie Click); Keith O'Brien (Keith Rogers); Laura Benedict (Linda); Ron Burr (Ron); Titus Moede (Motorcycle Officer Frank West/"Yes" Man at Party/Cripple); Erina Enyo (Erina Devore); Atlas King (Dennis Kesdekian); Nancy Crawford (Mrs. Kesdekian); Gene Pollock (Detective); Force McCall aka George Caldwell (Officer Wells); James Bowie (Officer Freeman); Lonnie Lord [Ron Haydock] (Officer Tracey); George J. Morgan, Arch Hall, Sr. (Themselves); Barry Barnett (Drunkard at Party); Brenda Renay (Girl at Party); Coleman Francis (Narrator)

Production: Producers: George J. Morgan, Arch Hall, Sr., Ray Dennis Steckler. Associate Producer: Titus Moede. Screenplay: Ray Dennis Steckler, Gene Pollock. Additional Dialogue: Ron Haydock. Photographers: Joseph V. Mascelli, Lee Strosnider. Editor: Austin McKinney. Art Director and Titles: Tom Scherman. Production Manager: Frank West [Titus Moede]. Music: Henri Price [Andre Brummer]. Sound Engineer: Lee Strosnider. Gaffer: Jack Cooperman. Key Grip: Ray Wickman. Assistant Director: Don Russell. Director: Ray Dennis Steckler. 70 minutes. Black and White (with color inserts in some markets).

The Film

People are no good. I hate people, they're no good.... I hate you and I'm gonna kill you.—Mort "Mad Dog" Click from *The Thrill Killers*

There is little doubt that *Incredibly Strange Creatures* is the film by which Steckler's career will forever be bound and tethered (or tarred and feathered, depending upon opinions). This is not to short-change *Wild Guitar*, a fantastic debut by a fledgling moviemaker who was obliged to answer to a strict producer. By anyone's standards, Steckler had begun cinematically with a proverbial one-two-punch.

Steckler had a few more tricks up his sleeve. Nineteen sixty-four would be a good year; the Beatles laid waste to *The Ed Sullivan Show* (the Rolling Stones following closely on their coattails), the Civil Rights Act was signed into law and Steckler filmed and released *The Thrill Killers*. Steckler's third cinematic offspring was conspicuously and, for no good reason, less notorious than its predecessor.

With a reported budget of almost zero, Steckler cashed in with his most technically adept film under the Hollywood International Star Pictures banner. The success of his previous venture assured that, once again, producer George J. Morgan was at the ready, greasing the palm of his young friend. This Morgan-Steckler cocktail was mixed, shaken and strained into a tall cool glass that is forever half-full.

The Thrill Killers has been repeatedly, and unjustly, compared to Alfred Hitchcock's 1960 runaway horror success *Psycho*. Hitch's film is definitely a

Poster art for *The Thrill Killers* (1964) (author's collection).

Strangler quietly came and went; Herschell Gordon Lewis' splatterpiece *Blood Feast* screamed its way to the bank. However, by Steckler's own admission, "I've never even seen one of that guy's movies!"

Onward and upward into the fog that is *The Thrill Killers*: Art director Tom Scherman provided yet another stark and creepy title sequence. This one, like the last, drives the unmistakable face of Cash Flagg straight into, and past, the theatergoer's comfort zones. Unlike his earlier arrangement, there is no animation here, just grainy black-and-white stills that fluctuate between over-saturation and just plain negatives. The film's star Brick (Joe) Bardo doubled as the still photographer and his work features prominently within the frames of Scherman's engaging footage.

A typed flashcard fills the screen informing viewers, "Events in this picture are said to be true ... and to have transpired back in the year 1965 as here-in depicted." It is odd that Steckler would date this 1965 when the film was shot and released in 1964.

Steckler's initial establishing shot is an overview of the bustling Hollywood that dissolves into the legendary Grauman's Chinese Theater. Those images give way to the highly recognizable footprints and handprints of the famous stars in front of the theater. These frames are quite similar to the opening sequences of *Wild Guitar* and Steckler revisited them again a couple of years later. Incidentally, Walt Disney's *Mary Poppins* (1964) was that week's featured film.

A narrator (B-movie actor-director

"thriller" and the Norman Bates character is certainly a "killer" and it is even plausible that Bates killed for a thrill. Nevertheless, Steckler maintained that while he loved *Psycho* (which kept him awake a few nights), it was never his intent to copy or even pay it homage.

Fact is, *Psycho* ushered in a glut of crazed-killer films and Steckler was simply staking his claim alongside his fellow low-budget exploiters. The 1963 James Landis–Arch Hall, Jr., vehicle *The Sadist* would have surely been on Steckler's radar. Ben Parker's 1964 *Teenage*

Coleman Francis) introduces the viewer to the character Joe Saxon. He is an aspiring actor with his head in the clouds: "Caught in the web of non-reality ... non-reality." With Steckler's lens as Saxon's eyes, a POV shot lingers on the foot- and handprints of Ray Milland, James Mason and Nelson Eddy. Are they favorites of Saxon's, favorites of Steckler's or simply unoccupied spaces to aim his camera? The jury is still out on that one, but the latter is more likely the case than not.

Joe Saxon is played by Brick Bardo, who had recently been the boyfriend of Mae West and "a few others," as Steckler quips. Steckler's sarcastic remark implies that Bardo had "many" other girlfriends and romantic encounters. Bardo certainly had the good looks and personality to take him where he wanted to go in the dating department. According to Steckler, Bardo lacked the focus and drive to formally study acting. So his career languished as he showed up for cinematography, acting, directing and producing gigs on a myriad of low-rent features. Some of these skin-flicks included *Teenage Seductress* (1975), *Alice in Wonderland: An X-Rated Musical Fantasy* (1976) and *Do You Wanna Be Loved?* (1978). It is interesting to note that Bardo and Steckler were on a parallel-porno trajectory during the 1970s.

Joe Saxon finds no work in Hollywood that day and calls his wife Liz (Liz Renay), a "former horror star turned artist," to break the news. The film cuts to Liz sitting before an easel painting poolside. The phone rings and Liz makes her way from the pool to the house. For an unemployed actor and a stay-at-home wife, it is one heck of a spread. Joe and Liz are on the verge of losing their home. In reality, the house belonged to the daughter of producer George J. Morgan. This is one of the daughters who later gave Steckler litigation grief over who owned the Morgan-Steckler productions. While the outcome was favorable for Steckler, the ordeal was frustrating.

Actress Liz Renay's involvement in *The Thrill Killers* is legendary. She had just spent 27 months in prison for perjury. Her then-boyfriend, mobster Mickey Cohen, who once held court with Al Capone and "Bugsy" Siegel, had been arrested when she refused to squeal. So it was off to Terminal Island for the tight-lipped moll. Renay may have refused to squeal in front of a judge, but had no issues penning her tell-all memoir *My First 2,000 Men*.

Steckler lore has it that Brick Bardo picked Renay up from prison and whisked her straight away to the movie set. It is a fanciful story but unfortunately Renay's timeline and dates simply do not support it. Cohen was arrested in 1959, and even if Renay's sentencing was not until 1960, she was out by 1963 (the same year she married her fifth husband Read Morgan). Less than three years later, Morgan was "out" and number six was "in."

Prior to Renay's fling with Cohen, the Arizonan had been crowned Miss Stardust of Arizona and scored some bit parts in low-budget films and TV. Renay's minor celebrity status simply was not translating into more acting roles so, for a while, she turned to stripping. She would re-visit this career choice later in life with her daughter Brenda beside her in perhaps the first mother-daughter striptease act. This successful and highly unusual floor show came to an abrupt end in 1982 when Brenda took her life on her 39th birthday.

From the Saxons' lavish dwellings, the film shifts to the modest home of Dennis Kesdekian (Atlas King). He's a faithful husband, doting father and traveling salesman who is "caught in the world of reality." The Kesdeckian character is introduced at the five-minute mark and by the seven-minute mark his grim fate becomes a reality: Traveling along a largely deserted highway, he encounters a lone hitchhiker and stops to give him a lift. Later it will be revealed that this mysterious man is Mort "Mad Dog" Click. The good Samaritan who stopped his car is shot and killed before *he* ever finds out his assailant's name. Apparently the Kesdekian character's only assignments were to provide a "reality"-based paradox to Joe Saxon's "non-reality" and a car for Mad Dog.

After Mad Dog dumps Kesdekian's body face-down onto the pavement, he whips the car away into the direction of Los Angeles. Steckler orchestrated a remarkable shot here that would be at home in any one of David Lynch's films. Joseph V. Mascelli was still manning Steckler's camera and between these two talented neophytes, *The Thrill Killers* was given a tactile look and feel far and away beyond its low, low budget.

That bleak scene, Atlas King's last for Steckler, segues into a raging party at the Saxons' swanky pad. The pool area is jampacked full of young adult extras Steckler neither knew, nor would see again. Liz Saxon goosesteps about the immature and unruly bunch like an incensed member of Hermann Göring's Gestapo. Liz is clearly not pleased with the evening's festivities.

Eventually, Liz concedes and lets her guard, and evening jacket, down to reveal her apprehensions as well as some skin. She sashays into the lounge room and catches another eyeful of partygoers she does not necessarily want or need in her house. The Saxons' home has become a convoluted mess of sweaty dancing youths and sweaty drinking dudes on the wrong side of 40.

Liz's husband Joe is attempting to impress some of Hollywood's elite, but

Steckler as Mort "Mad Dog" Click in *The Thrill Killers* (1964) (author's collection).

evidently not impressing his wife. Exasperated Liz seeks an answer: "Joe, what are you trying to prove with this party? You're just spending money we don't have and there's no one here but a lot of crazy people." Liz is at the end of her rope and Joe is so caught up in the "world of non-reality ... non-reality" that he flippantly responds, "Just let me worry about that."

Joe leaves his peeved wife to talk shop with his two guests of honor, producers Arch Hall, Sr., and George J. Morgan. Both older men are playing themselves; a comely and giggly woman is nestled between them. Liz Renay's daughter Brenda is their captive and while she was 21 years old at the time, she barely looked 16. Watching these old slobbering hounds toy with this lass is uncomfortable at first, but then Brenda *did* wind up stripping with her mother, so out with the vestiges of purity.

During this party scene, one record ends and someone drops the needle on Ron Haydock and the Boppers' "You're Running Wild." Ron and his Boppers were, only a few years earlier, Chicago's answer to Gene Vincent and had released a handful of singles on the Cha Cha Records label. This stomping rockabilly relic would figure much more prominently in a future Steckler project, but here it is a barely audible afterthought.

The gaiety of the party scene is cut short by a shot of a uniped using crutches along a crappy sidewalk in a seedy part of L.A. Steckler's old friend Titus Moede had been pegged for another small role (at the party he played George J. Morgan's assistant), but why a cripple? Who knows? Steckler's visions can be curious at times and downright confounding at others.

This crummy part of L.A. is chockfull of flashing neon signs announcing "Girls Inside," "Burlesque" and "Dancing Girls for Partners." Most of these establishments double for nests of call girls and their handlers. Mad Dog strolls out of one with Erina Devore at his side. Erina is played by Erina Enyo of "Carmelita" fame.

Erina leads Mad Dog down the street to her rundown apartment. "It's a great place you have here," a discerning Mad Dog says. "Yeah, for the rats," Erina responds. At least she is self-aware of her situation. Mad Dog, however, is either completely delusional or one oddball complimentary psychopath.

After a couple of Cutty Sark cocktails served up in tall plastic tumblers, Mad Dog puts the moves on his earmark. Erina responds accordingly, then Mad Dog snaps and slaps her across the tiny room, onto her bed, exclaiming, "You're cheap!" "Cheap!?" "What's so cheap about 50 dollars?" More self-awareness from Erina.

Mad Dog points out, "I hate you and I'm gonna kill you." The crazy cops a pair of scissors while approaching his quarry, and then smacks and bats her around like a cat bats its toy. Steckler has actually created a genuinely demoralizing sequence of events and is in no hurry to end it. Finally, Mad Dog begins stabbing, and that is the end of Erina the character. It was also the end of Erina Enyo's employ as one of Steckler's stock players.

As Mad Dog continues his work, the camera closes in on a transistor radio as a newscaster interrupts the scheduled programming with a news bulletin. "At 10:29 this evening, three inmates from the asylum for the criminally insane, successfully made their escape after slaying five guards and hurdling the 20-foot barbed-wire wall that surrounds the institution. Authorities have identified the escapees as Herbie Click, Keith Rogers and Gary Barcroft."

The Mort Mad Dog Click character was not initially intended for the movie, nor was another psycho performance by Cash Flagg. Steckler realized the film's running time needed some padding, so some additional action had to be devised. And thus Mad Dog was born. *The Thrill Killers* was facing a 60-minute mark just as *Wild Guitar* had, two years earlier, and Steckler added the kidnappers. As pointed out in the previous chapter, *Incredibly Strange Creatures* also runs a scant 60 minutes if the musical numbers are removed.

Back at the Saxon pad, Joe and Liz quarrel over money, bills and career choices. Liz just wants to "go away for a while." But Joe cannot leave the telephone unattended: "It might ring any minute with the part I've been waiting for." Liz is not buying it, and her tone of voice and eyes tell it all. She has become disheartened by her husband's pipe dreams. To Liz, Joe is a wanna-be that never will be.

Come morning, Liz leaves Joe a "Dear John" letter as he sleeps away with a *Movies Illustrated* magazine draped across his lap. This magazine, with Richard Burton on its cover, also featured an article on Steckler and *The Incredibly Strange Creatures*. Also of note is that the magazine is home to his old movie title nemesis Stanley Kubrick and his *Dr. Strangelove* film. Steckler's right-hand man Titus Moede pulled some strings and arranged for the impressive three-page spread. Knowing Steckler's panache for self-promotion, it is surprising the periodical was not visibly opened to that very article, perhaps the camera zooming in on it as the scene comes to a close. This time Steckler showed restraint, or maybe it did not even cross his mind. In any event, Steckler self-promotion *is* coming up.

Mad Dog takes time out of his leisurely day to terrorize a couple of kids on their front lawn. They smile, having no idea of his intentions, and then their mother snatches them away. The mother is played by Mary Morgan, wife of George J. Morgan.

The young boy is played by Carolyn Brandt's little brother Tony Flynn, who went on to play guitar for the rock bands Steppenwolf and Deep Purple ... well, sort of. In 1977, Flynn and keyboardist Geoff Emery put together New Steppenwolf *sans* the band's leader and lead singer John Kaye. This largely bogus incarnation of the early '70s hard rock band ran its course on the touring circuit in a matter of years with the majority of "Born to Be Wild" fans satisfied with the new lineup's performances. Then in 1979, Flynn and Emery looked to revive Deep Purple with its original singer Rod Evans.

Rod Evans would be the only legit member of Deep Purple, with Emery standing in for Jon Lord and Flynn supplanting the legendary and fiery Ritchie Blackmore. There simply was no reason to believe that this would go well and it did not. Unlike the largely passive Steppenwolf fans, Deep Purple's followers rioted at nearly every performance that would ultimately be cut short by the violence. Author Dave Thompson recounted this vicious scene in his book *Smoke on the Water: The Deep Purple Story* (p. 229–30):

> No matter where the group went, audiences remained furious at the deception. The Quebec show, at the Capitol Theater on August 12, was punctuated throughout by a hail of chairs raining onto the stage, a dire situation Tony Flynn only exacerbated when he grabbed the microphone

to admonish the crowd, "Whoever wants to see the real Deep Purple is welcome to stay ... the rest of you can fuck off." Inevitably, it was the band who fucked off....

It would be interesting if Tony Flynn had requested the services of Uncle Ray and his Bolex camera at some or even one of these ill-fated events. Steckler would have most assuredly captured the action both on and off the stage. If any such footage actually exists, perhaps it will surface one day to help explain what all the fuss was about.

Back to *The Thrill Killers*: On the run and on the road through Topanga Canyon, Liz manhandles her convertible towards the Pleasant Inn. Steckler christened this establishment after an inn in Mount Pleasant, Pennsylvania, near his hometown of Reading. The diner interior was constructed on a small stage on Santa Monica Boulevard called Smith Brothers' Studios. Erina Devore's "rat-hole" apartment was also a product of the inexpensive facility.

Liz's cousin Linda is the restaurant's owner and operator. Linda is played by actor Gary Kent's wife Laura Benedict (real name: Rose Mary Gallegly). For her first and last time in front of the camera, she projects as well as a seasoned performer. Plus, like many of Steckler's actresses, she is quite easy on the eyes.

Linda scoots over to the jukebox, revealing a pressbook of *The Incredibly Strange Creatures* hanging next to it. Steckler never disappoints in the shameless self-promotion department. Along with the pressbook, several 8×10 glossies of Brick Bardot, and one of Brick with Mae West, are haphazardly pasted to the wall. They will soon figure into the film's narrative.

Linda chats up her only customers, soon-to-be-wedded Ron and Carol. Ron is played by Ron Burr, who was a friend and student of actor Herb Robins. Robins ran an acting workshop and many of the *Thrill Killers* players were culled from his stock. No great surprise: The character of Carol is portrayed by the lovely Carolyn Brandt.

Ron and Carol vacate the diner to scope out their new digs. As they pull away, Liz pulls in. Over a cup of coffee, Liz tells Linda the woes of Joe and Hollywood life. When asked how her "handsome husband" is, Liz divulges, "I wouldn't know. I left before he got up this morning. I left him a note." So much for broken hearts and subtleties, Liz has clearly moved on.

Ron and Carol park their Ford pick-up truck in front of what appears to be an abandoned house. Carol is less than enthused by its outside condition so in they go, looking for the owner Hank. Hank is a lousy housekeeper and the inside looks even more dismal than the outside. Ron continues to try and sell his bride-to-be on the lean-to: "For a hundred bucks down, what more could we ask?"

An excited Ron has a big surprise for Carol in the backyard. What is better than one dilapidated house? Why, that would be two dilapidated houses. Carol can hardly contain her glee (sarcasm). This couple's romance is about to be cut short by "The Head Choppers Three" (as *The Thrill Killers* radio spot described them).

A sidenote about these houses is in order as they were not originally in the script. Steckler recalls on Media Blasters' *Thrill Killers* audio commentary,

> George [Morgan] and I were looking for locations and we drove down to Topanga Canyon and we're driving by and I just look over to my right and I say, "Hey, wait George. Stop. Turn around." Then we turn around and I say, "Go down that road." So,

I'd spotted the old house and the other old house, two of them. We were looking for roads to do the chase sequences and everything. "Oh, no, no, no, no. We have to stop here. We have to shoot here."

The two houses were seemingly abandoned, but the actual owners (or squatters) were located and settled on $50 a day as a rental. Steckler maintains that members of the Charles Manson family were living there as they migrated back and forth from nearby Spahn Ranch. Incidentally, exploitation alumni Herschell Gordon Lewis shot his all-nude lesbian Western *Linda and Abilene* at the same movie ranch three years later.

Still looking for Hank, Carol and Ron climb a rickety flight of stairs and locate him. Well, part of him. Looney Toon Keith Rogers sneers, "Looking for Hank? Here he is." Then the lunatic sends Hank's severed head down the stairs with the blade of a bloodied ax. It is a simple but effective way to let Ron and Carol know they are in for it.

Nutcase Keith Rogers was really Keith O'Brien (who was really Keith Pierce), who had really been the soundman on *The World's Greatest Sinner*; it is likely that Steckler met him on that shoot. Steckler remembered him as "a trained actor from the Pasadena Playhouse." As good as O'Brien's performance is, and it is good, it appears as though he was a one-and-done.

Now the rest of "The Head Choppers Three" are introduced. First up is Herb Robins, giving it his all as the nervous Herbic Click. It is odd how Click appears to be the leader of this motley crew but at the same time fidgety and timid. While this off-kilter characterization could easily be chalked up to Steckler's erratic directing style, it is more likely that Robins was dialing in his improvisational skills.

Steckler always referred to Robins as "Ted V. Mikels' boy," but the fact is, he only showed up for two of Mikels' films (*The Doll Squad* and *The Worm Eaters*). Robins stuck by Steckler's side for four of his features as either actor, writer or assistant director. Robins' birth name was Herb Rabinowitz and his brother Mort Rabinowitz was a production designer who found work on Tobe Hooper's sleeper horror feature *The Funhouse* (1981). Herb found work there as well, playing the carnival manager.

Regarding Herb Robins' left eye, the black one, the one with stitches: Robins had upset some big fellow a few days earlier and the guy let him know it when he ran into him on the sidewalk with his fist. Robins wound up in the hospital with a bum eye and the notion that Steckler would not use him because of it. On the contrary, Steckler thought the eye looked great and added more color to Robins' character.

Finally, rounding out "The Head Choppers Three" is Gary Barcroft, played by Gary Kent. Kent's name and face should be familiar to all outré cinema fans. He has been in the movie trenches since the late 1950s and is a veteran of films by cult favorites Steckler, Mikels, Al Adamson, Stephen C. Apostolof, David L. Hewitt and Richard Rush. He went on to become a sought-after stuntman (an attribute Steckler would utilize later), a production manager, writer, producer and even director. Some of Kent's better-known features include *Hells Angels on Wheels* (1967), *Satan's Sadists* (1969), *The Incredible 2-Headed Transplant* (1971) and *Bubba Ho-Tep* (2002). He has well over 100 credits under his cinematic belt and recounts those adventures in his book *Shadows & Light*.

Herbie is the nervous one while Keith is a complete loon. This makes

Gary the heaviest-handed of the nuts. His crazy-eyed stare, coupled with the caressing of his over-sized hunting knife, adds up to a visibly sadistic figure. Gary's glare slathers on the foam of fear as his body language works it into a thick lather. Herbie and Keith are no walks in the park but Gary is the one to not be left alone with.

With all three psychos in motion, Ron and Carol's minutes are numbered. There is very little in the way of tension-building. Gary quickly tires of Herbie and Keith's near-playfulness with their captive. When Ron tries saving Carol from an attempted rape, he accidentally slams the back door closed. Apparently, this is a very bad move on Ron's part.

Gary's eyes bulge even further from his skull while punching the living daylights out of Ron. Helplessly, Carol watches the carnage. The worst for Ron is yet to come: The beating culminates with Ron's head being lopped off with an ax smack dab in front of his mortified fiancée.

Even Gary's partners seem uneasy with his current mental state. While these wackos bicker it out, Carol makes a mad dash for the front door. The cat-and-mouse game lasts but only a few minutes but Carol gives Herbie and Keith quite the workout. The more she alludes them, the more she seems to excite them.

Currently, Gary is MIA but he returns once Carol enters the main house. She dashes upstairs (worst idea ever) and is cornered by Keith and Gary. Herbie has found a transistor radio broadcasting a reading of *Little Red Riding Hood* and plops down for a listen (Ron Haydock provides the narration). The implication is that Herbie is either

Herb Robins as Herbie Click in the foreground with Carolyn Brandt as Carol and Keith O'Brien as Keith Rogers in a chase scene from *The Thrill Killers* **(1964) (author's collection).**

bored by this particular heinous crime or he is a feeble-minded simpleton whose focus is easily diverted.

Carol is screaming bloody murder while the menacing Gary terrorizes her. The action is out of view and out of control, so what horrors Gary is administering is a mystery. Keith, watching the activity, bounces around manically, giving Gary a deranged pep talk. Then, with ax firmly in hand, Keith bolts in for the kill. The schizo swings, the blade connects with the wooden floor and the screaming stops. One room—one ax—one outcome.

The action shifts back to the Pleasant Inn. Liz is still there lamenting that she remained with Joe as long as she did. Joe and George Morgan are en route to intercept her. Once the men are inside, Liz's eyes, facial expressions and general demeanor suggests she is not at all thrilled to see them.

Joe strolls right up to Liz. He is plainly there to retrieve her and take her to her proper dwellings. Producer George Morgan is there to scope out a location for his latest picture. He finds the Pleasant Inn to his liking though it appears he finds its proprietor even more so.

Linda notices Morgan's subtle advances and flirts in a self-effacing manner. She is implying she might just like to be in his movie too. Before this party can blow full-steam ahead, the Head Choppers Three crash the shindig. Herbie asks Linda about a pay phone (to call his brother in L.A.). Keith states, with bloodied ax in hand, "Poor Hank. He had dandruff," then he and Gary slide into a booth. An unwitting and unknowing Linda closes the door behind them. Big mistake.

"Now, you listen to me, you little tramp. If I had wanted that door closed I would've closed it myself." Gary's sneer, at this point, is merely a warning. Herbie, hearing the conversation and his partner's temper escalating, races over to defuse the volatile situation. What Gary's beef is with a closed door might be puzzling at first, but appreciation of his tenure in a mental home tends to clear things up—a little.

Herbie attempts explaining Gary's outburst away with "claustrophobia," then he is back to the pay phone and Gary's back to the table. Linda is not accepting Herbie's lame excuse and approaches Keith and Gary's table asking, "What'll you fellows have?" They both want beers and the unshaken Linda moves to get them, indicating that the customer *is* always right.

Herbie Click reaches out to Mad Dog Click, via Ma Bell, and implores his brother to back him: "I need your help bad. I got a couple of nuts with me." An unmoved Mad Dog cracks, "So, what do you want me to do about it? I've got problems of my own." Herbie, sensing his brother's indifference, assures him that he has money. It seems things are tough all over.

Linda returns to the table of ill repute with two unopened cans of brew. Confused, Keith examines the vessel, inquiring, "Now, how do you expect me to open it without an opener?" The loon's server offers, "Why don't you just pop the top?" Actress Laura Benedict delivers this line with an effervescent verve usually saved for, and employed by, a product spokesperson. The product is Schlitz beer.

The Schlitz brewing company was one of the earliest to employ Ermal Fraze's invention the "pop tab." Fraze, from Muncie, Indiana, had patented his creation in 1963 and immediately sold it to the Alcoa Corporation. He and his "pop tab" made history while simultaneously helping make the union of the "churchkey" and the beer can history. It is quite likely that Steckler's film was the first to demonstrate Fraze's new gadget on the silver screen.

Off the phone, Herbie beelines it to the cash register, hits SALE and loots the cash drawer while insisting on coffee. Keith plays with the jukebox and Gary continues swilling the beer. Liz and Joe have deduced that the three intruders are the asylum escapees. Nothing to do now but wait for the arrival of Mad Dog Click, or so Herbie thinks.

In actuality, Herb Robins was tiring of the *Thrill Killers* shoot and wanted to find himself elsewhere. Like so many times before, Steckler found himself at odds with his actor. Nothing to do now but alter the already altered script and narrative.

Keith, still goofing around with the jukebox, notices the portraits of Joe Saxon–Brick Bardot on the wall beside it. Keith lunges over to Joe and Liz's table, brandishing his ax and demanding, "Hey, you, Curly. You a movie star or something?" Herbie gets in on the activity: "Hey, Curly. You a movie star?" The two brainiacs put their noodles together and conclude that the pictures are indeed of their handsome male captive.

Keith wants to chop Joe's head off and hang it on the wall next to his glossies. Herbie has other plans that includes a bit of role-play. At gunpoint, Joe is forced onto a bowling pin game to be used as a stage for his final performance as Samson. Demeaning the rookie actor, then killing him, in front of his friends, is a distillation of Herbie's scheme.

Keith is still pestering Herbie for Joe's decapitated head. Keith, pointing to Liz, barks, "The girl! The girl! She's got hair." Between this admonishment, Hank's dandruff and mocking Joe's "curly" hair, it is obvious what Keith's favorite pastime is. This loon-goon enjoys scalping his victims after beheading them. Would Joe Saxon's noggin be displayed with his promo photos without his rug, and if so, what does the halfwit Keith do with his collected scalps?

Herbie continues amusing himself with a troubled Joe Saxon, who doubtlessly wishes he was currently in a "web of non-reality ... non-reality." Herbie carries on the demented charade: "When the director says 'action,' that means death." It is here, the close-up of Joe's face, that Bardot's true acting abilities come forward. Without a word uttered, Joe is clearly distressed, even grieving as the reality of his mortality begins caving in on him. In what appears to be one last act of prolonging Joe's agony, Herbie gulps his coffee. The gunman barely mumbles the word "action" before collapsing to the floor grunting and groaning, "Poison." Linda had *wittingly* laced the coffee with strychnine. Now Steckler has obliged his antsy actor and killed off his character.

Joe snaps out of his catatonic daze, charging Keith while instructing Liz to run for the hills. With a dead Herbie, there is nothing left for Steckler to do but send the mean-spirited Gary after her. This is where the director learned of Kent's prowess as an actor, stunt-coordinator *and* stuntman. Kent provided Steckler with the perfect trifecta at just the right time.

Post haste, Liz is out the door with Gary running a very close second in this race of doom. Steckler sent his actors through some of the worst terrain Topanga Canyon had to offer. Rocks, logs, thorn-infested underbrush and every manner of detritus imaginable are all hurdled or crushed under the high-heeled feet of the film's screaming

Gary Kent as Gary Barcroft and Liz Renay as Liz Saxon in *The Thrill Killers* (1964) (author's collection).

heroine. As Kent put it in his autobiography, "She never complained, wimped out, or ruined a take."

Having finished with Keith, Joe hears his wife's cries for help and makes a mad dash for the canyon. There is little reason to believe that Joe can catch up, but after shedding his sport coat onto the desert floor, his pace accelerates. Liz will be happy to pick up and pay that dry cleaning bill as her husband miraculously catches up with her hunter.

Joe snatches Gary and the Topanga Canyon fistfight-rumble to the death is on. The two adversaries punch, kick, scratch, bite, claw and crawl their way towards the top of the mountain while Liz shows a lot of leg. Gary breaks away, chasing Liz to a ledge. Liz outwits her stalker and flails herself into her husband's arms. He orders her to get help, and away she goes.

Joe, getting it together once more, pummels his wife's assailant to the dusty ground. Up and down these two go, slapping and jabbing one another until Joe lands a couple of punches that take the wind out of Gary's sails. Yet again, "Joe has found himself tapped"; this time it is at the same precarious spot where, minutes earlier, he had found his wife. Gary leaps for Joe and they tussle, then off the cliff goes the worst of the Head Choppers Three.

Gary is dead at the bottom of the ravine. Liz reaches the dirt road in search of help and Joe remains alone atop the canyon wall. Liz flags down a car and implores the driver to get her help. Liz does not know that she has just put herself in the hands of Mort "Mad Dog"

Click. Joe watches from a distance as his wife steps into the stranger's car and pulls away.

Mad Dog has Liz at gunpoint and wheels his Plymouth station wagon recklessly through the canyon roads. What his intentions are remain unclear, but it will probably involve him deciding she is "cheap" or "no good" and then stabbing her to death with whatever is handy. Of the film's four psychos, Mad Dog seems to be the one with the least focus, possibly making him the most unpredictable and dangerous.

Joe fumbles his way back down to the bottom of the canyon, stopping to pick up his sport coat, and then into the Pleasant Inn. The police have arrived and apprehended Keith, who is screaming maniacally: "No! No! I don't want to go back! I don't want to go back! They'll want my ax." This is all the more reason for Keith to go—back.

The police officers are played by Force McCall (aka George Caldwell), James Bowie, Titus Moede and Lonnie Lord (aka Ron Haydock). A couple of years later, these four actors would become the nucleus to the zaniest of Steckler projects. Also in tow is actor Gene Pollock playing the detective; Pollock had also helped Steckler and Haydock pen the script.

Mad Dog speeds his car through the canyon with a screaming Liz. Motorcycle Officer West (Titus Moede) is in hot pursuit, but Mad Dog outmaneuvers him. He then ditches his car, dragging Liz along. The self-reliant Liz smacks Mad Dog right in the kisser and makes her escape.

En route to his fate, Mad Dog first shoots and kills Officer Wells (McCall) who had been firing a shotgun in his direction. Up next, Officer Freeman (Bowie) is shot indiscriminately, not once but three times. Then Officer Tracey (Haydock) is gunned down almost as an afterthought. The crazed killer stumbles upon a cowboy, levels his gun, blows him away, and steals his hat and horse.

Initially the fellow playing the cowboy was to double as Mad Dog on the horse as he was a professional stuntman currently working at the Spahn Ranch. Steckler recalls that he jumped onto the back of the horse and rode out of the scene like a pro. Of course, he was a pro and that is not at all what the director wanted. Mad Dog had stolen the horse out of desperation to shake the police, but that did not mean that the character could ride a horse properly.

So Steckler decided to perform the stunt himself, having only ridden a horse once in his life. Galloping through Topanga Canyon on horseback was a dream come true for Steckler. He finally got to play an on-screen cowboy for all to see. He was a cowboy kid living his childhood dream with Republic, Monogram and PRC Westerns going through his head.

Steckler asserts that cinematographer Vilmos Zsigmond captured all the horse action with a handheld camera while riding in the back of a pick-up truck. Simply put, there is no evidence to support this claim either in Zsigmond's credits or *The Thrill Killers'* credits. Whoever did it, the shots are remarkably well orchestrated, further illustrating *someone's* command of his hardware and his craft. The most likely culprit? Joseph V. Mascelli.

Mad Dog, on horseback, comes to a dead end and ditches his four-legged ride like he had ditched his station wagon. He then heads out on foot. Officer West has finally caught up with the deviate and a short chase is on. Mad Dog loses his hat, loses his balance, then loses his life to a bullet fired by Officer West. The thrill-killing ends with Mad Dog tumbling into a shallow drainage ditch fabricated by assistant director Don Russell. Mad Dog's expiration into his temporary resting place is very similar, in theme, to Jerry's death oceanside in *Incredibly Strange Creatures*. The director pondered the two endings: "It's interesting [but] I don't know what that means."

More *déjà vu*: Just as producer Mike McCauley found work for his client Bud Eagle at the end of *Wild Guitar*, George Morgan found work for Joe Saxon. Joe will star in Morgan's next picture alongside his "new discovery," Ms. Transylvania (Linda from the Pleasant Inn diner). Liz resists but at five grand a week (for ten weeks), the high-maintenance gal relents. In addition to the fat scratch, Liz should be satisfied knowing that her husband is no longer "caught in a web of non-reality … non-reality."

Steckler skipped the standard film distribution route and took *The Thrill Killers* out as a roadshow engagement. Roadshows generally involved a live cast of some sort or the other. Steckler had learned a thing or two with his previous feature and had hopes of duplicating its success.

One of the most infamous and successful of these attractions was Kroger Babb's *Mom and Dad*. This fairly innocuous film was touted as the antidote to premarital sex and teen pregnancy. However, Babb spiced and spliced it up with scenes of live baby birth and venereal disease casualties. Also on hand, live

A newspaper ad mat for *The Thrill Killers* (1964) (author's collection).

at theaters, was an expert called "Elliot Forbes" who sold educational pamphlets to the moviegoers. Obviously, "Forbes" could not be at every showing so basically anyone willing to deliver the schtick was in the employ. One of the reasons this film was so popular was that it offered many young men their first glimpse at female genitalia. The fact that another human being was being pulled out of it did not seem to matter much.

As time went on, the cheapie roadshows gave way to the more involved and elaborate spook shows and/or ghost shows. These performances usually involved magic, anything macabre and some good ol' Grand Guignol theater (some beheadings and a bit of gore were on the menu). Once the performance (usually 30 minutes) concluded, the feature film or films were screened.

The Thrill Killers probably had more in common with the ghost show than the more restrained and tame roadshow.

Promoter Joe Karston sent Steckler to the "Godfather of Halloween," Don Post, to create some glow-in-the-dark Mort "Mad Dog" Click rubber masks. When Steckler himself could not attend a screening, he would send a mask of himself and a rubber murder weapon for a theater employee to use.

Post had been responsible for some the first latex Halloween masks in production, his most famous being Swedish wrestler-actor Tor Johnson and the William Shatner mask that later became the face of *Halloween*'s Michael Myers. Steckler's "Mad Dog" lookalike disguise was certainly in good company, but unfortunately few, if any, have survived. The director lamented in *Incredibly Strange Films* Boyd Rice (p. 51), "Yeah, I had one, but recently I pulled it out of the box and the rubber had just deteriorated after all these years. See, we used them in the drive-ins. They would have guys running around looking like me. ... [Don Post] has probably still got the mold." (During Steckler's *Incredibly Strange Film Show* episode, he holds up a mask that appears to be in good condition. He must have located another one.)

The original mold was destroyed, as per company policy, in 1974 after one final casting made by special effects technician Rob Tharp. Tharp was working at Don Post Studios and stumbled across an unmarked mold of an unnamed person's head and asked to cast it. Post granted Tharp's wish and so to this day Tharp may have the only sportable Mort "Mad Dog" Click mask in existence. Thirty-nine years later, Tharp

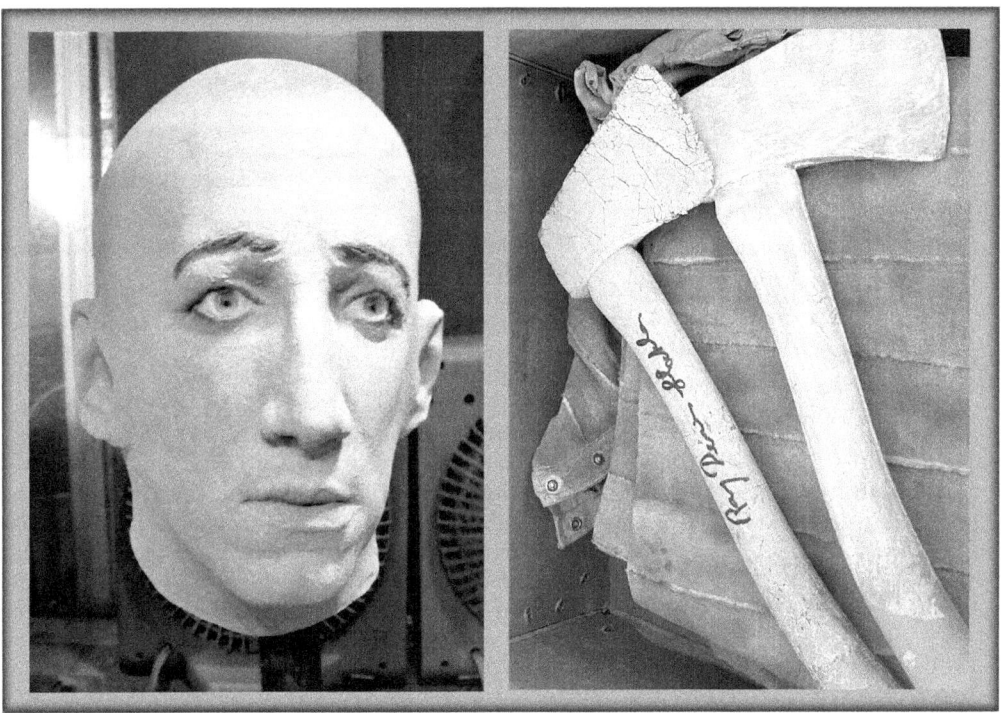

Former Don Post Studios employee Rob Tharp's final casting of the Mort "Mad Dog" Click mask. A set of two rubber prop axes that would accompany the mask to theaters while the film roadshowed as *The Maniacs Are Loose* (mask photograph courtesy Rob and Cathy Tharp; rubber axes photograph courtesy Laura H. Steckler).

had the mask cast and a few display pieces made. They sold in the area of $200 apiece.

Asked in a recent interview what Steckler might have paid for the masks, Tharp replied, "I'm thinking between one and two hundred dollars for the life cast and clay sculpt and mold, and another hundred for the ten masks. Don Post, Sr., wasn't one to overcharge. If it was over 500 for the job, I'd be shocked. I'd say probably 300."

What prompted Tharp to cast one more Cash Flagg mask? "I knew Don Post had made those masks for Steckler. I don't remember now how I learned it. I was able to recognize Cash Flagg just from looking into the mold. He's got a very distinctive face! Once I got the casting out of the mold, there was no doubt: Mad Dog himself."

This brings the story back around to the term Hallucinogenic Hypnovision which has been attached to *The Thrill Killers* for decades. As with *Incredibly Strange Creatures*, *The Thrill Killers* did not originally play in that format. Was Steckler and/or his rubber-faced lookalikes charging audience members at projected times while wielding plastic weaponry? Yes, indeed they were. Still, there is nothing in the theatrical trailers, radio spots, one-sheets or pressbooks to suggest any such form of promotion was in order ... yet.

Once *The Thrill Killers* exhausted its rounds, there was a change in moniker to get more mileage from Steckler's third feature film. One briefly used title,

On November 24, 1972, Indianapolis was home to four theaters showing *The Thrill Killers* (1964) in its roadshow shocker form as *The Maniacs Are Loose* complete with the Amazing Ormond getting you in the mood for Hallucinogenic Hypno-Vision. The film had special midnight screenings at the Indiana, Sherman, Tibbs and Greenwood drive-ins. The Sherman closed in the late '80s; the Greenwood was demolished and the land used for a car dealership. The Tibbs is still in operation (image and commentary courtesy film historian and archivist Raleigh Bronkowski).

The Monsters Are Loose, could have just as easily been used for *Incredibly Strange Creatures* as well. Years later, Steckler assembled a "director's cut" and called it

Mad Dog Click. But the film's best-known alternate title is most likely *The Maniacs Are Loose,* and this was another Joe Karston roadshow idea.

With *The Maniacs Are Loose* comes Hallucinogenic Hypnovision—finally. Take note of the expressly different excerpts from the *Thrill Killers* trailer vs. *The Maniacs Are Loose,* the most succinct and telling of the lot being: "Hallucinogenic horrors not only on the screen, but in the audience all around you!" The puzzling mystery of this film's promotion is almost at its conclusion.

"The Amazing Ormond" needs addressing to help unravel the yarns and conundrum of Hallucinogenic Hypnovision. Famed hypnotist Ormond McGill had traveled the country with spook and ghost shows for over 20 years before deciding that the rigors of the road were no longer for him. He appeared as Dr. Zomb with his show "London Hypnotic Séance" and later Dr. Zomb's "Seance of Wonders."

Joe Karston brought the Amazing Ormond aboard to provide a prologue describing the feature. Hallucinogenic Hypnosis was used to enhance the enjoyment of the upcoming film:

> Now, concentrate toward my eyes and as you watch my eyes they will seem to become larger and larger than before. Watch the eyes and, as you gaze deep into the eyes, the two eyes will converge becoming one gigantic eye. Ladies and gentlemen, look deep within that eye, and in the iris of the eye you'll begin to see revolving around and around and around a swirling disc. This is the Hypno-Disc ... Ladies and gentlemen, it is now my pleasure to present, for your entertainment, this very thrilling motion picture *The Maniacs Are Loose* and remember your psychological cue. When you see the Hypno-Disc appear before you, that is a time to look about and observe closely around the theater because you will truly see maniacs on the loose.

Dr. Zomb aka Ormond McGill (circa 1942) (author's collection).

The black and red Hypno-Disc would appear on-screen, alerting the Mad Dog lookalikes, or Steckler himself, to burst out from behind the screen and into the audience. Though quite similar, the Hypno-Disc should not be confused with the black and white Hypno-Wheel from *Incredibly Strange Creatures.* The Hypno-Wheel hypnotized Jerry, while the Hypno-Disc had the daunting task of hypnotizing an entire room full of moviegoers. Interviewer Boyd Rice got this from Steckler for the *Incredibly Strange Films* book (p. 38):

> I traveled with it for a couple of months. There was a point when I would jump out of the screen with a girl just like in the movie and we used to just run 'em out of the theaters. But one time near Sacramento someone shot me with a pellet gun—I think that's when I retired.

But in 1983 he told interviewer Johnny Legend in *Fangoria* #28 that he quit that type of performance because he had scared a man into a heart attack. (The fellow did live to tell the tale.)

In their 1980 book *The Golden Turkey Awards*, brothers Harry and Michael Medved nominated Hallucinogenic Hypnovision as one of "The Most Inane and Unwelcome 'Technical Advance[s]' in Hollywood History." The Steckler-Karston gimmick was one of several nominees that ultimately lost to William Castle's new and revolutionary technique "Percepto" which he employed for his 1959 film *The Tingler*.

All of this spook show business was masterminded by promoter extraordinaire Karston. Karston was a veteran of the spook, ghost and horror shows of the 1940s and '50s and at one point initiated his own religious revival, the Spiritual Psychic Science Church. Still, Karston was most known for shows with titles like "Dr. Macabre's Frightmare of Movie Monsters," "Dr. Satan's Shrieks in the Night" and "Dr. Jekyll and His Weird Show." By the time Karston and Steckler crossed paths, the ghost show had seen better days, so the two surmised that a fusion of the horror show and a novelty film would do the trick. And it did.

Steckler said in his *Thrill Killers* audio commentary, "I just wanted to make a crazy movie. We shot everything in black and white and to this day everyone tells me that those old house scenes were the scariest. They were the scariest because I shot them during the daytime instead of the night with all the shadows and stuff." (Note: By shooting during the day, Steckler would not have to put up the dough for light rentals either.)

At the time, *The Thrill Killers* was undoubtedly the darkest chapter in Steckler's cinematic career. A year later he would concoct an even darker story. But the director reportedly tired of doing another "psychopath" plotline and turned the film into an unhinged action-comedy of sorts.

Gary Kent claims in his book *Shadows & Light* (p. 71) that *The Thrill Killers*

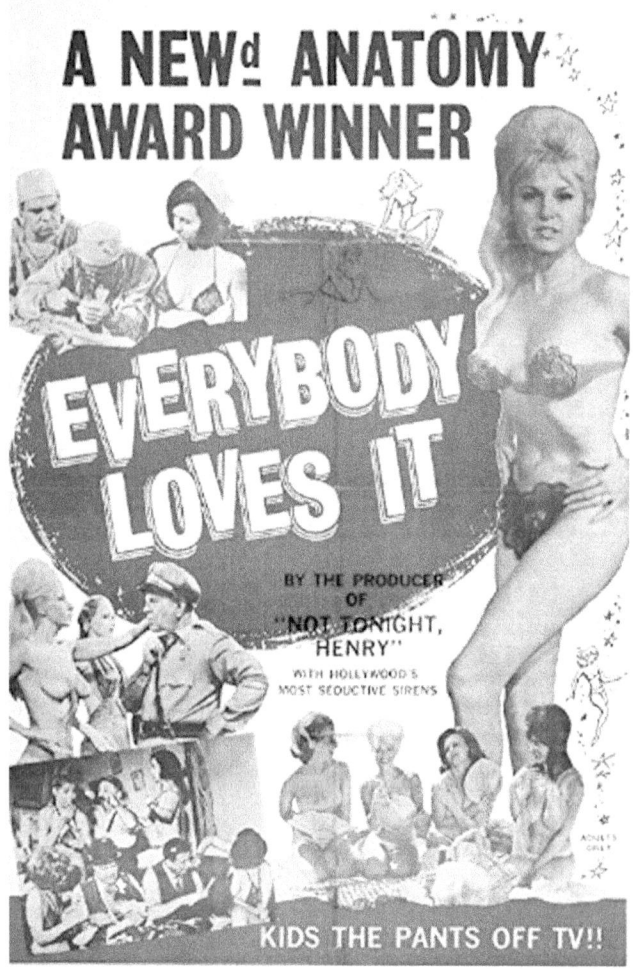

Poster for *Everybody Loves It* (1964). Steckler did some camerawork for this feature (author's collection).

"received a hearty endorsement from Bob Dobbs, the mysterious leader of the Church of the Sub Genius." Also of note is that Steckler handled some camerawork on director Philip Mark's 1964 sex-sketch comedy *Everybody Loves It*.

The Morgan-Steckler marriage forged yet another winner from absolutely nothing but talent, will and an unwavering desire to succeed. Steckler's family, friends, associates and neighbors trusted his wacky vision to the very end. This trust afforded them the opportunity to view the fruits of their labors on the silver screen. For all the right reasons, as fantastic as *The Incredibly Strange Creatures* is, *The Thrill Killers* is even better or, at the very least, racing neck and severed neck.

Rat Pfink a Boo Boo (1966)

Synopsis from Pressbook

When Cee Bee Beaumont (Carolyn Brandt), girlfriend of singing idol Lonnie Lord (Vin Saxon), is kidnapped by the Chain Gang (James Bowie, Mike Kannon and George Caldwell), Lonnie and his friend Titus Twimbly (Titus Moede) swing into action. They become the mightily costumed superheroes Rat Pfink and Boo Boo. Champions of women and children everywhere. Between rock and roll songs at wild Watusi go-go parties, Rat Pfink and Boo Boo search for Cee Bee in their Ratcycle. After many harrowing escapes they finally rescue Cee Bee and end the Chain Gang's reign of terror—only to face the fanged fury of Kogar the Ape, escaped from a jungle compound. But Rat Pfink saves the day as well as Cee Bee from the escaped ape and all zing over to the city-wide parade held in their honor, as once again Rat Pfink and Boo Boo prove that crime does not pay!

Credits

Cast: Carolyn Brandt (Cee Bee Beaumont); Ron Haydock [as Vin Saxon] (Lonnie Lord, Rat Pfink); Titus Moede (Titus Twimbly, Boo Boo); George Caldwell (Linc); Mike Kannon (Hammer); James Bowie (Benjie); Mary Jo Curtis aka Mary Demos (Irma La Streetwalker); Romeo Barrymore [aka Don Snyder] (Ape Trainer); Bob Burns (Kogar "The Swinging Ape"); Keith A. Wester (Cowboy); Larry M. Byrd (Commander Byrdman); Berri Lee, Alan Neal (Boys on Beach); Rox Anne (Girl on Beach); Linda Steckler, Tony Flynn (Children on Beach); Keith A. Wester aka Dean Danger (Narrator)

Production: Screenplay–Assistant Director: Ron Haydock. Original Story-Producer-Director-Photographer: Ray Dennis Steckler. Editor: Keith Wester. Music: Henri Price [Andre Brummer]. Wardrobe: Ruth Flynn. Publicity: Joe Bardo. Makeup: Mary Demos aka Mary Jo Curtis. Production Manager: Frank West. Second Unit Director: Herb Robins. Second Unit Photographer: Don Snyder aka Romeo Barrymore. Optical Effects: M.F.E. Titles: Tom Scherman. Title Photography: Rod Jolliffe. Re-Recording: Sound Transfer, Inc. Sound Recordist: Keith Wester. Associate Producers: Lillian Jackson, Bernard Benesch, Jeremy Lepard and John Rhinos. Executive Producers: George J.

Morgan and L. Steven Snyder. 67 minutes. Black and White (some versions have multi-colored tinting). Filmed: 1965.

Featured Music

"You're Running Wild," "Rat Pfink," "I Stand Alone" by Ron Haydock

"Big Boss A-Go-Go Party" by Ben Ralleigh and Bob Halley

"Eaffin' and Surfin'," "Bazooki" by Charles B. Tranum

The Film

> This is a job for you know and who.
> —Lonnie Lord from *Rat Pfink a Boo Boo*

With the success of *The Thrill Killers*, Ray Dennis Steckler cycled into 1965 with a sidecar of violence, action and good humor to deliver his zaniest madcap mash-up to date. *Rat Pfink a Boo Boo* (sometimes called *The Adventures of Rat Pfink and Boo Boo*) as a movie is certainly reminiscent of the filmmaking form, but ultimately seems to reside in some asymmetrical parallel universe. Steckler plays fast and loose with the rules of cinema and emerges with a film that is singular in its tones and arrangements.

This is a groovy, herky-jerky affair that can once again be blamed on the Morgan–Steckler damage duo. Steckler managed his third feature with far less moola than his second, and with his fourth film the bread was all but non-existent: He had 20 bucks to start, 2000 to finish, then 10,000 to blow it up to 35mm. Twelve thousand twenty smackers is not bad for a legend of ultra-low budget cinema, considering it was filmed in black and white using the not-so-inventive "RegularScope" technique. And, man, this romp is anything and everything but "regular."

Steckler repeatedly went on record stating that *Rat Pfink a Boo Boo* was partially influenced by his love of the original *Batman* theatrical serial from the 1940s. *Batman* was a 1943 black and

Artwork for *Rat Pfink a Boo Boo* (1966) (author's collection).

white 15-chapter cliffhanger series from Columbia. Producer Rudolph C. Flothow chose Lambert Hillyer to direct, Lewis Wilson to star as Batman and Douglas Croft to play his sidekick Robin. After seeing it, Steckler said he wanted to do something with Batman and Robin. "I tried to get the rights to Batman and Robin but didn't have the cash. What I really wanted to do was a Broadway musical with Batman and Robin. The studio executives didn't like that idea," recalled Steckler on the audio commentary track for the Media Blasters DVD release of *Rat Pfink a Boo Boo*.

Leaning into the film, a shot of a full moon dissolves as Irma La Streetwalker slinks out of the Lark Cocktail Lounge primping her hive, swaying her hips and generally looking to get *it* going. Irma is portrayed by Mary Demos (also credited as Mary Jo Curtis). Demos was a Las Vegas showgirl.

Without warning and out of the blue (Steckler tinted this scene blue for its re-release) come Linc and Hammer. These two menaces respectively brandish links of chain and a claw hammer. Hammer is played by relative newcomer Mike Kannon. Returning from *The Thrill Killers* is Force McCall (credited here under his real name George Caldwell) as Linc.

This pair of giddy and persistent delinquents relentlessly pursue Irma into a dark (dark blue) alleyway where she is accosted by a third derelict, Benjie. This miscreant scares the living daylights out of Irma by launching upward and out of an overflowing garbage can. James Bowie had small parts in three previous Steckler films, but in *Rat Pfink a Boo Boo* he finally got his cinematic day in the (tinted) sun. Bowie was now starring as the head honcho of a severely demented motley crew.

Irma backs away from her attackers, up a concrete staircase, but her time is short. Linc wraps his chain-linked appendage around her throat, rendering her unconscious. Benjie snatches her purse while Hammer threatens to install his namesake weapon into Irma's skull. As dark and violent as the scene is, and could have been, Steckler pulled the reins in regards to the expected carnage.

This portion of the pre-credits sequence certainly explains the film's original working titles *The Degenerate* and *The Insane*. Steckler is skating up to roughie subgenre territory with the authority of the Findlays or Joseph P. Mawra. The *Flesh* trilogy, the *Olga* series and a host of other psychosexual 1960s features immediately come to mind. The initial thought is that Steckler was attempting to outdo his previous work in the bleak and uneasy departments, but that would be all too simple and obvious.

Next up: another outlandish but alluring animated title sequence by Steckler favorite Tom Scherman. Scherman's work is accompanied by the trippy surf rock instrumental "Eaffin' and Surfin'." This number and "Bazooki" were penned by the virtual unknown Charles B. Tranum. Judging by these ditties, Tranum should have been at least as well known as the Astronauts or the Sentinels or perhaps Santo and Johnny.

Observant viewers will notice that Scherman's title card is misspelled and incomplete. As the story goes, the lab inserted an *A* between *Rat Pfink* and *Boo Boo* instead of an ampersand, and Steckler did not have the funds to rework it. Why a film lab would not own up to their obvious mistake has never been addressed. Additionally, there was not only the lab issue but possibly an issue of copyright. In the '50s and '60s, artist Ed "Big Daddy" Roth had a very character popular amongst hot rod enthusiasts,

Rat Fink. Presumably, Steckler added the *P* to *fink* to keep the artist off his case. Roth was as silent on the matter as the *P*.

In an effort to practice truth in advertising and garner some additional monetary miles, Steckler rechristened his abnormal cinematic offspring *Rock and Roll Super Heroes*. But later in life, he claimed the film was always titled *Rat Pfink a Boo Boo*. The one-sheet, the comic book (included in the movie), a prop cardboard placard and the copy written for the pressbook proposes differently. To further compound and confound the issue, Steckler later insisted that the real story involved one of his daughters chanting "Rat fink a boo boo, rat fink a boo boo" during one of the fight sequences. Meanwhile, Carolyn Brandt claims that the oddball title was partly a takeoff on the name of a Hollywood hot spot, Whisky a Go Go. There is simply too much evidence to offer otherwise, but still Steckler persisted: "That was the original title. No matter what you hear, that was the original title."

What's more likely is that Steckler was attempting to re-write and clean up a bit of his history. It is hardly an uncommon practice as many filmmakers have tried washing their hands of dirty laundry and/or outlandish accusations. Herschell Gordon Lewis denounced ever having an abortion clinic referral hotline (the Medved brothers, authors of *The Golden Turkey Awards*, threw that rumor out there) by inquiring, "Why would I have such a thing?" When Ted V. Mikels was asked if he had a fetish for women's

A highlighted caption from the *Incredibly Strange Films* book illustrating the conundrum surrounding the film's title (courtesy Boyd Rice).

high heels, he dodged the question altogether, stating, "I knew people who did." Simply put, it was damage control.

Rearing their heads once again, the Medved brothers nominated *Rat Pfink a Boo Boo* and *Incredibly Strange Creatures* in their "Worst Title of All Time" category. The other nominees: *I Dismember Mama* (1974), *Jesse James Meets Frankenstein's Daughter* (1965), *Matango, the Fungus of Terror* (1963) and *Wine, Women and Horses* (1937). According to those Medved boys, none of those titles could topple *Rat Pfink a Boo Boo*.

Tom Scherman's two-minute title sequence drags itself into one of Steckler's favorite establishing shots. At this point in his career, it is usually Hollywood and this film is no exception. Steckler's camera concentrates, yet again, on the Capitol Records building just as he had done three years earlier on *Wild Guitar*. Narrator Keith Wester begins, "This is Lonnie Lord. Lonnie is a rock'n'roll singer. Last year he sold ten million records. His fans are legion. Lonnie lives in Hollywood, the entertainment capital of the world. It's his town. Everywhere he goes, he carries his guitar with him because he never knows when he will be called upon to sing. Lonnie will sing a song any time, anywhere. Lonnie likes to sing."

Lonnie, played by Chicagoan Ron Haydock, had experienced minor fame in the Windy City as a wanna-be Gene Vincent. He was a rockabilly cat with his band The Boppers. The act scratched a few grooves for the Cha Cha label including "99 Chicks" with the unthinkable line, "Ninety-nine chicks, it's just my luck, not one of the girls I wanna fuck!" The expletive is nearly inaudible, but the mind fills in the blank. For its time, the song could have been quite the controversial coup had enough people heard it.

Haydock was also a contributing writer to *Fantastic Monsters of the Films,* which was a stylish knock-off (or an affable nod) to Forrest J. Ackerman's go-to mag *Famous Monsters of Filmland.* Stretching himself even thinner, Haydock penned numerous adults-only sex novels with such lurid titles as *Caged Lust*, *Sex-a-Reenos* and the head shaker *Ape Rape*. For these off-color endeavors, he usually hid behind the nom de plume Vin Saxon. Since Haydock used the Saxon name in *Rat Pfink a Boo Boo,* one could conclude that he was attempting to hide here as well. At the very least, Haydock was separating these projects from his true love: rockin' and rollin'.

Haydock *did* have talent. To what degree depended upon the listener, the viewer and/or the reader's threshold of accepting his jagged-around-the-edges creative abilities. Haydock was the stereotypical tortured artist with all of the compulsory trimmings and accouterments. He could be difficult, erratic and headstrong, but he and Steckler developed a bond that lasted for years, on and off the screen.

As the film carries on, Steckler's camera pans down the elaborate Capitol Records structure revealing Lonnie Lord signing autographs for fans. "His fans are legion." Here we see only three of them. Once placated, the trio turn in the opposite direction, one nearly trips and falls while Lonnie is all smiles and laughs. The rocker spins his hot heels and heads across the sidewalk of stars, pounding across Gene Vincent's first. James Arness' star receives a hot-heeled stomping as well.

The film quickly fixes itself on a carousel with Lonnie and his girlfriend Cee Bee Beaumont (Carolyn Brandt). The carousel was situated in Los Angeles' Griffith Park. Griffith Park was founded in 1896 by investor Griffith J. Griffith and sprawls for over 4300 acres. It has been seen on the silver screen numerous times over the years, from Billy Wilder's *Sunset Blvd.* (1950) to Danny DeVito's *Throw Momma from the Train* (1987). Steckler gave the park its only screen appearance of 1966.

Lonnie and Cee Bee ditch the carousel and engage in numerous activities including hide and seek, basketball, football and a bit of cat-and-mouse. These physical workouts are backed by the song "You're Running Wild." The sequence ends with the couple on a hilltop with Lonnie strumming a guitar and lip-syncing his song for Cee Bee. You see, "Lonnie likes to sing."

The active couple vacates the park as Lonnie manhandles a fourth generation Ford Thunderbird through the streets of L.A. This prop actually belonged to producer George J. Morgan and the house where Lonnie drops off Cee Bee was the home of Carolyn Brandt's parents. Carolyn lived in that house until she married Steckler.

Steckler returns the viewer to the deranged gang, lounging around their squalor in search of some kicks and chicks on the cheap. One of the dopes flops a phone book open and points to the name Cee Bee Beaumont. Cee Bee has unwittingly become these thugs' quarry and they deduce that she is in for a lewd phone call. Hammer does the honors.

This is where the film's second influence comes into play. At some point, Brandt began receiving indecent phone calls whenever Steckler left the apartment. Steckler, the makeshift sleuth, deduced that it was the one and only neighbor they knew. Steckler ambushed the creep, catching him red-handed in the naughty act. "This guy calls Carol and loves saying obscene things to her."

Cee Bee has a quick exchange with her gardener Titus Twimbly and then she is off the grocery store on foot. Titus is no dummy and catches more than an eyeful of Cee Bee's backside as she glides out of his view onto the sidewalk. If Brandt looked fetching in the previous Steckler films, "wowzah!" applies here. It is little wonder Titus seemingly lost control of his spewing garden hose.

Twimbly is portrayed by Titus Moede (pronounced and sometimes spelled "Moody"), who was born in 1938 in Chicago and migrated to Los Angeles 17 years later. His pilgrimage with cinema began in 1958 with a couple of juvie movies by director Bernard Girard. Next up was three years of uncredited roles; he shared the screen with Gregory Peck in *Pork Chop Hill*. Then a short run into television prior to Moede appearing before the purest of the outside Hollywood enigmas: Timothy Carey.

Carey had been toiling away for years on his incendiary masterpiece *The World's Greatest Sinner* when Moede made his presence known. Carey gave Moede a bit part as Follower Teddy. ("There's no use kidding ourselves. We've gotta hate someone.") Carey also gave him the uncredited job of associate producer. Even short-term memories should recall that Steckler was on hand with a camera to document Carey's clashing visions of the human condition. In all likelihood, this is where Steckler and Moede met.

Steckler went on to make *Wild Guitar* while Moede returned to uncredited screen roles. These two played brain games between the years 1963 and 1965 on *Incredibly Strange Creatures*, *The Thrill Killers* and now *Rat Pfink a Boo Boo*. Moede carried on in front of the camera and behind the scenes, with low-cost productions. His more notable efforts include *Pit Stop* (1969) and *The Dirtiest Game* (1970) before he surrendered to the easy monies of sexploitation and triple X features. Prostate cancer brought Titus Moede's mercurial celluloid career to an end in February of 2001.

At roughly the 17-minute mark, Cee Bee is stalked and pursued by one of the thugs. Hammer executed his duties as the lewd crank caller and now Linc is up to bat lasciviously grinning (literally) from ear to ear. Actor George Caldwell has a toothy grin that simply will not stop and Steckler zooms in close, making good use of it all.

Linc shadows Cee Bee for four and a half reel-time minutes before she reaches the supermarket. He patiently (or impatiently, it is impossible to know as he says nothing) waits and drags down four cigarettes. Cee Bee emerges from

Alternate artwork for *Rat Pfink a Boo Boo* (1966) (courtesy Media Blasters).

Later that evening, Cee Bee is awakened by the phone and sleepily makes her way to answer it. It is Hammer again and he instructs her to look at the door. Cee Bee does so and is startled to see Benjie there taunting her by beating and banging on her screen door. Cee Bee is suitably spooked this time, and rightfully so, but manages to muster the grit to dash into another room and call the police. Benjie takes a flying leap off the staircase and Steckler cuts to a leopard print bikini bottom, replete with shaking buttocks and hips.

This is an odd edit even by Steckler's standards, but then this film was started with 20 bucks, two rolls of 16mm film and no script or storyline. The first scene Steckler shot was a poolside sequence with Lonnie Lord rocking out to "Rat Fink" with some cutie-pie dancers gyrating accordingly. One of the girls is even wearing a monster-zombie mask from *Incredibly Strange Creatures*. Of some interest is that Ron Haydock returned to Chicago to re-cut and rat-tease the lyrics to a few Boppers songs for inclusion in the film. Also, continuing his self-promotion and branding, Steckler prominently placed an *Incredibly Strange Creatures* pressbook on a garage door.

Naturally, Cee Bee was at the pool party and at the song's conclusion a guest informs her that she has a phone call. Cee Bee cautiously takes up the receiver and Hammer does his thing. Cee Bee drops the phone, runs past Lonnie and the store with groceries in hand and walks directly past Linc, who inexplicably throws in the towel and walks away. Linc's sudden indifference begs the question, "Why follow her at all?"

As it is, this lengthy POV tracking shot appears to exist simply to show off Brandt's tightly wrapped posterior. Steckler blithely re-visited this motif later in the film. It is obvious that Steckler had a love affair with Ms. Brandt through the lens of his Bolex. This becomes even more clear as time moves on and the parameters of their union becomes murky, but still she remains the center of his camera's attentions.

into the street, leaps into a Chevy Corvair and speeds away. Cee Bee arrives home, races past Titus and straight into Hammer ... with his hammer. Cee Bee flees past Titus with Hammer on her tail, but her attacker makes a pit stop long enough to knock the daylights out of the gardener with his signature weapon.

Cee Bee is still in escape mode but lands directly in front of Benjie, who toys with her long enough for Hammer to catch them. Linc shows up in a truck, gets out and waylays Titus the gardener one more time for good measure. Meanwhile, Benjie and Hammer are unceremoniously escorting Cee Bee to the getaway vehicle. Cee Bee is tossed into the front seat, Linc and Hammer on either side with Benjie in the truck bed.

Lonnie arrives at the scene far too late and Titus briefs him on the situation: "Lonnie, they got Cee Bee." The exchange plays out as though Lonnie is wise to who "they" are, but there is no way for him to be in the know. All Lonnie can be aware of, is that Cee Bee received a distressing phone call at the party. Either that or there's a missing sequence where Cee Bee divulges the crank calls to Lonnie. She may also have mentioned the alarming visit from Benjie. In all probability, it is a continuity glitch in a script that did not exist.

The terror trio hustles onto the highway as Linc smirks and smacks a distraught Cee Bee around, ordering her to "Shut up!" Steckler zooms in even closer on Linc's big-toothed, unhinged grill. Not only does Cee Bee have Linc to deal with, but Hammer is mauling her all the while insisting she relax. Back at Cee Bee's pad, Titus nurses his wounds and Lonnie performs "I Stand Alone." Even when Lonnie is sad, "Lonnie likes to sing."

Once Lonnie's finished singing, the phone rings and this time it is Benjie: "Man, if you want your girlfriend back in one piece, you'll put 50 grand in a black case and put it in the garbage can behind 1213 North Highland tonight!" Lonnie balks, not at the amount, but the short time frame, but Benjie persists, "No! Tonight! Man, it's got to be tonight, baby, before dinner or she's had it—for good." A smidgen of the *Wild Guitar* narrative should come to mind.

Lonnie fills Titus in on the situation and says, "This is a job for you know and who." The duo darts into a closet, zip into some new threads and materialize as the apocryphal characters Rat Pfink and Boo Boo. "Together they play the four-fisted campaign against the enemies of truth, justice and the American way of life." Later prints of the film are tinted in pink once Rat Pfink and Boo Boo appear in full regalia. Rat Pfink sports a cape and ski mask while Boo Boo's indescribable get-up comes complete with flashing lights.

When searching for superhero character names, Steckler looked at Ron Haydock's tune "Rat Fink" and decided that would be his stand-in for Batman. Boo Boo received his unusual tag from the best softball team in Reading, Pennsylvania, the Boo Boos. However, in at least one interview Titus Moede recalled that his character's original name was Bobin. As inane as any of these labels are, they are really no more or less goofy than their initial inspirations.

At this point, the film begins to detach itself from its dark stalk-and-slash trappings to become something wholly unique. In the early '80s, Steckler confessed to Boyd Rice in *Incredibly Strange Films* that he was unsure of his decision to shift from thriller to comedy-spoof. By 1988, he had reconsidered and told *Incredibly Strange*

Film Show host Jonathan Ross that he had merely grown bored with how the film was progressing. For even more food for thought, actress Carolyn Brandt had her own take as to why her husband made such an abrupt change to the film's storyline (more on that later). Whatever his reasoning, *Rat Pfink a Boo Boo* has become an endearing and enduring cult movie classic.

Rat Pfink reminds his partner of the obvious: "Remember, Boo Boo, we only have one weakness—bullets." Then they are off "to fight crime" and presumably retrieve Cee Bee. The not-so-dynamic duo hop onto their Rat-Cycle and motor over the city streets with Boo Boo in control and Rat Fink standing in the sidecar posing and pointing.

Some of the Rat-Cycle scenes were shot by second unit cameraman Don Snyder hanging out of the back of a truck. Snyder had edited *Eegah* as well as *Incredibly Strange Creatures* and *Goof on the Loose*. So he was no stranger to the director's unorthodox manners of filmmaking. Dangling from the back of a pick-up clutching a Bolex camera was hardly anything to ask of a friend and colleague.

From here the film cuts back to Benjie making his way to the Dumpster behind 1213 North Highland (in real life, a film production building that housed Steckler's editing studio). Benjie dives into the Dumpster for the briefcase of ransom loot, but then the lid closes and locks.

Rat Pfink and Boo Boo watch from a distance as a cowboy (Keith Wester) leaves the building. Benjie yells for help and the good buckaroo releases him. It is worth mentioning that Benjie also launched out of a garbage can earlier in the film. Was Steckler implying that the character, Benjie, was garbage?

On a sidenote: While working for an ad agency making commercials, Steckler asked his boss for some financial assistance on his latest picture. The man in charge politely directed his employee to a novice film editor named Keith A. Wester. Steckler's employer was in no way interested in being an executive producer. However, Wester was a sacrifice he was willing to make. In the future, Wester later assisted Steckler as producer on two more features.

Rat Pfink a Boo Boo was shot silent, so every single solitary sound effect and piece of dialogue had to be painstakingly placed in post-production. This was Wester's first real gig and he made good on it as sound effects engineer, editor and even narrator. In years to come, he was Oscar-nominated six times for Best Sound: *Black Rain* (1989), *Waterworld* (1995), *The Rock* (1996), *Air Force One* (1997), *Armageddon* (1998) and *The Perfect Storm* (2000).

The 62-year-old Keith A. Wester rolled tape one final time 36 years after his career had started proper. Steckler admired the young sound effects wiz and was tickled to have him aboard. Steckler was just as happy to see him move onto bigger and better things. Steckler never had any sour grapes issues, but he did wish Wester had stuck around long enough to get that damned Academy Award—he deserved it.

Returning to the film: Benjie is getting away and it is back to the Rat-Cycle for another drawn-out chase sequence. Again, Boo Boo handles the driving and Rat Pfink directs the way while yelling, "Fight crime!" Benjie lands at the nest of misdeed and presents his fellow criminals with the satchel full of goods. They open the briefcase to find no money but a bunch of comic books, an issue of *Monster World* magazine with a *Munsters* cover and another featuring *Batman*. How apropos.

The film's first rumble begins and numerous times within its four-minute duration makes its way over to some pigeon coops. There is no particular reason to shoot around pigeon coops but they (or more precisely *other* pigeon coops) figured into Steckler's cinematic future. The later coops proved to be as perplexing as the first. It is only worth mentioning because Steckler makes sure the cages and their inhabitants get plenty of coverage, but why?

The rumble itself is as campy and full of slapstick comedy as any from the *Batman* television series, but *Rat Pfink a Boo Boo* predates the legendary show by at least a year. It is unlikely that *Batman*'s producers, Lorenzo Semple, Jr., and William Dozier, saw Steckler's low-rent homage to the Caped Crusaders. Still, it seems worth pointing out that *Rat Pfink a Boo Boo* was there first.

The brawl ends with the apprehension of Hammer. Linc and Benjie hustle Cee Bee back to the getaway truck. The final motorized chase is on and the kidnappers have quite the lead. Their truck tires inappropriately squeal and squall on dirt roads and the Rat-Cycle's engine cuts in and out, sounding like a flushing toilet. Then, when Rat Pfink and Boo Boo encounter a four-way traffic stop, they show they are always on the right side of the law or at the very least cautious. They stop, look both ways, then proceed—to "fight crime!"

Left to right, Vin Saxon [Ron Haydock] as Rat Pfink, Bob Burns as Kogar the ape, Carolyn Brandt as Cee Bee Beaumont and Romeo Barryman [Don Snyder] as the ape trainer in *Rat Pfink a Boo Boo* (courtesy Carolyn Brandt).

The hunt leads to Topanga Canyon exactly where *The Thrill Killers* was lensed. According to Steckler, that area was a Boy Scout ranch and they struck a deal with the troupe to the tune of $50 a day. Steckler considered it his back lot. Seven minutes into the sequence, the Ford truck actually sticks in the mud. Steckler gets the applicable coverage and then a script change is in the works. The goons and Cee Bee are now on foot, as are Rat Pfink and Boo Boo. The problem is solved—easy as mud pie.

The foot chase culminates in a fistfight between the sworn enemies. "Let justice prevail!" decries an amped-up Rat Pfink as he launches into his double-clenched blast against the criminals. Linc and Benjie are down for the count but now Cee Bee is seized by Kogar the Swinging Ape, escaped from a nearby zoo. Yes, Steckler has just introduced a gorilla into the storyline.

Actor Bob Burns occupies the monkey suit. He's an archivist and historian on the props and costumes of horror and sci-fi cinema. In this department, and others, he is akin to Forrest Ackerman. Both men had immense collections of authentic movie memorabilia and both had acted in film and performed consultant duties. Even still, of the two, only Burns had a recurring character, Kogar. Burns donned a furry primate suit dozens of times over the years and even as recently as 2009.

Rat Pfink and Kogar's handler (credited here as Romeo Barrymore) collectively stomp the desert floor in hopes of saving Cee Bee from the hairy anthropoid. Rat Pfink gets within earshot of Kogar and shouts, "Ape! Drop that girl!" Kogar complies, beats his chest, snarls, then slugs Rat Pfink square in the jaw. The scene concludes with an unmasked Rat Pfink and Cee Bee cooing and smooching with lots of kissy sounds. In the end, Kogar's inclusion was reduced to carrying Cee Bee on his shoulder with her rear end front and center.

As the film draws to a close, Steckler hijacks an actual Christmas parade putting Rat Pfink, Boo Boo and Cee Bee on the Rat-Cycle and sending them out. There are lots of shots of "fans" waving and screaming "Rat Pfink!" but there's no way they could have known who they were looking at as the film had not been completed or released. The keenest of viewers will catch a glimpse of Steckler and his Arriflex camera.

Just as *Wild Guitar* and *Incredibly Strange Creatures* concluded on the beach, so does this picture. The wafting sounds of Ron Haydock and "Big Boss A-Go-Go Party" can be heard. Lonnie, Cee Bee and Titus convene on the sand to celebrate with two dudes, two children (Linda Steckler and Tony Flynn) and a chick who had no other parts in the film. And that is how Steckler ends his fourth feature—with three characters

Carolyn Brandt as Cee Bee Beaumont being carried away by Bob Burns as Kogar the ape in *Rat Pfink a Boo Boo* (1966) (courtesy Carolyn Brandt).

the viewer knows and five they do not. It is almost as though the director had not had any of it planned in advance, but the film's tidy 67 minutes of running time makes the thing a marvel of low-budget cinematic precision.

Unlike Steckler's previous two features, *Rat Pfink and Boo Boo* did not get the roadshow treatment. Instead it was promoted throughout the Los Angeles area's supermarkets and their parking lots. Ron Haydock and a stand-in for Titus Moede appeared in costume, signing autographs and jamming the applicable Rat Pfink tunes. Carolyn Brandt would shake and move to the beats and her grandfather, dressed as a cowboy, would do the same.

Some critics did toss the film a few bones. According to *Variety*, "As an experimental film, *Rat Pfink* has its interesting moments and cinematic devices. Unfortunately they are few and far between and aren't quite enough to keep the viewer's

Vin Saxon (Ron Haydock) performs as Rat Pfink in front of an audience in a grocery store parking lot (1966) (author's collection).

attention fixed." The review went on to praise Carolyn Brandt's performance: "It's evident that she can easily go on to bigger and better things." Comedian Patton Oswalt described *Rat Pfink a Boo Boo* as "subversive brilliance" in his 2011 book *Zombie Spaceship Wasteland* (p. 122).

Rat Pfink a Boo Boo and grocery store appearances was not all Steckler had going on during this period. He also was cinematographer on *Scream of the Butterfly* (1965). The gig was for directors Eber Lobato and Howard Veit, collaborating on their only film together. This one did not initially set theater box offices ablaze, but the *Shades of Grey* movie review site cited Steckler's prowess behind the camera: "[T]he film is made even more entertaining by some consistently creative camerawork and direction that drive the story almost by themselves." *Fangoria* #28 (1983) called it "a sensitive black and white love story deemed unreleasable until a few seconds of accidental nudity (photographed by Ray in slow motion) were inserted and then—Boffo Boxoffice!" Ron Haydock had an uncredited bit part as a partygoer.

A newspaper ad for *The Velvet Trap* (1966), paired with *The Fickle Finger of Fate* (1967) starring Tab Hunter at the Center Drive-In Theater, 1603 Mechanical Drive, in Raleigh, North Carolina. This ozoner opened in 1956, concentrated on adult fare in the '70s and closed in 1985 (image and commentary courtesy film historian and archivist Raleigh Bronkowski).

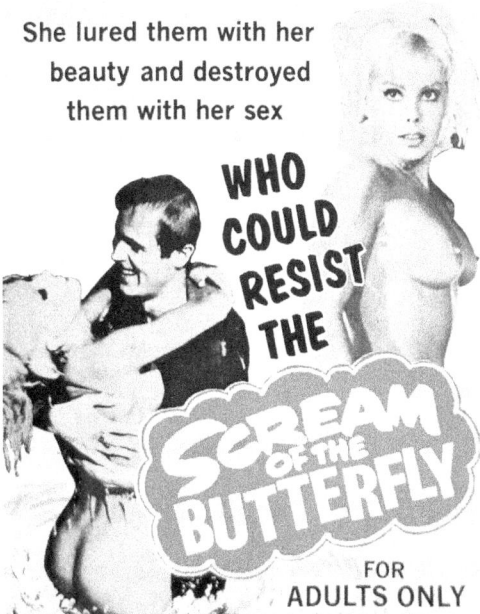

Artwork for the 1965 film *Scream of the Butterfly*. Steckler was cinematographer on this Eber Lobato-Howard Veit film (author's collection).

Around this same time, Steckler lent his cinematography skills to director Ken Kennedy's film *The Velvet Trap* (1966). Kennedy's rape-prostitution drama was filmed on location in Las Vegas and was quite likely Steckler's first time filming in his future home city. For this movie, he went by the pseudonym Sherwood Strickler, an anonym he did not employ again.

There seems to be some evidence that *Rat Pfink a Boo Boo* made its rounds through regions of Mexico. There exists a lobby card depicting Rat Pfink, Boo Boo, Kogar and the Rat-Cycle. However, the title is *Baty y Roby Contra El Crimen* which translates into *Baty and Roby Fight Crime*. It is interesting that the lead roles have been reversed where Boo Boo is Baty (as in Batman) and Rat Pfink has been switched to Roby (as in Robin). Carolyn Brandt remembers seeing the lobby card and to her recollection only *Rat Pfink a Boo Boo* and *Incredibly Strange Creatures* made their rounds south of the border. With Mexico's love affair with lucha libre (masked wrestling), it is easy to imagine the film playing very well there. Plus, there was a whole lot of attention and love given to that artwork and it would be unfortunate for it to have never been officially used.

Wrapping things up, cinematically speaking, *Rat Pfink a Boo Boo* is the oddest concoction of seriousness and the absurd, creating a unique collision of the senses for the viewer. The gritty on-screen violence is punched up with a heavy hand that stirs the cinematic stew to the boiling point. To bewilder the viewer or out of sheer boredom, Steckler skims the surface of this slapdash

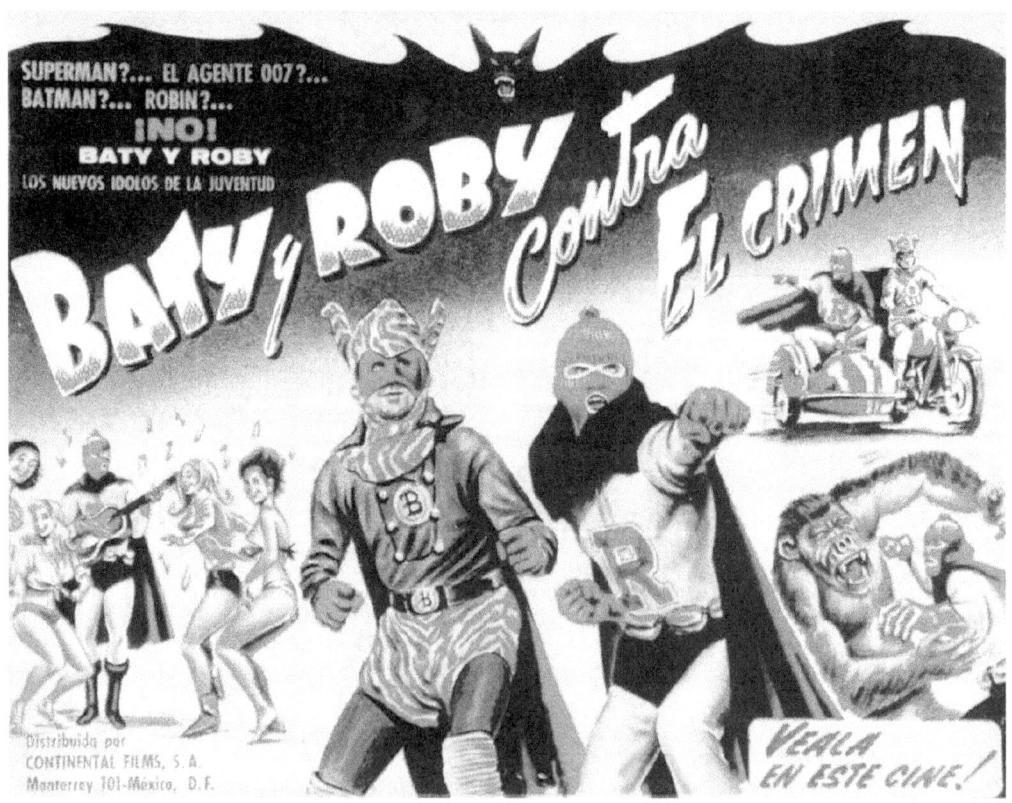

Mexican lobby card for *Rat Pfink a Boo Boo* (1966) (author's collection).

mixture, then adds a dollop of comic book super hero-stuff with pinches of action and humor. With *Rat Pfink a Boo Boo,* all of Steckler's film noir tendencies are fully realized, inextricably careening with his droll whimsy and camp senses.

The Lemon Grove Kids Meet the Monsters (1967)

Synopsis from Pressbook

(Note: The pressbook only contained the rundown of the film's first sketch, *The Lemon Grove Kids at the Big Race.*)

To settle their differences, Slug (Mike Kannon), Gopher (Cash Flagg) and the Lemon Grove Kids agree to participate in a cross-country race with their neighborhood rivals, Killer Krump (Herb Robins) and the East Lemon Grove Kids. But Duke Mazaratti (Bart Carsell), formerly a member of Slug's gang and now working for Big Ed Narzak (Coleman Francis), local bookie, has plans to make a lot of money on the race. He takes bets on Slug's gang to win the race while secretly placing his own money on Killer Krump's group, even though it's Slug's boys who are the better athletes of the two teams. Duke is confident of making a pile of money on the race because he has hired the Saboteur (Ed McWatters), who can fix anything, to fix the race against Slug and the Lemon Grove Kids. It's a riotous race through city, beach and desert as the Lemon Grovers heroically overcome the many plots hatched against them by the notorious Saboteur and the race to the finish line, neck and neck with Killer Krump's Kids.

Synopsis for *The Lemon Grove Kids Meet the Green Grasshopper and the Vampire Lady from Outer Space*

Strange things are occurring in Lemon Grove land. One by one the Lemon Grovers are vanishing. Where are they being taken and what is happening to them once they get there? Slug (Mike Kannon), Gopher (Ray Dennis Steckler), Jocko (Kedric Wolfe), Marvin-Marvin (Keith A. Wester) and Skinny (J. Jay Hartford) plan on getting to the bottom of this mystery with some half-pint help from Tickles (Laura H. Steckler). Along the way, the gang encounters a flying saucer, the Vampire Lady (Carolyn Brandt), a giant grasshopper (David Miles) and a myriad of other groovy ghoulies up to no good. Slug and Gopher find the rest of the Lemon Grovers in the basement of Mr. Miller's (Coleman Francis) house in a trance while the Vampire Lady and the grasshopper perform bizarre experiments on them. Gopher breaks up their inhospitable activities, causing chaos in every direction. It takes Tickles and some good old-fashioned magic to get Lemon Grove back on track.

Synopsis for *The Lemon Grove Kids ... Go Hollywood!*

The dazzling movie star Cee Bee Beaumont (Carolyn Brandt) needs some chores done around her estate and calls on the Lemon Grove Kids for help. Gopher (Ray Dennis Steckler), Don (Don Snyder), Pee Wee (Tony Flynn), Linda (Linda Steckler) and Tickles (Laura Steckler) all show up for work. What they don't know is that Killer Krump (Herb Robins) is back on the scene and he has a new accomplice—Nick the Gyp (Eric Morris). These two derelicts plan to hold Cee Bee ransom for a cool one million dollars. Killer and Gyp nearly succeed but Gopher, with the help of the other Lemon Grovers, thwarts their plan and save Cee Bee from peril, thus freeing her to take the role of her lifetime as Cleopatra.

Promotion (taken from theatrical trailer)

1. "It's coming! The world's craziest fun and fright show. *The Lemon Grove Kids Meet the Monsters.*"
2. "It's so scary, so crazy we dare you to see it. We dare you to see *The Lemon Grove Kids Meet the Monsters.*"
3. "The screen's funniest and wildest teenagers in the craziest fun and fright show you've ever seen."
4. "You'll see weird and frightening movie monsters not only on the screen but in the audience—alive and in person."
5. "See the horrifying mad mummy come to life and go into the audience to get you."
6. "We warn you, don't come if you're chicken. This show is not for sissies!"
7. "If you're not afraid, be sure to see the world's craziest fun and fright show, *The Lemon Grove Kids Meet the Monsters.*"
8. "A thousand and one laughs, thrills and chills."

Credits

The Lemon Grove Kids at the Big Race

Cast: Cash Flagg [Ray Dennis Steckler] (Gopher); Mike Kannon (Slug/Sylvester); Bart Carsell (Duke Mazaratti); Coleman Francis (Big Ed Narzak); Larry Pearson (Larry); Mary Morgan (Ma); Rox Anne (Roxy); Herb Robins (Killer Krump); Kirk Kirksey (Sunshine); Jim Plunkett (Stretch); Ed McWatters (The Saboteur); George J. Morgan (Officer Clancey); Bob Burns (Kogar "The Swinging Ape"/The Mad Mummy); Edward C. Wagner (Grandfather); Keith A. Wester (Cowboy and Man Shaving); Carolyn Brandt (Cee Bee Beaumont); Ron Haydock [as Lonnie Lord] (Rat Pfink/Guitar Player); Tony Flynn (Pee Wee); Berri Lee (Berri/Phony Blind Man); Cindy Shea (Girl Carried by Mummy); Mary Demos (Patio Dancer); Jim Harmon (Chubby Sucker Sucking Lemon Grover); Don Snyder [as Romeo Barrymore] (Check Point #1 Attendant); Dick Williams (Lemon Grover); Alan Neal, Don Bouvier (Killer Krump Gang Members); Anthony Cardoza (Big Ed Narzak Gang Member); Linda Steckler (Girl with Balloon); Larry M. Byrd (Carnival Vendor)

Production: Producer: George J. Morgan. Screenplay: Ron Haydock, Jim Harmon. Associate Producer–Editor: Keith A. Wester. Photographer: Jack Cooperman. Second Unit Director: Ed McWatters. Music: Andre Brummer Sound: Lee Gilmore. Sound Effects: Frank A. Coe. Assistant Producer: Alan Neal. Assistant Director: Berri Lee. Associate Directors: Don Russell, Sidney G. Koss. Director: Ray Dennis Steckler. 30 minutes. Color. 1967.

The Lemon Grove Kids Meet the Green Grasshopper and the Vampire Lady from Outer Space

Cast: Ray Dennis Steckler [as Cash Flagg] (Gopher); Mike Kannon (Slug); Keith A. Wester (Marvin-Marvin); J. Jay Hartford aka John Williams (Skinny);

Kedric Wolfe (Jocko); Joe Bardo (Brick); Felicia Guy (Flower); Beverly Carter (Dum-Dum); E.M. Kevke [as David Miles] (Green Grasshopper); Carolyn Brandt (Vampire Lady); Coleman Francis (Mr. Miller); Herb Robins (Chooper #1); Doug Weise (Chooper #2); Estelle Cooperman (Witch #1); Patricia Wells (Witch #2); D.J. Scord (Witch #3); Tony Flynn (Pee Wee); Linda C. Steckler (Linda); Jeff Scott (Jeff); Lisa Yesko (Lisa); Kevin Miles (Kevin); Keith Miles (Brian); Peter Christoph (Pete); Derek Quinn (Derek); Moni Christoph (Moni); Laura H. Steckler (Tickles)

Production: Producers: Ray Dennis Steckler, Keith A. Wester. Associate Producer–Editor: John Williams. Screenplay: E.M. Kevke [as David Miles]. Photographer: Gil Hubbs. Art Director: Herbert Rabinowitz [as Herb Robins]. Makeup: Carolyn Brandt [as Carol Flynn]. Sound Engineer: Sam Kopetzky. Music: Andre Brummer. Music Editor: Jack DuFrain. Director: Ted Roter. 24 minutes. Color. Released: 1969.

The Lemon Grove Kids ... Go Hollywood!

Cast: Ray Dennis Steckler (Gopher); Don Snyder (Don); Tony Flynn (Pee Wee); Linda Christina Steckler (Linda); Jeannie Rae aka Laura H. Steckler (Tickles); Carolyn Brandt (Cee Bee Beaumont); Herb Robins (Killer Krump); Eric Morris (Nick the Gyp); Keith A. Wester (Swami-Marvin); Boris Balakoff aka Ted Roter (Mr. Carstairs); Beverly Carter (Secretary); Jack DuFrain (Film Editor); George J. Morgan (Reporter #1); Mary Morgan (Reporter #2)

Production: Producers: Ray Dennis Steckler, Keith A. Wester. Associate Producer: John Williams aka J. Jay Hartford. Photographer: Keith A. Wester. Editor: Ray Laurent. Art Director: Anthony Flynn. Makeup: Carolyn Brandt [as Carol Flynn]. Sound Engineer: Blayne Alexander. Music: Andre Brummer. Publicity: Howard Wormser. Screenplay-Director: Ray Dennis Steckler. (Note: The film incorrectly credits Ted Roter as director.) 24 minutes. Color. Released: 1969.

The Film

> Don't worry, Gopher. If they kill you, we shall avenge you.—Slug from *The Lemon Grove Kids Meet the Monsters*

As mentioned in the previous chapter, Steckler filled up part of his down time with some camerawork on *Scream of the Butterfly*. The gun-for-hire was also behind a camera on *The Velvet Trap* and the William Shatner horror vehicle *Incubus* (1966). Rounding out these extraneous activities was the comedy *Ski Fever* (1966), which Steckler co-produced under the alias Wolfgang Schmidt. This

The title card for *The Lemon Grove Kids* (1967) (courtesy Media Blasters).

unusual handle would figure more frequently in Steckler's later works.

Steckler's *The Lemon Grove Kids* began as many of his past and future projects did—with a camera, *some* film, his friends and a short-sighted concept of what to shoot. Nineteen sixty-seven would prove to be a problematic year for Steckler, but at this point he could not know *how* problematic. Ignorance is/was bliss, so the director *et al.* forged on until the bottom of the $8000 barrel had been scraped.

Undeterred, the low-rent auteur downshifted his projected 90-minute feature to a 28-minute short. The plan was to sell the idea to a television studio for complete realization and eventual weekly series. The studios were not buying it. In fact, no one was buying it, and two more years would pass before Steckler would have enough money to lens a second in the *Lemon Grove Kids* series, which incidentally was patterned largely after the East Side Kids and Bowery Boys franchises.

Also, in 1967 Steckler was solicited to direct and edit a music video for Jefferson Airplane's "White Rabbit." Almost all of the action takes place at the beach looking like outtakes from *Incredibly Strange Creatures* and some of it may very well have been. Later in 1968, while still shopping *The Lemon Grove Kids* for funding, Steckler was hired by the Nazz to create a video for their song "Open My Eyes." Steckler worked on a surfing documentary, then turned his camera's lens to the after-hours party and recorded a young Janis Joplin. These, and various other projects of the type, busied the director until his old roadshow buddy Joe Karston came to the rescue.

Karston had great success roadshowing Steckler's seminal films *Incredibly Strange Creatures* and *Thrill Killers*. As stated earlier, these two features had been all around the country and back again under a revolving banner of titles and promotions. Karston was up for something new, so for whatever reason, Steckler showed him *Lemon Grove Kids* as opposed to the completed *Rat Pfink a Boo Boo*.

Karston recognized *Lemon Grove Kids*' potential as a kiddie-matinee feature rife with promotional gimmicks and exploitation angles, filmed entirely in "Laugh-O-Color." Steckler agreed as he longed to see his East Side Kids–Bowery Boys tribute on the screen. As Steckler recalled to an interviewer on the *Lemon Grove Kids Meet the Monsters* DVD, "Leo Gorcey and Huntz Hall. I saw all their movies when I was a kid. I never enjoyed anything more than those movies, because they always made me laugh. They were overgrown kids and they always got into trouble, but they never hurt anybody." (Note: Huntz played the dim-witted sidekick of Leo in more than 80 Dead End Kids–East Side Kids–Bowery Boys movies in the span of 20 years.)

When the East Side Kids form of comedy emerged, it resided within the realm of a cinematic two-way mirror. Really, it was a masterstroke for the creators. These writers mined and discovered a deposit of comedic gold by which they could simultaneously tickle the young but also amuse and maybe even embarrass the old. Take for instance this fairly innocent and innocuous scene from *Spooks Run Wild*. Huntz Hall and the gang are flirting with the pretty soda jerk but there is no way they were looking to split a chocolate malted with her. Adults, in the audience, knew that much, but the kids in attendance may have figured a game of spin the bottle at most. It is largely light-hearted stuff but it is punched up a bit with some double entendres, and for the 1940s and '50s this was just fine.

The late 1960s were a very different social climate from the *Leave It to Beaver* era of times gone by. The Vietnam War was in full swing, as were the Civil Rights and women's equality movements. These were turbulent times and a more poignant realism and reflection was required for laughs (nervous or otherwise). In short, American moviegoers had resistantly (perhaps even unwittingly) become more sophisticated; sight gags, pratfalls and general tomfoolery were no longer cutting it. Steckler had toyed with this stuff on *Wild Guitar* with the kidnappers and the overall effect of *Goof on the Loose* but *The Lemon Grove Kids* saw it to fruition.

None of the above figured into Steckler's creation whatsoever. He just took the slapstick, one-liners and absurd antics and ran with them for a pacey 90 minutes (or 60 minutes as it was originally released). *The Lemon Grove Kids Meet the Monsters* (the title lifted directly from the 1954 feature *The Bowery Boys Meet the Monsters*) was geared strictly for kids and adults who would enjoy the nostalgia of it all. Steckler's fifth film, and the final Morgan-Steckler production, was as different from his previous outings as it would be to his future projects.

After a 25-second stylized cartoon credit sequence, the film is literally up and racing at full speed as Cash Flagg's Gopher zips back and forth with a push mower. As Gopher, Steckler does a great

Kirk Kirksey as Sunshine and Steckler as Gopher listen as Mike Kannon as Slug provides details on the great race in *The Lemon Grove Kids* (1967) (author's collection).

job of channeling Huntz Hall. If anything, he is funnier, gilded with Hall's trademark foolishness, ball cap and schnoz. The opening scene is actually on Lemon Grove Avenue in Los Angeles near the Steckler home, 5057 West Lemon Grove Avenue. Steckler's neighbor's dog Lemondrop the basset hound makes his screen debut.

Next up is Mike Kannon doing his best Leo Gorcey impersonation as Gopher's boss Slug. Slug first catches an eyeful of his sister, Roxy, sunbathing and tossing her long locks before retiring to the kitchen for breakfast. "Hey, Ma! You see what Roxy's got on?" While he awaits the grub, Slug cracks open an issue of *Fantastic Monsters of the Films*. This prop was no doubt a Ron Haydock plant as he was still moonlighting as a staff writer and editor for the magazine.

Roxy's mother (Mary Morgan, George J. Morgan's wife) adores Duke Mazaratti (played by Bart Carsell who, with so many other Steckler finds, was a one and done). This guy, as the film progresses, proves to be a veritable human grab bag of nefarious deeds, dealings and misgivings. He is the proverbial "snake in the grass," only this one stood upright and slinked on two legs. Nonetheless, Ma thinks he is a finer catch for Roxy than her other suitor Larry, who seethes at the sight of Duke.

An aside about Roxy, Rox Anne as she was professionally known for a minute, involves Steckler helping her land a commercial agent who put her right to work. One day Steckler received a call for some union work on an advertisement. He went down, took up the camera and, while loading it, noticed that Roxy was the girl he would be shooting.

Thinking they were friends, Steckler attempted some small talk, but Roxy snubbed him because she was the "star" of the shoot. Not long afterwards Steckler ran into her at a waffle house where she was "Roxy the Waffle Waitress" serving *him* his breakfast. Now, that is karmatic justice at work and her new *stage* name had a much better ring to it. Carolyn Brandt had an altogether different take on the Roxy-Ray dynamic; more on that to come.

Gopher and Slug and the whole bunch of Lemon Grove Kids convene on a basketball court where they yuk it up as characters in these types of films always do. One of the overgrown kids is played by celebrated author Jim Harmon. Harmon wrote a host of short stories for sci-fi magazines in the 1950s and '60s and rounded out his oeuvre with Westerns and even some erotica. He was also well known for his research books on the golden age of radio (he was the only one penning such material at that time). *The Lemon Grove Kids* was his only movie.

Another to-be famous Lemon Grove kid was Dick Anthony Williams who would go on to amass nearly 100 acting credits. He showed up on the big and small screen for over 40 years in such movies as *The Mack* (1973), *Dog Day Afternoon* (1975), *The Deep* (1977), *The Jerk* (1979) and *Edward Scissorhands* (1990). No role was too small for the prolific, hard-working actor.

The kids tire of shooting hoops and Slug sends Gopher into East Lemon Grove Kids territory for two six-packs of Dad's Root Beer. The kids on the East Side are rivals and are headed up by Killer Krump, who is played devilishly by Herb Robins. To no one's great surprise, Gopher is captured by the competing gang and they steal the soda, cracking them open, one by one, with Gopher's teeth. Gopher returns empty-handed (and with a sore tooth) explaining his plight as well as informing his guys that Killer Krump's bunch want to rumble.

The two groups assemble on a hill underneath a bridge and immediately begin pummeling one another in a myriad of kooky ways. As with most of Steckler's fight sequences, this is staged fairly well, but it is mostly for laughs this time around. The police break up the ruckus and who but producer George J. Morgan is Officer Clancy. Clancy convinces the troops that they should have a race to determine who is the real powerhouse party.

That slimeball Duke overhears the plan and quickly calls his bookie Big Ed Narzak, played by Coleman Francis. The idea is to sabotage the race in their favor and therefore win big at the finish line. Initially, when the film had a projected 90-minute running time, it was worked under the title *The Lemon Grove Kids at the Big Race*. Obviously this did not stick, the title was changed but the segment is commonly known as *The Great Race* or *The Not-So-Great-Race* as Steckler has quipped in interviews though there is nothing on the film to actually indicate as much.

The rivals have to get into shape for their physical rendezvous and they do so in some quirky ways. They jump barrels, they pump barrels, they run around merry-go-rounds, they crash and burn skateboards and bikes alike. Rest assured, these antithetical crews will goof it up before they get it right.

The day of the race arrives and all converge except for Larry, the star athlete amongst the West Side Lemon Grove Kids: Four goons have kidnapped him. It is worth pointing out that the act of kidnapping, in some form or another, has figured into every Steckler feature thus far. There were the kidnappers from *Wild Guitar*; Madame Estrella kidnapped and disfigured victims, turning them into incredibly strange creatures. The thrill killers had kidnapping on their brains but gave in to their deranged needs, murdering their quarry instead. Then the central drive of *Rat Pfink a Boo Boo* is the kidnapping of Cee Bee Beaumont. The observation of this common thread is necessary in understanding the closure of this era of Steckler's cinema. Steckler's winking, impish side would soon give way to stories that were thematically darker in their tone and presentation and this was not always welcomed.

But Steckler was still in Los Angeles, he was still hopeful and he was still shooting the race sequence of his pet project *The Lemon Grove Kids*. The kids on both sides of the fence do everything in their power to interfere or louse-up their opponents' progress. They dump buckets of water on unsuspecting heads; there is also tripping, kicking, sitting-on and even the delivery of an atom bomb. Along the way, Larry escapes his four antagonists and rushes lickety-split straight towards and into the race.

Incidentally, one of Larry's abductors was none other than Anthony Cardoza of *Night of the Ghouls* (1959) and *The Beast of Yucca Flats* (1961). There was no way that *Lemon Grove Kids*' inclusion on Cardoza's résumé would in any way harm the young producer's credibility. On the contrary, Cardoza continued producing films such as *The Skydivers* (1963) and *Night Train to Mundo Fine* (1966). Cardoza's *finest* work would come while coupled with director Robert F. Slatzer on *The Hellcats* (1968) and *Bigfoot* (1970).

With Larry in the race, Duke and Big Ed panic and move on to plan B in order to make the killing: Enter the Saboteur. This disingenuous character, played by newcomer and one-timer Ed McWatters, is dressed to the nines,

A newspaper ad for *The Lemon Grove Kids Meet the Monsters* (1969) at Loew's Cinema 70 in West Palm Beach, Florida. The theater opened as a single screen in 1966 and expanded into a triple in 1977. Cinema 70 was closed and demolished in the early 1990s (image and commentary courtesy film historian and archivist Raleigh Bronkowski).

looking every bit a beatnik caricature that certainly cannot be trusted. The Saboteur is released to clean up the job Big Ed's men could not do. With Larry working double-time to catch up, he has his work cut out for him.

The hunt for Larry drags the Saboteur kicking and screaming and falling along the oceanside checkpoints. The Saboteur, so sure of himself and his abilities, has one Wile E. Coyote moment after another as Larry hurries along, Road Runner–like, without incident. McWatters choreographed and directed the beach scenes while Steckler was off doing who knows what. It is obvious that McWatters understood the project, and the ultimate goal, as his footage fits seamlessly within the frames of Steckler's.

As Larry beelines it towards the finishing goal, and appears to be winning despite Duke's crooked efforts, he trips and falls, giving the lead to the East Side kid Stretch. Stretch was played by Jim Plunkett, who not only appeared here but also in the 1965 Jean Harlow bio pic *Harlow* as Stan Laurel. Larry really fell and Steckler did not have the film to re-stage and re-shoot. So what is to be done about it?

Steckler's silver bullet solution: write a scene involving an overzealous female fan who runs up and hugs Stretch hard, driving the wind out of him. Stretch topples over from lack of oxygen and Larry recovers to cross the finish line. Now, this off-screen scenario poses an obvious question. This is a query that could been asked earlier, but had this particular change-up not occurred, the film might well have ended differently.

So, was it really a more inexpensive and expedient way to continue or did Steckler simply seize the opportunity to add a bit more comedy and drama to the film's conclusion? Sometimes it seemed as though Steckler expected the holes and lulls in his script to fill themselves with SNAFUs. This type of off-the-cuff procedure had been commonplace with Steckler but was fast becoming his storytelling cornerstone.

Not surprisingly, all is well in Lemon Grove except for Duke and his corrupt cohorts. They have just lost a ton of winnings and Duke's about to lose his girl, Roxy. Roxy's mother finally realizes what Duke actually is and berates him while braining him with her purse. Roxy runs into Larry's arms and Gopher runs into a sequence from *Rat Pfink a Boo Boo* with Kogar the Swinging Ape pawing Cee Bee Beaumont and Rat Pfink himself pulling up the rear. The skittish Gopher flees from this bizarre scene and catches himself within eyeshot of a mummy—and everything is tinted red.

There is a flash of stock footage lightning that reveals the mummy's face filling the entire screen. At this point, a theater employee lumbers through the aisles, in a mummy costume, taunting the kids. The on-screen mummy continues pursuing Gopher as he screams and more flashes of lightning (12 in all) crash into the eyes of the moviegoers. With the additional electrical bolts comes more in-person mummies. The kids are screaming, popcorn and sodas are flying and this whole crazy scheme is a success.

The aforementioned was all insert-footage to complete the roadshow version of *The Lemon Grove Kids Meet the Monsters*. At this point, Steckler leads the viewer from the real-time footage and returns them to the reel-time footage … or has he? The mummy carries a hapless girl into a clearing and inexplicably into the daylight, where Gopher stumbles in to find that he has interrupted an amateur film club just out having some fun.

Of interest is that during the nighttime sequences, the mummy has Carolyn Brandt in his clutches but once he breaks from dark to light he is clasping a different girl. Through the lens of Steckler's memory, Brandt's terminal friend, Cindy Shea, temporarily abandoned her hospital bed for a chance at cinematic immortality. Two weeks after Shea was granted her last wish, she passed away. Her appearance in the film, can be seen as Steckler's homage to one of his earliest fallen comrades.

Steckler's camera reveals an assembly of familiar and unfamiliar cast and characters. On hand to chastise the witless Gopher are Brandt as Cee Bee, Keith Wester as Cowboy, Ron Haydock as Rat Pfink, Bob Burns as Kogar (*and* the mummy) and Edward C. Wagner, Steckler's grandfather. Predictably, Gopher is flustered and sprints into the woods as far away as he can get from this gnarly bunch who seem to live in a co-extending world not that far into the future. It is surrealism to a degree, but more on that subject later.

As mentioned before, this second part of the series was made two years later, in 1969 (or so says the copyright on the film itself). With the Morgan-Steckler tag team

Bob Burns as the Mad Mummy grabs Steckler as Gopher in *The Lemon Grove Kids Meet the Monsters* (1967) (courtesy Laura H. Steckler).

laid to rest, Keith Wester had become Steckler's right-hand man in the production department. Wester, who had been Steckler's sound recordist and editor, would act as producer on their next three projects, all completed in 1969.

The Lemon Grove Kids Meet the Green Grasshopper and the Vampire Lady from Outer Space beat out Steckler's previous lengthy title by three words. Mike Kannon and Steckler (as Cash Flagg) return as Slug and Gopher while an entire cast of newcomers joins the party as the remaining Lemon Grove Kids. This revolving door of Slug-Gopher accomplices would continue into the third and final chapter. Even the director's chair was spinning on this episode. Enter Ted Roter.

Roter (real name Peter Balakoff) was the founder of the Santa Monica Playhouse in 1962. Steckler was impressed with Roter's stage work and offered him the job of directing the second *Lemon Grove Kids* installment. Roter's stage talents did not necessarily translate well to the screen as he possessed zero knowledge of camera operation and placement.

There is no real opening to the film, just a title card, a few credits and the thing is up and running. The kids are having a backyard party complete with hula hoops, badminton, darts, a pool table and lots of shaking and moving to an incredibly young Surf Rock band. Soon the camera fixes on a makeshift business sign, "Lemon Grove Kids Handy-Man-Shop," and there is the primary plot. The kids take on odd jobs they are completely unqualified for, but bumble and fumble their way through it all to the bitter end.

Mike Kannon returns as Slug, leader of the gang and proprietor of the Lemon Grove Kids Handy-Man-Shop. The ever-serious Slug sits at a desk awaiting business calls while the rest of the Lemon Grovers clown around as par for their abnormal course. The phone *does* ring: A Mr. Miller (Coleman Francis) needs some hazardous debris removed from his property.

Slug calls his troops to attention, informing them of the job. His "employees" revolt by throwing everything (literally) but the kitchen sink at their boss. The disgruntled workers reluctantly throw themselves in, on and generally pile themselves atop the company truck—arms, legs and heads sticking out in every direction. This human pile is headed straight to Miller's house at 5867 Hill Drive which was actually Steckler's house on Spring Oak Drive.

The Lemon Grovers reach their destination by crashing directly into one of Miller's trees. Surely he did not want *it* chopped down and removed. Even with their less-than-impressive arrival, Mr. Miller barks his demands at them, insisting the job be completed as soon as possible. Slug assures him, "It's as good as done!" and barks *his* orders at *his* inept bunch.

In the ineptitude department, Slug's crew never disappoints. Gopher hangs a chair on a pole and haphazardly stacks tree limbs cut by Brick while Jocko push-mows a gravel pit. In great frustration, Slug yells and blows maniacally into a sports whistle in an effort to maintain order. Gopher shirks his duties and slips into a kiddie pool with two bikini-clad cuties who declare themselves "The Gopher Girls." It appears Gopher is really no dummy after all.

As an aside, the character Brick is played by Joe Bardo (sporting a Pigmeat Markham T-shirt) returning to Camp Steckler from his turn as Joe Saxon of *The Thrill Killers*. Now, while Bardo and Steckler were about to embark on their off-color cinematic co-existences, Kedric Wolfe was just getting started with his career by giving it his all as Jocko. Wolfe, born in Ohio in 1939, went on to star in some pretty impressive exploitation vehicles. His most notable include producer David F. Friedman's *The Ramrodder* (1969), Charles B. Griffith's *Up from the Depths* (1979) and Richard Elfman's bizarro *Forbidden Zone* (1980).

In Mr. Miller's backyard, the Gopher Girls fall prey to the Green Grasshopper and the Vampire Lady who, according to the film's title, are from outer space. Some of the other Lemon Grove Kids are also snatched. The abductors' motives are unclear at this point. In time, Gopher spots a large red, shiny disc and calls over Slug, Skinny, Marvin-Marvin and Jocko to witness his unusual find. The Green Grasshopper and the Vampire Lady are both aboard the spaceship and it appears the kids may find out more about these interplanetary kidnappers. And there it is—more kidnapping.

As Steckler tells it, he bought the spaceship from an ill-fated filmmaker whose film never got made. Twenty-five smackers later, Steckler had a flying saucer (of sorts) and the Green Grasshopper and the Vampire Lady now had transportation around the cosmos. Chances are the two antagonists were originally to enter and exit the Earth telepathically, but now Steckler had an almost impressive prop and he *would* make good use of it.

The remaining Lemon Grovers

Coleman Francis as Mr. Miller encounters the Vampire Lady from outer space played by Carolyn Brandt in front of her transportation in *The Lemon Grove Kids Meet the Green Grasshopper and the Vampire Lady from Outer Space* (1969) (courtesy Carolyn Brandt). Note: In contrast to Steckler's flying saucer origins, Carolyn Brandt remembers the prop was actually taken from an old carnival ride.

look on slack-jawed and advance towards the UFO with caution but mostly just slack-jawed. Mr. Miller arrives to see what all the commotion is about and finds himself caught in the Green Grasshopper's bug-eyed gaze. The oversized insect has hypnotized Miller from afar. He walks away zombified muttering some sort of gibberish. None of this is really making any sense but for Steckler's part it was only kid stuff.

The actor in the Green Grasshopper get-up was E.M. Kevke, who used the screen credit David Miles. Kevke was also responsible for this film's screenplay as well as scribing the original story to *Incredibly Strange Creatures*. He had worked with Steckler as far back as 1962 on *Wild Ones on Wheels*. The Vampire Lady role was undertaken seductively by the radiant Carolyn Brandt. Brandt reprised this Vampira-type character in a far less kid-friendly feature four years later.

The two space intruders have set up shop in Mr. Miller's basement. The Vampire Lady bites Miller's neck and Gopher takes her ride for a spin, then lands and poses in a myriad of goofy fashions. Slug urges the remaining gang members to follow through with an investigation of the house. They split up to cover more territory, leaving Jocko and Marvin-Marvin vulnerable to capture.

As with everything else these subnormals do, their sleuthing techniques range from the unorthodox to the downright silly. The overweight Skinny finds an undersized footlocker to hide in, but actually hides nothing. Like a couple of snakes, Jocko slithers across the filthy

Getting up close and personal with Carolyn Brandt as the Vampire Lady from Outer Space from *The Lemon Grove Kids Meet the Green Grasshopper and the Vampire Lady from Outer Space* (1969) (courtesy Carolyn Brandt).

floor pushing up dirt and gravel with his noggin while Marvin-Marvin slithers around with binoculars. These two human serpents meet eye to binocular, then slither over and under one another.

Slug and Gopher finally stumble upon their friends and discover that they too have been hypnotized. The Vampire Lady again bites Miller and the Grasshopper waves a plastic flower-wand over him, reeling off, "Now, it is time for us to send you back to our planet." Was Miller on the lam, hiding out on Earth, masquerading as a human? It is a question probably best not pondered much.

Marvin-Marvin is strapped to a gurney and the Vampire Lady drains his blood while the Grasshopper begins ghoulish medical experiments of some variety. Slug shoves Gopher towards the scene and the Vampire Lady bites his neck. Gopher retaliates and bites her neck. She lets out a blood-curdling scream that breaks the hypnotic spell of his Lemon Grove friends.

Havoc breaks out as the Lemon Grovers flee the basement. Gopher is cornered by Herb Robins in silver face-paint and an oddball furry suit, repeating, "Choop. choop. choop." This whimsical character from this children's comedy would be transported three years into the future and transformed into a horror film for adults. Also, more of Steckler's self-promotion is on display as a *Rat Pfink a Boo Boo* pressbook hangs visibly on a back wall.

In all of the hullabaloo, the Vampire Lady and the Grasshopper hightail it to their ship and blast off from Earth, leaving behind a bunch of confused Californians and moviegoers. Tickles (Laura Steckler) locates the magic flower wand and begins flicking it at various aliens, sending them careening into the stars. Gopher is now a vampire with plastic dime store fangs which he promptly sinks into Slug's hand. When the film freezes on this image, it is the end of the second Lemon Grove Kids segment and the "monsters" of the film's title.

This portion of the film is the one Steckler had the opportunity to screen for Huntz Hall. A friend of a friend knew Hall and helped set up a dinner date for the two. Steckler idolized Hall, but once he got the chance to meet him, the old-timer began a series of emotional blows that would deflate the young filmmaker's enthusiasm.

Over dinner, Hall divulged a scheme by which he was capable of squeezing additional moneys from the studios. Hall beamed that he knew exactly where to flub his lines in order for production to go into overtime. The studios would have to pay "meal penalties" to the cast and crew if filming went over and into their lunch period.

Hall's colleagues were impressed but Steckler was not. Hall had managed to squander more studio money, in one day's shooting, than Steckler could hope to have over the course of a half dozen pictures. What soured Steckler further (and proving that Hollywood has always mismanaged their finances), was that

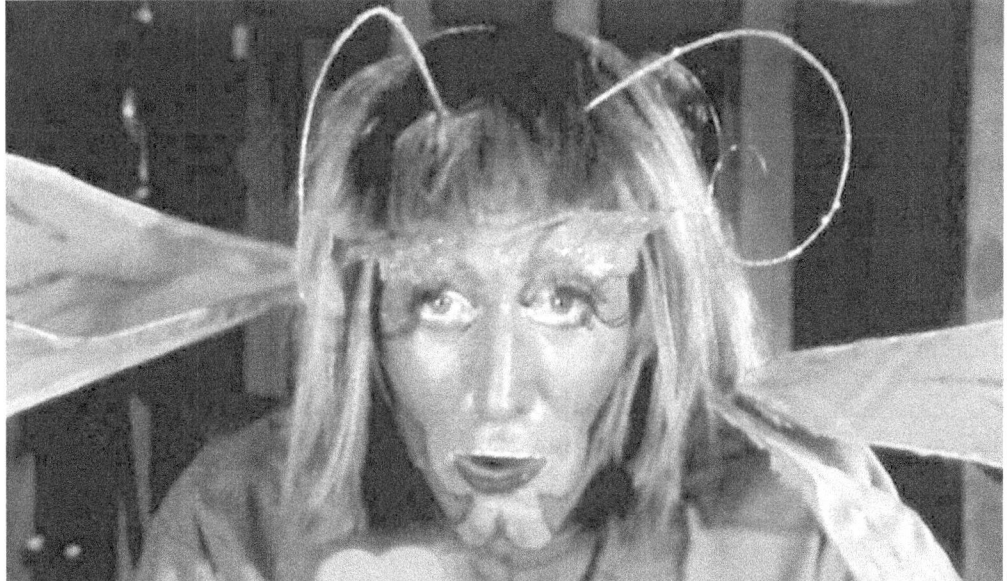

A close look at the Green Grasshopper played by David Miles (E.M. Kevke) in *The Lemon Grove Kids Meet the Green Grasshopper and the Vampire Lady from Outer Space* (1969) (courtesy Carolyn Brandt).

Hall was pulling down $25,000 a week in the 1940s and '50s.

Steckler still asked his hero to be in his little movie. Hall shot back an exorbitant cost, insisting on his same five-digit salary that he had acquired a decade or more earlier at Monogram and Allied Artists. A dejected Steckler declined. A week later, Hall's wife called and told the director to cease wearing the ball cap on film, or prepare for a lawsuit. The steadfast Steckler, remedied the disheartening situation in an easy fashion. He wore a different hat (a crumpled porkpie hat, to be exact) for the third in the series.

Steckler bares his Gopher fangs at the conclusion of *The Lemon Grove Kids Meet the Green Grasshopper and the Vampire Lady from Outer Space* (1969) (courtesy Carolyn Brandt).

The second *Lemon Grove Kids* sequel has a bare-bones storyline when comparing it to its predecessors. Not that those two short films or their narratives would ever find themselves lionized amongst its decades-old forerunners. The Three Stooges' *We Want Our Mummy* (1939), the Bowery Boys' *Spook Busters* (1946) and/or *Abbott and Costello Meet Frankenstein* (1948) are all examples of what Steckler was attempting to achieve, and to a very modest degree he did just that.

The Lemon Grove Kids' swansong has whittled the gang down to four members with about double that number comprising the remainder of the cast. This addition to the saga is short on narrative, cast, crew and naturally money. The whole thing seems to be running out of steam and it was probably a good call on Steckler's part to pull the plug on the entire project. He decided it was high time to put an end to this silliness and try his hand at something dark, serious and gritty. Five familiar faces would return to the fold but for the most part the old crew had departed for bigger or blue things.

The last Lemon Grove Kids movie *The Lemon Grove Kids ... Go Hollywood!* was filmed in 1969. It opens with a shot of a Bengal tiger at an L.A. zoo. As the credits affirm, Ted Roter is at the helm again, or is he? Steckler insists that he directed *Go Hollywood!* and that Roter's name remained because he did not have the funds to change the credit card. Since Roter's name appears over similar zoo footage, it can only be deduced that he was indeed originally slated to direct. Still, how much could it possibly cost to change that credit?

Young Tony Flynn, as Peewee, walks alongside Steckler's even younger daughters Linda and Laura (again as Tickles). While Steckler's offspring appeared in the previous two Lemon Grove pictures, they figure more heavily in this one. Flynn had some minor screen time in *The Thrill Killers* and *Rat Pfink a Boo Boo* as well as the two earlier Lemon

Grove Kids movies, but here he is front and center.

The trio bump into Gopher (Steckler) and they all decide to pay a visit to the nearly washed-up movie star Cee Bee Beaumont. Cee Bee is played again by the slinky and seductive Carolyn Brandt. En route to Cee Bee's home (actually Carolyn's mother's home), the quartet encounter street guitarist Don "How Do I Stand with Your Heart" Snyder, who decides to tag along and also meet the (falling) star of the silver screen. Ms. Beaumont's movie career may have been sinking but after *Incredibly Strange Creatures* and this picture, Snyder's had all but sunk.

The five are headed over to Cee Bee's place to assist in some handiwork around the grounds. This will not be the only recycled bit from the previous outing. Hiding in the bushes are Herb Robins as Killer Krump and Eric Morris as Nick the Gyp, who are planning to (big surprise here) kidnap Cee Bee and hold her for ransom.

Robins was a Steckler veteran with a few more rounds to go with the director, but Eric Morris was a different story altogether. According to Steckler, Morris was almost enamored of him and his abilities in getting his movies made. Morris wanted to follow suit and learn from the low-budget legend, so a flattered Steckler gave him the go. There is no indication that Morris ever did make his own movie but he did have several acting credits before and after his collision with Steckler.

At Cee Bee's, the Kids and Don vacuum, dust and rearrange furniture while Gopher makes a general nuisance of himself. Cee Bee smiles at the flaky floor show and continues reading what can only be a movie script. Then completely out of the blue, Don picks up his guitar and begins singing the Lemon Grove Kids' theme song. Again, Cee Bee smiles while continuing to read.

On a break, the Kids approach their employer for an autograph, which she is all too happy to oblige. Gopher attempts to help Cee Bee read for the part of Cleopatra, but naturally he botches the entire ordeal ending with the two of them crashing to the couch in a flurry of pages. The balance of the Lemon Grovers head into the yard to mow. Killer Krump and Nick the Gyp are still hanging around doing basically nothing.

Cee Bee feels her career is going nowhere and if only she could see into the future, she would know which parts to accept. Gopher mentions his fortune-telling friend Swami-Marvin (Keith A. Wester) and they give him a ring. "Hello? Swami-Marvin here. All the secrets of the future for only 25 cents." A bargain by any standard and this fortune teller makes house calls.

Outside, the Kids rake leaves, dig holes wherever, aggressively prune trees and cut the grass at an angle. Killer Krump and Nick the Gyp are still putting their pea brains together planning the perfect crime. Swami-Marvin arrives, bangs around on a piano and reads cards to Cee Bee while Krump and the Gyp hogtie Gopher in the side yard. Slipping into the house, the would-be kidnappers toss Swami-Marvin into a broom closet and corner a distressed Cee Bee.

The Gyp makes out with a more-than-resistant Cee Bee while Killer makes a call to Steckler-Wester Productions. Mr. Carstairs is hard at work looking over the edits of his latest picture and berating the decisions of his production assistant. Carstairs is played by Ted Roter (credited as Boris Balakoff) in an over-reaching fashion perfectly befitting this over-the-top film. After mustering up some old-style Hollywood charm, the moviemaker takes Krump's call: "Hello, Lionel Carstairs here. Producer of all your favorite flicks."

Killer Krump lays it on thick: They have Cee Bee Beaumont, the studio's number one actress, and they want money, one million dollars to be precise. Carstairs laughs hysterically and then even rather maniacally. Cee Bee's most recent features have tanked at the box office and as Carstairs flippantly puts it, "Her last few pictures have been the greatest invention since the sleeping pill."

Don Snyder and the three youngsters have been witnessing the action through a window while Gopher remains tied up in the yard. The quartet swings into action with Snyder taking on the Gyp and the three kids giving Killer Krump what for. Once Swami-Marvin is freed, the entire bunch is running aimlessly in and out of frame, up and down halls and over and around furniture. It is total bedlam in that Keystone Cops–Charlie Chaplin–Buster Keaton sort of way and it is just the way Steckler wanted it.

By now, Gopher has fumbled, mumbled and stumbled his way out of his bindings and is checking out the chaos through another window. Suddenly he has a plan. He ties the rope with which he was bound across a walkway and as the kidnappers come running towards it, he pulls it tight, tripping them. He begins shackling and restraining the not-so-tough guys with their very own rope.

The others catch up, join in and it appears to be a joyous occasion. Steckler's asking the silliest of them as actors, yet they are delivering as though Chaplin or Keaton were at the helm. In short, if Steckler believed in them, they believed in Steckler. It was a perfectly operating symbiotic union.

At this point, Steckler speeds up the film and does some inspired editing, and the scene kicks into excess. For what it is, it works. In fact, these techniques and others are what helps all three vignettes move along. As mentioned before, the film was (at times) sped up for the physical gags; the removal of entire body movements also aided in accelerating the action for comedic effect. All of this works very well in a cartoonish sort of way, just as it had with *Goof on the Loose*.

In the next-to-last scene, tabloid reporters (George and Mary Morgan) interview Carstairs and Cee Bee. Apparently this near-kidnapping incident has raised the public's awareness of Ms. Beaumont, and Carstairs promises to put her in his most expensive picture ever, *Cleopatra*. Cee Bee has but one request: She picks her leading man. Carstairs begrudgingly accepts the terms and asks the obvious question. The answer is clear: Gopher. Cute.

Steckler takes the film, and the series, out with the Don Snyder–penned theme song. It is a primitive one-take real-time recording that is quite catchy. This version differs slightly from the one Don performed for Cee Bee as this one features Steckler's daughters and Tony Flynn on back-up vocals. Snyder's lyrics really capture the essence of these movies and probably should have been played at the film's beginning: "We're the Lemon Grove Kids, and we love to have fun. We're the Lemon Grove Kids and we get the job done. So, look out whenever we're around. There's no problem we can't compound. A simple task you need done today, that's so easy we'll find a harder way." Yep, that about sums it up.

Clarification on the sequence of

On August 9, 1969, *The Lemon Grove Kids Meets the Monsters* had a matinee showing at the Charlottetown Mall in Charlotte, North Carolina (image and commentary courtesy film historian and archivist Raleigh Bronkowski).

these sketches seems to be in order. The film originally ran in theaters as *The Lemon Grove Kids Meet the Monsters* with only two segments hitting the silver screen. When youngsters bought a ticket, they were first treated to *The Lemon Grove Kids Meet the Green Grasshopper and the Vampire Lady from Outer Space*. If the moppet's attention could be sustained for a further 30 minutes, a second featurette was up and running, *The Lemon Grove Kids and the Great Race*.

Now, when this thing hit video cassette for the home viewing market, Steckler tacked on his third part, *The Lemon Grove Kids ... Go Hollywood!* So now it was finally a trilogy but it is completely out of order as far as when this stuff was actually shot. First up, on the VHS, is *The Lemon Grove Kids Meet the Green Grasshopper and the Vampire Lady from Outer Space,* then *Go Hollywood!* and finally *The Lemon Grove Kids and The Great Race*.

Eventually, the Media Blasters DVD release of *The Lemon Grove Kids Meet the Monsters* set the record straight. Steckler's kid-flick anthology is seemingly complete and now in perfect form. Good thing too, because Steck-heads here and abroad were vying and dying to know. Steckler gave away time and again that there was a fourth part of the compilation with possibly enough footage for a fifth. Furthering the ludicrousness of it all, could Steckler have not released his kiddie compendium as *The Best of the Lemon Grove Kids* and squeezed some more extract from this particular fruit of his labors?

A look at Luis Buñuel and Alejandro Jodorowsky seem ripe for the peeling. Buñuel's *Simon of the Desert* ends with the camera revealing the characters as actors on a set. Jodorowsky's *The Holy Mountain* zooms out and away from the ending scenario to show the cast and crew merely making a movie.

Steckler's film ends with the lead character, Gopher, gaffing an "Amateur 8mm Movie Club, U.S.A." gathering. Buñuel's film was released in 1965, Jodorowsky's eight years later. Steckler *may* have seen and been influenced by *Simon of the Desert*, just as Jodorowsky had been. It is a stretch, but Steckler is anything and everything but predictable.

Some naysayers have suggested that *Meet the Monsters* is a convoluted mess of a movie. To the contrary, Steckler's string of short sketches is actually a fairly accomplished project that very well could have been a television series as originally intended. The fact that it played theaters for seven years is testimony to its staying power.

Writer Scott MacGillivray pointed out in *Filmfax* #57 (p. 54), "This crude compilation of glorified home movies is not Academy Award material, or even good second-feature material, but Steckler and his crew do their best with no budget, some well-meaning friends and a lot of enthusiasm." Sadly, this would end Steckler's playfully defiant era. His later films would either be dead serious or simply unwatchable for viewers with prudish tastes.

Body Fever (1969)

Synopsis

Charlie Smith (Steckler) private eye, is in need of a break. However, he's not about to get one because one beautiful femme fatale is about to enter his life and change it forever. Receptionist by day and sexy cat burglar by night, Carrie Erskine (Carolyn Brandt) has decided to take on drug kingpin Big Mack (Bernard Fein) by swiping his stash of heroin. Once in the know, the Mack sends his henchmen to retrieve the booty, one way or the other. Carrie is as good as dead.

What Big Mack doesn't know is Carrie's also been ripped off and now the scumbag dope-pushing pimp Frankie Roberts (Gary Kent) has the drugs. Big Mack's fall guy Harris Fergeson (Alan Smith) knows the score and hires Smith to find Carrie. Fergeson hopes to recover the drugs before his allotted time is up. After three days, he too is as good as dead.

Smith interrogates numerous derelicts and lowlifes: Fritz, the smut photographer (Ron Haydock), Herbie the drug smuggler (Herb Robins) and a dubious talent agent (Wade "Doc" Watson). He also examines (in bed and otherwise) prostitute Shawn Call (Julie Conners) and druggie Julie Richards (Pat Jackson). The answers don't come easy and they don't come quick or cheap; every greased palm and trick question leads Charlie closer to Carrie and the outcome. But will the outcome include the prime movers, or will they end up like so many of the others, dead?

Credits

Cast: Carolyn Brandt (Carrie Erskine); Bernard Fein (Big Mack); Gary Kent (Frankie Roberts); Brett Pearson (Brett); Herb Robins (Herbie); Ray Dennis Steckler (Charles Smith); Coleman Francis (Coley); Dina Bryan (Stella); Julie Conners (Shawn Call); Brett Zeller (Carol Hollister); Alan Smith (Harris Fergeson); Ron Haydock (Fritz the Photographer); Larry Chandler (Waco); Wade "Doc" Watson (The Agent); Julie Roman (The Agent's Girl); Brick Bardo (Moose and Party Guest); Liz Renay, Pat Dobie, Stan Gilbert (Party Guests); Laura Steckler (Girl in Hallway); Linda Steckler (Girl with Chalk); Keith A. Wester (Sammy)

Production: Producers: Ray Dennis Steckler, Keith A. Wester. Executive Producers: William J. Libby, R.A. Barrett. Associate Producer: John Williams. Screenplay: William Edgar, Ray Dennis Steckler. Photographers: Keith A. Wester, Jack Cooperman. Editors: John Williams, Ray Laurent. Makeup: Carolyn Brandt [as Carol Flynn]. Negative Cutter: Alice Keillor. Script Supervisor: Pat Dobie. Key Grip: John Andrews. Gaffer: Stan Gilbert. Music: Andre Brummer, Don Snyder. Sound: Blayne Alexander. Director: Ray Dennis Steckler. 77 minutes. Color.

Featured Music

"Charlie Smith and Carrie Erskine Theme" by Don Snyder

The Film

Three days, $3,000. Okay, where have you heard that one before?
—Charlie Smith in *Body Fever*

By 1969, Steckler had five features to his credit and in retrospect it was quite obvious he was not interested in building a following or a fanbase. Each film differed wildly from the one before, with only a handful of connective qualities to tie them together. Mainly, it was Steckler's name in the director's slot (should anyone be paying attention). Though one must not forget Carolyn Brandt's face gracing and branding these pictures, and from any theater seat it is a damned fine brand and product.

As the Summer of Love came and went, Steckler busied himself with commercials, photography, music videos and any camera work he could drum up. The restless director was earning a living at his Sunset Boulevard office, but he needed to make a feature film. So the impatient maverick enlisted the aid of his in-house producer Keith A. Wester and screenwriter William Edgar and off they went into the territory of the private eye movie. Incidentally, Edgar went on to write the 1973 potboiler *Stacey* starring Anne Randall as a tough-as-nails P.I.

Steckler had yet to make a film that was not cartoonish in one way or another. And while his sixth feature may have been loaded with 1930s and '40s clichés, it provided yet another look into the mind's eye of this unique filmmaker. His first films, however successful some of them may have been, were still albatrosses about his neck. Hollywood had remained elusive for nearly a decade while Steckler made shot-on-a-shoestring movies and raised a family. The twinkle of Tinsel Town was fading fast.

Steckler adored the process of making films and he felt he had the talent, knowledge and background to be among the good ones in Hollywood. But Hollywood was not answering and Steckler

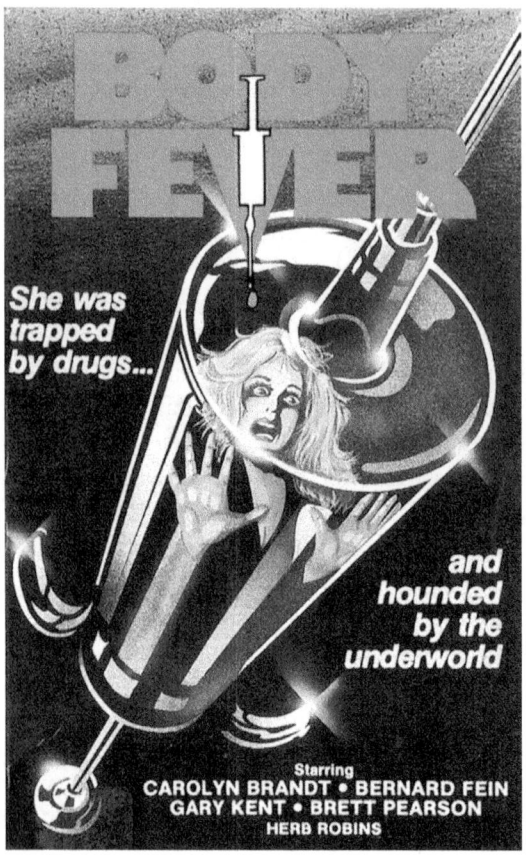

VHS box art for *Body Fever* (1969) (author's collection).

was tired of calling. The mere experience of making a movie, and the adventures it held, became Steckler's dominating drive and this is why he *needed* to make what became *Body Fever*.

The film abruptly opens with Carolyn Brandt as Carrie Erskine robbing a safe and dashing back to her apartment with the goods. Gary Kent as Frankie Roberts has been tipped off and he is awaiting her arrival. Before Frankie can get his mitts on Carrie, Steckler continues his love affair with Brandt through the lens of his camera. He offered the viewer some striking images of his wife prowling through the web-like shadows of the night. Brandt looks so darned good in her custom-made catsuit and costume party mask that it is easy to overlook the 1930s villain cliché vibe. Nevertheless, Frankie roughs Carrie up and snatches the satchel full of what is later revealed to be a large amount of heroin. The film has been on the screen no more than 60 seconds and it is apparent that Steckler is treading cinematic waters that are unlike any of his previous features. There had been a modicum of drinking in his films before, but never hard street drugs.

Steckler cuts from Erskine's pad to Frankie Roberts': He is cooking up some of the smack and getting the works together in order to fix his "friend" Carol Hollister (Brett Zeller). Zeller may have had a brief career, but her exploitation pedigree is cemented by her other roles in *Sinthia; The Devil's Doll* (1970), *The Doll Squad* (1973) and *The Virgin Cowboy* (1975). Two films were made with Steckler, one with Ted V. Mikels and another alongside Liz Renay. Zeller consistently found herself amongst good company.

From here the film moves to pug mug Bernard Fein, who is playing the film's heavy Big Mack. Big Mack's a name which seems in line with some of his other roles such as Biggie Gaines in *The Music Box Kid* (1960), Fat Man from *Man-Trap* (1961) and "Fat Thug" in a 1961 *Michael Shayne* episode. Fein was a creator of the hit television series *Hogan's Heroes* which ran for six seasons (168 episodes) from 1965 to 1971. Fein was another meeting through Herb Robins. Robins seemed to know anyone and everyone willing to clock in for a Steckler picture.

Fein attempted, with no luck, to get Steckler work on the set of *Hogan's Heroes* but Steckler refused, feeling there was nothing funny about prisoners of war. This is a curious mindset for a man who was willing to show men and women beaten, tortured, mutilated and murdered all in the name of entertainment. Sure, Steckler was not going for the bellylaugh but it is still there for the sheer enjoyment of it all. Not to mention, with all low-budget cinema there is at least some *unintentional* humor, so....

The Mack has been awakened and is half-naked screaming into his phone about who knows what. "Now, you listen to me, you imbecile. You're telling me that some girl went in and stole that stuff out from under your nose?" The Big Guy pauses, then Steckler zooms in for a closer look at the pug's mug. "Carrie Erskine? Who the hell cares about Carrie Erskine?" Steckler's going for broke now and Big Mack's big mouth is all over the screen. "I don't care if you ever find her. As far as I'm concerned, Fergeson, you're dead. Dead!"

Between the robbery, the fix and this telephone exchange, Steckler is establishing his story nicely and neatly in a film noir type of way. This is not at all like Steckler, as writer Jim Morton pointed out in *Incredibly Strange Films* (p. 57): "Unlike most of Steckler's films, *Body Fever* seems to have a carefully structured plot." Whether it is considered film noir, California noir or neo-noir, the film's creator appears to have an unusual (for him) death grip on its narrative.

Chugging the story along, the Mack crashes a back-room party, turning over a card table and screaming. Everyone is thrown out except Brett. Brett is played by Brett Pearson, whose biggest claim to fame is strangling Steve McQueen in *The Cincinnati Kid*. That film came out in 1965 and this one was made four years later, making it safe to say that Pearson's more notable days as a feature film actor were behind him.

Now it's just Big Mack (still half-naked) and Brett sitting in this seedy private speakeasy of sorts (which is actually Steckler's den). It is dark, the screen is grainy, and the walls are splashed with shadows; it is the perfect atmosphere to discuss the murder of the careless Fergeson. Mack wants him knocked off, but in a slight act of defiance Brett disagrees, thinking Fergeson is better alive with knowledge of the stuff's whereabouts than simply dead. The Mack reluctantly agrees by acknowledging, "That's a real good point. Okay, you find Fergeson and you tell him he's got three days to get that stuff back. If he doesn't, it's gonna be his last three days."

With Brett on Fergeson's case, Steckler shifts the film to the pivotal character Charles Smith. Smith is played rather dubiously by Steckler himself and not under his usual *nom de screen* Cash Flagg. Smith is a private investigator in the vein of authors John D. MacDonald's Travis McGee or Dashiell Hammett's Sam Spade. In 1941, Humphrey Bogart took on the role of Spade in *The Maltese Falcon*, creating a defining moment for himself and on-screen private eyes for years to come. Not surprisingly, Steckler loosely patterned *his* character after Bogie's.

The traditional belief is that Steckler was never slated to play the *Body Fever* lead. Steckler said as much time and again but always refused to divulge the original actor's name. This guy may have been a first-time or has-been actor, but he was a three-year fixture working around Steckler's studio. Steckler noticed the "mystery man"'s enthusiasm and generously offered him the lead role of Smith. Apparently, the man-with-no-name was about Steckler's size and, despite being handsome silver screen material, he needed a hairpiece. Steckler splurged, and a visit to Max Factor and 400 bucks later, this guy had hair. Steckler also picked out the guy's wardrobe and realized he was basically projecting himself onto his actor. This curious bit of vanity is not at all uncommon among filmmakers. (Tim Burton's *Edward Scissorhands* and David Lynch's *Eraserhead* are perfectly applicable comparisons here.)

Three days into shooting, which had been problematic enough (25,000 worth of camera lenses stolen on the first day), this guy decides to question Steckler's direction. It seems he was not warming to Steckler's vision and told him as much. A patient Steckler reminded him that he was the director and it was his money. Again, the ingrate refused and a now short-on-patience Steckler ripped the $400 toupee from the insolent actor's scalp and put it on his own head. Script girl Pat Dobie assured her employer that it looked great on him and thus Steckler became private detective Charlie Smith. Then, as if on cue, the former Charlie Smith ran into the street screaming, "I'll never work for you again, Steckler!" It is unlikely anyone cared, least of all Steckler himself.

It has been assessed that Steckler gave his Charlie Smith character an apathetic quality that at first glance appears to be listless and lazy. As the film progresses, it becomes more obvious that the gumshoe is merely cautious. Perhaps this innate caution is derived from years of experience, involvement and know-how, though it is improbable as this P.I. looks entirely too fresh-faced and young.

Steckler attested that in real life, he was dangerously impulsive and that his portrayal of a slow and methodical Charlie Smith was wholly intentional. Oft-times Smith seems aloof and confused, he appears to have no clue what he is doing. Surely this was more projection on Steckler's part, even if in a subconscious sort of way. Somewhere along the line, a producer, cinematographer, editor, actor (or all of the above) must have looked at Steckler curiously and questioned his visions and his motives, and at least *one* actor did.

As a means to an end, Steckler indiscreetly took the lead role but he was not altogether comfortable with his decision. There seems to be little reason for his doubts. In 1995, James Elliot Singer of *Cult Movies* magazine talked up Steckler's acting in issue #15 (p. 12): "Steckler is good in the lead role of Charlie Smith.... Unlike his earlier psychomaniac roles, Steckler portrays his first and last hero type who gets to make time with some attractive actresses." In his autobiography *Shadows & Light*, Gary Kent was succinct in his appraisal of Steckler's performance (p. 71): "[He] was quite touching as a private eye down on his luck."

In *Cult Movies* #8 (p. 31), Steckler told interviewer James Elliot Singer,

> Most people who have panned me as an actor, and that's their prerogative, have only ever seen me once. People who have seen me in five or six movies and pull all these different characters together like the Lemon Grove Kid, Preacher Man from *Wild Ones on Wheels*, Mad Dog Click from *The Thrill Killers* or Lost Jerry from *Creatures*, and really look at the films, find it hard to believe that the same guy is doing all of that.

In Steckler's opening shot of himself, the soles of his sneakers take up the majority of the screen while propped up on a desk. Soon, the shot makes sense as Charlie is affirmed as a private dick who will need those tennies to search for clues, but there is a deeper context to this footwear.

Just as Big Mack was startled awake by a ringing phone, so was Charlie Smith. Smith's secretary Stella (Dina Bryan) suggests answering since he has not had any work in some time and is broke. Smith is not the least bit interested (there is that listless quality coming out) and says that a weekend alone on his boat is the ticket. Incidentally, Travis McGee, the self-described "salvage consultant," lives on a 52-foot houseboat called *The Busted Fish*. Meanwhile, Smith holidays on the quainter environs of his *Rogue* sailboat.

Closing up shop early, Smith's looking to get a head start on his weekend getaway by driving straight to the pier. Stella reminds him that he is currently without a car, "Oh, yeah, the friendly finance company got me again." Again? Well, it looks like he is hoofing and hitchhiking his way to the boat slip and *that* is why he needs those deep treads on his dogs.

A narration by Steckler begins to unravel a bit more of the yarn involving Charlie Smith:

> Okay, you've got my name. Now, here it is 7:32 in the morning and I'm tired and I'm cold and if I had any brains I'd be back there with Stella. But, man, she is just so unreal. I mean, whoever heard of a chick waking up and looking like that, not a hair out of place? I like a funky broad who lets you know what a really rotten night's sleep she's had. Well, someday I'll make it and have the finer things. In the meantime, I get by on the necessary luxuries. Take my boat, for example, the *Rogue*. That's my security thing. It lets me say to myself, 'I'm a lousy private detective with a lousy little sailboat,' but it gives me class. And, you know, nobody outside of Stella knows I've got her stashed here. Nobody comes around and nobody bothers me. No finance company's gonna get this one. They got Charlie's wheels, but they're not gonna get Charlie's sailboat.

Well, somebody *is* about to come around and bother Smith, and that somebody is Harris Fergeson. Fergeson is played convincingly by Alan Smith, who returns to the Steckler fold from his turn as *Incredibly Strange Creatures*' choreographer. Fergeson offers Smith $1,000 a day for that three-day countdown to locate Carrie Erskine. Looking at a sexy head shot of his quarry, Smith says, "The illusive Carrie Erskine looks dangerous enough to be fun."

Fritz the photographer (Ron Haydock) is the first on Smith's list to question. He knows that Fritz exclusively photographs fast women and fast cars, presumably at separate times. Smith hitches a ride into the desert to lean on Moose (Joe Bardo) to direct him to Fritz. Moose is unwilling to cough up any information. With that, Smith once again puts his thumb to work and grabs a lift in the bed of a pick-up truck.

This desert scene was not shot in Hollywood or even California. Steckler

A pensive (or bored) Carolyn Brandt as Carrie Erskine leans against a post while sporting her handmade catsuit in a *Body Fever* outtake (1969) (courtesy Carolyn Brandt).

had been in Utah shooting a documentary on race car driver Craig Breedlove, the first person ever to set the land speed record of 500 miles per hour. Steckler used the opportunity to shoot a few scenes that could later be woven into *Body Fever*.

Smith goes back to Fritz: After some coercing and a 20, the cameraman aims Smith in the direction of Carol Hollister, who used to be Carrie's roommate. Hollister is still shacked up with her drug-pushing pimp Frankie Roberts and he is not the least bit interested in Smith's impromptu visit. The scene between Smith and Carol literally takes place across state lines. Smith is outside her door, asking questions, in Utah while Hollister is indoors in California. For a short time, the scene jumps back and forth from state to state. It is obviously planned very well in advance (a rarity), proving yet again that Steckler is not nearly the hack some critics have inferred.

On another side of town, Brett stalks and talks with Carrie. Apparently, Brett and Carrie were in cahoots to swipe the dope from Big Mack and then sell it themselves, splitting the take. Of course, this all went awry. Brett starts to rough Carrie up, and she pulls a gun on him. Carrie slips out of the scene as more of their profits slip into Carol's veins.

Charlie visits a brothel run by a lethargic gypsy king–looking dude named Waco (Larry Chandler). Waco knows Carrie and he also knows she has been doing some sort of business with Big Mack. After having his palm greased, Waco sends Charlie to a local pool hall owned by the Mack. Before Charlie can vacate, Waco offers his comrade some quality time with a couple of his quality "girls."

Steckler gets some nice shots of downtown L.A. after dark before entering Big Mack's seedy pool hall. Once inside, he sees Brett, Herbie (Herb Robins) and the Mack though he has no idea who any of them are ... yet. Charlie strikes up a conversation with Big Mack, claiming to be an old friend. Mack laughs it up while nearly skewering Charlie in the gut with the business end of a pool cue. Brett tosses the inquisitive intruder into the alley and begins a beating. Then Charlie lays some good old-fashioned jujitsu on the big guy and he is down for the count.

The next morning, Charlie is on the go again and downtown L.A. looks far less foreboding in the sunlight than it had only hours earlier. En route to speak with old friend and confidant Coley (Coleman Francis), Charlie passes the Gordon Theater with *The Maltese Falcon* on its marquee. The naive private eye stops to give a nod to his idol Humphrey Bogart as Sam Spade. These types of shots really give Steckler's films a time-capsule sort of charm that cannot be derived from looking at an artificially manufactured set.

After Coleman Francis' initial involvements with Steckler, the actor and his career were on a collision course with alcohol. Francis was more than down on his luck when Steckler and Ron Haydock happened across him drunkenly occupying a sidewalk bench. At first, Steckler and Haydock were unsure who they were eyeballing, but as they walked closer they realized it was their old friend and colleague.

Steckler offered his luckless pal a double sawbuck but the actor declined any charity. Steckler's mind began to reel and he instantly created a scene for Coley at an abandoned Sunset Boulevard laundromat. Francis graciously accepted the work and was told to be on location at

9:30 a.m. sharp. Haydock was quite vocal about his reservations concerning Francis' ability to show up on time or at all. Steckler concurred, assuming the old man would spend the dough on booze.

Both the young ones were more than surprised and pleased to see Francis show up not only on time but early. Then, to their astonishment, it seemed that instead of spending the 20 bucks on liquor, he bought a nice used suit from a thrift store. It was also apparent that the oldtimer had gotten some rest, sobered and cleaned up. Francis took his work very seriously whether he was working at Universal or in a burned-out building that once housed coin-op washing machines.

Francis loved his drink and Carolyn Brandt recalled him tasting a bit like alcohol when she had to nibble his neck as the Vampire Lady in *The Lemon Grove Kids*. To Gary Kent's recollection, it was the "old demon rum" that was about to sink this poor man into cinematic obscurity. Still, for two decades Francis stood in front of, and behind, the camera on such memorable titles as *This Island Earth* (1955), *Motorpsycho* (1965), *Beyond the Valley of the Dolls* (1970) and of course his largest creative investment, *The Beast of Yucca Flats* (1961).

Francis had two more movies in him after *Body Fever*; the last one was *The Dirtiest Game* for Titus Moede in 1970. Francis would pass away three years later under quasi-mysterious circumstances. Friend and associate Anthony Cardoza claims that Francis' body was found in the back of a station wagon at the Vine Street Ranch Market. Gary Kent recounts in his *Shadows & Light* autobiography (p. 71), "During the filming of *Body Fever*, Ray and a buddy went to Hollywood Ranch Market, then an open air market on Vine Street, to pick up a late night snack. As they walked away ... they noticed a big, poorly dressed derelict sitting on a bench. 'Hey, isn't that Coleman Francis?'" Of course it was Francis, leading one to believe this area was one of his final haunts.

Back to the narration: "A girl named Shawn Call was an old friend of Carrie Erskine. They used to dance together in a chorus line in Las Vegas. Now, it is a bit questionable as to her trade." It seems that Charlie has to continue seeking new depths of human depravity in order to dig up any information involving Carrie. Julie Conners, who played Shawn Call, mined her own cinematic depths with Herschell Gordon Lewis and David F. Friedman projects, respectively: *Miss Nymphet's Zap-In* and *Trader Hornee*, both 1970.

Charlie strikes out with Shawn, or so he thinks, and he beelines it to a swanky poolside party with a dozen or more dolls in some mighty skimpy swimwear. A scruffy-looking movie agent (Wade Watson) is on the hook and points Charlie towards another would-be actress, Julie Richards (Pat Jackson). Jackson later became a minor celebrity on the California club circuit as lounge singer Patty Romero.

Before Julie Richards makes her way onto the screen, Steckler sidesteps the story and returns us to the territory of Fritz the photographer. Fritz is doing the exact same thing as he had done in his previous scene: manhandling his camera for some sassy cheesecake. The big difference here is that the photographer is visited by Herbie. Fritz will not suffer *this* fool gladly. Herbie's looking to move some junk on the cheap, but Fritz is not buying. Actually, Fritz seems perturbed by *this* particular visit and makes his disdain known. An irritated Herbie declares, "I can't talk to you ... any more." An agreeable though generally indifferent Fritz responds, "You never could, Herb." Apparently, this is how these two guys were in real life; there was no love lost on- or off-screen. Regardless, it should be seen as a testament to their respect for Steckler and their abilities to soldier on just the same.

Somewhere on Ventura Boulevard, Charlie tracks down Julie Richards, who appears to be on some kind of a mystery drug that makes her think she is a bird. It is most likely Steckler's reference to LSD as many drug scare films warned of its fictitious side effects; thinking one could fly was a popular one. History has proven it to be governmental terror tactics, but in 1969 (the height of the drug culture) Steckler probably believed it true.

Steckler's quickly shifts the scene from an (squ)awkward bird-dance to a fairly arresting love scene. Since Steckler is in front of the camera, the photography was handled by Keith A. Wester. Jack Cooperman was also on hand to lend an eye to a lens. It is trippy stuff almost in the vein of *Incredibly Strange Creatures'* hallucination sequence. Also of note: These types of extreme close-ups involving intertwined body parts would suit Steckler's needs in the coming months.

Once the unlikely union is satiated, Charlie's first conquest of the film cautions him that if he still wants to find Carrie, he will have to look up her ex-boyfriend Frankie Roberts. No one who has experienced Frankie wants anything to do with him, but Charlie is not in the know and speeds straight over to a subterranean drug den. Steckler makes a salient transition here by zooming in on the fireplace, and then squeezing the flames out of focus before cutting to an acrylic painting of Satan.

Charlie lets himself into what appears to be a private club (Steckler's basement) and bellies up to the bar for some free libation. Frankie eyes the stranger and leaves his post that is inhabited by Liz Renay, Joe Bardo and an *Incredibly Strange Creatures* one-sheet. It is uncertain whether or not Bardo is the same character from the land speed race or if Steckler hoped viewers simply would not notice him in two separate roles. Either way, Steckler largely wastes Renay's on-screen charisma on a bit role as a partygoer with no lines to speak.

After a mostly civil verbal exchange with Frankie, Charlie still does not know who or what he is up against. Frankie's faux candor is a usual occurrence for this violent, thieving, drug-pushing pimp. Charlie leaves the scene once he homes in on Shawn Call. After the Julie Richards victory, his confidence is up, an attribute he intends to keep up by putting the make on a very loopy call girl.

Carrie's been eavesdropping on Charlie and Shawn's conversation and begins devising an arrangement that Charlie will find more inviting than anything Harris Fergeson could ever offer. The jig is about up, but neither Charlie nor Frankie know that. And Big Mack? Well, he has an appointment with a big meltdown, but until then, Charlie locks arms with Shawn and heads for the door while Frankie slips them the evil eye and Liz Renay slips a nip.

From Liz's on-screen indiscretion, Steckler takes the film back to the harbor where Charlie continues to put the moves on Ms. Call, eventually leading her to the *Rogue*. After some more hanky-panky, Charlie's latest carnal acquisition spills the beans on Carrie's whereabouts: She is at home in her apartment. Charlie goes there forgetting the room number, makes a guess at seven, then simply saunters in on Carrie in a black leotard dancing Marge Neilson–style. Astute viewers will catch the tiki idol from *The Incredibly Strange Creatures* making an encore appearance in Carrie's apartment.

Carrie wastes little time in unveiling her plan to steal back the heroin—$150,000 worth—and splitting the scratch with Charlie if he is willing to help. Charlie is all in. Carrie knows that Frankie keeps the stash hidden under a pile of debris in the psychedelic drug den. So it's back to Steckler's basement with a *Pfink* sign above its door. Why Steckler has this hanging on his house is a mystery. That *Pfink* placard also shows up numerous times in the *Lemon Grove Kids* movies.

Charlie digs out the handbag and off he and Carrie go bouncing through a park as though they are in a feminine hygiene product commercial rather than about to unload a dangerous drug onto the streets. The scene is very reminiscent of Lonnie Lord and Cee Bee Beaumont frolicking in Griffith Park, but the tone here is off-putting. Up to this point, the film has been played straight, with little in the way of frivolous nonsense. That is unusual for a Steckler production.

Noticing that the drugs are missing, Frankie flies into a rage and terrorizes Joe Bardo's character, whoever he is at this point, and Shawn Call. Shawn's lips get loose again and she spills more beans: the location of Charlie's boat. Frankie lets her go with a word of warning: "If I don't get it back, baby, you're dead." And if he does get it back, his little junkie trick Carol will likely be dead

Carolyn Brandt as Carrie Erskine and Steckler as gumshoe Charlie Smith overlook the irreparable damage to Gary Kent's Frankie Roberts in *Body Fever* (1969) (courtesy Carolyn Brandt).

from an overdose. There has been a lot of big talk about killing people, but 50 minutes into the film no one has died. That is about to change.

Frankie heads over to the harbor and quickly spots the *Rogue*. Charlie and Carrie, en route to the boat, see Frankie snooping around. Once Frankie spies *them*, a foot chase is on, through a railway station and lots of mud. Frankie catches up, landing a punch and throwing Charlie to the ground. The satchel flies into the air and Carrie looks on in a panic. Charlie retaliates with a fist to Frankie's face. Frankie cries out, "You're dead, Smith!" More talk of the dead and then it finally happens, a bullet to the back of Frankie's head.

It is fairly obvious that Carrie's the one who pulls the trigger but she is not 'fessing up and Charlie does not even consider it might have been her. They flee back to Carrie's apartment for another love scene. This one is nowhere near as stylish as the previous ones, but then this *is* Steckler's real-life wife, so the scene is far safer and pedestrian than the others. This form of prosaic filmmaking is in complete opposition to what Steckler would do in the very near future.

Charlie gets it in his head that rather than move the stuff themselves, he and Carrie should make a 50-50 deal will Fergeson. Carrie is not impressed, but shows little resistance. Charlie takes the stash to Coley's place for safekeeping while he works out the particulars with Fergeson. Arriving at Fergeson's home, Charlie discovers him dead on the floor from a knife to the neck. "I wonder why anyone would want to cut his throat."

Charlie leaves the scene of the crime for a strip club. Herbie has followed him there with what could only be nefarious intentions. Herbie takes a seat right next to Charlie and they both down some swill and gaze at the naked eye candy on the stage. Charlie exits with Herbie directly behind, following the private eye to Coley's where he is picking up the heroin. Charlie should have recognized Herbie from Big Mack's pool hall, but alas he does not and suspects nothing.

At this point in the film, things are starting to meander a bit as though Steckler is having difficulty wrapping up the story. Herbie picks up speed, snatches the satchel, nearly throwing Charlie off an overpass. The middle of a Los Angeles freeway is nowhere for a pedestrian to be, so Charlie chases Herbie into Bronson Canyon which is on the southwest section of Griffith Park. This particular canyon has been host to over 100 movies from 1919 to the present. Steckler helped the Arch Halls shoot their cult classic *Eegah*, barely seven years earlier, in this craggy, remote-looking setting.

Charlie is hot on Herbie's tail and, one right after the other, into a Bronson Canyon cave they go. Posthaste, they are both trapped in a cave, which is once again Steckler's basement. The external to internal transition is remarkable for any filmmaker, but more so for Steckler and his zero budget. Steckler has proven to be no slack in the cinematography or editing departments, but the burning question remains: Why the hell does his basement look like a cavity in the side of the Earth?

Charlie and Herbie are going to engage in a knife fight and only one of them has a knife and it is not our hero. Fret not as Charlie has a plan: "Give me the bag, man." With that, Herbie seemingly thwarts Charlie's plan. "Move or you're gonna end up like a little piece of sliced-up meat in a butcher shop window just like my ex-boss Fergeson did." Charlie surprises his attacker with a jujitsu-style chop to the arm, seizing the switchblade.

Another line of narration seems to position Steckler in the mirror of his lead character: "If I could go through one day without being confused, life would be much simpler." This voice-over is probably more Steckler's screaming thoughts than anything he intended for Charlie Smith. The fact is, Steckler attacked a mystery-crime story with little production time and even less production money. By his own recollection, many scenes were played and shot off the cuff, which worked on some of his earlier madcap efforts. But on *Body Fever*, more preparation may have lowered some tensions on the set, and there were inescapable tensions.

Charlie's internal dialogue is cut short by the sight of Brett assaulting a catsuit-adorned Carrie in the hall of her apartment building. Carrie begs for mercy, insisting that the double-cross was not her fault while Charlie launches into attack mode. Charlie lands a few solid blows before the big guy Brett gets his meat hooks into Carrie's wanna-be savior's throat. Charlie is about to be choked out when Carrie unloads her tiny handgun and curtly does away with the cretin. Steckler's daughter Laura closes the scene upon spotting dead Brett: "Mommy, there's a man on the floor."

Steckler brings the story back to Big Mack, who is in his office putting the make on a blonde cutey-pie. "When Big Mack likes somebody, he likes them and he goes all the way with them. Just remember that, sweetheart." Before the Mack can go all the way, the phone rings introducing yet another character to the narrative: Sammy. Sammy is played by Keith A. Wester in his final on-screen performance.

Sammy needs to talk biz with the big guy about drugs, Brett, Carrie and Charlie Smith. "Smith? Who's he?" The only Charlie Smith Sammy knows is the private eye: "He's got a big nose. You ever see any of those Bowery Boys movies? Remember the guy who played the dummy klutz?" That is some nice self-deprecating humor (or a retaliatory swipe at the deserving Huntz Hall) to close out the scene.

Brett Pearson as Brett manhandles Carolyn Brandt in her Carrie Erskine catsuit in *Body Fever* (1969) (courtesy Carolyn Brandt).

Back at Charlie's office, Carrie takes out the drugs and daydreams of all the scratch they will have after selling the junk on the streets. Charlie is starting to get cold feet about being a dope pusher and suggests they merely dump the stuff. In a slapdash exchange, Charlie realizes Carrie shot Frankie Roberts. Carrie professes her love. The two are on the verge of an agreement when Big Mack crashes their party.

"That's Big Mack. The kingpin. The master criminal. The big wheel." He is there to collect, but our protagonists are not giving in quite that easily. Carrie levels her gun at the intruder: "Big Mack, you're out of the ball game." Charlie begins dumping the drugs into the toilet as the "big wheel" pleads with Carrie to stop him while standing in front of a framed *Wild Guitar* lobby card. Strange behavior for "the master criminal."

The stash is flushed, and the Mack is out of luck. Carrie and Charlie hit the door: "Let's get out of here before we get contaminated." The two leave Big Mack laughing and shouting, "I'm gonna be around a long time. You know why, Smith? Because there's a sucker born every minute and they need me. *They need me!*"

Steckler closes the scene on what is arguably one of his best shots: Big Mack steps over to the upright water cooler and Steckler shoots from the other side as the glass bottle bubbles distorting the Mack's face and mouth as he continues his laughing tirade. It is a marked image that should have been the end of the picture but Steckler simply could not resist one more love scene and a montage recap. It should be noted that Steckler *did*, however, resist throwing in a kidnapping.

Of Steckler's feature-length films, *Body Fever* has for years remained an enigma. Even during the 1980s resurgence of these types of movies, *Body Fever* was seldom discussed at length or at all. Perhaps the writers did not know *to* ask. Often, when Steckler himself brought the film up, very little back and forth occurred between the interviewer and the interviewee. There just did not seem to be a whole lot to *Body Fever* that was capturing the imaginations of Steckler's dyed-in-the-wool admirers.

Some of the film's messy history could involve its myriad of largely misleading titles. Steckler has gone on record stating that the film was originally *Snowjob* which may have made sense had the film centered around cocaine as opposed to heroin. *Cheat for Life* was also considered. Next was *The Last Original "B" Movie*. Although an interesting banner, this title should have been saved for any other movie. Next in line was *Super Cool* which is as confusing and confounding as the former appellations but was perhaps a stab at cashing in on the Haskell Wexler 1969 film *Medium Cool*. Lastly, *Body Fever* is an obviously deceptive cash-grab for video store patrons looking to ogle Melanie Griffith in Brian DePalma's *Body Double* (1984).

The film screened one single time as the B feature to Richard Rush's college campus–political unrest film *Getting Straight* (1970). The film was most likely shown as *Super Cool* and did little more than run these activist theatergoers to the concession stands or completely out the doors. The critics, what few bothered to mention the film, panned it. However, Steckler maintains that one critic was prompted to label the film "The greatest invention since the sleeping pill." This seems like more self-created Steckler lore as he had Mr. Carstairs from *The Lemon Grove Kids Meet the Monsters* describe Cee Bee Beaumont's latest feature in the exact same terms.

Steckler lamented in the Media Blasters DVD audio commentary for *Body Fever*, "I didn't have enough money to do that picture correctly, but I finished it." Years later, critic Michael Weldon was kind to Steckler's 1969 effort in his *Psychotronic Video Guide* (p. 71): "It's a typical dumb-fun Steckler production with an oddball cast." James Elliot Singer had this to say about the film in *Cult Movies* #10 (p. 10): "*Body Fever* is certainly a detour from the predictable private detective formula and a change of pace for Steckler. While producers of A-level crime movies spend considerable sums to effect a nasty, seedy look, *Body Fever* achieves that goal effortlessly, by dint of necessity."

More accolades *may* have come from Quentin Tarantino and his reworkings of Elmore Leonard's 1992 novel *Rum Punch* into his 1997 film *Jackie Brown*. There is no bait-and-switch in Steckler's heist film but there are other similarities in characters and their motivations. Carrie is a lowly secretary working for a drug front and looking for a way out. Tarantino's Jackie Brown (played magnificently by Pam Grier) is in a very similar situation. Jackie attempts making ends meet by working for a crappy airline while smuggling drug money into the States for Ordell Robbie (the inimitable Samuel L. Jackson). The commonalities hardly end there.

Jackie Brown is busted for bringing money from Mexico to the States and Carrie Erskine is caught stealing Big Mack's heroin and now both women are in a sling. Ordell Robbie sends bail bondsman Max Cherry (Robert Forster in his crowning achievement) to fetch Ms. Brown. Big Mack's lackey Harris Fergeson is sent to do the same but does so by way of Charlie Smith. In this instance, Max Cherry and Smith take on almost identical roles. The relationship that develops between Max and Jackie all but mimics Charlie and Carrie's.

Sure, it seems to be a long shot, but knowing Tarantino's courtship with low-budget exploitation cinema draws the target a wee bit closer. Consider this: In the 1980s, Tarantino worked at Video Archives in Manhattan Beach, California, and Steckler's *Body Fever* finally saw the light of day on VHS during those years. It is completely plausible Tarantino saw the lurid cover with its obvious stab at *Body Double* (1984), flipped the box over and spotted Steckler's name.

It is also plausible that Tarantino took that baby home, watched it and subconsciously pasted some of it to the back of his mind for use some years later. He did the same thing with his ending of *Kill Bill: Vol. 2* (2004) vs. Ted V. Mikels' *The Doll Squad* (1973) and he has admitted as much. Perhaps Steckler's film all but slipped his mind except for the characters, their actions and nuances. Maybe these four claptrap paragraphs should simply be heaped upon the pile of coincidence.

This was erroneously called the last film Steckler made with Carolyn Brandt as his wife. Not at all true as the two remained a married couple until 1980. Even still, it seems that the monetary stress of living with a low-budget filmmaker was getting the better of Brandt. Unfortunately (and uncomfortably), her nervousness manifested itself into a disagreeable rash that covered most of her body. Her catsuit and turtleneck sweater hid this unsightly fact from viewers. It was also his last film to be credited to Ray Dennis Steckler for nearly 28 years.

While Steckler felt that he had made a dud, he was still suitably crushed at the cool reception it got. Steckler tossed his work on a shelf and once the sting of rejection had dulled, he sold it to some folks in England. From there the film mysteriously wound up on French television in dubbed form. Ten years later, Steckler sold the film to TV in some stateside territories. Of course the film gained *some* legs later on VHS and DVD.

Sinthia: The Devil's Doll (1970)

Synopsis

At the age of 12, a sexually confused Cynthia Kyle (Shula Roan) viciously murders her parents in a fit of jealous rage. Cynthia possesses an unhealthy love for her father (Boris Balachoff) and fully expects him to reciprocate. When he does not, he and his wife (Diane Webber) are stabbed and their house set afire.

Cynthia spends the next eight years in a mental home. Upon her release, she sees a psychiatrist (Brett Pearson) tasked with stopping Cynthia's nightmares. Cynthia's recovery from her guilt will prove to be no easy undertaking.

What follows is a series of hellish hallucinations and walks through demonic dreamscapes. Here her parents appear in various guises and she even meets the dark lord himself, Lucifer (Herb Robins). The psychiatrist convinces Cynthia that she must commit suicide within one of her dreams to atone for her sins. Cynthia does as she is asked and with that she is freed of her stigma.

Credits

Cast: Bonnie Allison [as Shula Roan] (Sinthia/Cynthia); Ted Roter [as Boris Balakoff] (Lennie); Brett Pearson (The Psychiatrist); Brett Zeller (Carol); Gary Kent (Mark); Maria Lease (Liz); Diane Webber (The Housewife); Herb Robins (Lucifer); Lynn Levin (Asagorah); Theresa Thaw (Dancer #1); Kim Lynn (Dancer #2); Charles Reynolds (The Devil's Messenger); E.M. Kevke [as David Miles] (The Minister); John Andrews, Barbara Mills [as Barbara Caron].

Production: Executive Producer: Dorothy K. Sonney. Screenplay: Herb Robins. Assistant Director: Bernard Glow. Production Designer: E.M. Kevke [as David Miles]. Music: Andre Brummer [as Henri Price]. Costumes: Carolyn Brandt. Director-Photographer: Ray Dennis Steckler [as Sven Christian]. 77 minutes. Color.

The Film

> The Devil is in my brain! Oh, God! He's burning me alive!—Cynthia from *Sinthia: The Devil's Doll*

The end of the 1960s was a pivot point for director-producer-writer-cinematographer-actor Ray Dennis Steckler. His working relationships with the Arch Halls, George J. Morgan and Keith A. Wester had slowly succumbed to the fatigues of ultra-low-budget filmmaking. While Wester went on to become one of the most sought-after soundmen in Hollywood, the Halls were about to run out of steam and Morgan had already raised his white flag.

Enter producer Dorothy K. Sonney, assistant director Bernard Glow and Sun Art Enterprises in what appears to be their second of two productions. The first was director Ron Scott's foray into adult cinema, *The Sex Shuffle* (1968), which was also known as *The Love Shuffle* and then simply *The Shuffle*. Their second junket into adult cinema was led by Steckler, who let interviewer James Elliot Singer in on the scoop in *Cult Movies* #15 (p. 71), "Dorothy Sonney out of Texas came to me to make a movie, 'something weird,' but with more nudity than I had ever shot before."

This is a curious statement from

Poster art for Steckler's trippy sex and Satanism flick *Sinthia: The Devil's Doll* (1970) (author's collection).

Some cinematic mysteries may never be solved but the title of Steckler's seventh feature film will forever remain conspicuous, *Sinthia: The Devil's Doll*. The title's play on words is bawdy by nature, but the horror element is most assuredly intact. This is the type of territory Steckler had been working towards for nearly a decade whether he really knew it or not. If *Body Fever* was a 90-degree turn from *The Lemon Grove Kids*, then *Sinthia* was a complete 180.

Sinthia seems to have been made over a period of time spanning *The Lemon Grove Kids* and *Body Fever* as it is copyrighted 1969. It was not released until the summer of 1970 and the carry-over of cast and crew members indicate as much. Ted Roter, Brett Zeller, Gary Kent, Herb Robins, E.M. Kevke, John Andrews and Henri Price all busied themselves with Steckler to close out the tumultuous late 1960s.

Steckler knew the type of girl he needed for the lead, but after four weeks of interviews with nearly 200 hopefuls, the leading lady slot was not yet filled. In an attempt to move forward, Steckler called Ted Roter over to his office for a chat about his role as Cynthia's father Lennie. As luck, bad and otherwise, would have it, Ted's car broke down and good Samaritan Bonnie Allison stopped to give him a lift.

Ms. Allison could have merely dropped her hitchhiker off and sped away but was intrigued enough to accompany him into Steckler's office. There is little doubt that Roter informed his attractive roadside savior of his destination. Once Steckler got an eyeful of Bonnie Allison, that "Eureka!" moment occurred and he offered her the part. Fate had seemingly dealt a hand, and a promising one at that.

Roter was somewhat shocked at the prospect and informed the starry-eyed

Steckler since, except for *Body Fever*, none of *his* films, up to that point, contained any nudity whatsoever. In any event, this was about to drastically change. In the interview, Steckler may have been referencing a film he had lensed in 1964. Between *Incredibly Strange Creatures* and *The Thrill Killers*, director Phillip Mark hired Steckler as a camera operator on his nudie-cutie *Everybody Loves It*.

Whatever Sun Arts' output, one thing becomes obvious when perusing the credits of their second feature: a large portion of the folks on board are Steckler alumni. The two that remain the proverbial wild cards are Dorothy Sonney and Bernard Glow. Perhaps these two were all there was to Sun Art by the turn of the decade.

Steckler that Allison was a Sunday school teacher by day and possibly was not right for the role. The fact that Roter knew all of this about Allison furthers the notion that their en route conversations were more than just small talk. Ted may have been dragging his feet on the subject, but Allison made her stance quite clear: She had always wanted to give acting a try but never had the guts. And with that, Bonnie Allison became Shula Roan and thus Sinthia or rather Cynthia.

Ted Roter (credited here as Boris Balakoff) went on to direct some adult doozies: *Prison Babies* in 1973 and *Hollywood She-Wolves* (with Titus Moede) in 1976. He did this before going the hardcore porn route like Steckler and Joe Bardo. Roter; unlike his screen mates, actually managed to work with some hard-hitters in the industry like Ron Jeremy, Veronica Hart and the legendary Georgina Spelvin. His highest-profile films were 1981's *Ring of Desire* and 1984's *Endless Lust*.

Another holdover from the *Body Fever* shoot was Steckler's key grip John Andrews. Andrews was the son of "Arkansas Slim" Andrews, Tex Ritter's cowboy movie sidekick. No doubt Steckler took an immediate liking to Andrews and his connection to those classic B-Westerns. Andrews' movie career was short-lived, but he did put in some additional time with Ed Wood on *Orgy of the Dead* (1965) and *Necromania: A Tale of Weird Love!* (1971). Andrews also worked alongside Stephen C. Apostolof on his sleazy 1966 *Suburbia Confidential* and Al Adamson on his 1970 mess-terpiece *Horror of the Blood Monsters*.

Actress Brett Zeller turns in her final role for Steckler as the character Carol. In *Cult Movies* #15, the director remembered her for James Elliot Singer: "Brett Zeller ... went on to do some leads in a few movies. She was an artist and did all of the paintings for *Body Fever* and *Sinthia*."

Another notable newcomer to Team Steckler was soft-core adult screen actress and model Barbara Mills. Mills was known for her long mane of brown hair and her willingness to fully undress in front of a camera. Some of her more interesting titles are *Wild, Free and Hungry* (1969), *Don't Just Lay There* (1970) and *Chain Gang Women* (1971). The free-spirited Mills has over 40 credits to her name as well as her aliases: Barbara Caron, Gabriella Caron and Leona Tyler.

Steckler opens the film in a precipitous manner with two naked bodies in the act of copulation while a female voice narrates, "Flesh upon flesh. My mother, my father and I captive in a brain that we cannot see. The eyes of the Devil watch us closely." Not exactly titillating stuff

Shula Roan aka Bonnie Allison plays the cute but wildly disturbed and deadly Cynthia Kyle in *Sinthia: The Devil's Doll* (1970) (author's collection).

for the viewer but actually more on the uncomfortable side of things. This preface places the film perfectly within the parameters in which it will reside for its 70-minute duration.

Riding a wave, Steckler followed his confusing influx with Ted Roter and Gary Kent in their respective roles as Lennie and Mark pulling and pawing at various naked women. These scenes are voiced over with Cynthia declaring Mark her first love, then amplified with cries of, "Daddy, oh Daddy, oh, why Daddy?" *ad infinitum*. Again, it is all more unsettling than remotely arousing, which even in this short pre-credit sequence is leading the audience down an unexpected path.

From this confounding two-minute introduction, Steckler pushes the film into a dense, forest-like setting where Cynthia dances about completely in the buff. More of Cynthia's psychosis is revealed with her words, "Years have passed. My life was one of searching through dreams and fantasies, which had no end, only lost waves that kissed the shores of a clean virgin sea that I could never bathe in." In an obvious attempt to appease the raincoat crowd, Cynthia's dance in the dark leads the film back to a bedroom where Lennie is at it again with his wife (Diane Webber).

Ms. Webber had previously been a Playboy Playmate twice over, once in May 1955 and then nine months later in 1956. Her second *Playboy* pictorial (credited as Marguerite Empey) was photographed by none other than Russ Meyer. Steckler eyed Webber's talents in the film *Mermaids of Tiburon* six years later as she worked as a topless mermaid. The diehard nudism advocate and belly dancer's showbiz course was quaint but it did include seven film appearances, numerous television spots and a spate of modeling for vinyl album covers.

Finally arriving at the core of this film's hysteria, Lennie reveals that he is Cynthia's father. Mother feels he dotes on the little one too much as Cynthia is now 12. The troubled tween feels otherwise and quietly sits at the end of their love nest contemplating the worst. The *worst* she could muster up was stabbing her parents to death, then setting the family home ablaze, destroying their bodies and the evidence. Where are those raincoaters now?

This is Steckler's set-up for his first adult feature; something he would not dream or dare of showing his daughters Linda and Laura. For reasons discussed below, Steckler would put a

This Les Baxter album cover from 1961, *Jewels of the Sea*, is an example of Diane Webber's modeling career. Ms. Webber played the Housewife in *Sinthia: The Devil's Doll* (1970) (author's collection).

lifetime of effort into detaching himself from this film, though he apparently put zero effort into the credit sequence. This indifference to detail had reared its dull head during *Lemon Grove Kids* and *Body Fever* which was especially disappointing after the bombast of *Creatures*, *Thrill Killers* and *Rat Pfink*.

Steckler briskly pushes the film forward. Cynthia's psychiatrist (Brett Pearson) reads aloud from her medical charts regarding the events which led to her being in his care. He recites these passages not for his or Cynthia's benefit. They already know the facts. Steckler included this reference for the viewing audience.

The inclusion of this scene and two others like it were insisted upon by the producers in order to help explain the film's "Euro-style" narrative. This move on the producer's part infuriated Steckler and is the primary reason he removed his name as director, or so he maintained. One could argue that he was simply distancing himself from a skin flick, a tactic he would become all too familiar with in the coming years.

Sven Christian was Steckler's first *nom de screen* as director and he begrudgingly applied it to *Sinthia*. He would hide behind this name at least four more times over the next three years in a clandestine effort to separate his legitimate work from his off-color titles. For the most part, Steckler's simple act of subterfuge worked and it would be years before any dots were connected revealing his aliases.

Steckler may have been pitching a bit of a tantrum as he had not experienced any resistance from a producer since his days with Arch Hall, Sr. Even still, those spats were ironed out in the interest of finishing the film and saving their friendship. This arrangement was altogether different. Steckler felt his hands were tied and did not like it at all as he bemoaned to Boyd Rice in *Incredibly Strange Films* (p. 44): "I had no control over the film because I didn't produce it; a sorry lesson I learned. I made a film I really cared about, yet they took it away from me and changed it. I swore I'd never do that again."

Back at the doctor's office, Cynthia's therapist believes he can help relieve her anxieties through his understanding of her merciless nightmares. "Just relax, Cynthia. Relax and think about that very first time you saw your father and your mother in bed." At this point, it has been strongly suggested that Cynthia's love for her father went beyond the usual parameters of a parent-child relationship. Again, the raincoaters are being led down a cinematic path they had likely not bargained for.

Ten minutes into the film, Steckler unleashes the first of many hallucinatory dream sequences. This one is an electric inferno of garish colored lighting, painted laughing faces and writhing naked bodies in a myriad of sexual positions. Steckler twists his camera in and around the action, which is far more psychedelic than sexually stimulating.

In addition, Steckler employs some nifty kaleidoscopic optical effects, variable camera speeds, double exposures and superimpositions that blast furiously from the screen. All of these visuals are backed with a wild experimental jazz score by Henri Price. With all there is to see and hear, Cynthia merely runs from one side of the hallucination to the other crying, "Please! Daddy! Where are you taking me?"

Steckler grinds this course on for a full seven minutes before maniacal laughter breaks the mood and shifts the film a bit. At this point, *Sinthia* is an outright art film anchored in a Freudian narrative that turns the tables on the doctor's Oedipus complex theory. Throwing in more than a dash of Kenneth Anger and very low-rent Federico Fellini, Steckler attempts advancing the film into *Satyricon* (1969) territory. Of course, Steckler does not have the resources, monetary or otherwise, to see the sequence to its fullest potential but he gives it a go and the results are not entirely awful.

Herb Robins as Lucifer presides over the whole infernal affair with a look and demeanor of devilish glee. The orgy people drag Cynthia to Lucifer, mocking and taunting her: "Cynthia wants her father. Cynthia loves her father." These jeers are brought to a halt as the naked gang throw their arms up in some sort of a satanic salute and chant, "We love Lucifer! We love Lucifer!"

Lucifer and his wife tell Cynthia that both her parents are there. The demonic wife puts forth, "You are one of us, child. You have murdered your parents and have not atoned. You are rightfully ours, Cynthia." This stern assertion gives way to more chants, "Welcome, Cynthia! She is one of us!" Lucifer demands she be whipped. The nude brood sneers, "Child of the Devil, Cynthia." The S&M audience gets jilted here as all the action is off-screen.

A large portion of the film's cast appear in the Hellscape scenes, which were shot in Steckler's basement. One face is conspicuously missing: Carolyn Brandt's. As mentioned in the previous chapter, the Stecklers' honeymoon was over, their marital union was on the rocks. Perhaps spending evenings in her basement surrounded by naked men and women spouting sacrilegious chants was not what the doctor had ordered for her. Still, Ms. Brandt would have been right at home in Lynn Levin's seat as Asagorah, Lucifer's wife.

Next, Steckler moves Cynthia and her evil dream to a deserted pathway overlooking the ocean. In grand contrast to the darkened scenes within the bowels of Hell, Steckler chooses to shoot this sequence in broad daylight. Cynthia awakens on her back, then stands and walks to the edge of the pathway. She looks over the cliff at the jagged rocks and the violently crashing ocean waves. It is a scene Steckheads will find familiar from *Wild Guitar, Incredibly Strange Creatures, Rat Pfink a Boo Boo* and a film he will shoot nine years later.

Cynthia's tweaked psychosis is off and running again as she peers into the ocean: "The waters are a fat, clean virgin sea I once dreamed of." Cynthia turns and walks into the distance only to encounter a soothsayer (Brett Zeller). Zeller, whose character is later named Carol, warns Cynthia, "I wouldn't go that way if I were you. Danger lies waiting for you in that direction." Cynthia ignores the admonishment and strolls on into danger.

The danger she encounters this time is in the form of an amplified and animated man in gaudy '60s mod attire and multi-colored face paint. This character's motive is unclear. However, chasing Cynthia in and around the rocks while pulling her sun dress off seems to be his M.O. During this pursuit, Steckler employs his handheld camera to great effect. He quickly zooms the lens in and out then twists the camera in numerous directions, creating a scene that is as disconcerting as this dream is supposed to be for Cynthia.

Cynthia escapes her attacker and finds herself in the arms of the soothsayer: "Poor, dear little child. The cards said that pathways of trouble would open up for you, but still you walked blindly towards the depths of Hell. Your world is so full of evil, so terrifying, so empty of love, so troublesome. Come with me, my child, into my world." It is all so poetic, almost.

Now the dream maneuvers to what appears to be a small makeshift art studio exhibiting nude paintings. This scene, like all the others, is completely surreal in its appearance and execution. This is the third level of Cynthia's nightmare and while things seem less unstable, they are no less bizarre. It is here that the soothsayer is recognized as Carol.

Cynthia gets some art critic time in before Lennie enters. Lennie, as mentioned before, is played by Ted Roter but here he is not recognized as Cynthia's father but merely an artist who paints nudes. Wasting no time, he asks his young attractive guest, "Do you model?" On the surface it appears as though a father is requesting the naked modeling talents of his daughter. But it is not that simple. This is where the parallels between Cynthia's reality and this damnable dream begin to mix and blur in an off-kilter fashion.

Carol decides to give Cynthia a tarot card reading and the cosmos seems to have no better events in store for her than it did for Marge in *Incredibly Strange Creatures*. Showing her the "devil" card, Carol tells Cynthia, "The lovers are chained together and the evil one controls their destiny." Cynthia flips at the news and runs into Lennie's arms. Carol

On September 4, 1970, the Downtown Cinema in Tampa, Florida, screened *Sinthia: The Devil's Doll*. The Downtown was one of Tampa's many Adults Only theaters during the early '70s. In the summer of 1971, its name was changed to the Mini Sun Art; later, it was sometimes called the Mini Downtown Cinema. After Tampa introduced an obscenity ordinance in March 1973, the theater made news by showing *Deep Throat* (1972). It was the Mini-Burlesque from 1974 until its final days in 1976. The building reportedly became an office building before its demolition (image and commentary courtesy film historian and archivist Raleigh Bronkowski).

continues her reading: "With the coming of the full moon, you will reap your rewards. The darkness and night filled with cleanliness and peace for you. The moon is on the way, I bid you go." With that, Cynthia is out of Lennie's arms and into the blackness.

Steckler cuts to a house in flames (presumably Cynthia's) and then back to the thicket where Cynthia dances, again completely in the buff. In an attempt to tie up some of this non-cohesive narrative, the thicket dancing could have been used as a conduit for one dream dimension to another. Alas, it was not. What remains is a repeated sequence that reveals some skin but no more about the film's story.

Cynthia returns to the art studio only to find that the paintings have been rearranged and the bed that she had murdered her parents on has appeared. Before she can begin piecing more of the mystery together, an incredibly well-endowed and curvaceous beauty steps into the room. For now, the raving vision is only a visitor in Cynthia's unbalanced mind but soon enough her role will become far more significant, though unsettling.

What follows is as uneasy a sequence as Steckler would ever shoot. After some small talk about home life troubles, the two ladies move in on each other and begin kissing and petting. Cynthia proclaims that no one has ever been nice to her before and her partner pulls out a breast. Cynthia looks into her new lover's eyes and sighs, "Mommy." Cynthia takes Mommy's nipple into her mouth and suckles and nurses infant-style.

From incestuous lesbian sex, Steckler moves the film back to the beach and then back to the art studio where Lennie is about to lay a brush stroke or two on canvas. There's a nude cutie posing on a stool and Lennie's asking that she expose more of her naked chest; then he asks Carol to bring him Cynthia. He wishes to paint her in the raw as well. This may well be all in Cynthia's disrupted mind, but it is still forging an account of a most dysfunctional family arrangement.

For whatever reason, Lennie asks Cynthia if she would attend a play with him and Carol. Once they are seated, the show begins and out walks Mark (Gary Kent) and Liz (Maria Lease). These two had been getting it on in the pre-credit sequence, which made no more sense than this floor show does. Liz begins to berate Mark and again Cynthia flips out, storming the production in an attempt to circumvent the on-stage aggression.

Trailing this madness is even more madness. Now Cynthia and Mark are marrying. Once the minister, old Steckler standby E.M. Kevke, delivers the vows, Cynthia decides Mark is her father and begs him never to leave her. He insists that he would not and then a topless Liz begins making out with Mark in front of Cynthia. Yet again, Cynthia flips.

Cynthia awakens screaming from this portion of her nightmare into the arms of Lennie back at the art studio. "Oh, I'm sorry. I get these attacks so often. I lose all self-control. It's almost as if I were slipping away. Am I all right now?" Lennie comforts her, "I guess God has left you for a while and the Devil wants to claim you as his own." More comforting words have never been spoken.

Cynthia revives back at the shrink's office, crying, "Help me, Father! Help me, I'm burning up! The Devil is in my brain!" The good doctor attempts calming her: "You're not burning up. There's not a devil in you. Wake up! Wake up! Everything's gonna be okay. You have to kill yourself." Before any rational person can ask what kind of lame-brained advice this is, the doctor clarifies that this suicide be performed within one of her dreams. Somehow he has deduced, while observing her nightmare in a chair, that this will rid her of her guilt.

Doctor whatever-his-name-is instructs Cynthia, "Go back into your world of nightmares and destroy yourself." More anguished cries for Daddy lead Cynthia back into the hellish world of Lennie, Liz, Carol and Mark. They take turns telling Cynthia that her father is dead. Cynthia gets an eyeful of Lennie's latest creation, a painting of her parents burning alive in their home. Cynthia screams, then dances naked, for the third time, in the thicket.

Cynthia returns to the scene of the crime and repeats the murder. She then asks, "Is God dead now, Daddy?" Daddy insists, "Do not say the word 'God' in front of me. You don't know his presence. You are a child of the Devil." Lennie advises Cynthia, "You must give to someone who is also possessed by him. You must destroy the Devil in someone else with your purity and love." This guidance leads Cynthia to lay on a white shag rug and masturbate.

After Cynthia's self-gratification, she and Mark are alone and in love again. Cynthia goes to Carol and tells of her new beau and they wax seriously about first kisses. Then Carol declares that *she* is Cynthia's mother and a naked Lennie finally declares he is her father. There is a quick strip tease act from Liz and then Steckler returns the film to the deserted walkway on the beach. At 60 minutes in, the wheels have come completely off this thing.

A recap of the first oceanside chase with the amplified and animated man in gaudy mod attire and face paint gives way to more pawing. Lennie makes it with Liz. Mark makes it with Liz. Mark makes it with Carol. Cynthia makes her way through the thicket for a fourth time. Mark makes it with Cynthia. Mark and Liz get it on once more and Cynthia contemplates murdering them Mommy and Daddy-style but decides better of it and starts screaming again.

Steckler returns us to the beach as the mod man pursues a topless Cynthia through the surf. Liz performs topless again and warns Mark that she will kill Cynthia if he goes near her. Mark beckons Cynthia and she comes to him. "Little angel God-child. Thank you for letting me kiss you this afternoon." If the wheels of this thing are off, the nuts and bolts are letting loose now.

Lennie asks Mark to give Cynthia to him. He cannot and so he asks Carol. She cannot, *will* not. She will kill Cynthia before she gives her back to Lennie. Lennie observes, "The moon is no longer full of life. The Devil is gone from her. She has been purified with the fires of Hell." Cynthia's mind then returns yet again to the scene of the crime, and she murders her parents for a third time. She sets the house aflame and then commits hara-kiri. A three-minute nutzo jump-cut recap ensues.

This cinematic insanity finally begins to wind down in the shrink's office as Cynthia careens back into the real world. She tells the doctor of her suicide and burning up in the fire and that she somehow feels different now. Apparently Doc's unorthodox plan worked and Cynthia is no longer pregnant with possession. This viciously slick and supernaturally hip psychedelic sexploitation psychodrama has come to its end.

Steckler's seventh feature made its rounds through the grindhouses of America and even found itself in some U.K. territories under the *Where the Devil Toils* title. The *Dark Eyes of London* Internet blog reported on April 21, 2019, that the British theater chain Tatler ran their version of *Sinthia* alongside an Ed Wood–scripted softcore comedy, *One Million AC/DC*. This particular pairing made a Gary Kent double feature of sorts as he had an uncredited role in *One Million AC/DC* as the character Olaf. Some video releases employed the *Teenage She Devil* designation. While Steckler considers *Sinthia* the best example of

A newspaper advertisement for *Sinthia: The Devil's Doll* (1970) on a double-bill with *The Exotic Dreams of Casanova* (1971) at the Mallet's Bay Drive-in in Burlington, Vermont. Mallet's Bay opened in 1949 playing standard first-run films before switching to more adult-oriented fare in the 1970s (image and commentary courtesy film historian and archivist Raleigh Bronkowski).

his photography skills. The critics were mixed on the film as a whole.

Writer James Elliot Singer said this of *Sinthia* in issue #15 of *Cult Movies* (p. 70): "[B]izarrely delirious...." He also pointed out that *Sinthia* was among his [Steckler's] later features to have "a dark atmosphere populated with unpleasant characters in grim settings." Actor Gary Kent briskly mentioned in his autobiography *Shadows & Light* (p. 71) that *Sinthia* was "a seriously flawed art piece."

Critic Michael Weldon wrote about the film in his *Psychotronic Video Guide* (p. 509): "*Sinthia* is a plotless sex-trip movie. Some of you might enjoy *Sinthia* more than I did. Drugs might help. Maybe not." It is certainly worth noting that up to this point, Weldon had been a staunch supporter of Steckler's work but the director's future endeavors would not be spared the writer's pen nor his opinion, which did not improve after *Sinthia*.

Backing up a tad, this was actor Gary Kent's third and final performance for Steckler. Kent went on for many more years as an actor and stuntman for fellow exploiters such as Al Adamson, Anthony M. Lanza, Richard Rush and Don Coscarelli. Of late, Kent has been the subject of a celebrated documentary entitled *Danger God: The Lives and Love of a Hollywood Stuntman* (2019) by filmmaking newcomer Joe O'Connell. Even later, director Quentin Tarantino based part of his character Cliff Booth on Kent and his rough-and-ready stay at the infamous Spahn Ranch movie set for his 2019 film *Once Upon a Time ... in Hollywood*.

As it is, the film's over-saturated colored lighting, wrenching camerawork, garishly painted faces, seaside foot chases and tarot card readings all seem quite familiar. So in the end, the whole thing comes across as sort of an unbalanced sister-piece to *The Incredibly Strange Creatures*. *Sinthia: The Devil's Doll* can be fun, but Steckler was to continue moving into darker cinematic territory. Some fans of his kookier works just were not going to stick around for it.

Blood Shack (1971)

Synopsis

One hundred fifty years ago, on a Death Valley ranch, an accidentally murdered Indian boy incites a local medicine man to put a curse on the killer's family and their home. One by one, the Walton family dies by the blade of the malevolent Indian spirit known as the Chooper. The medicine man's curse has ordered the Chooper to allow no one in the Walton house ever again.

One hundred fifty years later, horror scream queen Carol Craig (Carolyn Brandt) is looking to get away from the hustle and bustle of Hollywood. Her uncle, Jim Craig, recently passed away and willed his ranch to Carol. The old, haunted Walton house still stands.

Ranch hand Daniel (Jason Wayne) looks over the property. Tim Foster (Ron Haydock), owner of a competing ranch, wants to buy the land, but Carol is not selling. Tim devises a scheme to scare her away from the Blood Shack.

The Blood Shack has had many visitors who died at sword point, the same fate as the Walton family. Daniel keeps the Chooper and the old house's secret by quietly disposing of the bloodied bodies.

Credits from Blood Shack

Cast: Carolyn Brandt (Carol Craig); Ron Haydock (Tim Foster); Jason Wayne (Daniel); Laurel Spring (Connie); John Bates (Charlie); Linda Steckler (Margie Potts); Laura Steckler (Barbra Potts); Ray Dennis Steckler (Mr. Potts); Steve Edwards (Constable); Peanuts the Pony (himself); Sugarplum the Puppy (himself)

Production: Producer: Carolyn Brandt [as Carol Flynn]. Screenplay: Christopher Edwards. Photographer-Editor: Ray Dennis Steckler [as Sven Christian]. Music: Frank A. Coe. Sound Effects: Frank A. Coe. Director: Wolfgang Schmidt [Ray Dennis Steckler]. 55 minutes. Color.

Credits from The Chooper

Cast: Carolyn Brandt (Carol Craig); Ron Haydock (Tim Foster); Jason Wayne (Daniel); Laurel Spring (Connie); John Bates (Charlie); Linda Steckler (Margie Potts); Laura Steckler (Barbra Potts); Ray Dennis Steckler (Mr. Potts); Steve Edwards (Constable); Peanuts the Pony (himself); Sugarplum the Puppy (himself)

Production: Producer-Director-Photography-Editor: Ray Dennis Steckler. Executive Producer: John Foty. Co-producer: Steve Edwards. Associate Producers: Robert Compton, Hank Cartwright, Gene Cartwright. Titles: Larry Fisher. Screenplay: Ron Haydock, Ray Dennis Steckler. Makeup: Carolyn Brandt [as Carol Flynn]. Sound: John Bates. Assistant Director: Robert Fisher. 70 minutes. Color.

Featured Songs

"Carolyn Brandt's Theme" by George Hernandez
"The Chooper" by Ron Haydock
"Dream Your Dreams" by Don Snyder

The Film

> Stay away from that old house. Bad things happen in there!—promotional tagline from *Blood Shack*

In 1962, Steckler's career as director revved-up with *Wild Guitar*. In '63 he punched the accelerator and shifted gears into *Incredibly Strange Creatures*. The young director then slid up to third gear and roared into 1964 with *The Thrill Killers*. Maintaining the previous year's velocity of unpredictable entertainment value, Steckler's cinematic engine seemed to top out in '66 with *Rat Pfink a Boo Boo*. Just five years after a promising start and a rousing race from the camera to the cinema, Steckler's moviemaking machine was on cruise control.

Nineteen sixty-seven and *The Lemon Grove Kids Meet the Monsters* represent a change in Steckler's direction. By the time of *Lemon Grove Kids'* third vignette, Steckler was losing co-workers left and right. The pit crew that had helped Steckler across the finish line with his first four features were now finding other courses to run. Steckler's drive and determination to win seemed to wane through the end of the 1960s. In the early '70s, it sputtered into a full-service station.

That full-service station resided in Pahrump, Nevada, which is also home to a portion of Death Valley. How completely apropos; it appeared as though Steckler was bringing his legitimate film career to its final resting place. Sure, he tried resurrecting it eight years later but by then the drive-in market had all but dried up. Shady theater owners and even

Three very different VHS boxes for *Blood Shack* (1971) with the middle one representing one of the film's alternate titles *Curse of the Evil Spirit*. This was the same artwork used when the film was also released as *The Chooper* on VHS (author's collection).

shadier distributors effectively muscled small-time moviemakers off of the track. Sad to say, Steckler was one of those small-time moviemakers who got muscled out.

However, 1971 saw Steckler at his most prolific with at least seven new movie credits. None of them could be accredited to him as his alias was on full display. Apparently Steckler's relocation to Las Vegas had its pros and cons as six of those seven titles were "adults only" features. Six from seven leaves one and this tiny balance left Steckler with his lone and last gasp at legitimacy. It was a cheaper-than-normal horror flick called *The Chooper*.

Steckler started the film with the low, low sum of 500 bucks and claimed it was his lowest budget ever. But nothing had *really* changed as he recounted to Boyd Rice in *Incredibly Strange Films* (p. 36): "It's not easy to make any film. Even if you have $20,000,000, you've got the same problems as some kid with 10,000. There's never enough money; you never get what you want. And the more money you have, the more pressure you have. At least that kind of pressure I don't have."

The Chooper was likely the first legit film Steckler shot after moving to Sin City. It was also the next-to-last legit Steckler film that Carolyn Brandt was involved in. After working with and under the guidance of four different producers, Steckler found himself without a partner in 1971. Brandt took on the faux role of producer, but Steckler was essentially foraging his barren cinematic landscape alone.

Ron Haydock, despite knowing squat about Native American legends, was nevertheless pegged to pen the script about a bogus Indian curse. Evil deeds were carried out by the Chooper, but what the hell is a Chooper? At a cursory glance, a list of demonic Indian spirits will not produce a Chooper, but rather Atasaya, Baykok, Okeus and/or Matchi Manitou. So, what is in this name?

Apparently, Steckler had a leftover *Lemon Grove Kids* costume that Herb Robins wore as he jumped around repeatedly saying, "Choop! Choop!" So they called him the Chooper. Haydock later donned the costume and executed a very different take on that character. Steckler just used what he had on hand and as usual it was not very much.

Steckler's waste-not-want-not ethos dictated the direction of the title and costuming departments. It did not matter to Steckler that the costume was ill-fitting or that the antagonist's name meant nothing whatsoever. He had managed to scrape together five big ones and it was time to make a movie.

Steckler's original cut of the film clocked in at barely 55 minutes with the working title *Blood Monster*. No distribution company was remotely interested in what amounted to a made-for-television movie. Finally, one distributor showing *some* interest in handling the film insisted on a 70-minute running time. Yet again, Steckler found himself in the dicey situation of padding his already completed movie. This time, musical numbers, parades and/or additional characters and plotlines were out, and rodeos were in.

Next, the film's title was on the proverbial chopping block. The distributor figured most people would mistake *The Chooper* for *The Chopper* and while they may have been correct, the latter is far more befitting the film. So Steckler's eighth feature became *Blood Shack* and Ray Dennis Steckler became Wolfgang Schmidt. This handle was recycled from his stint as co-producer on Curt Siodmak's 1966 comedy *Ski Fever*.

Steckler lore maintains the name

Wolfgang Schmidt came to him while drinking at a party. The director's drink of choice that evening was the first vodka introduced to the U.S. around the turn of the twentieth century. This inexpensive, though award-winning, elixir was originally made in Latvia and bore the name Wolfschmidt.

Steckler had changed his name on *Sinthia: The Devil's Doll* to Sven Christian in order to distance himself from a production he was ultimately unhappy with. As mentioned before, Steckler was a hired gun for *Sinthia* and felt very little connection to it once the producers demanded changes he was not comfortable with. This time, however, Steckler was in complete control of his film and yet he still felt a name change was in order. He recounted on the audio commentary of Media Blasters' DVD release of *Blood Shack*, "I told Ron Haydock that no one would even steal our movies. So we took three 16mm prints of *Lemon Grove*, *Rat Pfink* and *Creatures* and we put them on the bus stop at Hollywood and Vine. Then we stopped back three hours later and nobody had even stole them. And they were marked. They don't even want to steal Ray Dennis Steckler movies." However, in 1983 Steckler had a slightly different version of the story to tell Johnny Legend for *Fangoria* #28 (p. 27): "I unloaded every print of every movie I had made, with my name in big letters on each film can, and we left them there. Four hours later, no one had even touched or tried to steal my movies."

Nobody wanted *The Chooper* so Steckler had to take what he could get out of it. The fun and sun of Steckler's earlier ventures had been replaced by the gloom and doom of his three latest pictures. With very little money in the budget, Steckler was forced to shoot his latest film with "short ends" left over from those productions and others.

Making matters even worse is that some of these "short ends" were so old that it was impossible for the film lab to color correct them properly. This left many of the scenes with an odd and/or improper color palette. This obstacle along with the fact most of the film was shot at high noon (for inexpensive lighting purposes of course), gave *Blood Shack* a murky, washed-out look and feel.

The film appears to have been run through the grimiest of projectors around the country and back again. But this was not the case at all as Steckler recalls it receiving only one showing in Denver, Colorado. Although *Sinthia: The Devil's Doll* garnered a fair amount of screen time, *Body Fever* and *Blood Shack* quickly wound up in the "where are they now" files.

As with Steckler's previous outings, *Blood Shack* was shot on 16mm and blown up to 35mm for its one and only theatrical viewing. Steckler opens the film with his camera aimed directly into a raging sun, rewarding the viewer with some fantastic spheres of multi-colored flares. Three years later, a virtually unknown director named Tobe Hooper opened *his* little horror film in a similar manner; this little film was to become the runaway success known as *The Texas Chainsaw Massacre*. Could Hooper have been influenced by this sequence? This seems unlikely since the film only played once in Colorado and Hooper was 800 miles away in Texas.

Then, without warning, Steckler jams the movie straight into the credit sequence. As *Blood Shack,* the film's titles are as simple as they come—yellow print on a black background. MCMLXXX appears under the *Blood Shack* title indicating that it had been re-released on VHS in 1980. The early '80s was a perfect time to cash in on the slasher craze that had been kickstarted by John Carpenter in 1978 with his never-say-die classic *Halloween*. Artist Larry Fisher created some amazingly ghoulish and striking paintings depicting a grisly humanoid creature brandishing a myriad of bloodied weapons for the credits of *The Chooper*.

If the Chooper of the film's title looked anything like these gruesome full-color images, then the audience was in for a shocker. Alas, the Chooper will not be anywhere near as menacing as its painted representation suggests and the audience will be nowhere near shocked. In the end, it is a moot point as theatergoers never got to actually see the original title sequence that also announced the director's real name, Ray Dennis Steckler.

During both title sequences, some unconventional sounds and noises emit from the speakers. It is hardly music but it still somehow manages to construct an unsettling tone for the low-rent film. Steckler's longtime music coordinator Henri Price must have been busy that year working on Art Lieberman's 1971 sex comedy *Up Your Alley* as he turned the reins over to Frank A. Coe. Coe returned to Steckler from his sound effects duties on *Lemon Grove Kids* to provide *Blood Shack* with more of the same in addition to music. In between those two films, Coe stayed close to the Steckler crew by working on *Hell's Chosen Few* (1968) with Gary Kent and Titus Moede. Two years later, Coe worked on *The Girls from Thunder Strip,* also with Kent.

Steckler's camera roams a mountain range while Carolyn Brandt's familiar voice chimes in with a lengthy narration to set the story up:

There is a legend about Death Valley. A tale carried across the winds of time. A legend strange and sinister. The legend of the Chooper. A long time ago, a pioneering family named Walton settled these lands and built this house. One evening Ed Walton heard someone sneaking around outside and fired his rifle into the darkness. He heard a scream and then nothing but silence and the wind. Walton investigated the darkness and found a body, that of a little boy … the son of an Indian chief. When the chief learned of his son's death, he vowed revenge. The medicine man placed a curse on the Walton family, calling upon the powers of their god of vengeance, the Chooper. Within two days, the neighbors found the hideously slain bodies of the entire Walton family. But since that time long ago, others have been murdered in the old house. For the legend says that whoever stays within the cursed walls of the house shall find only monstrous death awaiting them. Death at the hands of the Chooper. When my Uncle Jim came into this property, he built a new ranch house but because he was always interested in history, he never had the old house torn down. Today, I can only wish that he had.

An unfortunate aspect of the *Blood Shack* edit vs. *The Chooper* version is the omission of three original musical numbers. Brandt has a lovely theme scored specifically for her by composer George Hernandez. Singer-songwriter Don Snyder makes it yet again onto a Steckler movie soundtrack with his tune "Dream Your Dreams." And then there is room for one last Ron Haydock rockabilly scorcher; "The Chooper": "You better look out world, there's a menace on the loose. Women better run and hide. Men, prepare to defend yourselves from a terror from the other side. Well, here I am, baby, I'm the Chooperman."

As Haydock bangs on his acoustic guitar singing the somewhat foreshadowing lyrics, Steckler focuses his lens on his daughters Linda and Laura as they dash across a desert floor. It *could* be deduced that they are running from the Chooperman but their smiles and laughter tell otherwise. Up to this point, Steckler hardly missed an opportunity to include his adorable daughters in his films. *Sinthia: The Devil's Doll* was the obvious exception.

As Haydock's song comes to a close, Steckler moves the film to a shoddy ranch house where a shirtless man swings a shovel into the air, striking a dead tree. Soon it will be disclosed that this tree-attacking man is Daniel, the foreman of Craig Ranch. Daniel will spend a great deal of the movie leaning on his shovel, heaving rocks into rusty buckets, chasing his hat and screaming at dead people.

Daniel is played by small-time actor Jason Wayne. Wayne managed a local movie theater when not propping himself up with a shovel handle in Steckler's movie. He continued working off and on with Steckler until 1976. Some of Wayne's off-color ventures with Steckler included *"Daisy Lay": Ozark Virgin?* (1971), *Peeping Tom* (1973) and *South of the Border* (1976). The frames of *Blood Shack* display plenty of Wayne's lanky build. Should an even more revealing look be necessary, check out one of his latter films.

After Daniel's rock-tossing is completed, some shovel-leaning is next on the agenda. Linda and Laura Steckler show up as Margie and Barbra Potts. The girls want to know if they can play around the ranch, but they like the old, haunted shack in particular. Daniel's having none of it: "I told you kids before to stay away from that old house. Bad things happen in there."

Margie and Barbra decide on a game of musical chairs with one chair. Margie points out that they cannot play that game without three people though she seems to think one chair will do just fine. So they attempt this activity without enough players or props. It is a silly but cute scene that is likely only there for the viewing pleasure of their real-life parents.

Jason Wayne as Daniel oversees the Craig ranch in *Blood Shack* (1971) (courtesy Carolyn Brandt).

Daniel exits the scene to answer the telephone and the Potts girls find the lure of the dilapidated house irresistible. Daniel returns in time to stop them and then yell at them. "I told you kids to stay away from this house! That was your mother on the phone and she wants you home, now! If you wanna play around here any more, stay away from this house!" Daniel is clearly angry and kicks an old, battered washtub to the side. Then it is back to the shovel.

As with Steckler's previous cinematic ventures, he was scouting around for locations and happened upon an abandoned house situated upon what appeared to be an abandoned ranch. Steckler only wished to rent the lean-to but wound up having to cough up the dough for three months rental on the entire ranch. At 275 bucks a clip, Steckler insists that it was a kosher arrangement as he had several friends who needed a place to stay. So, when not filming, the ranch became the Steckler compound.

Back to the film: Daniel pokes his favorite farming implement repeatedly into the ground as some old jalopy turned hot rod races onto the ranch and parks in front of the haunted shack. Daniel seems largely indifferent to his uninvited guests, three men and a young woman who discuss spending the night in the house on a dare. The two men decide it is not in their best interests and speed off, leaving the woman to fend for herself.

The woman's name is Connie and she is credited as Laurel Spring; her real last name was Bates. She was married to actor John Bates and it was he who brought those two men and the hot rod–jalopy to the set. The two young men did not receive a screen credit and will likely stand nameless but not faceless. These presumably wanna-be actors will forever remain framed between Steckler's 16mm sprocket holes.

After Laurel's scenes were shot, she stayed on as script girl and attended to the makeup department. Laurel's husband John had an even smaller role, and spent the remainder of his time on set running sound. He was able to operate the tape machine after Steckler taught him the ropes. Bates stuck around long enough that year to play Zeke in one of Steckler's earliest forays into the adult film world, *"Daisy Lay": Ozark Virgin*? (1971).

Connie makes her way into the house and Daniel makes his way over to scream some stuff and push her to the ground. Daniel fusses about the house being haunted and Connie fusses, "I'm staying here, baby." Daniel sees that the determined woman will not budge and relents: "Well, go ahead and stay, but if the Chooper does come to get you, well, you deserve it. But I warned you. The Chooper will get you and I know it"

Finally, Connie is back in the house and Steckler's camera exposes some of the old shack's amenities. The *niceties* include windows with no dressing, busted drywall, peeling wallpaper and the filthiest mattress this side of John Waters' *Female Trouble* (1974). This abhorrent excuse for a bed appears to have already had someone or something murdered on it. Nonetheless, Connie spreads her sleeping bag across its puke-inducing stains.

Night falls and Connie begins to undress but the mood is quickly soured as she plops her backside straight onto the soiled pallet. This entire sequence is as gritty and gnarly as they come. The abandoned house Steckler found for *The Thrill Killers* was a palace compared to this repulsive shanty. As one of Connie's friends noted earlier, "What kind of ghost would haunt a place like this? It's a dump."

As the night wears on, Connie becomes increasingly spooked by the sounds of the desert. She thinks she has nothing to worry about but an ancient Indian curse is about to make her reconsider. Enter the Chooper with its monosyllabic roar, wielding what appears to be a shiny medieval knight's sword. Even for a Steckler movie, that's a strange choice for weaponry. Why not a spear, war club or even a bow and arrow? Surely someone on the set could have fashioned a fairly realistic-looking tomahawk. Hell, even a rubber prop ax from the roadshow days would have sufficed.

The howling Chooper and his blade steadily pursue the frantic Connie, who eventually dies a bloody death. This first on-screen murder discloses the malevolent Indian spirit to be in some sort of human form. It walks and kills like a human and later it will reveal another human ability no other on-screen ancient spirit, evil or otherwise, could possess.

The sun rises and Daniel saunters into the house and screams, "No! I warned you! I told you the Chooper would get you but you wouldn't listen! No!" Daniel vacates the murder scene to retrieve his pick-up truck and pitch Connie's mangled body into its bed. He then buries the body, *after* rifling through the victim's purse. "I sure am glad the Chooper couldn't use this money, 'cause I sure can." Daniel is all heart and all class.

From Connie's makeshift gravesite, Steckler takes the film to a Texaco station where Carolyn Brandt is basically playing herself as Carol. Carol kicks around some gravel (in her stylin' white go-go boots) to the wafting sounds of George Hernandez's "Carolyn Brandt's Theme." More narration is employed to further the plot as character development and a cohesive script are MIA once again on a Steckler production. By now, Steckheads know the drill.

Brandt stars as washed-up scream queen Carol Craig. She has had it up to here with Hollywood and is hell-bent on retiring from Tinsel Town to the filthy, abandoned ranch that she has recently inherited from her Uncle Jim. It is a telling storyline that almost mirrors Brandt's real-life circumstances. This will be Brandt's last quasi-legit role in a film for Steckler or anyone else for eight years.

Daniel drives up to the gas station: He pulls in alongside Carol and helps her into his truck. He then whisks her away to her new home. Tim Foster is waiting on them, especially Carol, as he wishes to purchase her property. In fact, his first words to her are, "I wanna buy your ranch." No beating around the bush for this competitive rancher, played by Ron Haydock.

Carol is not interested in selling, but Tim seems to hardly notice her resistance. He yammers on about cleaning the place up, tearing down the inoperable water tower and especially the old shack. Daniel hollers, "That's a historical monument! It's been there for over 150 years!" Tim's response is less excited though far more pragmatic: "You know the only history that place has got is about 150 years' history of death in it."

Tim leaves the premises in a cloud of dust and Daniel moves Carol's belongings into the ranch house guest room. He points out the john and then the office where her uncle used to write his horror pictures: "You know, my Uncle Jim wrote some of the best horror films I ever acted in." After zero self-promotion in *Sinthia:*

The Devil's Doll, Steckler went for broke in this room. Viewers will clearly see a framed *Lemon Grove Kids* 8×10 glossy and *Incredibly Strange Creatures* and *Thrill Killers* pressbooks. Daniels points to *The Thrill Killers*: "*The Thrill Killers* is where those crazy men got you out in that old haunted house and started butchering you all to death." Daniel continues his morbid description of Carol's career: "Then in *The Incredibly Strange Creatures* when you were that exotic dancer and Cash Flagg comes in and starts butchering you and your blood is splattering all over the place. Those are some great ones."

Tim pulls over to blankly stare at the side of the old shack; Daniel lobs more rocks into a bucket, and Carol takes a tour of the grounds while her theme song plays once more. Carol makes it to the porch of the house but is startled by a sound that only winds up being the Potts girls. They ask Carol if they can play in the creepy old house and she gives them permission. The two girls stand in the front doorway and Barbra chatters some unintelligible babble about dead children and the Chooper. Then they find the sickeningly repulsive mattress and play on it.

Carol returns to the ranch house and showers. This first of the two shower scenes was left over from *Body Fever*. After Carol is freshened up, Daniel takes her on a tour of the ranch and explains why Tim Foster so desperately wants to buy her property. Tim believes the grounds to be his even though *his* great grandfather lost it in a bet to Carol's great grandfather over 100 years ago. Bad blood still runs deep between the Fosters and the Craigs much like a modern-day Hatfields and McCoys.

Later that evening, Carol basically sleepwalks to the Chooper's domain but is stopped short of the front door by Daniel. Some of Carol's walking scenes are so dark that she is practically swallowed entirely by the immense blackness of the night. Steckler usually lit his films more effectively than this but since the house had no electricity, they had to run power from 200 feet away and were only able to use two stage fill lights.

While this particular lighting job did not quite work, Steckler prided himself in being able to illuminate any scene anywhere with only a pair of lights. Eight years later, while he was teaching at a film university, a student asked how he could possibly accomplish such a feat. Steckler said, "I'll show you how." So, he went out one night, set up a camera, two lights and a bloody murder scene. He returned to class the next day and screened his example. That short sample eventually blossomed into an entire film.

Carolyn Brandt, as former scream queen Carol Craig, scopes out her new digs at the Craig ranch in *Blood Shack* (1971) (courtesy Carolyn Brandt).

The next day Carol, Mrs. Potts and the girls attend a rodeo. Daniel is visited by Connie's husband Charlie (John Bates). Charlie is convinced that his wife is still in the old house and sets out to investigate. Daniel delivers his usual refrain, "You stay away from that old house! Stay out of there you hear me! Stay out of there! The Chooper'll getcha!" At this point, it's unclear as to whether Daniel *is* the Chooper or merely its gatekeeper.

Charlie ignores Daniel's admonishments and proceeds to the front porch of Chooperdom, but this time the cantankerous old spirit is waiting outside. The Chooper launches into action, pushing his quarry into the house. He meets the same fate his wife did. In broad daylight, the Chooper's furry black ninja-like get-up can be inspected and that inspection reveals that the costume is about two sizes too small.

Once again, Daniel trundles over to the shack: "Oh my God! I warned you! I told you the Chooper would get you! Oh my God!" Then, just as before, he races to get his truck, hurls Charlie's carcass into the back and tears across the desert floor. Presumably Daniel will steal Charlie's money and deposit him into the ground. This thing is starting to resemble the 1993 Bill Murray comedy *Groundhog Day* as much as it is a slasher flick.

Steckler brings the story back to Carol and the Potts girls. There is more unintelligible talk from Barbra, then it is back to the rodeo for this thrill-seeking bunch. Tim Foster pesters Carol again over the ranch. Carol, to herself: "I wondered what was really ticking in his head behind those weird sunglasses."

Local Johnny Law shows up at Craig Ranch to query Carol about missing teenagers Connie and Charlie. She knows nothing of their appearance *or* their disappearance. The lawman decides the answers to his questions and the investigation lie within the walls of the old shack. The constable, as actor Steve Edwards is credited, gets back into his unmarked patrol car and putters over to Chooperland. Edwards managed a radio station in the Pahrump area, and was also one of its announcers. This film is loaded with local *talent*.

The inquisitive police officer gives the Chooper's lair a once-over, then decides to check out the surrounding grounds. Then from off the roof, with a not-so-mighty roar, comes the Chooper. Daniel is out of a job today because after the constable is offed, the Chooper puts his body in the car, takes the wheel and frantically drives away. What 150-year-old evil spirit knows how to drive an automobile?

From this head-scratcher of a scene, Steckler again applies the "family fun" angle to the film. Carol goes to the Potts ranch to meet the Margie and Barbra's new pet, Peanuts the pony. Here they cavort (for nearly three minutes of screen time) on their acreage with various animals and neighborhood children. Mr. Potts (Steckler himself) shows up to tell Carol that his kids "really dug her." Peanuts was an unexpected gift from a "working girl" (as Steckler described her) whom he had helped out of a jam. The director would not expound upon this story but to his recollection Carolyn Brandt was not interested in the full explanation anyhow.

Daniel is back on the scene, or the porch of the murder shack anyway. Here he ruminates over the fate of the historical site, the Chooper's continual reign of rural terror and his part in the whole bloody affair. Jason Wayne gives it his all: "That's okay, Chooper. You keep knocking them off and I'll keep burying them.

Laura and Linda Steckler as Barbra and Margie Potts sit atop Peanuts the pony while their mother Carolyn Brandt playing Carol Craig holds their new puppy Sugarplum in *Blood Shack* (1971) (courtesy Carolyn Brandt).

So, you just kill all you want and I'll just keep burying them but they'll never knock this old house down. It will be here forever and ever. There will always be this old house and I'll be the protector of it."

Steckler continues to pad the film with more footage of the Potts girls running around, Carol showering and Tim Foster being a pest. Daniel informs Carol that she is the owner of 10,000 acres with a lake 100 feet underneath. She is briefed on the water's credentials. It is Artesian water filtered through limestone and she has enough to irrigate half the state.

It is becoming clearer as to why Tim Foster insists on owning this ranch. It is becoming *clearer* that Steckler is, yet again, starting to lose control of his narrative. Simply put, there should never be protracted conversations about irrigation and filtered water in a horror film. Steckler is doing everything in his power to stretch his original 55-minute version to the demanded 70. Whether or not it is working, is definitely up for debate.

At Craig Ranch, the Potts girls dig holes and it appears they are about to unearth Daniel's secret—the buried bodies. But no, they are just digging holes as Foster chases Carol around blathering about the same old thing until Daniel has had enough of his bullying. The ranch hand and the ranchman square off for a showdown in the desert sun. The tussle goes on and on until Carol's had enough. She slings a wooden 2×4 towards Foster and makes contact with his ankle.

The defeated Foster limps away from Carol, "You're gonna sell. You're gonna sell, baby," as the film limps back to the rodeo. Here, Tom Snyder's schmaltzy "Dream Your Dreams" makes its silver screen debut, adding the oddest aural atmosphere to any cattle-wrangling footage ever. After four more minutes of these barnyard festivities, Foster shows up again in his "weird sunglasses" to deliver a half-hearted apology. Carol's not having it.

The next morning, Daniel, with shovel in hand, traipses his way towards the shack but is stopped short by the growling Chooper. The Chooper is in full-on attack mode and stabs Daniel in the gut. As with the constable, Daniel is struck down outside the house, proving that victims are not necessarily required to enter the Chooper's domain in order to be eligible for liquidation.

Carol, sporting skintight stars-and-stripes pants, hears the commotion and sashays towards the shack. Here, Steckler continues his love affair with Carolyn, through the lens of his camera; he records her every provocative movement. It is not the frantic walk of someone making their way to a crime scene, but it is obviously *the* walk that Steckler desired to document. It is reminiscent of Cee Bee's long stroll to the grocery store in *Rat Pfink a Boo Boo*, but those were somewhat happier times behind the scenes.

Carol reaches the front porch and cautiously enters the shack; viewers get a final peek at the sick murder mattress. Back on the porch, she hears Daniel struggling and follows the sound of his cries but is descended upon by the yowling Chooper. Chooperman chases Carol around the corner and is immediately stopped dead in his tracks by Daniel, who, despite bleeding profusely,

The Chooper (Ron Haydock) attacks Carol (Carolyn Brandt) in *Blood Shack* (1971) (courtesy Carolyn Brandt).

manages to tackle the demonic menace (whose footwear includes dress socks and white sneakers).

Sneakerman leaps from Daniel's grip and begins pummeling the terminally wounded man's face with one fist after the other. Carol grabs Daniel's shovel and plants it onto the Chooper's back with all the might she can muster. The injured assailant rolls away, revealing the face of Tim Foster. Daniel sweeps up the Chooper sword and brings an end to Foster and presumptively the ancient Indian Chooper curse. Or did he?

A dying Daniel does not believe it is the end of the evil scourge: "That's not the Chooper. He's not 100 years old. That's Tim Foster, he's just trying to scare you off your ranch. Don't let anyone ever tell you different. Don't ever go into that old house or the Chooper will get you." With that, Daniel takes in his last gasp of air and drops his dead head directly into the desert sand.

Steckler bookends the film with more shots of sun flares as Carol delivers one last narration in an exhausted and indifferent tone. "Tim is dead. Daniel is dead. I don't know what I'm going to do. Oh, well, I think I'll just worry about it tomorrow, that's if tomorrow ever comes." The film ends with a reprise of "Carolyn's Theme" and Larry Fisher's lurid yet highly stylized visuals and credits. As the music swells to a crescendo, the short list of cast and crew drags itself to term with the ominous question, "The End?"

There is a finality and sadness that comes with the closing of *Blood Shack*. Steckler had relocated from the town that had more or less turned its back on him to a place that ultimately would not fully embrace his talents either. His family ties were coming apart before his eyes, as were his ties to the legitimate film industry. Add to that, a failing furniture business that he had opened with his long-time friend Ron Haydock. The once jaunty cameraman was spiraling downward into a blue abyss he likely never dreamed of exploring.

As a bridge over future troubled waters, Steckler manned a camera for Corey Allen's sex romp-a-rama take on the classic *Pinocchio* story. The Medved brothers wrote in their book *The Golden Turkey Awards* (pp. 164–65), "We are pleased to see that as recently as 1976 [sic] Mr. Steckler could still find work as a cameraman on this *Pinocchio* project—a film in which he should feel entirely at home." Carolyn Brandt had an uncredited role along with sex goddess Dyanne Thorn as the Fairy Godmother. This is also the period where Steckler reportedly made the elusive serial killer film *Bloody Jack the Ripper*. Herb Robins starred alongside Brandt and Steckler in a reprisal of his Charlie Smith role from *Body Fever*. This project reads like it possesses a deluge of charm and potential but alas remains lost.

By 1971, what there was left of Ron Haydock's career was grinding to a halt. He bemoaned his position in life to Steckler: "Nobody cares about me anyway. Nobody wants me no matter what we do." Steckler fired back, "You know what, Ron? This has gotta stop right now. I have hocked my house. I have hocked our cars and almost my kids to put you in the movies because I believe in you." Steckler stated this while recording the audio commentary for Media Blasters' DVD release of *Blood Shack*.

Steckler's friend, confidant and moviemaking partner was only 31 when they lensed *The Chooper*. The *Chooper–Blood Shack* was Haydock's last cinematic dance with Steckler. It was also his last screen credit. Six years later, he died

Poster art for Corey Allen's *The Erotic Adventures of Pinocchio* (1971), on which Steckler was cinematographer (author's collection).

while hitchhiking from Monterey, California, on his way to L.A. Some have suggested that he was inebriated when he was hit by a semi on an exit ramp. At least one person (Steckler) has suggested it was suicide.

Haydock died on August 13, 1977, and was quietly buried three days later. The tortured artist's remains lie on Chicago's periphery in an old Catholic cemetery. Haydock's untimely death forever plucked him from any future grooves, pages or silver screens.

Over time, *The Thrill Killers* has been hailed as Steckler's darkest film but if that was the case, then *Blood Shack*, coupled with its behind-the-scenes back stories, is his most somber. It is gritty and it is grim—it is depressing and the critics are all over the place on this one. Joe Bob Briggs wrote, "Depending on how big of a Steckler fan you are, [this] is either his minimalist masterpiece filmed in the style of Michelangelo Antonioni or a 70-minute snooze-fest disguised as a horror film." Jim Morton from *Incredibly Strange Films* (p. 57): "The Chooper has a few Stecklarian moments, but pales beside his earlier efforts." But Miriam Linna saw the film in a positive light, writing in the Norton Records bio notes of *Ron Haydock and the Boppers: 99 Chicks* (p. 26), "The desolate Death Valley setting and Ron's unnerving portrayal of a bloodthirsty, sword-wielding, supernatural psychopath make it a genuinely scary movie, although it certainly doesn't live up to *Rat Pfink*. Still, it's a bleak psychological chiller easily capable of causing haunted dreams."

Critiques aside, Steckler managed once again to fly directly in the face of adversity to assemble and release a movie with almost no money. His 1971 horror film, made under horrible duress and conditions, may have had only one screening but it found an audience on the video market in the 1980s. Sometimes the film was for rent as *Curse of the Evil Spirit* or *The Chooper* but it mostly made its rounds as *Blood Shack* with the tagline, "Open the Door to a New Kind of Terror!"

The Hollywood Strangler Meets the Skid Row Slasher (1979)

Synopsis

The sleazy, crime-ridden streets of Hollywood's Red-Light district host a killing spree by *two* serial murderers. The Strangler (Pierre Agostino) has been done wrong by his previous lover Marsha and plans to exact his revenge on Hollywood's harlots. The heartbroken (and mad) man poses as a nudie photographer to gain his victim's trust; he then launches into a rage, choking them to death with whatever is handy. One by one, hapless and helpless lasses fall prey to the Strangler.

Another part of town, another killer: The Slasher (Carolyn Brandt) runs a used bookstore by day, then by night slices her way through Skid Row's bums, winos and weirdos. The Slasher catches the pensive eye of the Strangler, who longingly pursues her in hopes of replacing his promiscuous Marsha.

Night after night this psychopathic duo kill their respective quarry in their own respective fashions. In a final act of desperation for attention, the Strangler cautiously approaches the Slasher. The two killers face one another and lock eyes. Will they fall in love or will they fall in their own blood?

Credits

Cast: Pierre Agostino (Jonathan Click); Carolyn Brandt (The Slasher); Lori Morris (Strangler Victim 1); Chuck Alford (Slasher Victim 1); Snowy Sinclair (Strangler Victim 2); Jim Parker (Slasher Victim 2); Bonnie Smith (Strangler Victim 3); Forrest Duck (Slasher Victim 3); Joanne Hiatt (Strangler Victim 4); John Leeman (Slasher Victim 4); Jean Roberts (Strangler Victim 5); Denise Alford (Strangler Victim 6); April Grant (Strangler Victim 7); P.J. Parker (Streetwalker and Strangler Victim 8); Trish Lope (Strangler Victim 9); Ray Hughes (Man in Bookstore); Laura Steckler, Ruth Flynn (themselves)

Production: Producer: Carolyn Brandt [as Carol Flynn]. Executive Producer: "Dutch" Niemann. Photographer-Editor: Ray Dennis Steckler [as Sven Christian]. Screenplay: Christopher Edwards. Music: Andre Brummer [as Henri Price]. Theme Song: Alberto Sarno. Makeup: Laura Steckler. Director: Ray Dennis Steckler [as Wolfgang Schmidt]. 71 minutes. Color.

The Film

Soon she will be out of her misery. Slow ... don't rush it. Yeah, I'll give her

The Hollywood Strangler Meets the Skid Row Slasher (1979)

what she wants. I'll give her what she needs. Wait! Wait! Wait!—Jonathan Click from *The Hollywood Strangler Meets the Skid Row Slasher*

After an eight-year hiatus from the horror genre (and legit films altogether), Steckler finally decided to try paddling back into the mainstream. Being his last feature *Blood Shack* languished in complete obscurity until the 1980s video craze, who exactly was going to notice him missing? He had not used the Ray Dennis Steckler handle for nearly ten years.

In fact, between 1970 and 1979 he had operated under nine aliases on 25 different films. For *the Hollywood Strangler Meets the Skid Row Slasher* he opted for the old standby Wolfgang Schmidt. So, while Steckler was extremely busy during this time, it was by design that no one knew it.

As it turned out, *Hollywood Strangler* really did not deviate from his tried and tested voyeur-porn formula. Steckler had continuously driven home that cinematic recipe between 1973 and 1979. This is not to suggest that his return from the bowels of the underground was completely baseless. Steckler was going to get away from the adult film industry, but it appears as though he was going to make this transition in baby steps.

In his new feature, Steckler has his antagonist Jonathan Click lumber about the streets of Hollywood (sometimes literally Las Vegas) looking for promiscuous women. He buys these women's time under the guise of a photography shoot and then chokes them to death with whatever is handy. The camera parallels the voyeurism and the strangulation represents the sex.

Naturally Steckler could not resist putting his wife in the film, so the Skid Row Slasher is presented as the second of the two serial killers. Carolyn Brandt's character appears to be clearing the streets of the homeless by stabbing them in their drunken stupors. Steckler has suggested that this psychosis was

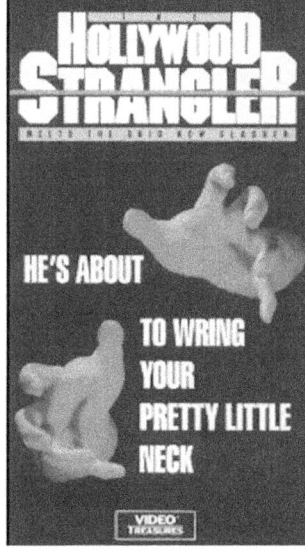

Three different VHS covers for *The Hollywood Strangler Meets the Skid Row Slasher* (1979) (author's collection).

brought on by the need to murder any man who reminded her of her abusive father. This is not explored in the film as Steckler's narratives are never quite that complex. Convoluted at times but hardly complex.

True to Steckler's form and norm, the prudent director shot this entire film MOS (without sound) and literally shopped it to distributors as a silent movie. Naturally, no one wanted a silent movie in 1979, so Steckler was coerced into adding a soundtrack with voiceover dialogue exactly as he had done with his porno films. Various women provide voices for the strangler's victims while Steckler looms over a mic to give said strangler his. Interestingly, after all those years of lending her voice to Steckler's adult films, Carolyn Brandt's sultry purr is nowhere to be heard, thus leaving the Slasher mute.

Steckler may have reluctantly added the voiceover material, but in all actuality it lends an edge of uneasiness to the film as Click never actually speaks. Steckler's inexpensive remedy, whether cleverly executed or by accident, involves the demented thoughts of Click as he rants and raves in his own head. What's more, the dialogue from the women is muffled and at times completely inaudible. Again, this was either clever or accidental as it makes it appear as though Click is so damaged in the brain, he can hardly make out what the girls are saying.

Pierre Agostino was tapped for the Hollywood Strangler role. (Steckler insists that his last name is actually Agostini.) He also claims that Agostino was from São Paulo, Brazil, and relocated to Vegas to start a drywall-painting business. In 1970, Agostino starred (as Pierre Gostin) in Charles Nizet's Vietnam-vet-gone-haywire yarn *The Ravager*. Four years later, he returned to the Nizet team to play a sadistic hunchback in *Help Me ... I'm Possessed,* an early example of torture porn. Two more years would pass before Agostino would see himself on the silver screen and that would be within the frames of Steckler's raucous X-rated *Red Heat*.

Getting on with *Hollywood Strangler,* the pre-credits sequence reveals Jonathan Click's method of operation which involves snapping a camera, with no film, aimed at a floozy. His broken mind says things like, "She wants it. They all want it. They like it. She wants me to do it to her." Then once the working girl unknowingly crosses Click's self-imposed puritanical lines, he strangles her. Lori Morris is his first victim in the film and apparently the last thing she was to do in front of the camera.

Click leaves the scene of the crime and pretends to take pictures of passersby as he makes his way through a seedy part of Hollywood. From here he arrives at his home where he will cool down from the kill by petting his pigeons. This is a strange way for a murderer to spend his down time as well as an inadvertent nod to *Rat Pfink a Boo Boo*. In that Steckler classic, the not-so-dynamic duo rumbled in and around a pigeon coop. An additional nod to Steckler's past is Jonathan's last name Click, which is reprised from *The Thrill Killers* character Mort "Mad Dog" Click.

Returning to this pigeon business, possibly a more effective way of exploiting the cooling-down process might have involved Click fantasizing about the murder, but he did not. Perhaps another way of winding energies down is to look at pictures of the victim, if any were taken, but again he chose not to. Click could have easily done this as he always had a camera; he just needed to put film in the damned thing. If no pictures were taken and the fantasies have run their course, the last resort might be returning to the scene of the crime and yet he did not do this either.

That final cooling off method will lead to the murderer ramping up for the next kill. So, judging by the forementioned cooling down examples, Click's pigeon-petting can be seen more as an act of disassociation. This is a simple exercise that allows Click to mentally and emotionally remove himself from the heinous crimes that he has committed—for a while. Still, the cooling-down periods and acts of disassociation are subjective and vary from one serial killer to the next.

Then Steckler quietly introduces the Skid Row Slasher on the very beach where *Incredibly Strange Creatures* was shot a decade and a half earlier. Click peruses a sleazy sex paper, locates his next victim and telephones her. To help explain Click's lunacy, Steckler adds more voices in his head to the soundtrack. "She sounds anxious, too anxious, but she's no different from all the rest. They try to act so cool and different. Marsha tried to act that way when she told me they were just photo sessions. Just photo sessions, yeah, just photo sessions."

So, whoever this Marsha was, she has obviously done a number on Click, and all the other tramps in his life will pay for her sins and that is it—Jonathan Click's flimsy-thin motivation. Now, the anxious girl is about to extend a bit of hospitality, as only this type of chick can, before checking out altogether. Snowy Sinclair, a professional dancer who worked at the Cabaret in Vegas, lent Steckler her talents as Strangler Victim 2, then vanished from the movie business.

After the kill, Click returns home to cool down, this time by playing with his dogs. Click, the Hollywood Strangler, sure has a soft side to his psychotic personality. He then visits a used bookstore run by the Skid Row Slasher. "That girl behind the counter; maybe she's different. Maybe she isn't like the rest, like Marsha was." Click thumbs through a book he clearly has no interest in, while the Slasher stares blankly into space with clearly no interest in him.

The Skid Row Slasher's bloodied tool of the trade (courtesy Media Blasters).

A drunken bum wanders into the shop and offers the Slasher a drink. She pushes him away. Here Carolyn Brandt's character is dressed in a very drab-looking pale blue dress. She wears no makeup and has done nothing specifically stylish with her hair. This will all begin to change as her kills add up, but not before actor Chuck Alford becomes the Slasher's first victim of the movie.

Click leaves the shop and loiters in front of the Flick Theater on Freemont Avenue in Las Vegas. One-sheets for *Deep Throat* and *The Devil in Miss Jones* hang behind him. Supposedly, *Deep Throat* played there continuously for over ten years. The films on the marquee are the forementioned plus *Behind the Green Door* and *The Resurrection of Eve*, both starring Marilyn Chambers.

A streetwalker strolls by. "Hey, honey, looking for some action? I can outdo Linda Lovelace any day!" Click declines. Still, she is just the kind of gal that Click likes to sink his mitts into. P.J. Parker, who plays the propositioning prostitute, was in real life married to Jim Parker, "The Vegas Vampire." Mrs. Parker played Jim's female counterpart "Satana" on the local Vegas *Shock Theater* show. Jim had previously turned in a memorable performance as Count Dracula in one of Steckler's earliest adult film efforts, *The Mad Love Life of a Hot Vampire* (1971).

Click continues to loiter outside the porno theater next to the used bookstore. The bum stumbles by and lands in a patch of grass in hopes of sleeping off his drunk. The Slasher closes up shop and makes a beeline to the grass patch in order to conduct a bit of street-cleaning in her own messy way. A shiny silver switchblade is brandished and plunged directly into the bum's throat; Slasher Victim 1.

This scene (the first one shot for the film) interestingly serves as a cinematic pipeline into how Steckler's mind could work. Steckler had been giving a lecture at the University of Nevada, Las Vegas, on film production and instructed his class that anything could be photographed with a camera and only two lights. One incredulous student questioned his ability to do such a thing at night. Steckler assured his inquisitive pupil that it could indeed be done and he would prove just how. Later that week, Steckler hauled his two lights and 16mm camera into a darkened alley and filmed his friend Chuck Alford being murdered by a faceless killer with a switchblade knife. This short sequence was then screened at his next lecture and presumably the members of the class were satisfied with the results. Since Steckler does not waste a thing, this footage became

Jim Parker played Slasher Victim #2 in *The Hollywood Strangler Meets the Skid Row Slasher* (1979). Note: Here he is in his Vegas Vampire getup (author's collection).

the genesis of *The Hollywood Strangler Meets the Skid Row Slasher*.

The Slasher character appears to be somewhat patterned after England's most notorious serial killer, Jack the Ripper. While the Ripper preferred to murder and mutilate working girls in the night, the Slasher has her bloody way with drunken street people. Both of these factions of humanity have been described at times as undesirables, so the Ripper and Slasher have a similar endgame. Also noteworthy is that there was a real-life Skid Row Slasher: Vaughn Greenwood, who murdered nearly a dozen victims between 1964 and 1975.

What follows next is a fairly lengthy montage of Click driving around Hollywood, taking pictures of random things and random people. Incidentally, as with all of Steckler's footage of this type, none of these people (other than Agostino) are aware they are being photographed for a movie. Steckler just poses as a tourist with his Bolex camera filming Agostino ducking in and out of X-rated theaters and bookstores as unknowing passersby wander in and out of view. This is guerrilla filmmaking 101.

Apparently Click has exhausted his previously purchased sex trade paper and grabs the latest edition of *Playhouse*. This issue, full of young and willing hopefuls, will surely yield another satisfying kill for the crazoid Click. He slips into a phone booth with the sleazy magazine and his unbalanced thoughts. "I keep trying ... searching, and I know their routine. Yes, I won't forget to bring my camera and I won't forget to bring the money. They never forget to ask about the money ... honey. Now, let's see what I'm gonna give her. Let's see what I'm gonna give her."

Click locates the applicable house and is somewhat disconcerted to find there are two girls living there and he had not bargained on that. "Ah, just another piece of garbage. I'll have to get rid of both of them now." The sharp eye will notice Steckler's adult one-sheets hanging on the wall: *French Fantasies*, *Teenage Massage Parlor* and *Paranoia*, which inexplicably changes to *Teenage Hustler*. This is further proof of Steckler's sordid celluloid past which he forever insisted he wanted to disassociate himself from.

The first girl (Bonnie Smith) gets Click's murderous motor running while her roommate (Joanne Hiatt) takes a cold shower. Bonnie moves through her clumsy peekaboo peepshow type of dance until Click has had quite enough and strangles her with her own scarf. This exercise in murder may have been influenced, in part, by the Boston Strangler. Killer Albert DeSalvo supposedly strangled 13 women to death in the 1960s, and many times he utilized an article of their clothing.

Bonnie gives it her all under the attack of Click but ultimately becomes Strangler Victim 3. Joanne is still in the shower and could not hear her friend's stifled cries for help. Once Click's work is done, Joanne exits the shower and wraps her wet body in a beach towel emblazoned with a logo from the popular shock rock group KISS. It is now time for Click to go into overtime and Joanne is summarily suffocated with a pillow. "I wonder if she ever saw that movie *Pillow Talk*?" Steckler closes out the scene of Strangler Victim 4 with a close-up of KISS's *Destroyer* album cover.

Click's after-kill cool-off is literally his consumption a cup of frozen yogurt while he eyes the filthy streets of West Hollywood. After night falls, Steckler cuts back to the used bookstore where wino Jim Parker saunters in and offers the Slasher (this time wearing a lavender colored dress) a drink. As with the first vagrant, she again declines the offer of a brown paper bag–covered libation. Unhappy with her refusal, out the door the derelict goes. He passes the porno house and the P.J. Parker prostitute, then into an alley and up some stairs to await his fate as Slasher Victim 2.

The Strangler has been seen cooling off from his kills by petting his pigeons and dogs and eating frozen sweets. The Slasher, however, chooses to take her anxieties to the beach for a jog. While the Slasher winds down, the Strangler winds up by calling another number in another of his many trashy rags. "The ad said photo session cheap—many poses—many positions. Sure, I just know what that means. She sounds nice but she's going to be just the same as the others but I've gotta keep looking. I mean, I have to keep looking until I find someone like Marsha. Someone pure—caring—like Marsha—was."

Steckler then returns Click to his pigeons as the Slasher struts her increasingly more stylish stuff about the seedier parts of Hollywood. Apparently Click tires of his birds and stalks the Slasher as she makes her way to her used bookstore. Click surmises, "This one is different. Marsha was different too. So different too, until she cheated on me with all those men ... all those men."

The Slasher is once again at work and the Strangler is once again on the prowl. Armed with his bogus camera, Click convenes upon what will become Strangler Victim 5. "She looks so young and innocent, but she's no better than a slut." This particular slut (Jean Roberts) is gagged to death, Albert DeSalvo–style, with her own bikini top. "Die, garbage."

Then like a broken record, Click once again turns his attentions to his caged pigeons: "You, my loves, are the loyal ones. Why can't I find someone loyal like you? Yes, I know, they all must die. The world must be cleansed of all its garbage."

The entrepreneurial Slasher closes up shop in the middle of the day and takes a stroll into the shopping district of L.A.'s Chinatown. The ever-attentive Click is there to eyeball her every move until she checks out the Happy Lion arts and crafts store. Here Click seems to lose interest in the Slasher and stalks his next prey in a grocery store parking lot. Denise Alford (daughter of Slasher Victim 1, Chuck Alford) becomes Strangler Victim 6.

After this kill, Click reacquaints himself with the squalor that is his apartment and downs some liquid courage in the form of canned Budweiser beer. Once his nerve is up and running, it is time he pays the Slasher another visit. High on the adrenaline of his most recent kill and buzzed on Budweiser, Click steps into the Slasher's bookstore. With an obvious determination and intent, he locks eyes with his fellow murderer and they stare blankly at one another until Click retreats back out onto the sidewalk.

The Slasher seems intrigued by her curious suitor, who is now nervous and shaken back to his apartment where he guzzles vodka straight from the bottle. "Why couldn't I bring myself to talk to her?" Once Click's head is screwed on straight, he moves the party over to Plato's Retreat West for a topless roller-skating disco affair. This footage is snatched directly from Steckler's 1976 X-rated film *Sex Rink*.

One curious bit from the *Sex Rink* footage involves "Big Tits" Malloy making eye contact with Click as she skates up to and past him. This second sequence of events more than suggests that Steckler had been working on *The Hollywood Strangler Meets the Skid Row Slasher* at least three years earlier. Either the forementioned is true or Pierre Agostino had originally been slated to appear in *Sex Rink* or perhaps the celluloid evidence applies to both cases. After all, Agostino was, at the time, in Steckler's orbit as he had also appeared in *Red Heat* from that same year.

Back at the bookstore, the Slasher concludes her work day with a bit of fun (for her) with local Las Vegas movie critic Forrest Duke, who becomes Slasher Victim 3. Steckler then shows the Slasher walking directly towards the camera's lens with an almost happy smirk on her face. Then it is, once again, back to the beach with the progressively more attractive murderess, who seems to somehow assimilate the spilled blood of her victims into a beauty all her own.

After her seaside jog, the Slasher dons her snazziest dress yet and hits the streets for some more shopping. After more pigeon time, the Strangler grabs his camera and tries to catch up with her. At one point the Slasher strolls in front of a bench where a young girl and an older woman are seated. In real life, these two are Laura "Tickles" Steckler and her grandmother (Carolyn Brandt's mother) Ruth.

While Click is en route to locate the latest edition of *Playhouse,* he walks (and drives) up and down Santa Monica Boulevard. This is ground zero for porno everything at this time. It is interesting to note that Steckler may have shot the last footage of the Venus Movie Arcade, the Sin-O-Ram and/or the Cave Adult Movie Theater. The Cave, previously been known as the Haunted House, was featured prominently in Ted V. Mikels' 1968 film *Girl in Gold Boots.*

Another nightlife hotspot Steckler highlighted numerous times over the years was Plato's Retreat West. L.A.'s unofficial satellite swingers club, it had been initiated in Manhattan around 1977. The original Plato's was shut down in 1985 by the city of New York during the height of the AIDS epidemic but soon found its new home in Fort Lauderdale, Florida. It is unclear as to whether Plato's Retreat or Plato's Retreat 2 encouraged or even allowed roller skating.

Click moseys into a modeling agency (actually part of Steckler's movie studio) and points to a black-and-white shot of Trish Lopes. The agency's bikini-clad receptionist (P.J. Parker in her second role of the film) informs Click that Ms. Lopes is unfortunately not available. "Lots of photos but no real bodies. You take what's available or nothing at all."

Click decides the special of the day is better than nothing at all. "I wonder how long she'll take before she gives me the come-on?" Actress April Grant wastes little time in getting Click's motor running hot. She licks her lips, peels off her one-piece bathing suit and becomes Strangler Victim 7. Grant was in nearly 20 films between 1973 and 1984 including *Wham Bam Thank You Spaceman* (1975) and *Little Orphan Dusty* (1978). The attractive brunette also operated under the stage names Lois Grant, Maria Schell, Ginger Leigh and Brandy Lee.

Click vacates the scene of *this* crime and strolls past a hanging *Incredibly Strange Creatures* pressbook and straight up to receptionist Parker. "Okay, blondie, it's your turn now. I'm gonna show you a real good time." It is certainly a good time for Click, but not so much for Parker as she becomes Strangler Victim 8. "Ah, that was really something, two so quickly."

This tandem kill has Click's

emotions and sensibilities wound to the hilt. He swipes, Trish Lopes' head shot from the studio wall and proceeds to a phone booth. On the horn with Click, Ms. Lopes relays directions to her pad (then, in actuality, Steckler's bedroom) and forthwith becomes Strangler Victim 9. "She looks good now. Too bad I don't have film in my camera, I'd really take her picture."

Click's third murder of the day apparently gives him more courage than any number of Budweisers as he waltzes straight into the Slasher's bookstore. He gives her a half-smile and then returns home to his beers, pigeons and thoughts. "Why can't I get her out of my mind? She's not like Marsha, she'd listen to me. Marsha ... Marsha."

Then as the day gives way to night, another street urchin catches the evil eye of the Slasher. This soon-to-be martyr without a cause was played by Steckler's friend, a former boxing trainer, John Leeman. The Slasher closes up and follows Leeman up a darkened staircase to a sordid and presumably abandoned room where she executes her specialty. Leeman has become Slasher Victim 4.

The next day, the Slasher frolics once more at the beach while the Strangler swills beer, cavorts with his dogs and ponders, "She's beautiful but would she be loyal?" Soon the Slasher lets down her hair, slips into a slinky blue dress and struts over to an occult supply facility before opening her bookstore for the day. This fourth kill has the Slasher feeling (and looking) particularly radiant.

The Slasher passes through the main floor of the store and past an S&M bondage room. The walls of this area are covered in leather whips, chains and other devices designed for willing or unwilling servitude. What exactly goes on in this dungeon-like space is never revealed but Click has snuck in and observes all he needs in order to understand the Slasher's fate. "She's a tease just like the rest."

Click lunges for the Slasher's throat as she pulls her switchblade from her purse and plunges it into his stomach. Click steps back to assess his injuries and the Slasher goes in for the kill. She manages to stick him four more times but Click is choking her through the entire ordeal. Finally, the Slasher gives up the ghost and the Strangler skulks off to bleed out in front of the Flick theater.

The film abruptly ends with the swooning lounge song "You're My Love" by actor-composer-singer Alberto Sarno. This is a jarring way to end a film that possesses no highs or lows in aural or emotional delivery. *The Hollywood Strangler Meets the Skid Row Slasher* just kind of flatlines its way through its short 71-minute span.

This is in no way a negative observation of the film's tone and pacing, quite the contrary. Steckler wisely chose to insulate the film, and its viewers, by having no outside interference of any kind. There are no police investigations, newspaper headlines or radio reports describing any of the events as they occurred. The film takes place, almost exclusively, within the crazed mind of Jonathan Click with the Slasher's murders being the viewer's only real reprieve from the Strangler's movements.

Steckler oft-times describes *The Hollywood Strangler Meets the Skid Row Slasher* as his stab at a love story. Directors Paul Bartel and Gorman Bechard threw their knives at the same target with *Eating Raoul* (1982) and *Psychos in Love* (1987), respectively. Both films are better examples of this horror subgenre but in 1979 Steckler was three years ahead of the curve.

The Flick Theater in Las Vegas opened in 1969 and quickly moved to triple X-rated features. By 1976, it had added a second screen and even more adult features. It became a laundromat and then a 99-cent store before it was demolished in 2017. It is seen here in *The Hollywood Strangler Meets the Skid Row Slasher* (1979) (author's collection).

In *Incredibly Strange Films* (p. 57), Jim Morton seemed hardly impressed: "[It] is an amazing title, but the film—essentially a silent movie with narration—is little more than a curiosity piece." In *Cult Movies* #8 (p. 10), video reviewer James Elliot Singer saw far more in the film than Morton had: "This is Ray Dennis Steckler's most incredibly strange film and one of the weirdest sexploitation films ever made, period.... Shot in 16mm without sound and filmed on streets and locations in decrepit sections of L.A. with real pedestrians, skid rowers and prostitutes serving as unaware extras, *Strangler* has a sleazy quasi-documentary look to it that's light years away from any conventional murder pic ever made."

The book *Cult Flicks & Trash Pics* (p. 243) gave the film two and half bones out of four: "While Steckler's earlier features were lively entertainments, only occasionally showing a dark side, this one is almost all dark side. There is not much in the way of blood and gore, but the atmosphere is reminiscent of more excessive serial killer films like William Lustig's *Maniac*, Abel Ferrara's *Driller Killer* and Lucio Fulci's *New York Ripper*."

J.A. Kerswell wrote in *The Slasher Movie Book* (p. 83), "Ray Dennis Steckler's burlesque slasher movie appears immune to *Halloween*'s influences. This decidedly low-budget production has a rather staid, almost documentary-like approach to the on-screen mayhem. It at least has the novelty of two killers—one who strangles models and the other, a woman, who slashes tramps."

Steckler claimed that he sold more VHS copies of this film (which is also known as *The Hollywood Strangler* and *The Model Killer*) than any of his other movies. He also claims that one of those copies wound up in Ted Bundy's prison cell.

So, over four decades later, the jury

is still out on this one. Is Steckler's 1979 effort transgressive or terrible? Could it be that it is subversive or is it simply silly?

Las Vegas Serial Killer (1986)

Synopsis

The Hollywood Strangler, Johnathon Klick (Pierre Agostino), has been released from the Nevada State Correctional Facility six years after his lock-up. Out on a technicality, he wastes little time getting back to his nasty habits of guzzling booze and murdering women. The Las Vegas strip is a veritable hotbed of hopeful models and seasoned hookers from which Klick will choose his kills.

Simultaneously, thugs Clarence (Ron Jason) and Jack (Chris Cave) trot out their less violent brand of terrorism in the form of muggings. The three criminals continually cross paths at strip shows, seedy street corners and night clubs, but why? The Las Vegas police are hot on the tail of Klick and his "Glitter Gulch Holocaust" but will they get to him before he kills again or *is* killed?

Credits

Cast: Pierre Agostino (Johnathon Klick); Ron Jason (Clarence); Chris Cave (Jack); April Grant (Flashback Victim 1); Denise Alford (Flashback Victim 2); Michelle Carlson (Flashback Victim 3); Glenda Savage (Strangler Victim 1); Julie ? (Strangler Victim 2); Verina Zenker (Mugging Victim 1); Leona Krskova (Mugging Victim 2); Tara McGowen (Mugging and Strangler Victim 3); Greg Dorchak (Mugging Victim 4); Suzee Slater (Photographer's Model and Strangler Victim 4); Tad ? (Mugging Victim 5); Kathryn Downey (Kat Carson and Strangler Victim 7); Toni Alessandrini (Miss World Burlesque); Jeannie Pepper (Photographer's Model); Hans ? (Photographer); Leigh Agostino (Waitress and Script Girl); Gabriella ? (Topless Sunbather); Andre Brummer (A John); Joseph Dvorak (Office Manager); Joe Harris (Pool Party Host); Joe Wilkerson (Partier); Jerry Carrol, Chuck Alford (Night Club Patrons); Matthias Merlin aka Gary Thompson (Radio Announcer) Tammy Lee, Laura Hoffman, Debra Brown, Laura A. Hetherington, Laura Steckler, Linda Steckler, Katherine Steckler, Morgan Steckler

Production: Producer: Katherine Steckler. Executive Producers: Salvatore Richichi, James Golff. Associate Producers: "Dutch" Neiman, Wyetha Lee Jaynes. Production Manager: Paul Bram. Story: Christopher Edwards. Photography: Ray Dennis Steckler [as Sven Christian]. Makeup: Jerry Carrol. Key Grip: Chuck Alford. Gaffer: B.J. Thomas. Continuity: Laura Coon. Wardrobe: Mary Louise Coon. Sound: Laura H. Steckler. Sound Effects: Greg Farina. Narration: Gary Thompson. Locations: Ron Kerns. Music: Henri Price. Apprentice: Hollie Stark. Caterer: Laura H. Steckler. Psychiatric Consultant: Laura A. Hetherington. Director: Ray Dennis Steckler [as Wolfgang Schmidt]. 76 minutes. Color.

The Film

Die garbage!—Johnathon Klick from *Las Vegas Serial Killer*

Nineteen eighty-six was another particularly quiet year for Steckler and his fading feature filmmaking career. However, it does appear as though he had finally removed himself altogether from the adult movie world. Steckler had also remarried to a woman named Katherine and had fathered another child. This one he named after his old friend and colleague George J. Morgan: Steckler's third daughter was christened Morgan Steckler.

Also around this time, Steckler opened Mascot Video, which later expanded into a three-link chain. The rental stores stocked all manner of videos but specialized in offering director's cuts of Steckler's films, newly produced documentaries and compilation tapes. Titles include *The Incredibly Strange Ray Dennis Steckler, Carolyn Brandt: Queen of Cult, Steckler Mania* and *Steckler Interviews*. Steckler also sold vintage promotional materials from his earlier films and was, by all accounts, a most affable host to customers yearning to discuss films—especially his.

Another nugget from the 1986 vault reveals that Steckler acted as a college professor in Dale Trevillion's sex comedy *Las Vegas Weekend*. Trevillion's film follows a computer nerd who finds himself increasingly more irresistible to women as his winning streak grows. Trevillion's crowning (filmmaking) moment was three years later with his action-crime-drama *One Man Force*. This 1989 exploitation potboiler starred a bona fide *who's who* of cult film actors including John Matuszak, Ronny Cox, Charles Napier, Sharon Farrell and

Camp Video's VHS release of *Las Vegas Serial Killer* (1986) (author's collection).

Richard Lynch. Too bad the inimitable Cash Flagg was not on hand for this raucous occasion.

After approximately 13 adult features following his last legitimate film *The Hollywood Strangler Meets the Skid Row Slasher*, Steckler deemed it necessary to lens his first sequel. The Strangler from said movie was granted a second go-round, six years later, in *Las Vegas Serial Killer*. Pierre Agostino returned as the eponymous Strangler while Steckler chose to return as director Wolfgang

Schmidt. Steckler probably only maintained this *nom de screen* in order to have *some* continuity with the previous film.

The film itself seems to reflect some of Steckler's state of mind and life's choices at the time. Similarly, when Steckler's marriage to Carolyn Brandt was unraveling, he delivered the largely grim and unpleasant *Blood Shack*. Then when the sting of their separation (they ultimately divorced in 1980) had subsided, Steckler made *The Hollywood Strangler Meets the Skid Row Slasher*, which is almost whimsical by comparison.

Flash-forward seven years to 1986 and Steckler unleashes on the straight-to-video market *Las Vegas Serial Killer*. He was then in a different place physically, mentally, emotionally and perhaps monetarily. The film is a complete patch job that echoes many aspects of his current life and situation.

Number one is that ex-wife Carolyn Brandt is nowhere to be found—not even in a flashback sequence. Two, the locations of the sister movies have switched, story- and production-wise, from Hollywood to Vegas. Three, Steckler has a new wife and child and he turns the camera on them numerous times within the film. Four, this new family along with his old (daughters Linda and Laura), were not only in front of the camera but also on hand production-wise as well. Lastly, Steckler's furniture business had failed and given way to his new video rental store.

Steckler furthers this cinematic family affair by including scenes with his mother, the woman who had, so many years ago, brought him defective product from the Yocum Brothers Cigar factory to peddle for spending money. This brings the narrative around to the dicey construction of the film.

Las Vegas Serial Killer was strung together with new footage, newly re-discovered footage, thought-to-be-lost footage and originally discarded footage. Its structure can be viewed as a visual metaphor of Steckler's life and his life in cinema. In short, Steckler had many irons in the fire and his newest film mirrored that ostensibly controlled chaos.

Steckler jams the film into gear with the title card and then the words "Las Vegas, Nevada—Six Years Ago" appear upon the small screen. This is superimposed over skyline footage of Sin City. Then the film cuts to flashback sequences of the Hollywood Strangler smoking and staring blankly at some of the neon-lit establishments on Santa Monica Boulevard in Los Angeles County.

Steckler continues with the flashbacks by cutting to actress April Grant's studio apartment where she falls victim to the Strangler. Then more old footage involves Denise Alford as another victim. Steckler wraps this montage up with some previously unused frames from *Hollywood Strangler* where Michelle Carlson is choked to death in a dumpster. Incidentally, this dumpster resided behind Steckler's office.

Eventually, Steckler pushes the film into the present with "Outside of Las Vegas, Nevada …Today" splashed across the screen. The next sequence opens with a shot of a small motor lodge on the outskirts of Jean, Nevada. This tiny town is located 12 miles north of the Nevada-California state line. (The motel was leveled years ago to make room for more casinos.)

Inside the motor lodge (actually, in Steckler's living room), central characters Clarence and Jack are introduced. Clarence is played by Ron Jason, Steckler's air conditioning repairman. His a.c. repairman assistant, former police officer Chris Cave, played Jack. The alleged idea being that if they worked together well on the job, they would work well together on screen. While Cave called it a day as an actor after *Las Vegas Serial Killer,* Jason continued for the next 32 years. Six of his on-screen credits would be for Steckler's old friend Ted V. Mikels: *Warcat* (1987), *Mission: Killfast* (1991), *Dimension in Fear* (1997), *Mark of the Astro Zombies* (2002), *The Cauldron: Baptism of Blood* (2004) and *Heart of a Boy* (2006).

Steckler zooms in on an antique radio that Clarence and Jack are listening to when an emergency news report interrupts their tunes:

> WQXU has just learned that the Nevada parole board has approved the release of self-proclaimed serial killer Johnathon Klick from the state prison in Jean. Klick has served only six years behind bars after claiming to have killed seven young women in a murderous five-day rampage in California and Nevada. Noting that the body of only one of his alleged victims was ever found, the parole board granted Klick's release from a life sentence after two court-appointed psychiatrists said that they believe his lurid claims of multiple murders are part of a misguided attempt to achieve notoriety. Klick was convicted of second degree murder in the strangulation slaying of Mary Jean Arbor, whose partially nude body was found in a waste container near his Las Vegas hotel room. In granting Klick's release, the parole board ignored the passionate pleas from parents of Kilick's other alleged victims.

The film's press materials state that Klick was sentenced to life in prison on August 28, 1980, and released August 31, 1986. Klick's reign of terror in Las Vegas was dubbed "The Glitter Gulch Holocaust." Also of note: Pierre Agostino's character name has been changed from Jonathan Click to Johnathon Klick.

This news spurs Clarence and Jack into action and they make a mad dash for Vegas in a red Nash Rambler. Steckler then shifts the film from the largely deserted town of Jean to the all-too-familiar travelogue footage of the Vegas strip. Cue the same old shots of the Dunes, Oasis, Flamingo, Imperial Palace, Barbary Coast *et al.* Steckler used these same frames no less than 20 times during his porno years, even employing the same music. Upon first-time viewing it is a wonderful snapshot of Las Vegas in its 1970s and early '80s heyday but by this point in Steckler's career it is merely padding.

Klick, just released from prison, decides to take in a topless dance show featuring Toni Alessandrini, who was billed as Miss World Burlesque. Ms. Alessandrini's next biggest claim to fame was her appearance in the 1984 Tom Hanks comedy *Bachelor Party.* The go-go club was actually Ron Jason's living room decked out with a few movie posters, a couple of tables and six or eight chairs.

Also, in the quaint club are Clarence and Jack along with Steckler's old friend Chuck Alford from *Hollywood Strangler*; Jerry Carrol, who was one of Steckler's

Pierre Agostino as the titular Las Vegas serial killer, Johnathon Klick, in *Las Vegas Serial Killer* (1986) (author's collection).

university students, and Pierre Agostino's wife Leigh Agostino as the night club's only server. This most unconvincing setting is edited together with shots of other people sitting at a bar and Jack playing the slots while watching Miss World Burlesque. Four rooms in total are used in an attempt to create a Las Vegas hot spot.

Clarence and Jack, tired of the old bump-and-grind routine, retire to the streets and walk around staring at pedestrians, diners and gamblers. These scenes, and there are several of them to come, are more travelogue-type footage that Steckler shot guerrilla-style with his handheld camera. The vast majority of the people in these frames have no idea they are going to wind up in a low-budget horror film.

Steckler then cuts to a pool party where two attendees are making out in a darkened area of the backyard. The handsy Joe Wilkerson (a real-life local Vegas stuntman) leaves his girl Glenda Savage to refresh her drink. Along the way, he flirts with every girl he comes in contact, leaving Glenda in a precarious situation. He is gone long enough for Klick to revive his tired-and-true strangler business.

The partygoers notice Glenda's freshly murdered body and just stare. No one screams and no one hurries to her aid in a scene that is oddly handled but also strangely chilling. Then Steckler cuts to a parade in Helldorado where he squeezes in a few frames of his new wife Katherine and infant daughter Morgan. Clarence and Jack are also in attendance, as is Ron Jason's father and brother, who stand behind them. This sequence serves no purpose other than to continue padding the film's short running time.

In another part of town, Klick lounges shirtless in his hovel of a room, listening to the news of his previous night's work:

> The highly publicized birthday party for Las Vegas film star Cash Flagg came to an abrupt halt late last night when celebrants discovered the body of a young woman in the backyard of Flagg's home. The name of the murder victim, who had been strangled with the top of her own bathing suit, hasn't been released, but metro police said that the woman disappeared from the party at Flagg's home shortly before her body was discovered in a grass-covered field less than 50 feet from the celebration. Mr. Cash Flagg was not available for comment.

Clarence and Jack mug an attractive lass (Veronica Zenker), flirt with two more and then hightail it to an air show to count the loot. Katherine and Morgan Steckler also appear to be interested in antique fighter planes. The new Mrs. Steckler supplies the oh-so-informative narration to the next round of cinematic filler:

> The confederate airport is having an air show at the McCurran field today where you can see historic combat aircraft that have been restored and preserved in flying condition. These are the same planes that defended our nation and won the skies over 40 years ago. So, go on out and give your support to help keep these flying monuments in the sky and preserved for future generations to see in action as they were flown to defend our country.

It is worth pointing out that Steckler's voiceover, while not nearly as bawdy as his pornos, still have an insensitive sexist and racist bent to them. For example, while Clarence and Jack look at a fighter plane called China Doll, one of them says to the other, "I bet that plane flies sideways." Throughout the entire film, these two goofy goons make one disparaging comment after another about the women they see on the street. "Bad legs. Bad legs. Definitely too old and that one waddles like a duck. Quack! Quack!" These are women who never consented to be in this film, much less be made fun of for audiences to see and hear. The inclusion of such remarks is unfortunate.

After the air show, the film settles back into more scenes of Klick, Clarence and Jack walking aimlessly up and down the Vegas strip. There are lots of shots of flashing lights, tourists and casino signs to help elongate the running time. However, their jaunts have pointed them straight into the same joint where they ogled Miss World Burlesque. This time the featured dancer is Kat Carson (Kathryn Downey), who entertains them while remaining in her blue one-piece bathing suit.

After Kat's rather frustrating no-strip strip tease, it is back to the Vegas pavement for Klick, who turns a corner and spots a sweaty prostitute. She propositions him; he does not like the steep $20 price tag. He then tightens his mitts around her neck. To no avail, the working girl screams and struggles. Her dead body is deposited behind an alleyway dumpster.

From Klick's nighttime crime, the film switches to a daylight sequence (presumably the next day) where Clarence and Jack lay the old purse-snatch routine on a female jogger (Leona Krskova). Katherine and Morgan Steckler can be seen lounging in Sunset Park. Why these people continually seem to occupy the same spaces in such a large town (Vegas had a population of 583,000 in 1986) will remain a mystery.

Clarence and Jack celebrate their good fortune by aiming their Nash Rambler towards the nearest Pizza-N-Pizza restaurant. This is the very establishment where Klick had earlier taken a delivery job. The two thugs settle down in a booth with a framed *Incredibly Strange Creatures* one-sheet on the wall above them. Steckler has stated in the past that he felt this to be the greatest movie poster ever for a low-budget picture, and he may be right.

Clarence and Jack wrap up their meal and take off in search of their latest criminal activity while Klick delivers a pizza. Klick locates the address and with pizza in hand rings the doorbell. A tall blonde woman answers the door and seductively leads Klick to the very Jacuzzi that had been used in *Hollywood Strangler*. It was here that actress Jean Roberts met her fate as Victim 5. Klick seems to be losing his touch as the tall blonde will not become a victim at all.

In his tiny apartment, Klick sulks over what could have been by washing his sorrows down with a few whiskey and colas. Then it is back to pounding the Vegas pavement, where Clarence and Jack have been making their rounds in search of whatever it is that they think they require at the moment. As luck would have it, actress Tara McGowen storms out of her boyfriend's office and straight into the thugs' clutches. They carry out their normal routine and stash the shaken girl in the trunk of her Mercedes Benz.

The two low-rent criminals then turn their attentions to their victim's boyfriend (Joe Dvorak) who they knock senseless before robbing him. Then Heckle and Jeckle are off and running, leaving Ms. McGowen in the car trunk for Klick to find. He hears her cries for help. Klick pops the trunk and is thanked by the girl: "I could have died in there!" And then she *does* die in there.

Following slightly in the hoofprints of *The Chooper*, Steckler and his camera visits, yet again, a bronco bustin'–bull ridin' rodeo. Due to the exceptional clarity of the footage and the hair styles, it can be deduced that this is newer rodeo footage rather than what can be found within Steckler's 1971 film. Still, it is no less obtrusive for a horror film than Steckler's first go-round with the redneck sport.

During this largely tedious sequence, Laura "Tickles" Steckler makes her first appearance in one of her father's films since 1971's *The Chooper*. She can be spotted wearing a white cowboy hat with dangling feathers, a white t-shirt and blue denim jeans. This ensemble is fairly standard rodeo attendee attire. The second point is that Clarence and Jack are in attendance, but Katherine and Morgan Steckler are conspicuously absent from this local event, as is Klick.

Klick stalks prudish dancer Kat Carson while Clarence and Jack tool around in the Rambler listening to police reports that are alleging their guilt in the murder of Tara McGowen. These two continue to cross paths with Klick and surely nothing good will come of it. They also continue to run across Katherine and Morgan Steckler but nothing will come of it.

At a backyard fashion photo shoot, female models are dressed fully or in bathing suits. It is odd that adult film star Jeannie Pepper appears here but bares no skin at all. Pepper had a 30-plus-year career in the porno business beginning in 1980. She has 173 credits under many different names and acted in 21 movies in 1986 alone. *Las Vegas Serial Killer* was her lone straight film for the year.

As bad luck would have it, Klick stumbles upon this gathering of fashion models and claims two more victims when they stray from the pack to change costumes and freshen up. Klick leaves their lifeless bodies on the living room floor, one lying on top of the other, then steals a camera. Now Klick is equipped to pick up his *faux* photography career where he abruptly left off in 1979. He is outfitted to snap pictures of the Vegas strip and its hordes of walking and gawking tourists. Cue more reels of travelogue footage.

Klick returns to the adult world trade papers for some numbers of models to call, photograph and murder. In a short scene before Klick reaches a payphone, Steckler's mother, Laura A. Hetherington can be seen perusing a newspaper with her granddaughters Linda and Laura. After Klick makes his call, he walks by the Steckler clan and they all exchange a glance and then return to their respective activities. The Stecklers will likely continue their tour of Las Vegas while Klick continues to terrorize the women of the city.

After more footage of Klick walking around fountains, casinos and dinner clubs, the psycho finally arrives at his latest earmark's studio, where she is posing as a tennis player. Klick, posing as a photographer, asks his subject to remove her sweater and when she does, she becomes Victim 6. Klick executes the old wring-around-the-neck in front of a chair with the letters "CEE" as in Cee Bee Beaumont. So, while Carolyn Brandt was not on hand to grace this film, her old chair was.

Klick makes his way back to his seedy apartment and drinks more whiskey while listening to more news reports about more dead women. After a round of cocktails, Klick hits the streets and snaps photos of jaywalkers, neon signs and flashing lights while Clarence and Jack pass by repeatedly in the Rambler. Steckler then cuts from this *ad nauseam* footage to yet another installment of the Kat Carson show.

Clarence and Jack finally give the

Chris Cave as Jack and Ron Jason as Clarence plan their next "deviate" move in *Las Vegas Serial Killer* (1986) (author's collection).

Rambler a break and take to the Vegas strip on foot while Klick does the same snapping away at most anyone and anything. The bogus photographer finally zeroes in on a couple of prostitutes. One of the ladies is being propositioned by Ron Jason's father while the other strikes a deal with Henri Price aka Andre Brummer. Price was Steckler's right-hand man in the scoring of nearly all of his movies; this film is not exactly one of his high-water marks.

Klick decides to stick around Prostitution Point in hopes of catching some more action with his camera and otherwise. True to criminal form, one girl returns to the scene of the crime to continue hustling. Klick murders her straight away, right on the pavement for anyone to see should they care to see. Apparently no one was watching and Klick gets away with Victim 7. It really is the Strangler's night.

Klick cools off with another Kat Carson show and after she performs her tired old routine he heads for the head. On the lavatory mirror is scrawled in lipstick "Fun–Kat Carson—739-8555," which is really the phone number for Steckler's Mascot Video store. There is little doubt about Klick's intentions, having just procured Kat Carson's phone number from the men's room of a sleazy strip joint.

He calls, Kat answers, he goes, he asks her to put her legs up; he puts his camera down, he then squeezes the life out of her in front of a stuffed Papa Smurf doll. This could have and should have been the crescendo of the film but alas it is not. Klick once again retreats to his humble digs to drink, smoke and ponder the life and death of his eighth victim. It has been a busy few days for the Strangler and he feels he deserves down time to relax and reflect.

Clarence and Jack stake out another ambush that yields them a briefcase full of who knows what. As they flee the scene, they literally bump into Klick. Clarence draws his gun and fires into Klick's stomach where seven years earlier the Skid Row Slasher had repeatedly stabbed him. This also could have been the end of the film, but it was not.

Heckle and Jeckle continue running and chuck the murder weapon into a dumpster. Two young boys have been watching the activity as it unfolded and head straight for the firearm. The adolescents are clearly thrilled with their new find and the film ends with a freeze-frame of them and the French word "Fin???" The question marks indicate that this is not at all the end. However, as the credits begin to roll, a shot is fired presumably by one of the boys at the other. A fairly bleak ending to a fairly dull movie.

At one point in the 1990s, Steckler decided to revisit, re-edit and re-title this clunker. Fortunately or unfortunately (depending on one's tolerances of such things), this was Steckler's final flirtation with what he arguably wanted to be an ongoing franchise. Pierre Agostino was slated to kill again in *The Return of the Hollywood Strangler* but decided better of it. Still, Steckler had his fourth installment in the works, *The Son of the Hollywood Strangler*. One can only imagine.

The film did not receive a lot of press but what does exist is in no way flattering. Author and longtime Steckler fan Michael Weldon put it this way in his *Psychotronic Video Guide* (p. 327), "It's narrated by a reporter, but this awful movie still makes no sense and has no ending. Parades, a rodeo, signs, models posing—anything is thrown in to fill up the time." Another Steckler defender, James Elliot Singer, was marginally more impressed. He wrote in *Cult Movies* #15, "Strangler/fake photographer Agostini continually crosses paths with two stupid street thugs, possibly the most jerked-up crime duo in weird movie history which kinda swings this entry into a comedy of sorts. A third Strangler epic was partly filmed then shelved. Guess the world wasn't ready."

Las Vegas Serial Killer was Steckler's final film to receive any sort of official release. This thing never saw a silver screen and was released straight to video. Camp Video wanted the releasing and distribution rights to *Incredibly Strange Creatures*, *Thrill Killers* and *Rat Pfink a Boo Boo*. All three of the forementioned films were clearly cash cows for the video company so there was no good reason for them to get involved with *Las Vegas Serial Killer*—or was there? Presumably, Steckler twisted Camp Video's arm and in order for them to get the films they wanted, they had to also take his latest one. This is merely speculation. While Camp was guilty of releasing low-rung exploitation films like *Goremet Zombie Chef from Hell*, *Las Vegas Serial Killer* was an all-time low for them and Steckler.

PART TWO

The Adult Films of Ray Dennis Steckler

Introduction

In many ways, this chapter in Steckler's film career is his most mercurial. While these "adult" titles represented a man paying his bills while quasi-flexing his creative muscles, they are also an important piece of the Steckler puzzle that has been largely ignored. Independent film legend Ed Wood, Jr., forged a similar path by first writing the "blue" novel *Orgy of the Dead* and then later "blue" films such as *Take It Out in Trade* (1970), *Necromania* (1971) and *The Class Reunion* (1972). Like Wood's "adult" titles, Steckler's also possess the filmmaker's left-of-center sense of quirkiness and humor. Steckler openly admits to admiring Ed Wood as an artistic visionary.

These films contain the usual humping, bumping and pumping, all of this augmented by mounds of unkempt curlys, arcing ropes of reproductive fluids, pimples, cold sores, in-grown hairs and lots of sweat. It is not pretty by any stretch of the imagination. In fact, Steckler does not seem at all interested in shooting stimulating sex scenes. It is all unattractive and it is as if Steckler is attacking his audience for forcing him into this cinematic corner.

In fact, most of the hardcore scenes glisten to the point that the screen appears to actually precipitate. The viewer's sense of smell is mercifully spared, but for the eyes and ears it is an all-out assault. It is debatable as to whether or not it was stimulating for the "raincoat crowd" of the early to mid-70s, but for audiences today the action is simply too personal and uncomfortably up close. So much so that every vein, crack, fold and crevice is on display appearing more angered than aroused.

The Sultan of Sleaze David F. Friedman, a man of dubious taste for sure, refused to delve into hardcore pornography. He was satisfied making softcore sex films with titillating titles like *The Ramrodder* (1969), *The Big Snatch* (1971) and *The Adult Version of Jekyll and Hyde* (1972). Still, as graphic as his films could be and the boundaries of common (Christian) decency they could cross, Friedman could not and would not go all the way.

Friedman was a consummate showman. He had worked in carnivals and roadshows and learned from the master showman Kroger Babb. When asked, "Why did you get out of the moviemaking business?" Friedman's canned answer was, "Because the hardcore pornography industry offered the 'steak,' to which we, the exploiteers, only attempted to sell the 'sizzle.'"

Unlike Friedman, Steckler stayed in there and offered up the "steak." It was not the greatest cut, but even with his minimal monetary resources he managed to serve up some oddball hardcore pornography. Taken in the context of Steckler's real and reel life, his adult films seem reactionary and negative by nature. Steckler teases his viewers with tantalizing promises that ultimately devolve into ugly images.

Reportedly, Steckler would get so incensed when asked about his involvement in the pornography world that he would oft-times end the interview. These titles are a long way from *Goof on the Loose* and are not for the faint of heart or squeamish. Proceed with great care and caution.

In 1970, Steckler dabbled in softcore pornography via *Sinthia: The Devil's Doll* but went full-on hardcore no less than six times in 1971. He topped that number five years later with seven porno titles to his name(s). It is literally impossible to know the proper release dates of these films, so they will be presented, by year, in alphabetical order.

The Films

> I'm a lady pornographer. You know, you've seen my films. I'm Cindy Lou Sutters.—Cindy Lou Sutters from *Red Heat*

"Daisey Lay": Ozark Virgin? (1971)

Steckler took no credit, *nom de screen* or otherwise, as director of this Southern fried porno quickie starring Maria Arnold as the titular Daisy Lay. Ms. Arnold has over 50 screen credits to her name; most of them are adult titles, including Ed Wood's *Necromania* (1971). Also on hand are George Peters and Starlyn Simone, seasoned veterans of the triple X-rated film world. Then for a closer look at some of the *Blood Shack* cast are Jason Wayne and John Bates as Lester (Daisy's brother) and Zeke, respectively.

Daisy Lay, as the title suggests, is a virgin. Curious about sex, she educates herself by spying on her brother's friends Harry (George Peters) and Zeke as they get it on with *their* girlfriend Thelma (Starlyn Simone). Daisy gives Harry a go at her goods before giving in to a foursome on the family couch. This eventually leads to the anticipated act of incest with her brother Lester. "Oh my stars! That's a goodin'."

The exteriors include several shots from the *Blood Shack* ranch as well as the blood shack itself. Jason Wayne successfully maintains the hat that he kept losing in his previous film. Steckler shot this one in full color and seems to be giving a nod to producer Harry Novak and his backwoods softcore features. *Tobacco Roody* (1970), *Country Cuzzins* (1970) and *Midnite Plowboy* (1971) are but a few of those classic Novaks.

There's a full 57-minute version

of the film as well as shortened 43- and 34-minute cuts. This hedonistic hayride has several alternate titles: *Daisy Lay & the 52 Pick-Ups*, *Hillbilly Sex Clan*, *Ozark Virgin* and, in Australia, *Inside Daisy Lay*.

The Horny Vampire (1971)

This comedy–horror porn spoof stars Victor Alexander (real name: Jerry Delony) as the title's vampire. Alexander's face should be familiar to exploitation fans for his turn as El Sharif in *Ilsa, Harem Keeper of the Oil Sheiks* (1976). No other cast or crew credits have surfaced, but Carolyn Brandt's voice can be heard in one scene. Steckler's silly cinematic stamp is all over this thing.

Count Dracula's under-sexed nephew Count Al-Kum (Victor Alexander) prowls Las Vegas in the daylight hours in search of loose women. The count's secret weapon, other than having no aversion to the sun, is the sex manual *1001 Ways to Seduce Women*. His powers of persuasion are not quite those of his uncle's and he repeatedly bungles the encounters. Always waiting in the wings is Count Dracula, who swoops in to sweep the ladies off their feet and out of their clothes.

Dracula takes a chick on her living room floor while his nephew hungrily looks on. Dracula nails another victim beside a red 1965 Mustang while Al-Kum gets his head slammed underneath the car's hood. Uncle Drac seduces a different girl in the same car while his nephew gets his member stuck in the keyhole of her apartment door. Al-Kum fantasizes about his uncle's sexual prowess and techniques while the old Count actually gets it on again. Dracula three, Al-Kum zero. Steckler wraps this production up with Count Al-Kum finally wooing a girl back to her apartment only to discover she is wearing a strap-on appendage.

In actuality, *The Horny Vampire* should be *The Horny Vampires* as there are two of them though one is successful with the gals while the other is not. Steckler cut the film at 45 minutes but there are also 41-, 21- and 13-minute versions. This sex-filled flick features several sight gags and contains many nighttime scenes of Las Vegas in 1971.

How to Make a Sex Movie!! (1971)

How to Make a Sex Movie!! stars Nora Wieternik, who has an impressive 30 screen credits to her name, 18 of them from 1971 alone. Her career in erotic cinema started in 1970 and culminated with her role as Queen Amora in the 1974 tour de force sex comedy *Flesh Gordon*. In that film, she was able to keep *some* of her clothes on while delivering such gems as, "These, my power pasties, are the only force that can stop the sex beam."

Early '70s porn fixture Buddy Boone shows up in *How to Make a Sex Movie!!* as Guy in Jeans. Boone has 14 credits under his belt; he was uncredited in 11 of them. Boone is seen in the Ed Wood–scripted *Undergraduate* (1971) as Bill Jeffers. Then there is Patty Snyder, whose short career ended with two more Steckler movies in 1973.

How to Make a Sex Movie!! follows the exploits of three filmmakers who intend to enlighten their would-be "stars" in the proper ways of the X-rated movie world. There will be hands-on "lectures" and "educational" films shown by way of sex loops as well as a group "test" at the end. In the interim, however, the wanna-be actors learn of the importance of the "up and down" movements during oral sex. They are also schooled on the effect of facial expressions and how the girls can "let him know you dig it." Who knew there was so much to know?

Steckler (somewhat) took credit for this nearly forgotten film as Sven Christian. He may have thought the name change would have kept his association with this film quiet, but he would be very wrong in that assumption. What Steckler did that *really* lets the pussycat out of the bag: He hung a *Teenage Psycho Meets Bloody Mary* one-sheet on the filmmaker's ugly wood-paneled office wall. *How to Make a Sex Movie!!* had a 54-minute running time.

The Mad Love Life of a Hot Vampire (1971)

The Mad Love Life of a Hot Vampire stars a minor Las Vegas celebrity, Jim Parker, as Count Dracula. Parker had made a name and a face for himself as the host of Shock Theater on KHBV Channel 5, Henderson, Nevada, from 1964 to 1972. Steckler figured Parker would be a natural for the role of the count as his persona on that station was "the Vegas Vampire." In 1970, Parker's wife P.J. (Paula) joined the show as Satana. Eight years later, Steckler immortalized the couple in a legitimate feature.

Steckler's second vampire porno also stars the dubiously named Will Long. Long spent additional time with Steckler on three more of his films ranging from 1973 to 2003. Then the ever-alluring Carolyn Brandt, here as Jane Bond, returns to the screen as Dracula's wife Elaina. The remainder of the cast (Rock Heinrich, Greta Smith, Fritz King, Kim Kim, Ken Moore, "Sam") and art director De Sade all appear to have vanished from the movie world. These people may have simply decided that once was enough with Steckler *and* those aliases.

This time around, the count is less horny and more in need of that vampire kind of sustenance. He runs a call girl agency and sends his three employees out to their respective callers to exsanguinate the unsuspecting johns. Their life's blood is to be returned to Dracula's cave in crystal vials (more resembling flower vases) for their master's nourishment. In a standard incoherent Steckler move, only two of the three girls are

The Busy "B" Theater showed *The Mad Love Life of a Hot Vampire* (1971) with the truncated title *Hot Vampire,* plus the second feature *The Little County Jail* (1970), which is also known as *In a Little County Jail* (author's collection).

seen working, leaving the third seemingly MIA. Dracula's hunchbacked assistant (Rock Heinrich) laughs, twitches and masturbates furiously.

As the girls do the count's bidding, a couple across town summons Dr. Van Helsing. Van Helsing believes that the disappearance of their loved one, Carmille, and other girls is the work of Dracula. The doctor lost track of the count in Paris and believes him to be in Arizona. In and around all of this action, Carolyn Brandt reprises her Vampire Lady role from *The Lemon Grove Kids Meet the Monsters.* Her character Elaina pops in and out of the story with lines like, "Dracula is groovy."

During the act of fellatio, the girls sprout plastic dime-store fangs that extracts the blood of their clients straight through their manhood. The third of Dracula's employees is caught by Van Helsing attacking a woman on a toilet. It is revealed that she is Carmille and she leads them to Dracula's lair. Van Helsing stakes two female vampires. Amidst all the hullabaloo, the count makes a hasty escape straight into the rays of the sun. he disintegrates, leaving only an empty cape. The hunchback cries at this sight, then flips off his master's killer: the sun.

Steckler shot this 50-minute doozie in 1971, again as Sven Christian, but it did not see the light of a projector until the summer of 1975. The film was always intended to be called *The Mad Love Life of a Hot Vampire* but has been abbreviated at least twice to *Love Life of a Red Hot Vampire* and/or *Hot Vampire.* This one is not as amusing as its sister film *The Horny Vampire,* but it does contain enough Steckler-esque moments to make it worth a day in court. The guys do not perform that well but it is not for a lack of the girls trying *really* hard.

Sacrilege (1971)

Sacrilege stars adult screen veteran Jane Tsentas as the witch Cassandra. Ms. Tsentas stayed quite busy between 1969 and 1975 racking up 48 credits to her name, 13 just in 1971. Cassandra, in her mousey librarian disguise, happens upon the dopey Jay as he sits in the middle of nowhere reading a book on witchcraft. Jay is played by Gerard Broulard, who managed 38 credits between 1969 and 1972 with 15 of them from 1971.

Jay and Cassandra immediately hit it off, with his interest in the black arts and her being a practitioner of them (though he does not yet know this). Cassandra lures Jay back to her house with the promise of fresh jasmine tea. Within moments they are in her den that she shares with her pet cat Lucifer. Jay drinks the tea, it is poisoned, and he begins to hallucinate.

Jay's first surreal visual is the cat transforming into a bearded man who sneers at him with an evil eye and grin. Cassandra has literally conjured the Devil through a cat. Satan is played by C. Davis Smith (here as Charles Davis). Smith has quite the body of work, but his biggest claim to fame is being cinematographer on 16 of Doris Wishman's sexploitation films.

From the cat's transformation to the Devil, Cassandra reveals her skin and her true identity as a witch. She climbs atop a coffee table and begins to gyrate seductively with only a black cape, gloves and go-go boots to get in the way. Jay is mesmerized and apparently aroused by the dance and pounces on the naked witch. Cassandra wears Jay completely out but is not satiated herself and insists that Jay call his girlfriend Maria (Ruthann Lott) over.

After drinking the tea, Maria falls

Los Angeles' Paris Theater hosted some screenings of *Sacrilege* (1971). The front of the theater was seen in the movie *Wanda, the Sadistic Hypnotist* (1969). The Paris was originally the Carmel. As the Paris, it was known for showing adult flicks and hosting stage shows. A second miniscreen known as the Paris Penthouse was added in 1967 (image and commentary courtesy film historian and archivist Raleigh Bronkowski).

into a trance and awakens tied to a picnic table getting shagged by the Devil. She is then roped to Jay on a green shag rug and there's a four-way with Cassandra and her dark lord. As the film draws to a close, Cassandra laughs manically and announces that her sacrilege is now complete. Jay and Maria awaken naked on the floor of what appears to be an empty house. They dress and walk into the daylight of the early morning sun.

Steckler closes the 56-minute film with one of his madcap, mash-up flashback sequences to revisit all that has happened. Reportedly some prints of the film were struck in black and white. Steckler, credited here as Michel J. Rogers, emphatically denied any involvement in the picture.

Triple Play (1971)

As an X-rated feature, *Triple Play* is a quickie even by Steckler standards. Steckler shot it entirely MOS (without sound) and had Carolyn Brandt provide the overwrought narration in her characteristically breezy voice. Giving his films the silent treatment had not been the norm up to this point, but it would become more common for the director. Steckler *had* assembled *Rat Pfink a Boo Boo* in this manner, but other than *Goof on the Loose* every other film had featured *some* sync sound.

What story there *is* involves wanna-be actress and sexual virgin Rosie Palmer as she ventures into "a certain house on Orange Grove Street in Hollywood." Here she "not only lost all her charming innocence, but also came to grips with a soul-twisting situation that was to affect her drastically for the rest of her life." Rosie is slipped a Spanish Fly that sends her into a sexual frenzy that takes up about a third of the film's running time. The remainder of the picture involves Rosie's *friends* convincing her to prostitute herself out for a sleazoid pimp and his busty-lusty girlfriend-hooker.

Actress Carmen Olivera managed 29 screen credits between the years 1969 and 1973. She played with and alongside Rene Bond, Liz Renay, Candy Samples and Maria ("*Daisy Lay*": *Ozark Virgin!*) Arnold. Nineteen of these movies were made in 1971 which makes this Steckler alumna the busiest beaver of the year.

One of *Triple Play*'s most intriguing aspects is Steckler's inclusion of British composer Syd Dale's song "The Hell Raisers" (he used it again five years later in *Red Heat*). Dale was not only a composer but also an arranger of easy listening, library and funk music. His sounds have been featured in TV, radio, movies and advertising for decades. Listen for his compositions in the original *Spider-Man* animated series (1968–1970), *The Ren & Stimpy Show* (1991–1994), *Black Dynamite* (2009–2011) and *Once Upon a Time … in Hollywood* (2019).

The Sounds of Syd Dale was released on March 1, 1966, and while it contained "The Hell Raisers," the song had already been in the public domain since 1965 as the theme to *Orlando*. This British television serial, a thriller for kids, ran for 76 episodes from 1965 to 1968. Who could have known that this piece of iconic music would wind up across the pond in a cheap-ass porno flick three years later?

Of course, Steckler would have known of the existence of "The Hell Raisers" as TV's *Wide World of Sports* used it in the late 1960s.

Devil's Little Acre (1972)

Steckler ushered in (and out) 1972 with this cornpone porn that could be seen as a companion piece to *"Daisy Lay": Ozark Virgin?* or an X-rated sequel to 1958's *God's Little Acre*. It stars the sultry Rene Bond in her first of two ventures with Steckler as Miss Frenchy Tiggler. Ms. Bond was one of the first adult film stars to get breast augmentation and as a result go on to bigger and better things. It is recorded that *this* Bond girl has been in nearly 100 films.

Returning to the team from last year's *"Daisy Lay"* is Maria Arnold in her final appearance in a Steckler film. Actor Doug Darush began his career a year earlier with the Richard Mailer–directed *Specimen: Female* with Carmen Olivera of *Triple Play* fame. Over the next five years, Darush appeared in just one more film and, not so surprisingly, it was for Steckler.

Devil's Little Acre tells the horny story of three subnormal farm boys who anxiously pick at one another and their respective noses. Eventually their libidos get the better of them and they head out, to God knows where, and catch a cutie (Arnold) posing naked for a camera club photographer. This greases the goon brothers' crankshafts, so they ring up the Ozark Maids Employment Agency presumably to scrub away their moist and muggy messes.

Frenchy Tiggler, president of the maid agency, sends over a one-woman clean-up crew who is gang-banged by the three dummies. More girls arrive and one breastfeeds a toy doll while another makes it with a hog. Frenchy orchestrates this bizarre sex madness that culminates in a three-way marriage that continues escalating into an all-out six-way orgy overseen by the local minister.

Steckler began and ended 1972 with an X-rated feature that was praised by some critics and loathed by others. The film runs a mere 45 minutes and was released in the early winter as a B-feature (in some territories) to Ed Wood's *Necromania*. This rarely seen piece of Steckler cinema can also be found under the banners *Devil's Acre* and in a 34-minute cut as *Oakie Maid*.

Baby Bubbles (1973)

Baby Bubbles is one of three Steckler features shot during 1973 and the only one of the trio where he took no screen credit at all. Steckler also gave his wife Carolyn a break from the microphone and provided the narration himself. By '74 Steckler had coerced her back into his sanctuary of sin.

Here, Steckler puts newcomer Jeanie Tulip in the lead role of Baby Bubbles, an undercover(s) agent for G.A.S. (a smelly acronym for Girls Against Slavery). The film also stars Marsha Hart, who went on to make three more adult films with Steckler over the next nine years. Actor Charles Orlando, featured as the Englishman, found himself in three more Steckler films in 1976.

Rick Clampton and Rufus Studley run a phony modeling agency, luring hopefuls into their pit of despair. The girls are drugged, caged and then sold as sex slaves. Ms. Bubbles infiltrates the den of deceit by acting, "a dingbat, a mental deficient" with "a body that would make a rich man drool," as Steckler's narration goes. This abysmal operation must be shut down immediately. This is a job for G.A.S.

Jason Wayne of *Blood Shack* fame returns as the clean-shaven Clampton. Wayne's face may not be immediately recognizable, but his unmistakable Southern drawl is. Then Rick Martino lays in as Studley. He laid around three years waiting for another turn with Steckler.

This entry in Steckler's sex movie series runs under an hour. It was elongated with several of the close-up hardcore scenes repeated. This title, reportedly, went out with one of the *most* presumptuous promotional taglines, "The Most X Film You'll Ever See!"

Peeping Tom (1973)

Peeping Tom possesses the most bare-bones narrative, for an X-tated film, to this point in the Steckler's filmography. There are literally four unrelated sex scenes that a voyeuristic pervert watches around the neon-lit surroundings of Sin City. This Tom is peeking while simultaneously peaking.

Once again Steckler provides the narration: "The man you are looking at is known to the public as a weirdo. Unfortunately, the public doesn't know what really goes on behind his mind. Deep into his being he has an insatiable desire to watch other people make love. Join him tonight as he takes a trip behind the many locked doors of the city."

First up, the protagonist takes in an amusing couple who argue their way into the sex act. *Blood Shack* veteran Jason Wayne bares all again with an unnamed actress who threatens to break wind in her lover's face. This is classy stuff all the way.

After those two bicker to the end, the seemingly unsatisfied ogler discovers a four-way orgy to spy on. This unhealthy-looking quartet appear to be on Quaaludes as the action moves along at a snail's pace with only two of the four actors actually engaging in copulation. This display is as frustrating for the viewer as it is for our Tom.

The peeper moves on and finds a middle-aged couple who seem as hopelessly confused as to what to do as a pair of early teens. Both were seen in *The Mad Love Life of a Hot Vampire*, the male as Van Helsing and the female as the woman on the toilet. (This *Peeping Tom* scene may very well have been shot during the *Hot Vampire* shoot.) Finally, a guy and a girl (Patty Snyder), whose faces (and other anatomy) are familiar from *How to Make a Sex Movie!!*, get it on in the basement of the gal's parents' house. She worries the entire time that her mother will walk in. As the sex act, the scene and the film draw to a close, the dreaded parental figure enters the room.

Steckler, who directed under the Sven Christian moniker, closes this seamy and extremely gritty 60-minute feature (aka *The Creeper*) with more narration. This time he warns, "You have just witnessed a strange man living a strange life through the affairs of other human beings. Who knows, maybe you'll be the one who Peeping Tom watches next. After all, sex is to be enjoyed by everyone."

Pleasure Motel (1973)

Steckler's final smut feature to be credited to Sven Christian takes place in a crappy room ... presumably a motel room. The manager assures his guests that Room 169 is the nicest in the building. This film, like *Peeping Tom*, has a number of performers from *The Mad Love Life of a Hot Vampire* and *How to Make a Sex Movie!!* Patty Snyder gives her final performance for Steckler as the character Maureen while Steckler again provides narration. He describes Room 169 as "a room that has many stories to tell. Stories of different lives. Lives that need living. Lives that become interchangeable and interwoven with the threats of ecstasy."

The first scene involves some prostitute-on-girl bondage with a few whirring battery-powered toys. The female customer is not satisfied with the hooker's performance and demands her money back. "You cheap hussy!" cries the working girl.

The second scene has the same couple who closed out *Peeping Tom*. Here they are a husband and wife and they argue about his gambling hang-ups. The husband contends that he can win his losses back if she gives him a hundred bucks. Then the argument ends and they are doing the horizontal mambo.

The gambler heads out to score big. "I'm gonna go back down there and I'm gonna win us enough money to stay in real style. Just wait and see. You ain't seen nothin' yet." Maureen, the gamester's wife, does not wait long before inviting a female friend over for some naked fun of their own. More buzzing and whirring sounds here.

The cardsharp returns with his pay dirt and some flashy new threads. Maureen decides that they should celebrate his good luck by stripping down and making it again. This is more or less a repeat of their first round with Maureen more enthusiastic this time. Apparently winning a few grand yields even more rewards.

The fifth and final scene sees the return of the prostitute with a male customer. These two go at it for over ten minutes of screen time and never fully realize the act. It is an odd way for

Steckler was cinematographer on Chris Warfield's sexploitation film *Little Miss Innocence* (1973), which was also known as *Teenage Innocence* (author's collection).

Steckler to end the film but it is fairly obvious that there was not a lot of love in this production. Steckler closes the film with more narration: "There's 365 stories a year from Room 169 of the Pleasure Motel. This has been five of them."

Like *Peeping Tom,* there is really nothing tying these segments together. The 58-minute, barely thought-out film was shot with what appears to be sync-sound. Some time this same year, Steckler stepped away from full-blown porn to exercise his abilities as a cinematographer on Chris Warfield's sexploitation picture *Little Miss Innocence.*

Perverted Passion (1974)

Up to this point, Steckler had employed a ragtag bunch to participate in his sex movies, which had threadbare stories and production values. His slipshod way of working this blue territory began to change in 1974 with *Perverted Passion.* Here the title alone is not the whole of the narrative as Steckler's directing skills begin to improve within this off-color cinematic world. This more mature world (for adults only) and approach point to his next two legitimate films.

Also having Carolyn Brandt return to the screen lent the film an air of Steckler-professionalism for the first time since 1970. Here Brandt plays a ginger-headed hooker aptly known as Red. The film also stars Will Long returning from *Peeping Tom* and *The Mad Love Life of a Hot Vampire.* Long portrays the film's mentally deranged antagonist simply called "Mr. Ordinary" by the narrator.

Speaking of narrators, Steckler takes a break from the mic and has Rik Tazíner do the voice-over honors. Tazíner was a porno veteran seen in such lurid titles as *Boys in Chains* (1970), *The Erotic Adventures of Hercules* (1971) and *Finger Licking Good* (1974). Eddie Bach, Rita Cummings, Anna Leeds, Franklin Margello, Henry Moran, Liz Swanson, Lenore Swink and Joan Woodman get off on their first and next to last film for Steckler.

Mr. Ordinary has just been released from a state mental facility, as the narration continues, because of governmental budget cuts that were demanded by voters. The narrator, identified as Mr. Ordinary's former probation officer, more than implies that it is the audience's fault that he is out on the streets. "You did it. Now you live with it!"

Like the *Peeping Tom* voyeur before him, Mr. Ordinary roams the streets spying on couples having sex. With each sneak peek he appears to become more agitated. This pervert then graduates to hands-on action by hiring a prostitute who cannot get the goods from his teeny piggly-wiggly weenie. The beer-bellied loony snaps and strangles the working girl.

After the kill, Mr. Ordinary retreats to the squalor of his apartment to drink booze and grimace dementedly into the camera. Steckler also allows the viewer a glimpse into the mind of our antagonist by providing the narration to his thoughts. Usually the man with the damaged brain thinks things such as "I like it. I like it! Wait'll she sees me. She's gonna love me!" or "I'm a real man." Oh, and he has more than a minor obsession with Bruce Lee, striking poses in the mirror *somewhat* like his idol.

Mr. Ordinary is anything but ordinary. He eavesdrops on his oversexed neighbors and spies on more copulating couples. At one point, the crazoid works himself into such a frothing frenzy that he is forced to murder a random woman living in a trailer. Mr. O's sexual frustrations are manifesting themselves into indiscriminate acts of violence.

Mr. Ordinary takes an instant liking to the red-headed hooker and follows her about town wondering, "What's she doing with that old son of a gun?" Around this time, Steckler introduces a second villain in the form of a motorcycle-riding thief who is out of prison due to more spending cuts. The biker seems to have zero interest in sex, more in robbing people blind.

Mr. Ordinary confronts Red and murders her too. Motorcycle Thief continues his reign of terror and winds up trying to rob Mr. Ordinary's neighbors. The burglar flees the scene of the crime as Mr. Ordinary opens his apartment door and is shot dead by the crook. The biker rides off into the desert, wrecks and presumably dies. The narrator chimes in, "Well, citizens, you were lucky this time. One problem cancelled out another."

One sequence is worth mentioning because it seems so out of place. A spindly, bespectacled introvert hires a hooker at a brothel and they retire to a seedy room. Mr. Ordinary is nowhere to be found and he misses quite the show. Spindly Man cannot perform properly and his hired hand berates him, "Nobody is as weird as you are! You've got to get that through your head right now!"

Ms. Hired Hand continues the dress-down: "If you can't get it up, then don't come to a cathouse! Personally, I can't stand you, but I need the money. Is that cool?" Mr. Spindly takes great offense to the chiding and begins sobbing and crying out for his mother as he suckles the working girl's mammaries. This scene appears to be a leftover from the *Pleasure Motel* shoot, haphazardly plugged in here to pad out the running time. Not at all an unusual move for Steckler.

Steckler directed this 62-minute feature under his new alias Cindy Lou Sutters, which he used seven more times over the next nine years. The film also made its rounds as *Fire Down Below*. The one-sheet with this title featured the misleading tagline, "An older man's search for a teenage lover in Hollywood, California (Middle age crazy). The true story."

The Sexorcist (1974)

Steckler only made two films in 1974 and *The Sexorcist* is easily the stranger of the pair. Carolyn Brandt (credited as Eva Gaulant) plays reporter Janice Lightning, who is investigating a Satanic cult. The determined journalist enlists the aid of Prof. Ernest Von Kleinsmidt, a sexorcist and a doctor of demonology portrayed

The New Cinema 295 presented a triple-X triple-bill of *Everything You Always Wanted to See in a Sex Film But Were Afraid to Ask For* with Steckler's *Fire Down Below* aka *Perverted Passion* (1974) and *Alley Cat* (author's collection).

by Kelly Guthrie. Mr. Guthrie performed six more times for Steckler between 1976 and 1982.

The remaining cast includes Lilly Lamarr, Wayne Williams, Lane McGarter and Richard Zufger. Now, either all of these are aliases that they never used again, or this fornicating quartet called it quits after a single Steckler picture. As with so many of Steckler's adult film actors and actresses, it is simply impossible to know who they are, where they have been and where they went.

The film opens with Janice and the demon doctor exploring a swamp that once was home to a group of devil worshippers. Brandt's unmistakable, racy voice comes over the speaker describing their foreboding and sultry surroundings. Janice snaps photos of the prof that will accompany her article for an occult magazine while additional narration continues the storyline: "Knowing the area was heavily steeped with legends about a sex-mad devil worshipping cult, Von Kleinsmidt said he was hoping to find some proof that these horrible satanic rites had taken place here."

Von Kleinsmidt locates a pirates' treasure chest full of ancient evil documents. Janice continues snapping her camera and the overwrought voice-over continues:

> The parchment was definitely of an ancient age and although he couldn't translate its meaning right then and there, he felt confident that once back in his study he would be able to read the parchment's true meaning. But if we could have known the horror that lay in store for us, Von Kleinsmidt would've destroyed the parchment immediately. Horror and misery not only for the professor and myself, but also for my friend Diane, a prostitute who never in her wildest drug-induced dreams could possibly imagine the evil that was soon going to visit her and take possession body and soul.

From here, Steckler moves the film to a backyard patio pool with a naked Diane (Lilly Lamarr) and her gangly and equally naked pimp Fritz Granger (Richard Zufger). Ms. Brandt's narrating voice tells of *her* recent divorce and how she came to live with a floozy who only seems to come alive during fellatio. "She was on drugs most of the time and I don't suppose that helped her disposition any."

Fritz gets *his* poolside while Diane's enterprising roommate snaps candid and profit-making photos of the two, before relocating to her office. Von Kleinsmidt is also in his office deciphering the archaic vellums while simultaneously awakening Volta (Wayne Williams), a disciple of Satan. Before Volta can descend upon

Newspaper ad for *The Sexorcist's Devil* (1974) with a slightly censored title. Detroit's the Mel was one of the many smaller theaters that turned from second run to adult in the early '70s. Based in Melvindale, it was part of the United Detroit chain which had some room for local events thanks to its stage in its more mainstream years. With the change to Adults Only movies came the usual complaints. By 1988, it was forced to close and it was soon demolished. The lot was next used by a strip mall (image and commentary courtesy film historian and archivist Raleigh Bronkowski).

Diane, the head-happy tramp gives her boss *his* once more, this time on a shiny brown pleather couch.

Diane awaits Theodore (Lane McGarter), her most important customer of the evening, when Volta abruptly materializes. "Who are you and how did you get in here?" Diane deduces that this is her expected John and begins administering her specialty. The demon announces that he is Volta and says, "You've never really known true passion, true fire, true hurt or anger until you've known the love of Satan himself." Diane receives the love of Satan through Volta in a variety of manners, angles and positions.

After receiving the unholy ghost, Volta declares that Diane a full-fledged member of the Prince of Darkness' brotherhood, "Hail Satan! Hail Satan!" they both shout to the heavens. Volta demands that Diane, as a representative of the sect, collect souls for their master. To Volta's annoyance, Diane is unwilling. Still, she is decked out in some black leather-and-chains bondage gear. Theodore does finally show up for his stabbing and soul possession.

During all of this sex action, Janice continues to work on her article while Von Kleinsmidt reads books, stares at macabre paintings and repeats the word "evil." Diane's mack returns and is summarily shipped to the world of the dead with a knife to the throat. Diane is on a roll and aims to please no matter who is pulling her strings.

Diane's roommate Janice has a feeling that all is not well and phones home. Volta puts his satanic sex slave on the phone. In a moment of strength, she cries out for help. An incensed Volta promises to punish Diane for her insolence by raping her in the name of Satan.

After Satan is satiated via Diane's sacrifice, Janice arrives to hear her roommate's pleas: "Janice, please help me. I'm being possessed by a devil." A not-so-frantic Janice phones the only sexorcist she knows, Von Kleinsmidt. The good doctor promises to convene upon the malignant premises but does not arrive before Diane takes her trusty knife to Janice's pretty face. Volta rewards his faithful disciple with more of that unholy ghost business.

Von Kleinsmidt arrives too late to save Janice but surmises that a spiritual cleansing is in order. With his *Encyclopedia of Witchcraft and Demonology* he begins the sexorcism. Earlier in the film, Janice described this religious liturgy,

Advertising artwork for Doris Wishman's Chesty Morgan vehicle *Deadly Weapons* (1970). This was one of two Wishman films Steckler lensed in 1970 (author's collection).

"Sexorcism is the removing of the Devil from your body while he's sexually possessing it." As with all the others before him, Diane will knife him to death too. Volta is pleased, the Devil is pleased and all is currently well in the world of Hell.

The film was directorially credited to Sven Hellström under its three *Sexorcist* variant titles while Max Miller was listed as director on the film's later run as *Undressed to Kill*. Before the *faux* director Max Miller's involvement, the film went out as *The Sexorcist*, *The Sexorcist Devil* and the full-blown possession version *The Sexorcist's Devil*. All four titles are reportedly in the 60-, 61-minute neighborhood.

As mentioned before, 1974 appeared to be a lean year for Steckler but he did manage some side-work for one of his peers. The First Lady of exploitation, Doris Wishman, flew from South Florida to Las Vegas and assembled a small film crew that included Steckler. This bunch shot some scenes for two of Wishman's most notorious films, *Deadly Weapons* and *Double Agent 73*. Both starred the incomparable Chesty Morgan and her 73-inch chest.

French Fantasies, French Heat and *French Throat* (1975)

Steckler directed, or rather compiled, his three French-themed films in 1975 under the phony alias Henri-Pierre Duval. All the performers were given French-sounding names and there is no way of knowing who any of these people actually are. Steckler swung low and on the cheap. The frugal director purchased 20 or so stag loops and strung them loosely together with travelogue footage of Paris, France.

Carolyn Brandt is once again handed a microphone, and with a French accent attempts to help the minimal storyline along with another Steckler-penned narration. Other than Steckler's production credits on *Trip with the Teacher* (as Erwin Jay Barer), the trilogy represent his entire body of

Poster artwork for *Trip with the Teacher* (1975). Steckler (credited as Erwin Jay Barer) was cinematographer on this *Last House on the Left* (1972) cash-in (author's collection).

work for 1975. These three films clock in at roughly one hour each and somehow made their way to Spain. Then they garnered their only legitimate French connection by finally being screened in France.

Paranoia (1976)

Nineteen seventy-six proved to be one of the busiest years of Steckler's X-rated career as he plowed through seven different titles. While the *Paranoia* cast of eight racked up a collective 321 screen credits under 99 different aliases, nothing else could be unearthed about the film. There appears to be a short trailer, currently in circulation, and even it may be under the film's alternative title, *The Seduction of Monica*.

Red Heat (1976)

Red Heat marks Steckler's most narrative-conscious film in over a year since *The Sexorcist* and most notably *Perverted Passion*. The Steckler pseudonym Cindy Lou Sutters reappears, along with the female filmmaker-narrator (Carolyn Brandt). It is an interesting slant on Steckler's identity-hiding technique that he would use six more times over the next seven years.

Red Heat boasts a ten-actor cast with eight of them returning from the *Perverted Passion* sessions. In repeated attendance were Eddie Bach, Rita Cummings, Anna Leeds, Frank Margello, Harry Moran, Liz Swanson, Lenore Swink and Joan Woodman. Actually, this cross-over suggests that Steckler had resigned himself to shooting his own loops to work with, as opposed to purchasing them as he had for his *French* trilogy.

The film opens with familiar travelogue footage of Las Vegas and a narration by female pornographer Cindy Lou Sutters (Brandt). Ms. Sutters and her cameraman, Habib, have relocated to Sin City from Los Angeles to shoot a porno film starring her latest find, a slender, fiery ginger dubbed Red Heat. Red was played by Lovie Goldmine, a quasi-famous dancer-showgirl on the Vegas Strip.

Reputedly, Goldmine left the film halfway through shooting. She was not required to perform any of the hardcore action but what did remain of her footage lends to the belief that Steckler was attempting to make a legit slasher flick. Steckler either wisely or accidentally shot a beginning, a middle and an end to his feature with Lovie before she bailed on everyone.

The penny-pinching Steckler took the footage that he had and strung it together with some newer scenes, and the movie was then padded with old stuff from *Perverted Passion*. The *Perverted Passion* goods involve the motorcycle-riding thief, which cements the notion that Steckler had this project in the works two years earlier. *Red Heat* also introduced actor Pierre Agostino to the Steckler fold. Agostino figured heavily into Steckler's next two non–X rated films.

Before Cindy Lou can wrap her camera lens around Red, the minx catches her boyfriend (the forementioned Agostino) messing around with another woman. The sleazeball boyfriend slaps Red around and hits the street in search of more strange. Habib and Cindy Lou shoot a couple of quickie porno loops to pass the time. Red catches her unfaithful beau in the shower and brutally stabs him to death with a switchblade.

Red takes to the glitter strip in search of more quarry as she has found the act of murder to be more arousing than sex. Cindy Lou and Habib shoot another loop. The *Perverted Passion* moto-thief robs Cindy Lou's talent agent, then stakes out and spies on Red hitchhiking. Red is picked up by a scuzzy photographer named Roberto and Motorcycle Man follows.

Back at Roberto's place, the flashbulbs flash and Red shows some skin, then gives her photographer the business end of a stiletto directly into his neck. Red is then back on the Strip. "Red was definitely writing her own script. All she needed was another leading man and she knew it was just a matter of time before she found the *right* one." Cindy Lou and Habib shoot another loop.

Another scuzzy dude picks up Red thumbing a ride and takes her into the desert for a little fun. Red has other plans and soon this not-so-good-Samaritan is knifed just like the others. Red cools off with a cigarette while Cindy Lou and Habib shoot another loop. This time they employ a couple of hookers. "The girls weren't much to look at, but we had to make good with them as we were running low on money." Squeezing every last cent out of a dollar, Habib shoots a POV loop with the nympho–Nancy who has been in all of the loops but two up to this point. Habib comes to the realization that he "now knows why he became a cameraman." This POV sequence begs the question, was Steckler himself shooting this scene?

More pennies are pinched as Steckler recycles the entire *Perverted Passion* scene where the motorcycle thug rips off Mr. Ordinary's neighbors at gunpoint. The two-wheeling criminal is back on the run, Red polishes her weapon of choice and Team Sutters shoots another loop. This time Cindy Lou claims that she jumped in front of the camera for some money-saving fun and action.

Steckler abruptly ends the film with the motorcyclist giving Red a lift into the desert only to be hit and killed by a booze-swilling delivery driver. Cindy Lou wonders "if Red would've made a good porno star." For whatever reasons, Steckler shot this one in 35mm and cut it to a lengthy (for a porno) 81 minutes.

Poster art for *Red Heat* (1976) (author's collection).

Sex Rink (1976)

Sex Rink opens with yet another narration by Carolyn Brandt who, this time around, is a high school guidance counselor. She tells of Senior Day and how a certain group of gals desired something more special than the tired old prom scene. This gaggle of girls, known as the Sweethearts, was mainly comprised of cheerleaders who "loved sports of all kinds, as you will see."

Brunette and voyeur Tina ogles the Homecoming King and Queen Mark and Holly as they get it on atop a "stairway to heaven." Cheerleaders Paula and Cheryl paw each other in an adjacent corner for Tina's leers. The school's star football quarterback, Patrick, makes an appearance to the glee of a handsy Jackie.

Tina's best friend Colleen arrives and is delighted at the floor show that she is greeted by. "Mark and Holly sure got the party off to a swinging start." Tina and Colleen retire to a couch and engage in some good old S&M. The cute Evelyn shows up to take in all that her friends have to currently offer but she is really on the prowl for Rico.

A shirtless but suspendered Rico makes the scene just moments before the leather-clad Bianca enters the room with her boyfriend Neil. Once Mark and Holly have completed the deed, the entire gang makes their way over to a skating rink where they are chaperoned by the vice-principal Mr. Dickerman. From here, loads of naked roller-skating ensues.

Tina and her new partner-in-crime Shezell tie up Mr. Dickerman for some off-campus fun of their own. "I think Shezell has got him right where she wants him." Evelyn finally locates Rico and the two begin wearing out the felt covering of a pool table. The resident quarterback finds his conquest. "By now Patrick was calling the play with Wanda and it wasn't the quarterback sneak. He was definitely going up the middle." Then Evelyn and Rico switch off with Bianca and Neil.

Some dude named Eddie makes it with Cheryl while the film's narrator does some business with her chosen beau Rodney and her student Laurie. Many of the satiated skate back to the rink for some goofy shenanigans and balloon bursting. Wanda tags Eddie while Mark gets tag-teamed by Paula and her big-busted blonde friend Jackie. Late to the party, Tammy Lee joins Laurie, Rodney and the counselor in a four-way.

Steckler bookends the film with a final word of narrative: "Everyone had seemed to have gotten a little closer to each other and in the end uncovered new things about each other and that's when the Sweetheart party started to break up."

The film's pivotal character Tina was played by Debbie Truelove, who over the next eight years did six more titles with Steckler at the helm. Mike Ranger, the film's biggest star-to-be, gave Steckler a go two more times before moving on to less budget-constrained fare like *Taboo* and *Insatiable,* which are both regarded as triple X-rated classics from 1980.

Sex Rink boasted one more rising star in the form of Rhonda Jo Petty. She was a dead ringer for Farrah Fawcett and her producers exploited this to the hilt. The real Farrah was married to actor Lee Majors and during that time went by Farrah Fawcett Majors. Rhonda Jo's handlers christened her Farrah Fawcett Minor and received a cease-and-desist letter from Majors' legal team. Despite this *minor* setback, Rhonda Jo Petty racked up over 70 screen credits.

The remainder of the cast: John Colt, Caylene Mariel, Desiré Elms, Sandy

Sunshine, Kelly Guthrie, Gene Miller, Millie Moon, R.J. Reynolds, "Too Tall" Teresa and Denise Swenson (who did even bigger business as Jenene Swenson). They all worked in and out of Steckler's adult film world for the next eight years. Steckler fashioned this 72-minute feature under the familiar Cindy Lou Sutters banner and would make its companion piece seven years later.

South of the Border (1976)

Steckler launches this film with more of his travelogue-type footage, only this time Vegas and L.A. are not the catch of the day. Instead he aims his camera at Tijuana. It could be stock travelogue footage though some of the shots do possess Steckler's by-now-familiar roaming eye lens. Narration begins but this time it is likely Carolyn Brandt doing her best at a Latin impersonation. "Every year thousands of Americans visit Mexico looking for fun and relaxation south of the border. Women and men alike come here trying to escape the everyday stress of business and personal problems."

From shots of a filthy and run-down Tijuana, Steckler moves the action indoors (presumably back to his Vegas home base). Cantina waitress Maria Moranda (Debbie Truelove) makes good with a sex toy while slum lord Anthony DeVille (Kelly Guthrie) puts his staring, slobbering hound routine into action. Steckler cuts to another less-than-appealing shot of this vacation destination and then it is back indoors where Anthony is now on the business end of Maria's mouth.

Steckler quickly moves the film back outdoors to the slums of Tijuana and then to another seedy room where "some of the most exciting escapades of sexual fantasy take place." Overly excited beach house handyman Pedro (Jason Wayne) and Kitty (Maria Arnold) do the deed in some seriously short order. This footage was archived from the *"Daisy Lay"* shoot five years earlier.

More external shots of Tijuana and its beaches give way to another crappy room. This time Andrea (Andrea True) is having car troubles and a salesman, Tony (Charles Orlando) is helping her save some scratch by scratching *his* itch. To tie these scenes together, Steckler cuts in shots of Maria appearing to peek in the window as Andrea and Tony close the deal. Actually, the Andrea and Tony sequence is more archival footage, this time from Steckler's 1973 *Baby Bubbles*.

Steckler prowls the beaches with his camera, then closes in on a stucco lean-to. Here cab driver Mario (Franklin Anthony) has a passenger (Nina Fause) work off her fare the old-fashioned way. Steckler lengthens the scene with more footage of Maria spying on them through a barely opened door. The Mario and his "paying" lady stuff is also archival footage but neither actor were in another Steckler movie so it is impossible to know where it originated.

Without fail, Steckler delivers more frames of Tijuana's underbelly only to later expose his viewers to an automobile junkyard where a men's magazine shoot is underway. The subject, Donna, poses naked atop the wrecked cars while the never satisfied Maria hungrily looks on. Maria is caught by the photographers and runs to a horse ranch.

This time Steckler abandons his tired transition material and allows Maria to make the move. The little Latin nymph is giving Lem (George Peters) and Wanda (Starlyn Simone), two horse traders from Arkansas, the eye. "Every time Wanda gets around horses, she gets the urge for a roll in the hay." Lem and Wanda's "roll" is courtesy of more frames from *"Daisy Lay."*

"Inside the ranch house is Cynthia and her little brother Billy. They like to play together. Today's game looks like doctor." This footage of these unknown actors is interspersed with shots of Maria invading their privacy. Once the action is completed, Steckler moves back to his shots of a scruffy desert as Maria runs towards the next crummy window to snoop into.

"Maria is off to see her friend José from the cantina where she works. José is a dishwasher there, but it looks like José has company." It matters not, Maria will loom and leer as José and whoever get it on. This is likely a leftover from Steckler's 1971 *How to Make a Sex Movie!!* Then it is back to the beach and Maria beelines it to her next free peepshow.

Airline stewardesses Tina and Marguerite show Maria, with the aid of their battery-powered toys, that "[a]fter long flights, they like to unwind together. They think ecstasy is the only way to fly." The Euro-Prog Rock soundtrack along with Marguerite's name coming from French descent more than lends to the notion that this stuff is rehashed from Steckler's 1975 *French* trilogy.

"Looks like Pedro's little trailer sure sees a lot of action": Pedro's grab this time would have been the dancer Carlotta (Rene Bond) if he were home. His stand-in is Miguel. Carlotta delivers the goods, seemingly unaware of the difference. These repeat frames are from *"Daisy Lay."* Then another shot of the beach leads to another shabby room. Maria's back at Anthony's place where he has procured the services of two Lone Star lasses who show them "how to have fun Texas-style." Steckler accidentally includes the familiar shots of Maria having a gander at the fun but her character is clearly smack dab in the middle of the activities. This sex sequence along with the first seem to be the only thing shot specifically for this film. It closes with another salvaged series of *"Daisy Lay"* scenes.

Steckler took no credit for *South of the Border*. To date, this is the biggest hodgepodge mash-up in his filmography and it runs a long 78 minutes.

Teenage Dessert (1976)

For *Teenage Dessert,* Steckler is back as Cindy Lou Sutters. As with all the other Sutters productions, Carolyn Brandt provides the narration:

> Venice, California, is a town where new adventures in life occur every ten minutes. The young lady you see roller skating, in the red blouse, is Mona Miller. She'll take you on a roller-skating tour that will set your wheels in motion. Actually, Mona is in search of her girlfriend Chrissy, but while she looks for her, she's going to introduce you, the audience, to some of her wild and exciting friends.

That is the set-up and that is the plot, as threadbare and paper-thin as it can possibly be. This will be Steckler's seventh "voyeur" film where stag loops are interspersed with cutaways of a Peeping Tom while the entire ordeal is explained by narration. It is a cheap maneuver on Steckler's part; he used it time and again.

Brandt continues her voice-over: "So let's skate along with Mona as she heads to Rita's pad. Rita's a waitress at the Doggy House down by the pier. However, right now she and her lover John, who fixes roller skates for a living, are taking their own lunch break. Let's check in on the action."

Mona is played by Sandy Sunshine on her return from *Sex Rink* and en route to three more Steckler productions. Orita

DeChadwick, as Rita, turns in her only performance for Steckler; she appeared in at least two dozen other films under six different aliases. Once John and Rita's lunches are consumed, Mona rolls over to Sylvia's for some fun with her and her friend Helen. These are two liberated women who make tacos for a living.

Since Helen and Sylvia have concluded taco time, Mona glides over to Chrissy's brother's place in her continued search for her friend. Jusepe, Chrissy's brother and pizza boy, *is* home but he is about to make a special delivery (involving a banana split) and an unnamed cutie is preparing to receive it. Jusepe is portrayed by R.J. Reynolds who has 66 screen credits to his name. While the majority of them are in the adult category, he did find himself in one episode of *Magnum P.I.*

Once Jusepe has finished with his (teenage) dessert, Mona beelines it over to a men haters club where three gals play choo-choo train. "Let's see where this locomotive is headed." Apparently this train was transporting fresh produce as bananas and cucumbers make their way into the scene. Mona tires of the food revue and decides to take a trip across town to Hollywood.

Plato's Retreat West is Mona's next den of sin and what she ganders at is an eight-person after dinner orgy. Club manager Mike Ranger also looks in on the event in footage left over from *Sex Rink*. The eight-person blowout finally peters out and Steckler moves the film to Plato's basement where there are showers, a sauna and a roller-skating rink.

Ranger chaperones the basement affair as Candy Clean showers. He leaves nothing untouched and three others, from *Sex Rink*, engage and disengage accordingly. After exhausting all that Plato's has to offer, Mona heads back over to Venice to continue looking for Chrissy. Chrissy has the same proclivities towards voyeurism as Mona, but this vixen is strictly into girls.

Chrissy is played by Desiré Elms who had previously been in *Sex Rink* and continued with Steckler for three more films. Other than Antoinette Maynard from Herschell Gordon Lewis' *The Ecstasies of Women* (1969), the balance of the cast, Gene Miller, Millie Moon, Denise Swenson and "Too Tall" Teresa, were from *Sex Rink*. Steckler takes this cozy 60-minute film out and closes with Mona and Chrissy and some whipped cream for more dessert—teenage dessert.

Teenage Hustler (1976)

Steckler shot (or, more aptly, assembled) this second film in his *Teenage* trilogy as Ricardo Malatoté. In some markets, *Teenage Hustler* went out as *Young Hustle*. It is a companion piece, of sorts, to *Rufus Potter's Hooker Scam* (more on that later). Whether the *Scam* or the *Hustle* came first is not known.

What *is* known is that regardless of Steckler's seventh bogus alias, this is undoubtedly his picture. One dead giveaway: The ever-present travelogue-type footage of Hollywood is narrated by the all-too-familiar voice of Carolyn Brandt. Plus, more carry-over performers from some of Steckler's previous films aid in letting the proverbial cat out of the bag.

Steckler's camera roams the streets of Hollywood in search of the film's resident "weirdo," English Billy Boynton. Along the way, Steckler again captures the Capitol Records building where only a decade earlier Lonnie Lord had happily signed autographs for his "legion" of fans. Then Brandt's narration begins to help guide the viewer through the film's lead characters and plot:

This is the story of one ... person who came to Hollywood. A wisecracking sex freak who has since gone on to become something of a legend in the glamour capital of the world. His name is English Billy. He's a con man, a hustler and freak who seems to always be getting himself into trouble, usually because of girls. English Billy Boynton just can't seem to keep his mind off girls. They're all he thinks about, girls, girls and more girls. He's a regular sex maniac all right and he's got some of the freakiest ways of meeting girls that you will ever see.

English Billy, a model who is obscenely behind in his rent, is hoofing it over to Rufus Potter's (Jason Wayne) photography studio to have some pictures snapped of him and some naked lasses. But first he has an overwhelming urge to peek in on a couple of ladies experimenting with one another's bodies. The eighth Steckler "voyeur" film is underway.

English Billy leaves *this* scene to make for the workplace and Carolyn Brandt introduces the film's co-star:

When Rufus Potter opened his photography studio in Hollywood three years ago, he made a vow to himself that it was going to be business first, fun later. He knew he'd be working with a lot of sexy young girls and that the temptation to put his camera down and go chasing after them would be a very strong one. But unlike English Billy, Rufus is a strong-minded person and he knew that once he made that vow to himself, he'd stick to it. Get the work done first. There'd be plenty of time later for balling. Rufus also made a pledge to be honest with his clients and models. Unlike Billy, Rufus played straight with everyone and always came out on top.

Soon both men are hard at work in front of and behind the camera. Billy is with Connie (in front of the camera) and Rufus is taking it all in with the lens and flash of his camera from behind. After the shoot, Billy and Connie are compensated. Rather than paying his rent, Billy insists he and Connie head out to paint the town red.

After his night out with Connie, Billy returns home to find a "For Rent" sign on his door. His landlord was not budging on his decision: Billy gets current on his rent or he and his belongings are out by noon the next day. Time for the shady Billy to hatch a hustle for some quick bread, but he will need Rufus' help to make it happen.

Billy pitches his game plan and Rufus is all in. Billy will call prostitutes over and Rufus will record the action on film. Then Rufus will have his way with the girls. After the festivities are over, each working girl will be monetarily blackmailed over the illicit pictures. Why a prostitute would possibly care about such photos is never explained.

First up and out of her clothes is Mary (Mary Monroe) and then the fox fur coat–adorned Vicki. The black-booted Trixie (Sunny Boyd from *Ilsa: She Wolf of the SS*) is the conspiring duo's next mark. Trixie catches Rufus and his camera and confronts the two shakedown artists. "You're gonna blackmail a prostitute? Who you gonna sell the pictures to anyway? Give me my bread so I can get out of this joint." So, the dream scheme was a dud and in the end Billy winds up losing his apartment.

Steckler made this 64-minute hodgepodge using a liberal amount of cast and character names from *Baby Bubbles*. The film's two leads and Marsha Hart as Francine are all veterans of that 1973 Steckler film. In fact, all of Hart's footage appears to have been culled from the *Baby Bubbles* archives. The remaining cast consists of Glenda Turner, Barbara O'Farrell, Liz Wilson and Maggie Williams, who either changed their names for further work or decided that their first stop in porno-world would be their last.

Teenage Massage Parlor (1976)

Teenage Massage Parlor is the second and final film Steckler made using the Ricardo Malatoté *nom de screen*. It follows the same template as many of his previous adult films in that a series of sex loops are inserted into a loose storyline. A voice-over is again employed to help the viewer follow said storyline. Most sources claim Carolyn Brandt is the narrator, but it is clearly a male's voice. Perhaps it is Steckler but it is certainly not Ms. Brandt's.

The narrator tells of Brooklyn native Helga Swartz (Brandt) and her penny-pinching trip to California. Once there, she opens a massage parlor with a photography studio above it. Helga interviews record industry executive Frick Overmeijer about his stay at her massage parlor. Frick, whoever he is in real life, is doing his best Groucho Marx impersonation.

Rufus Jordan (Jason Wayne) and Stanley Rajentski run the photo studio and take stag pictures that Helga then sells to popular men's magazines. One of Rufus' favorite subjects is Ginger, recently released from prison after doing time for seducing young boys. This actress also played Connie in *Teenage Hustler* and had a role in *Baby Bubbles*. Only two minutes into the film, it is apparent that *Teenage Massage Parlor* is going to be cobbled together from those aforementioned films.

Teenage masseuses *and* photo models, Sammi and Jenny are introduced as "workers" who are exceptionally popular with the customers. Steckler shifts back to Frick Overmeijer and his masseuse Tiffany as Helga gazes on. Back at the studio with Ginger and Stanley, Rufus "snaps off pictures of her action."

Then Steckler brings in another character and familiar face from *The Mad Love Life of a Hot Vampire* and *Peeping Tom*, Jeremy Von Ripple. He is in need of an inexpensive massage. Helga fetches Jenny. Jeremy is more than impressed and shows her as much by posing and flexing his muscles. "Okay, Jenny, let's get it on."

Not satisfied with nine characters, Steckler works a tenth one in with 16-year-old Babsy Blockman (Jeanie Tulip). A new girl in town, she's looking to become a model at Helga's studio. All of this footage is gathered straight from *Baby Bubbles* in which Ms. Tulip *was* Baby Bubbles. Steckler continues the recycling by throwing in more *Baby Bubbles* footage in the form of Ginger-Connie servicing English Billy Boynton. *Teenage Massage Parlor* is a real mash-up.

An eleventh character is added, Lucretia (Marsha Hart), via more *Baby Bubbles-Teenage Hustler* footage. Finally, all the characters have been brought on and what follows is one sex scene after another involving all the respective couples. There is all the standard stuff and then there is the Steckler weirdness. One such scene involves Tiffany playing "hot dog" with Frick complete with ketchup, relish and a bun.

Teenage Massage Parlor is a mess in more ways than one but it does have a campy charm that is, at times, amusing. Apparently, the film ran in some territories as *Massage Parlour* and even got some lip service from the 1977 Rik Tazíner film *Inside Baby Sister*. This 53-minute goofball porno concludes Steckler's adult output for 1976 and his *Teenage* trilogy. By the way, there is not a teenager anywhere in or near their frames.

Nineteen seventy-seven and 1978 appear to be Steckler's leanest years working within the film industry. He has no movies to his name(s) and no extraneous credits on any outside projects either. During this time, he may have been mourning the death of his good friend Ron Haydock and attempting to keep his furniture store afloat. Steckler reappeared in 1979 with three adult features and a return to the horror genre with *The Hollywood Strangler Meets the Skid Row Slasher*.

Deviates in Love (1979)

Deviates in Love sports a ghoulish two-minute pre-credits sequence that appears to take place in a medieval torture dungeon. This promising opener looks nothing like anything Steckler had ever shot before and in all likelihood he did not shoot this. This stylish (for a porno) reel is, naturally, accompanied by narration to help set up the storyline:

> The years of the Spanish Inquisition were a Hell on Earth for people who were accused of practicing witchcraft and being in league with the Devil. Many times condemned by their own friends and neighbors, they were tried and tortured by official inquisitors until they pleaded guilty to the charges against them whether they were guilty or not. What is not so commonly known about this terrible era, however, is that some of the inquisitors actually enjoyed torturing their victims. They derived great pleasure out of their prisoners' screams of agony and sometimes they would even force their unwilling captives to commit acts of depravity simply because beneath their righteous-minded exteriors they themselves were extremely depraved creatures. But as a psychiatrist specializing in all kinds of sexual psychoses, I've made a lifelong study of human history and I can assure you that while the era of the Inquisition is far behind us, the secret and suppressed sexual urges of mankind are still very much with us, even today.

The narrator goes on to tell of 23-year-old Claire Green, who suffers from an obsession with voyeurism. She seeks treatment from the psychiatrist who spoke earlier of the Spanish Inquisition. Steckler is about to revisit his old Peeping Tom formula, whereby shots of Claire peeking into neighbors' windows are intercut with purchased stag loops.

Claire first sneaks a peek at Fred and Angie. "Fred and Angie weren't really doing anything my husband and I didn't do in bed, but it was very exciting for me to watch someone else doing it. Then I suddenly realized something, and I thought it was odd that it hadn't struck me right away: Fred and Angie were brother and sister." To no one's great surprise, Carolyn Brandt is the voice of Claire Green.

Claire's attraction to her neighbor Bonnie Simpson began putting worrisome bi-curious thoughts into her head that drove her to drink. Still, Claire could not resist watching Bonnie and her husband's show. Steckler shifts gears here and introduces a group of young men and women (the Cycle Devils) on motorbikes. Moe Anderson heads up the Cycle Devils and they have recently kidnapped a young woman and strapped her to a bed in their secret hideout in the Pine Valley Mountains. The narrator explains, "The Cycle Devils are a band of freaked-out, maladjusted young people who three years ago rode their way into a hellish reputation of terror, sexual assault and even murder. Whatever they felt like doing, no matter what it was, they did it."

The Cycle Devils' captive is tortured and raped, and then it is back to

Claire and her problems. Claire is now "intrigued" by old schoolmate Annie Conway, who could get you "liquor and dirty magazines if she likes you." After Annie and her beau wrap things up, Claire turns her attentions to a six-person naked pile-up. Steckler then turns the film's attentions to the world of prostitution and Darla McEntire.

Darla was lured into a frightening situation with the promise of a massage, but *this* massage goes horribly wrong. Darla is bound, beaten, violated with a foreign object, raped and then choked to death. Steckler exits this dismal scene for more of his recognizable Las Vegas travelogue-style footage along with more on Claire and *her* sexual disorders and disfunctions.

Claire has a hang-up with another girl she knows, Cynthia. "Cynthia was something else all right. Completely free and uninhibited. She loved it." Claire tells of her husband purchasing a film projector and screening pornography in their bedroom in order to get things moving along. Claire enjoyed these stag films so much that she began watching them while she was alone. "I watched them over and over again and again. Oh, it was so satisfying."

Cynthia's sister Rosemary got Claire and her husband hooked on those old dirty movies by giving them a dozen films as a wedding gift. "Rosemary was something else all right. She had such a big appetite for life. I haven't seen her for years, but I bet she's doing what she likes to do and doing a lot of it too."

Claire finally succumbs to her Anne Conway desires and pays her a surprise visit which plays out exactly as she had fantasized. No matter how much Claire enjoyed her friend, she never saw her again nor had another lesbian encounter. Claire's shrink begins telling her a story of the New Yorker Josie and her repressed sexual urges that, "for the first time in her life, were about to become a reality." Josie was secretly into "water sports."

Yet again Steckler plays fast and loose with the parameters of the porno film and subjects the audience to a barrage of ugly situations and images. He made this thing under the Otto Van Dayan banner. He later re-cut the film as *Fade to Red* using the Max Miller alias. The film has two edits, 59 or 53 minutes respectively. The Spanish Inquisition sequence along with the "water sports" scene appear in some versions of the film and not in others. Voyeurism, urination, incest, sado-masochism and rape—deviates for sure, but in love?

Las Vegas Wives (1979)

Las Vegas Wives appears to be a lost film. Some information on the cast exists but the film currently resides in the "where is it now?" file. That's a shame, because any Steckler film available for viewing is another glimpse into the mind of this unique and unpredictable artist.

Actor Jerry Davis seems to have gotten his start in pornography with Steckler. While he only worked two more times for Steckler, he did amass 39 screen credits overall. Steckler veteran Kelly Guthrie gets into some more action after *The Sexorcist*, *South of the Border* and *Sex Rink*. Guthrie worked with Steckler two more times over the next three years.

Devon and Jim Mayer made their way back to the Steckler fold after time spent on *Perverted Passion* and *Red Heat*. It appears as though Mr. and Mrs. Mayer ended their movie careers with *Las Vegas Wives*. This is a familiar tale that echoes Steckler's legit movie days where cast and crew members would drop out of sight indefinitely after working for him.

Also included in *Las Vegas Wives* was Andrea True. One of the best-known actresses in the pornography field, she ended her adult film career in 1976. Ms. True recorded several disco records but "More More More (How Do You Like It?)" became a #1 hit for her during the American bicentennial. During this time, future Kiss guitarist Bruce Kulick was part of the Andrea True Connection touring band. At this point, Andrea vowed, "I'd rather be a waitress or a typist than make another adult film."

Now, since Andrea was true to her word, just how *did* Steckler get a retiree into his film? By procuring loops or scenes and dubbing in narration and dialogue to fit *his* film's narrative.

Lastly, actress Debbie Truelove made six of her eight screen credits under the direction of Steckler and closed out her stay with the porno industry in 1984 under the alias Chica Moreno. Perhaps, one day, *Las Vegas Wives* and *Paranoia* will rear their heads for all to see and hear.

Lust Vegas Joyride (1979)

This next feature presents a bit of a conundrum as it appears to be an edit of another film which Steckler had nothing whatsoever to do with. *Heavenly Desires*, an 85-minute vehicle for porn legend Seka, involved the Old West, the Devil, ghosts and the deflowering of two female college coeds. Somehow Steckler acquired this film and trimmed it down to 73 minutes, leaving the entire narrative on the cutting room floor.

Naturally Steckler used an alias, this time Bill Hunter, then changed the film's title to *Lust Vegas Joyride*. Apparently Steckler stripped the film of its original soundtrack and inserted a narration by a Jim Nabors sound-alike. "Shazam!" The narrator tells of four guys on a Lake Mead fishing trip who aim to catch more than just fish.

The group's driver, John, cannot wait to get into a motel bed, "alone or otherwise. Golly." Ted has his sights set on a small disco in Vegas while Steve is looking to get a massage once they arrive in Sin City. Bob is about to dig his way into a nurse's station.

Steve is dropped off at a newsstand where he can sort out what massage parlor he wishes to visit. Ted's disco destination is the Crazy Horse Topless Saloon. Bob sets up another date with his favorite nurse, and John locates his motel room and orders up some special room service.

Steckler bounces between the activities of the four men, adding new dialogue, more narration and rockabilly and disco music. In short, it is just another messy Steckler porno amalgamation. In the end, the film's biggest star Seka ("She can do the real Las Vegas strip") is only present for a scant few minutes (due to the Steckler edit). Steckler concludes *his* version of *Heavenly Desires* presumably on the beach of Lake Mead where the entire cast has gathered to do their deeds in the sun and on the sand.

So, between 1971 and 1979 Steckler had a hand in no less than 26 adult films of varying degrees in quality. Over the next decade, the filmmaker's output would slow drastically. Still, Steckler returned to mainstream moviemaking (well, mainstream for him anyway) with his 1979 feature *The Hollywood Strangler Meets the Skid Row Slasher*.

California Girls (1980)

Steckler closed out 1979 with four films (three smut, one legit) and managed to do even less movie business in 1980 with only two notches in his cinematic belt. First up is *California Girls* or *California Girl* (aka *The Champ*) as the pasteboard title card reveals. After the film's less-than-imaginative moniker has vanished, the most familiar name in the adult film world appears: John C. Holmes.

By 1980, Holmes' golden years in porno were behind him and his cocaine consumption and freebasing habit had rendered him a limp member on the majority of porno sets. His inability to perform properly on film led Holmes into a life of crime that included credit card fraud, drug-running, prostitution and possibly murder. The Wonderland Murders (the crimes took place on Wonderland Avenue in Los Angeles) were committed on July 1, 1981, and Holmes was a prime suspect.

Eventually Holmes was acquitted on all four counts of homicide. Still, by 1980 when Steckler would have been calling, the waning porn star was in no position to turn down any work, no matter how little the pay. Apparently co-stars Rhonda Jo Petty, R.J. Reynolds (both Steckler graduates) and Tiffany Clark were also in a tight monetary squeeze as they showed up for duty alongside Holmes.

Steckler opens the film with the roller-skating Julie (Petty), "a tough chick who will do anything to get to the top of the roller skating racket." Also there's Sally (Clarke), "who will sell her sweet young body to the highest bidder." This skating activity is quickly retired in favor of a water-conserving shower scene. The film then cuts to more roller-skating, but this time with John Holmes. Holmes is playing Paul Felbert, a national skating champ, and the girls think they can win a competition with his help, however a pit stop with Julie is the next order up.

Once the Paul-Julie show comes to a close, Julie bets Felbert $500 that she and her friend can beat him at a 400-yard dash, presumably aboard roller skates. Felbert accepts the challenge. In another room, Julie is (sexually) working out the details of waiving the entry fee into the skating competition with a promoter.

Julie and Sally pay a visit to the T-Birds' manager (Reynolds) and wager they can convince him to "throw the show" in order to join his team. They offer him ten percent of their earnings and then some pluses if he goes along with the deal. Julie and Sally begin administering the "pluses." The girl's scheme is a success and then it is on to some guy named Walter who also has a stake in this skate race. Curiously, Steckler chooses to use an instrumental version of the "Theme from *Shaft*" here.

As the "Theme from *Shaft*" concludes, softer music enters while Julie and Sally make out with each other in front of a raging fireplace. The girls are now T-Birds and the next day, at the race, they double-cross Felbert. They give the reigning champ the what-for by slamming him roller derby-style to the sidelines and taking the lead. Steckler ends this quaint 50-minute film on Felbert attempting to get up with a busted ankle. Once again Steckler took no screen credit.

Steckler shot this one entirely without narration or loops. While *California Girls* is no lost gem in the world of pornography, it does show Steckler sidestepping some of his tried-and-true formulas. Still, the film's trailer proudly exclaimed, "*California Girls,* where savage sex explodes on the screen in an orgy of orgasmic passion with scenes so bold, so hot, so incredible that you won't believe your eyes."

A Touch of Love (1980)

Steckler turned in his second 1980 feature *A Touch of Love* as Randall Hayes. Steckler used the Hayes handle only one more time, in 1982. This 89-minute sex looper is narrated yet again by then ex-wife Carolyn Brandt masquerading this time as Francois. Why Carolyn continues to come back for this type of business is the big burning question. However, Steckler may have simply had this recorded tape lying around for years.

Steckler begins the film with some awfully familiar Las Vegas travelogue footage and then quickly launches into Francois' narration:

> Las Vegas, Nevada, the entertainment capital of the world ... but a lot of people like to call it the sex capital of the world. The movie you are about to see is going to take you behind the glitter and the lights to show you the real Las Vegas. It's not all casinos and gambling. It's fiery passion and hot steamy sex, all done with a touch of love.

Francois explains that she is in public relations and it is her job to show what all there is to see—for a nominal fee, of course. Francois insists that she and the viewer get to know each other a bit better as the film cuts to a blonde (supposedly Francois herself) giving some lip service to her beau. This particular "beau" sounds suspiciously like Steckler himself. "Who said you can't get ahead in Las Vegas?" As the scene concludes, our faceless beau declares, "I love coming in Las Vegas."

Francois' voice reappears to push the Sin City sex underworld journey forward. "When people think of Las Vegas, our beautiful showgirls come to mind, but do you ever wonder what they do on their day off?" Enter Darlene and Nancy, a couple of dancers who are more than eager to shed their stage costumes for some birthday suit fun. "I think Darlene and Nancy can face work tomorrow a little better."

The tour continues with honeymooners Gary and Susan, who must decide whether to hit the casinos or to hit *it*. "It" wins and the gambling tables will have to wait as these two laugh-happy goofs get to know one another better. This sequence appears to be a leftover from *Perverted Passion*. "Well, by the looks of this, Gary won't have any trouble making Susan do the things he wants and I think Susan's got him right where she wants him."

Actor Mike Ranger returns as Mike, a tour guide who has arranged a banquet meeting of eight kitchen appliance sales representatives who have tired of conventional Las Vegas dinners and diners. The eight reps quickly finish their eats and get on with the treats. "This doesn't faze Mike, he's seen it all before. I guess it's something about Las Vegas that makes people go crazy." This entire scene is a leftover from *Teenage Dessert* which was partially a leftover from *Sex Rink* (the Mike Ranger parts anyway).

Francois continues with a Steckler-penned line: "A lot of people come to Las Vegas to make it big in show business. But it's tough to break in and a lot of them don't make it, but they keep on trying." This particular part of the narration is simply another peek into Steckler's mindset at the time. The days of the *Blood Shack* were dreary enough but seven years later, Steckler's movie career had come to this.

Enter Gwendoline, the wanna-be singer, and David, the self-professed professional lounge performer. David sees talent in Gwen and sets about showing her the casting-audition couch-type ropes. This footage appears to be from Steckler's 1975 *French* trilogy era: "Well, from the look of this, I think Gwendoline is going to be a big star."

Charlotte and Karen take front and center as they get some time away from their hubbies who work the graveyard shift at the casinos. These girls do some shuffling and rolling that doesn't require cards or dice. Then Francois cuts the scene short for whatever reasons and moves the action. "This is the other side of Las Vegas. The part not too many people get to see. Sure it doesn't have the glamour of the big hotels and casinos but it doesn't mean it's not as exciting."

Francois introduces her associate Louise, who is giving John Smith a private guided tour of what she feels to be the best of Las Vegas—for a nominal fee. "It looks like John and Louise hit it off real well. See how easy it is to make friends in Las Vegas?"

Speaking of making friends, Steckler could not have possibly remained friends with two of his performers. He had used this upcoming scene last in *Red Heat*, calling the players "low-budget hookers that weren't much to look at." Fast forward four years and he is using the exact same footage describing them as "Rhonda and Becky, two over-weight secretaries from Sacramento." Of course this is probably purchased footage but there is a bit of a biased mean streak on display here that is very uncommon for Steckler.

Character judgments aside, Rhonda and Becky's "fantasy is to meet a real macho hunk and have a threesome." This recognizable footage gives way to more lifted frames from *Red Heat*. In *Red Heat*, it is Nancy Regal and a local stud but here it's Jimmy Joe the used car salesman and Lydia something-or-another from "back East somewhere." Steckler disguises his voice as best he can as he enjoys verbally reacting to the on-screen action reprising the earlier line, "I love to come in Las Vegas."

Steckler's third *Red Heat* revisit initially involved two unknowns in a "quickie loop" but now the names have changed to Nick and B.J. "Guess how B.J. got her name." If in this footage, from 1976, hair styles and decor looked tired, imagine what it looked like four years later in 1980. The film then shifts to some Long Beach dude (Steckler again providing voiceover) named Harry, who likes the intimate company of two females even if he has to pay for it.

Steckler begins wrapping up this long feature with Francois stating, "Before we go, I think it's time again for you to have a little fun. This is Amanda and—well, I'll leave you alone for a little while." Once again Steckler turns in the male narration to what appears to be a *French* trilogy scene reprisal. In total, other than the newly scribed narration and dialogue, there is simply no reason to screen this picture when taking Steckler's previous adult features into account.

Black Garters (1981)

Steckler closed out 1980 with a whopper of a loopzilla in the form of *A Touch of Love*. It gives his 1976 *South of the Border* sex loops-gone-berserk feature a run for its money (in which there was none). Still, Steckler would go one better than he had in 1980 by cashing in on three adult films.

Black Garters is another Cindy Lou Sutters production that has most of the *Sex Rink* gang returning for some more skin-to-skin fun on wheels. Carolyn Brandt does the narration honors and

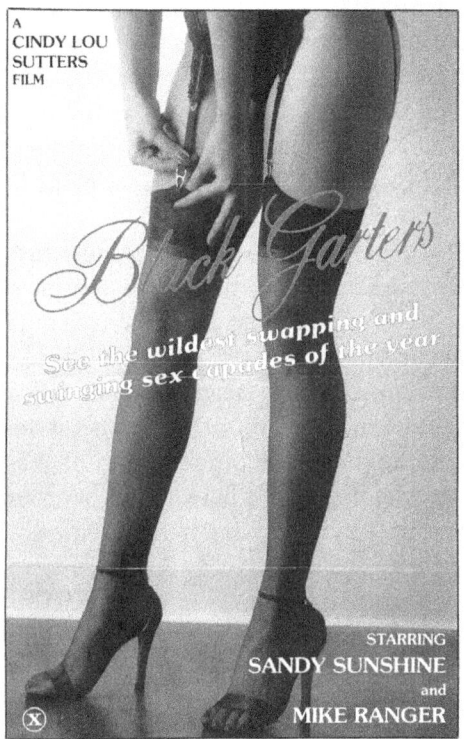

Poster art for *Black Garters* (1981) (author's collection).

dialogue, to date, for Carolyn Brandt to read and she reads it well. While this a tame example, it is how Steckler closes out this scene and moves onto the next: "Those black garters really turn men on, maybe women too."

Mike Ranger returns with his patented arm cast, that he has worn several times over, and skates his way over to the hottest swingers club on the West coast, Plato's Retreat West. Mike manages this joint and he and Sandy get quite naughty when she visits. Steckler's camera follows "Big Tits" Malloy and her friend as they stroll over to Plato's to get their evening's escapades underway lickity-split.

Tony and Tasha, regulars at Plato's, appear to be heading there just as their friends are. Steckler takes the film back indoors to Plato's Retreat West where Luscious Laura sits at a desk helping Mike run the club "like it's her own baby." Laura then shows a new customer just how luscious she *can* be. "Big Tits" Malloy does her own thing in the back with some shaggy dude.

Steckler leaves the club and catches up with Sandy as she glides over to Angela's place for some girl-on-girl activities. Angela's not home but her promiscuous sister Connie is there with her new boyfriend Tom. Naturally, Sandy cannot resist ogling these two as they investigate one another inside and out. Sandy leaves these two investigators and finally locates Angela: "C'mon, let's skate."

Off these two sex kittens go on wheels, in search of cheap thrills. Back at Plato's, Ranger brushes his hair (again) just as he has done in at least four previous films. Why Steckler continues to recycle this mundane footage is mind-boggling. Brandt makes it known that while Mike has the pick of the club, he is waiting impatiently for Sandy today.

Steckler settles the film into a

promptly introduces Sandy Sunshine as she skates her way around Venice, California, in skintight red satin pants. "Join us as Sandy takes us on a roller-skating tour of sexual enlightenment."

First Sandy spies in on Frankie (Steckler provides his voice) and the black garter–adorned JoAnne as they do what everyone does in an adult feature. Once Frankie and JoAnne have gotten their show to its obvious conclusion, Sandy takes to the streets again in search of more voyeuristic thrills and spills. Brandt introduces Sandy's best friend Angela, who enjoys the same pastime. "She thinks it's great to be a peek freak."

The freak first peeks on Mindy and Jake who are doing the same things as Frankie and JoAnne, but in their own time and way. It is worth mentioning that Steckler has written some of the filthiest montage of steamy action because "a picture is worth a thousand words and Plato's Retreat has a lot of pictures for you." No less than six couples make their way around one another and their partners as Ranger watches and "Big Tits" showers. One by one the couples' exercises crescendo and come to an end. This is only to have them all reignited and realigned in one room. Curiously, there is not one stitch of black garter material to be found anywhere in this writhing human pile-up.

Sandy and Angela retire to a private area of their own for that personal touch. Across the room, a brother and sister perform a bit of the old in-and-out for a small audience. The onlookers watch as the incestuous swinging siblings engage in their unholy act aboard a giant swing. Then, just as before, everyone and everything comes to an end.

If it were possible for Steckler to be proud of any one of his adult features, *Black Garters* should be it. The tagline: "See the wildest swapping and swinging sex capades of the year," and this time the advertising may have been spot on. It took Steckler 29 tries to get it right but *Black Garters*, at a pacey 60 minutes, delivers the goods just as any good porn should.

Debbie Does Las Vegas (1981)

Debbie Does Las Vegas is another Cindy Lou Sutters production with Steckler taking up the mike and providing the narration. Nude roller-skating queen of the year Debbie Truelove makes her way around the Las Vegas Strip and promises a guided tour through the city's seedier locales. "So, sit back and take in all of the action."

Debbie's first stop is the home of her friends Betty Sue Anna Mae and Bobby Joe Billy Mack. This couple is supposedly from somewhere down south as their ridiculous hillbilly-esque names suggest. Debbie spies on her friends as they conduct a largely vanilla display that nonetheless has her wide-eyed and grinning ear to ear.

Once Betty and Bobby conclude, Debbie's off and rolling again. She pays a visit to Andrea True and Helen Madigan as they provide a very different kind of show for Debbie's viewing pleasure. Even though Andrea was Debbie's first sexual conquest, she quickly tires of these two and beelines it back to her bedroom for some personal and private time with herself.

Next Debbie eyes in on an African-American couple (a rarity for a Steckler film) who give her just the type of presentation she had come to see. Steckler dubs in some fairly racist dialogue but also gives a shout-out to comedian Pigmeat Markham: "Here come the judge." Debbie moves on and catches an eyeful of two of her girlfriends who apparently just wanna have fun.

Debbie abandons this scene and arrives for her appointment with a psychiatrist who is helping her learn to relax and relieve stress. Here Steckler has more racist slurs tossed in, with Debbie's Native American ancestry the target this time. This type of tacky nonsense is not really normal for a Steckler film, though he has been guilty of chucking "beaner" around when describing a girl of Spanish descent. It is not very classy but then neither are these films.

After some more personal stress release (taking things in her own hand), Debbie watches a couple of porno actors rehearse their scenes together. Debbie approves and gives these two the green light and then finds herself smack dab in the middle of some action of her own.

Never quite satiated, Debbie looks on, in a hotel room, as three women have their way with a guy who then has his way with them.

In an act of sexual desperation, Debbie picks up a motorcyclist who refuses to remove his helmet and declares, "I've been captured by Injuns." More classy writing from Team Steckler. For reasons unknown, Debbie's psychiatrist peeps in on them and then decides to join the fun. "Hey, doc, get this Injun off me. She's skinned me alive." Good grief.

Steckler concludes this 62-minute sex loop compilation with Debbie seductively mawing a peeled banana. She then accidentally falls, busting her behind on the pavement. Obviously the *Debbie Does Las Vegas* title is aping the 1978 Bambi Woods porno *Debbie Does Dallas* and that is where the similarities begin and end. This one is not nearly as good as *Black Garters* but then, racist crap aside, it is a far cry better than *A Touch of Love*.

Indian Lady (1981)

Indian Lady closes out Cindy Lou Sutters' 1981 adult film trilogy with more roller skating from Steckler's current fave Debbie Truelove. The cast listing is identical to *A Touch of Love* with the exceptions of Toni Reenee, Charles Anthony and Jerry Davis. With so many familiar folks already in place, it should come as no surprise that Steckler has delivered yet another voyeur-and-sex-loops extravaganza.

Nudie photographer Charles (Charles Anthony) has his friend Jerry (Jerry Davis) pull off some poses with Sunshine (Toni Reenee). This is while Debbie gets on with her inexpensive jollies. Sunshine sports a full Indian warrior headdress as she attempts to orally keep Jerry's interest. Toni Reenee (aka Toni Alessandrini) would make one more film with Steckler two years later but weaved in and out of X- and R-rated features for the next decade and a half.

Sunshine spots Debbie in the wings and helps prepare her for some shots with her and Charles. This time Jerry mans

Poster art for *Debbie Does Las Vegas* (1981) (author's collection).

the camera for what will be his first of two performances for Steckler alongside his friend Anthony. Anthony appears to have called it quits on the porno industry by 1983.

Then, out of the blue, Steckler hands the mic over to Carolyn Brandt, "Debbie likes to witness other people making love. She has lots of friends in Las Vegas and each day she goes visiting in search of new and exciting ways to make love. Let's join her as she makes her first stop at John and Sarah's apartment."

Never mind the fact that this is Debbie's second stop, but it is also a recycled loop from *Deviates in Love* involving the brother-and-sister team Fred and Angie. John and Sarah provide Debbie with the proper ending; then the vixen on eight wheels tears across town to see her orgy-throwing friend Suzy (another *Deviates in Love* loop). "Debbie feels that this orgy could go on forever. Besides, she wants to get over to Harvey's pad."

Harvey and his new friend Sheila give Debbie what she came for and then it is back on the streets with the little skating lady. Debbie knows of a sleazy motel where Bobby and Mary will perform for her, just as the others have. Debbie has a knack for catching her friends in the act.

Debbie then catches Charlotte and Sonny as they slip in and out of a scene that has been lifted directly from *Deviates in Love*. Rick and Rene are next up and running in a sequence last seen in *Deviates in Love*. In a refreshing twist, Cindy and Louella keep things moving with a rehashed display from the *French* trilogy.

Debbie's on the move again, headed straight towards Jay and Felishia for a loop that was obviously shot in the '70s. The hair styles and the defiled couch with its wild patterns prove when this cheap thing was made. After Jay and Felishia achieve their goals, Debbie is off and rolling again.

Next stop is Bill and Stoney's where Debbie will finally join in on the action that has practically been promised since the film's beginning. Here Steckler's written dialogue again turns racist as Stoney undresses Debbie, muttering, "Hold still, li'l Injun. Now I'm gonna teach you the way of the whites." Then Bill and Debbie exchange, "Give that Injun a good one. Remember the Alamo." "That was Little Big Horn, you dumb shit."

Steckler and his films are nothing but bizarre but within the parameters of pornography it seems he let go of *some* tact that he appeared to have earlier in his film career. It goes without saying the adult film world is anything but tactful, though taking cheap potshots at someone's race, color or creed seems just that: cheap.

Race aside, what started out with shades of *Baby Bubbles* and *Teenage Hustler* wound up being more akin to *South of the Border* and *A Touch of Love* in terms of construction. Furthermore, within its 70-minute duration, nearly 50 percent of *Deviates in Love* is reprised. This makes *Indian Lady* a contender for Steckler hodgepodge of the decade. As it is, Steckler's film career, adult and otherwise, was running on fumes with only a handful of these types of babies left to go.

Steckler ushered 1982 in and out with a very minimal amount of film work. He managed to release two features and punch a clock for two other directors. *Skin Deep* and *Weekend Cowgirls* were his only cinematic offspring for the second year of the 1980s. The porno world was in the midst of a major upheaval that laid waste to some filmmakers and give rise to others.

But in the meantime, Steckler

worked as production manager for Gerd Wasmund's cash-in on *Footloose*: *Sexloose*. Then, more in Steckler's wheelhouse, a gig as cinematographer came up. This job was for Hal Freeman's *The Best Little Cathouse in Las Vegas,* an obvious cash-grab for *The Best Little Whore House in Texas.*

The adult film industry had a good ten-year run but the writing was on the filthy walls. So it is important to note that by the early '80s the video cassette was taking over the porno business. Further, there was very little need for 16mm or 35mm productions as grindhouse theaters had switched from film projectors to video.

Even though many crews had made the move to video production, it still was not profitable for the moviemaker to try and sell their product to the theaters. The old vanguard was gasping and grasping at anything and everything to stay afloat during this celluloid to magnetic media overthrow. Video rental stores were popping up everywhere and theater managers simply rented the tapes. Those make-a-fast-buck practitioners merely projected the movie for however long it was profitable. Then later, after figuring in the late fees, they would return the rewound product. Ultimately, theater owners, pornographers and producers realized that production values and the vast quality difference between film and video simply did not matter. Perhaps Steckler had always been on to something as far as his concern for quality.

Skin Deep (1982)

Rhonda Jo Petty stars as herself in a cast which includes Miss World Burlesque Toni Alessandrini (credited here as Toni Reenee). The plot involves the exposing of the day-to-day goings-on of porn stars on their days off. What do adult actors do with idle time? They practice their craft, that is what they do. Feisty Rhonda is riding this sex train straight into an awaiting tunnel.

Rhonda Jo and Toni Reenee attend a debauched pool party and play a little "hide and seek" with an English movie director who is a bit on the stiff side. Then actress Darling Darla stretches her "talents" in an unimaginable and unforgettable act of "sexercise." The pool boy shows up for work and is lasciviously "worked up" by an enterprising script girl. The lass was looking to get out from behind the pen and in front of the camera.

Some of the gang are tired of getting chlorine in their eyes and move the party to a lake. The aquatic antics turn into nautical naughtiness that turns into one hot and wet orgy. This human assemblage, which is connected in every way possible, concludes *Skin Deep*. Steckler directed this 72-minute "educational" film using the Randall Hayes alias for the second and last time.

Weekend Cowgirls (1982)

For *Weekend Cowgirls,* Steckler ... er ... Cindy Lou Sutters has Debbie Truelove (credited here as Debbie True Love) trade in her roller skates for a tiny moped. Debbie, along with being a weekend cowgirl, shirks a helmet in favor of a cowboy hat. What's interesting is, Debbie never loses her head gear, unlike Daniel from *Blood Shack* who cannot maintain his even while standing perfectly still.

Steckler's voyeur formula is in play here as Debbie gads around an Arizona desert scene spying on friends and neighbors as they have sex. Somehow Steckler convinced his ex-wife Carolyn to yet again sit with a microphone providing a voice for his increasingly unfunny and racist dialogue (more "Injun" crap) and narration. It seems as though Steckler has lost his sense of fun and humor.

The film begins with Debbie tooling the highway and locating her first point of perversion on a dusty old ranch. Here she watches a couple (Starlyn Simone and George Peters) in a scene straight from *"Daisy Lay": Ozark Virgin?* For no apparent reason, Debbie next visits the runway of an airport to watch planes land. She then scoots over to Andrea's (Andrea True) pad where she is about to give some business to a local chef named Clem (Charles Orlando). Clem says he would, "like to taste something spicier." Once Clem has had his fill of Andrea, Debbie literally cartwheels over to Elizabeth's (Nina Fause) house. Here she witnesses Elizabeth's oral specialty on male stripper Percy Rodriguez (Franklin Anthony).

Bruce's place is up next and Debbie's sure he will have a man with him, but today she is wrong. Debbie finds this scenario quite interesting and contemplates what it might be like to make it with Bruce. There is no time to fantasize. Debbie has to catch a couple of siblings doing what would probably get them grounded. "Damn, sis, playing doctor is more fun than Space Invaders."

Debbie's friends Kelly (Kelly Guthrie) and Pam are having a poolside party that involves skinny dipping, stag films, tether ball and topless swinging of the playground fashion. The outdoor exercises give way to indoor liveliness where everyone wears cowboy hats with little else while hillbilly banjo music threatens to never stop.

Soon Debbie abandons that scene for her boyfriend Whitey's place. Whitey also wears little to nothing but some western headgear and the banjo music

from the previous sequence has followed Debbie here. Steckler takes this feature out with a few more words from Carolyn the narrator: "Debbie's determined to make the whole world forget Linda Lovelace. At the rate she's going, it won't take long. But now it's the end of our story and we hope you've enjoyed the latest adventure of Debbie Truelove as much as we enjoyed bringing it to you. As they say in American Injun lingo, 'Sayonara.'"

At the film's conclusion, one more dig is delivered involving Debbie's native American heritage. Steckler probably thought he was just being cute, but in 2022 it just does not translate well at all. Still, over time, Steckler seems to have lost touch with the zany side of himself which helped create madcap characters that populated his early adult films. Long gone are the days of vampires, serial killers, demons, witches and (s)exorcists.

It is also worth noting that Debbie Truelove has worn the exact same red Miller Lite t-shirt and roller skates for at least four of these features. A case for a continuity *faux pas* could be made, but it is more likely Steckler shot all of Debbie's scenes at one time. He then later dispersed them accordingly throughout subsequent films. It is a cheap shot for sure, but then, when it comes to his films, Steckler is a cheapskate—for sure.

Las Vegas Erotica (1983)

For Steckler, 1983 proved to be an even less productive year than the previous regarding film production. *Plato's Retreat West* was the final chapter in the Cindy Lou Sutters collection while *Las Vegas Erotica* was produced under the Sergio Leonardo banner. Director James Kenelm Clarke called upon Steckler's cinematography skills for his comedy crime drama *Funny Money* and that would be it for Ray in 1983.

Steckler launches directly into *Las Vegas Erotica* with the Las Vegas travelogue footage he has used so many other times before. For years he has shown his raincoat crowd Caesar's Palace, the Oasis, the Imperial Palace, the Sahara and the Flamingo with little regard for what his audience might actually have paid their money to see.

Then predictably, and without haste, the sexy hum of Carolyn Brandt's voice can be heard reciting Steckler's narration:

> Well, hello there. I'm your tour guide. My name is Raven and I have only one job and that's to show you a good time, and that's exactly what I intend to do. You'll see the fabulous city of Las Vegas from the inside, through the eyes of the people who work here. We'll see the entertainers and what they do for entertainment. We'll see the restaurant and what they like to eat best. Then you'll see—well, you'll find out as we go along.

The tried-and-true voyeur-tour scenario has been set up but Raven wants to give the viewers a tour of herself before hitting the streets. This quickie leads to familiar scenes of Debbie Truelove (this time as Charlene) roller skating around the Las Vegas strip in search of something and someone to spy on. Charlene decides to give Lorna a visit, but she has a visitor of her own. Here Steckler reuses a loop last seen in *Debbie Does Las Vegas*.

Once Lorna and what's-his-face have finished their titillating tangle, Steckler turns the camera back to Raven. Raven continues her tour of herself before the film switches to a German restaurant and the after-hours exploits of the staff. Once the restaurant staff have finished their dessert, Raven reveals more of herself for the camera.

Frenchy (Darling Darla) and Gary (Jerry Davis) are up next for a bit of action. Simultaneously Andre (Charles Antony) and John (John Colt) make their moves for Rhonda (Rhonda Jo Petty) and Terri (Toni Renee). This foursome moves from the pool to a bedroom to attempt petting one another dry. Some girl named Samantha snoops around peeking at the quartet and gets so worked up that she has to give Lester, the pool boy, an additional job to do.

Steckler then cuts to Tamara (Sandy Sunshine) flitting about Las Vegas on her well-known roller skates. Tamara makes a stop at her friend Diane's place to see what she and her boyfriend, of the day, are *up* to. Steckler provides the voice of Diane's friend during this loop. Raven and her secret male friend give the viewers a smidgen more of what is going on in their room and then it is off to the movies for a reprise of some *Deviates in Love* footage.

More *Deviates in Love* sequences follow before the film returns to Raven's room and what it is she and her beau feel the viewers long to see. Steckler simply cannot resist introducing new characters even at the 70-minute mark of an 80-minute movie. So, now we have Shelia (on skates of course) giving two rock musicians, Michael and LaVonn, the wanton eye. "They have the best rhythm in town." Again, Steckler is the voice of the male participant.

Steckler takes the film out with more exploratory footage of Raven and narration: "I hope you've enjoyed this outsiders tour. I know I have." So ends another Steckler loop carrier in a long line of Steckler loop carriers. The more Steckler reclaims and reprocesses old footage, the more difficult it is to discern one film from the other. Perhaps this was by design or perhaps Steckler simply did not care.

Plato's Retreat West (1983)

Plato's Retreat West opens in true Steckler form with Sandy Sunshine roller-skating her way to the film's namesake. Steckler, giving his ex-wife a long-deserved break, provides the narration. After he introduces Ms. Sunshine, Natasha (Desiré Elms) and Tony (R.J. Reynolds) are brought into the picture. Inside the club, the camera settles on club owner Mike Ranger, and narrator Steckler claims to be him. "So why don't you, the audience, just lay back and watch the wildest and most exciting sexcapades ever filmed in Hollywood's number one sex factory Plato's Retreat West."

What follows are scenes culled directly from Steckler's 1976 film *Sex Rink*. Killer Miller (Gene Miller) and "Too Tall" Teresa do their staircase boogie while "Big Tits" Malloy (Denise Swenson) and April Schwartz (Millie Moon) skate in the buff. On another staircase, Natasha takes matters into her own hands as Ranger looks on wide-eyed.

An unsatiated Natasha follows "Too Tall" Teresa into the locker room where things get so heated that Killer Miller notices and joins them. In another room, "Big Tits" and April get to know one another better and a peering Ranger eats a sandwich. "Big Tits" and April disengage long enough to run upstairs to join a ten-person naked pile-up.

Mike polishes off his sandwich just in time for Sandy Sunshine to do some polishing of her own. Sandy then turns her attentions to Killer Miller while Mike gives Natasha the time of day. "Big Tits" abandons the human pile for a little one-on-one with some scruffy dude. Sandy decides to do the same after she has sent Killer Miller away happy.

More nude skating is followed by the tired footage of Mike looking in a mirror and brushing his hair. After the fun of skating wears off, five girls leave the dance floor for some heavy petting of their own. This scene segues into another group effort which threatens to outdo the film's previous pile-up. Mike oversees the festivities and eats more sandwiches.

Steckler abruptly brings the whole 60-minute breezy affair to an end. "That's all, folks. Hope you all come in and see us some time soon." Other than an alternate narration, dialogue and sound effects, this thing is basically a re-edit of the far superior *Sex Rink* which really was not all that superior to begin with.

Cathouse Fever (1984)

Cathouse Fever marks Steckler's only known work on a film in 1984 and here he takes no credit as co-director with Chris Warfield, who is masquerading as Billy Thornburg. Warfield started off the early '70s as director of a couple of R-rated features, *Teenage Innocence* (1973) and *Teenage Seductress* (1975). From here he directed another dozen X-rated films over the next decade. This includes *Black Silk Stockings* (1978), *Sheer Panties* (1979) and *Garters and Lace* (1980).

Cathouse Fever follows Becky (Becky Savage), who is a very shy and modest secretary from the Los Angeles area. Becky spends her free time fantasizing about sex. These fantasies are growing old and Becky needs a way to make them a reality. It is speculated that adult film legend Colleen Brennan provided the voice of Becky's thoughts. "I get so lonely sometimes that my body just aches. So, a fantasy gets me by until the next time—and the next—and the next."

This narration gives way to Becky at a candlelight dinner with lover Herschel Savage. The lover seduces her in a way she can only dream about. In real life, Ms. Savage starred in over 50 adult titles while Mr. Savage miraculously racked up over 1,000 using 50 or more aliases. Once Becky's imagination has run its course, the voice-over continues: "As I said, I fantasize—a lot."

Becky takes to the beach (which is awfully familiar territory for Steckler) with her guitar and her thoughts:

> I saw this "Help Wanted" ad for a cathouse in Las Vegas. So I gathered up my courage and after a couple of glasses of wine, I called. I told the madam I had great legs and would that qualify me for the job? She said, "When can you get here?" So now, I've got a problem. On the one hand, I want to do it. On the other hand, I'm scared to death and I just know that If I wait I'm going to talk myself out of it.

From the beach and Becky's brain, the film moves straight to Vegas with some new travelogue footage of Sin City's Strip. This footage is credited to Ziggy Zigowitz, but could this be a silly pseudonym for Steckler? Fact is, this film looks nothing like a Steckler production but there is enough by way of cross-over cast and the film's general silliness to help validate the claim that he co-directed.

In Vegas, someone's camera follows actor Tommy Drake (credited here as Gordon Miller) into the cathouse of Rhonda (Rhonda Jo Petty), the establishment's madam. Working girls Sherri (Marla Lee Gardner) and Brandy (Laverne Shields) immediately descend upon the young man and his money. Tommy's mouth is taped shut and he is brandishing a letter from his wife stating he will not speak to any girls today. Steckler favorite Debbie Truelove (credited here as Chica Moreno) will be using *her* mouth and this time there are no roller skates in sight.

Mr. Tape Mouth is lead away to another room just in time for Mickey Macho (John Colt) to enter in search of some new action. Becky is the "new action" and things get seriously heated seriously quick. "I came. I saw and I came again." Becky appears to be quite pleased with her first day on the job.

Brandy leads Tex (Jerry Davis) to Sherri's room for a little cowboy-type one-on-one fun as Madam Rhonda balances the books with her accountant (Art Parker) the best way *he* knows how. In the end he got *his* and the I.R.S. got screwed. Then Debbie and Sherri decide to spend some private time on themselves; however, before they can finish, the continuity of the film begins to derail: Now Debbie and Sherri are with Brandy and Mr. Tape Mouth while Rhonda is giving it to Mickey Macho for every dime he has. Once Rhonda finishes off the Macho Man, she departs for Tex's room where he and Becky are at it cowboy-and-Indian-style. Becky gives Rhonda a cat bath before finding herself in a sunken tub with bubbles and Brandy.

Becky is having second thoughts about her decision to make a life at a brothel, "I was beginning to think that I'd get the fever if I didn't leave the cathouse and come home." Mickey Macho's currently with Brandy and could not care less about Becky's reservations. "What I really want is some guy to love me and bring me flowers."

Then there's a Stecklarian moment: Becky picks up her 12-string guitar, begins strumming a tune and dreaming of Rick Cassidy. In her mind, they do their things to each other in an empty black room bathed in red, green, purple and blue lights. The setting is a total flashback to *Sinthia: The Devil's Doll* and the dream sequence in *The Incredibly Strange Creatures*. This scene, along with the Vegas Strip footage and six cross-over cast members, are additional indicators that Steckler had a hand in this production.

Becky leaves the rainbow-colored fantasy island of her mind. "As I said, I fantasize—a lot." She returns to the office from which she emerged earlier as though she had never left L.A. and perhaps she had not. Paralleling this notion is Steckler leaving this 78-minute feature *and* (presumably) the adult film world, returning to his former position as quirky though legit filmmaker.

While Steckler was no pioneer in the adult film world, he was there in the genre's infancy with six features of his own. He trotted those films out in 1971, a year before *Deep Throat* and the short-lived porno chic phenomenon. Also, it cannot be stressed enough that, for years, Steckler vehemently denied any involvement with these pictures. However, the advent of the world wide web helped begin the dissolve of Steckler's coveted safe space.

Steckler was unwilling to broach this subject even as late as 2006, just two years before his death. Romeo Carey, the son of Timothy Carey, was interviewing Steckler for a documentary concerning *his* father and *The World's Greatest Sinner*. Steckler knew Carey's father well and worked in many capacities on said film, but still presented this request: "Promise me you won't put him in any porno films. Give me your word." The full interview can be heard on the *Romeo Carey Podcast* which originally aired November 15, 2020. It is a possibility that Romeo was not even aware of Steckler's adult film career—but he is now.

Steckler's adult features are essentially a connective tissue to a large part of his work and should not be overlooked, particularly when examining his films from the '70s and '80s when he weaved in and out of the adult industry. Steckler eventually came to terms with the fact that people *could* and would find out about (what he believed was) his checkered cinematic past. So, while he would admit to creating *some* adult titles, he never discussed the whos, whats, whens or wheres. Still, with Steckler providing his voice for at least six of these films and Carolyn Brandt pulling down nearly 20, it is impossible to deny that these *are* his works—good, bad or otherwise.

Part Three

Unfinished Films, Unreleased Films and Compilations

Ray Dennis Steckler's proclivity towards employing every inch of film he had exposed has left him a curious filmography that is, at times, quite difficult to navigate. As early as *The Lemon Grove Kids Meet the Monsters* (1967–69), Steckler told interviewers that he had enough leftover footage to compile two more entries into the "franchise." Odd that he did not pursue this endeavor as by all accounts the *Lemon Grove Kids* roadshow was a success. Steckler instead focused on films that received little to no screen time and scores of bottom-feeder adult features.

By the early 1970s, Steckler's film career was on the wane. *Body Fever* had performed poorly, as did *Blood Shack*. Simply perusing Steckler's cinematic timeline will reveal these failures to be the catalysts for his making over three dozen pornographic films. As stated previously, Steckler tried desperately to distance himself from his rated-X past so it is impossible to know if he actually enjoyed making them, but he did make a lot of them.

Still, in and around all of these problematic times behind the camera and in the editing bay, Steckler attempted other projects that either fell short of his vision, money or interest. In all likelihood, it was all three factors that shifted several of these enterprises into the realm of the unfinishable. Never short on words, Steckler told any interviewer willing to listen about films that were in the works. Ultimately, however, these things never saw the light of day.

What follows is a compendium of films and videos that Steckler started and aborted. What is also included are titles that are merely compilations of materials that Steckler had lying around. The term "cinematic decoupage" comes to mind when attempting to describe much of Steckler's output in the '70s and '80s. The definition of "decoupage" is: the art or technique of decorating something with cut-outs of paper, linoleum, plastic or other flat material over which varnish or lacquer is applied. Steckler used "cut-outs" of "plastic" or film, as it is in this case, and "varnished" the finished product with a new title and/or cover art.

Some additional odds and ends are mentioned because there seemed to be no other proper place for them. Also, as with so many of Steckler's films, it is nearly impossible to pinpoint the actual date of production. So, having mentioned that, please know that every effort has been made to keep this guide as linear as possible. Also be aware that this is in no way a complete list. Even an in-depth archaeological dig through Steckler's vaults would only serve to generate far more questions than answers.

So getting on with it, Steckler had spoken at some length about his incomplete sequel to *Body Fever,* called *Bloody Jack the Ripper.* This film featuring the return of gumshoe Charlie Smith was lensed during the time between *Blood Shack* and *The Hollywood Strangler Meets the Skid Row Slasher.* This serial killer film is not likely to rear its head and it is a shame as it would be one more time to see Carolyn Brandt and Herb Robins on screen.

Also circa 1972, Steckler shot the first footage for *Revenge of the Ripper.* This is the film he deliberately planned to finish ten years later, but obviously did not. Then in February 1974, Ron Haydock reported in *The Monster Times* issue #30 (p. 29) that Steckler was working on a film entitled *The Bog People* and that he was certain "that it will maintain the same level of quality found in Ray's earlier films."

Next up, *Rufus Potter's Hooker Scam* is a 19-minute sex comedy with a tiny cast and another Carolyn Brandt narration. Charles Orlando returns from *Baby Bubbles* for his second of four gigs with Steckler. Sunny Boyd makes short work of this film and only one other with Steckler—*Teenage Hustler.* In fact, Boyd and Orlando's character names, Trixie and English Billy Boynton respectively, are the same in both films. The character name cross-over suggests that this is merely a shortened re-edit of *Teenage Hustler.*

A minimal amount of information exists on *Rufus Potter's Hooker Scam,* but with such a short running time, there cannot be much to know to begin with. What Steckler's intentions were or where an under-20-minute distillation of a cut-rate porno might be screened is the question. Still, Steckler would employ his waste-not-want-not recycling routine many times over the coming years.

In the early '80s, Steckler told Boyd Rice of *Incredibly Strange Films* that he was compiling footage for his ode to Hollywood called *Hollyweird.* Then in 1983, he told Johnny Legend in *Fangoria* #28 that he was working on a picture with the title *Warning: No Trespassing!* So many projects, so little money, so little time.

Face of Evil, considered a lost Steckler film, is merely a 33-minute edit of footage from *Red Heat, Perverted Passion, Sex Rink* and *The Hollywood Strangler Meets the Skid Row Slasher. Slashed,* another missing piece of the Steckler puzzle, clocks in at 30 minutes with frames culled from *Red Heat, Perverted Passion* and *Las Vegas Serial Killer.* All of the hardcore action has been removed from these, along with any reason whatsoever for Steckler to misuse his time on such efforts.

Still, *some light* can be shed on these two mysterious featurettes. Steckler shot a beginning, a middle and an end to what became *Face of Evil,* which had been the original working title for *The Incredibly Strange Creatures.* The film was to star the director's friend Will Long, who died of hepatitis shortly after filming began. Then, stripper Lovie Goldmine, entered the picture but skipped town before filming could be completed. Steckler was left to quasi-complete the work with his old standby Carolyn Brandt, who stepped in to double for the estranged stripper. Then in an experiment gone awry, Steckler cross-cut footage from *Face of Evil* to the other featurette *Slashed.* He then made 25 VHS copies of each and promptly destroyed the masters. Just as well.

In 1986, Jeffrey C. Hogue, attorney at law turned film producer, approached Ted V. Mikels in hopes of getting Hogue's ambitious exploitation movie project *Angel of Vengeance* off the ground. Ted's projected budget for the movie involving rape, revenge, a military outpost setting, a biker gang and lots of explosions and gore was too expensive at nearly a quarter of a million dollars. Hogue turned to Ray Dennis Steckler who said 20 grand would do the trick.

Rumor has it that Steckler spent the first two days of production shooting 16mm footage of locations and streets and passing cars. As Steckler recalled, "I was hired to do a Ray Dennis Steckler movie. Hogue wanted a Jeffrey C. Hogue movie. I gave it to Ted." Perhaps Hogue simply was not interested in more of Steckler's travelogue footage.

As things progressed, Steckler's projected budget increased drastically when the location was shifted from Las Vegas to Northern California. Also, a larger cast and crew were employed, making Hogue and associate producer Craig T. Keller extremely unhappy, as the changes were putting them in a difficult financial position. The businessmen were about to shirk their businesslike demeanor; fortunately the answer was waiting in the wings. Ted V. Mikels was back on the set.

For my book *Film Alchemy*, Mikels told me how the changeover was handled (p. 112):

> I told them I would only do it if Ray said that it was okay. I went to him and said, "Ray, they want me to take over directing this movie, but I won't do it without your good graces." He said, "Ted, we'll be out of here by tomorrow afternoon. Good luck with the movie." That was it, I was in

VHS box art for *War Cat* (1987). Steckler was originally hired by Jeffrey C. Hogue to direct this rape-revenge movie but was quickly replaced by Ted V. Mikels (author's collection).

charge of directing *War Cat*, which was at the time under the working title, *Angel of Vengeance*."

Very little remained of Steckler's mark on the film but the biker gang *was* called the Thrill Killers as a plug for his 1964 feature of the same name. Mikels relayed one more anecdote involving Steckler and what was to become *War Cat* in *Film Alchemy* (p. 112):

> I'll tell you this, and I'm not really proud of it, but it did happen. On my first day of shooting, after I'd taken over the project, the girl playing Tina literally got on her knees, kissed my hand and thanked me for taking over directing the film. Again, I'm not proud of this, as Ray is a friend, but it did happen that way. But I did appreciate the fact that she was pleased to have me as director of the movie.

In the late '80s, Steckler amped up his video compilation game. In *Cult Movies* #8, interviewer James Elliot Singer asked him about his ongoing production of his "glamor video series" which featured local models and actresses (p. 31). "Originally I just took the video camera to tape some rehearsals, kinda fun. I thought it would be kind of neat to be able that night to look at something of that day since I have to send the film to the lab. And then I thought, 'Well, what about somebody in Peru, Indiana, who always wondered what it would be like to be involved with a B-movie or to audition for these movies?'" (Considered the circus capital of the world, Peru, Indiana has been home to the Peru Amateur Circus since 1960. Little wonder that this quaint town of 11,000 inhabitants was right on the tip of Steckler's tongue, what with his obsession with carnivals and the circus.)

Another shelved project involved the return of Ron Jason and Chris Cave from *The Las Vegas Serial Killer* for *Las Vegas Thrill Killers* was supposed to be released in 1993. As pointed out in the *Las Vegas Serial Killer* chapter, Steckler intended to keep actor Pierre Agostino busy with more *Strangler* sequels like *The Return of the Hollywood Strangler* and *The Son of the Hollywood Strangler*. Then Steckler busied himself by re-editing many of his films, removing the color, shortening their running times and changing several of the titles. The list is as follows: *Wild Ones on Wheels* became *Desert Maniacs*, *The Thrill Killers* became *Mad Dog Click*, *Rat Pfink a Boo Boo* became *Rock and Roll Superheroes*, *Sinthia: The Devi's Doll* became *Teenage She-Devil*, *The Chooper* returned to its other alias *Blood Shack*, *Body Fever* became *Deadlocked* and *Las Vegas Serial Killer* became *The Hollywood Strangler in Las Vegas*.

In 1988, Steckler was the focus of an episode of a 12-part British series called *The Incredibly Strange Film Show* which was no doubt named after his 1963 film. Hosted by Jonathan Ross, it featured other directors including Mikels, Herschell Gordon Lewis and Russ Meyer, just to name a few. At the time, Steckler was working on a film titled *Dark Alleys in a Well-Lit City* with Ron Jason as a Las Vegas psycho sporting a leather biker jacket with "Thrill Killers M.C." emblazoned on the back. This film, perhaps never finished, has not seen the light of day.

Also in 1993, musician Boyd Rice teamed with former Strawberry Switchblade member Rose McDowall to record an album of dark-tinged 1960s pop tunes for Mute Records. The two christened themselves Spell and the album was called *Seasons in the Sun*. Mute execs felt that their cover of "Big Red Balloon" (originally by Lee Hazelwood and Nancy Sinatra in 1971) was hip enough to be the album's first single. The Mute people also wanted a video made for the song, and Rice wanted Steckler to direct it.

Rice, McDowall and her husband were all flown to Las Vegas to commence work on the project. Steckler had lots of ideas and the McDowalls did as well. This combination (or rather collision) of views pretty much doomed the endeavor from the get-go. Then for reasons unknown, even to Rice himself, Steckler saw fit to cut in sequences of his daughters Bailey and Morgan dancing around in silly witch get-ups. They play a game of Ring Around the Rosie with McDowall, who is also in witchy garb. These sequences are reminiscent of Linda and Laura playing musical chair 22 years earlier in *Blood Shack*.

As the video moves along, there are nonsensical scenes of a pensive Rice staring into nothingness and then running around aimlessly in the Nevada desert. Finally, as the video and song come to an end, Rice inflates a hot air balloon. While it *is* big, the damned thing is not red. As Rice put it, "At times it looked like a Ray Dennis Steckler movie and at other times it looked like a Ray Dennis Steckler home movie. Mute spent a lot of money for something that was completely unusable." (Rice also mentioned that in the early '90s, he and Steckler worked on a *Rat Pfink a Boo Boo* sequel entitled *Son of a Rat Pfink*.)

Around this time, Steckler opened Mascot Video, which stocked all manner of videos but specialized in his output. The store offered director's cuts of Steckler's films plus newly produced documentaries and compilation tapes. Some titles included: *The Incredibly Strange Ray Dennis Steckler*, *Carolyn Brandt: Queen of Cult*, *Steckler Mania*, *Steckler Interviews*, *Ray Dennis Steckler Is "The Teenage Psycho": The Steckler Collection*, *The Making of* The Incredibly Strange Creatures Who Stopped Living and Became Mixed Up Zombies!!?, *Ray Dennis Steckler's Reading, Pennsylvania: Take One*, *A Tribute to Ron Haydock* and *Two Lost Films by Ray Dennis Steckler*.

In 1997, Steckler appeared alongside some more well-known members of the horror industry (Joe Dante, Roger Corman, Wes Craven *et al.*) in the ten-hour British miniseries *Clive Barker's A-Z of Horror*. That same year, he made a film entitled *Summer Fun* (the title being the film's plot). It was also known as *Camp Robinson*. This low- to no-budgeter starred his daughter Bailey Steckler along with other friends and family members. Wife Katherine Steckler was on hand as associate producer and Herb Robins made his final screen appearance. There is no evidence that this G-rated silent movie was ever released other than through Mascot Video. Steckler's next project, to be abandoned, was entitled *77*

VHS box art for *Steckler Interviews: Volume #1* (1993). Interviewer John Roberts conducts an hour-long Q&A session with Steckler (author's collection).

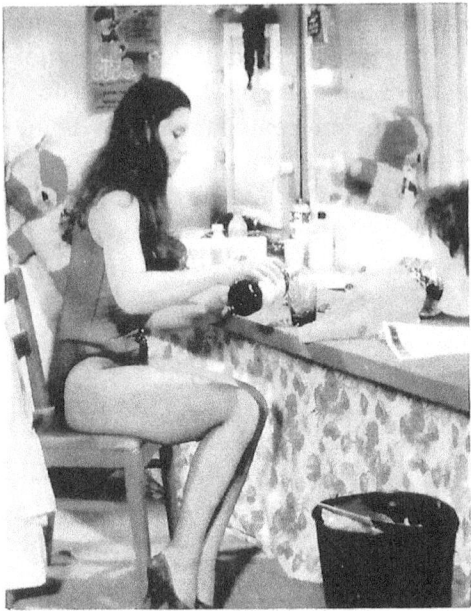

VHS box art for *Carolyn Brandt: Queen of Cult* (1994), a 60-minute compilation of Brandt highlights from Steckler's films (author's collection).

Sunset Park. He felt it was the most beautiful park in the country and he hoped to dedicate a document to one of Las Vegas' best-kept secrets. The *Las Vegas Sun* newspaper reported on August 12, 1998, that Steckler had also turned his camera towards former Utopia band member Todd Rundgren; the article failed to mention the title of the music video.

One very special evening was captured on tape at the Crest Theater in Sacramento, California, on the third day of August 2002 when a screening of *Rat Pfink a Boo Boo* was presented. Steckler had arranged for a tribute to his beautiful *Rat Pfink* star Carolyn Brandt, and he, Carolyn and Herb Robins posed for pictures and signed autographs. The Steckler girls Laura, Morgan and Bailey, were on hand to videotape the affair, which Ray edited down to two hours. Steckler released copies of the VHS in 2003 as *Ray Dennis Steckler Presents a Tribute to Carolyn Brandt*.

In the time leading up to Steckler's death, he was working on a multi-part series on his hometown Reading, Pennsylvania, and his friends and colleagues there who impacted his life. In 2005, Steckler and Ted V. Mikels made cameo appearances in Andre Perkowski's experimental film *I Was a Teenage Beatnik*. He also made his extension to *The Incredibly Strange Creatures* (for just under four grand, which was a tenth of the original's budget), calling it *One More Time*. This is another multi-media amalgam of travelogue frames, flashbacks to the original film and some newly shot Digital8 video footage.

The set-up is bare bones: Steckler's Jerry, nearly 70 years old, has nightmares of his past. He visits a psychiatrist and a busty tarot card reader to help him sort things out. These sequences run parallel to sequences of Steckler attempting to raise money for the very movie on the screen. It is a reality vs. non-reality motif that is reasonably effective in its obvious self-reflection.

Steckler's last cinematic go-around is still not without its charms. There is some fun footage of the Santa Cruz Beach Boardwalk (standing in for the Pike in Long Beach) and the Giant Dipper roller coaster (standing in for the Cyclone Racer). All this while a garage rock act, the A-Bones, churn out their rendition of Frank Zappa's "The World's Greatest Sinner." The song, backed with "Shanty Tramp," was released as a seven-inch single by Giant Claw in 1993.

Jerry takes in a floor show featuring a rockabilly cat by the name of Johnny Legend. Legend and his band perform H.G. Lewis' "The South's Gonna Rise Again," Ron Haydock's "Rat Fink" and a tribute to Arch Hall, Jr., called "Night of the Sadist." Then Jerry takes a seat at a pizza parlor where several patrons are attired in *Incredibly Strange Creatures* t-shirts. To the very end, Steckler rarely missed an opportunity to self-promote.

At one point, Ron Haydock's "I Stand Alone" plays as Steckler turns his camera once again to the streets and captures the hustle and bustle of California and Vegas. Katherine, Bailey and Linda Steckler make brief appearances and then Haydock's "Big Boss A-Go-Go Party" takes the movie out. Steckler chose to wrap this one with a recap montage and outtakes. The movie, copyrighted 2008, and it is less than incredible and more unbelievable.

It is obvious that Steckler longed to remain in the entertainment industry by any means necessary. He was always shooting footage and editing old and new sequences together in an effort to create something unique for his audience. It did not always work, but his tenacity always held it together. Even so, many of these later projects never saw an official release and are therefore very difficult if not impossible to track down.

Steckler, who had been fighting heart disease for several years, died of cardiac arrest on January 7, 2009, at the age of 70. He was buried at the Palm Mortuary–Cemetery Green Valley in Las Vegas. He was survived by his wife of 23 years, Katherine Steckler; two daughters from his first marriage, Linda Steckler of Maui, Hawaii, and Laura Steckler of Sunland, California; two daughters from his second marriage, Morgan and Bailey Steckler, both of Las Vegas; his sister, Judy Conrad of Reading; and two grandchildren.

Michael Weldon, who had largely championed Steckler's films, said in an interview after the director's passing, "He had this way of mixing childish things with really bizarre, kind of adult-oriented things. You didn't know quite where he was coming from." A MetaFilter Community blogger insisted, "He is not dead. He lives on in every dark glimmering heart of movie maniacs; his soul flickering across the surfaces of corneas and psyches scarred by the brilliance of his fiendishly bloody, brilliant cinema." That is a good way to send off Ray Dennis Steckler and his incredibly strange film career.

Part Four

Homage and Memorabilia

Homage: A Global Send-Up

Only a handful of golden era exploitation directors have managed to impact popular culture (most notably pop music) the world over. Russ Meyer, Herschell Gordon Lewis, Ted V. Mikels and Ed Wood all have numerous bands named after their well-loved films as well as a multitude of songs. Ray Dennis Steckler is no exception. The following list is primarily culled from the musical side of things but there have been other, non-musical shows of respect to the maverick filmmaker.

A common misconception is that punk band The Misfits recorded a cover of "Rat Fink" in honor of Steckler's film. In reality, "Rat Fink" was recorded in 1963 (two years before Steckler's film) by comedy singer Allan Sherman. Sherman's tune was a send-up of hot rod artist Ed "Big Daddy" Roth's seminal character Rat Fink.

It is certainly possible that the Misfits covered the song to pay homage to both "Big Daddy" Roth *and* Steckler. A similar argument could be made for heavy metal band White Zombie's "Rat Finks, Suicide Tanks and Cannibal Girls." Like the Misfits, White Zombie (and in particular Rob Zombie) are fairly transparent when it comes to their adoration for low-budget cinema and '50s–'60s hot rod culture.

My Life with the Thrill Kill Kult's main members, Groovy Mann and Buzz McCoy, have never been silent about their affinity for bizarre cinema. This leaves little doubt as to what influenced this Chicago-based electronic-dance band's name. Similarities to *The Thrill Killers* aside, the very length of the band's name could be seen as another nod to Steckler and his passion for long movie titles. In fact, My Life with the Thrill Kill Kult originated as such—a movie. Also, their 1997 "Dope Doll Jungle" music video is an obvious tip of the hat to *Incredibly Strange Creatures* with its beachside locales and goofy rubber monster masks.

A Swedish punk act, the Nomads, released an album and a single for their musically instrumental high-five to Steckler called "Rat Fink a Boo Boo." The band *almost* corrected the title on this Shake It Records 1984 release. Then Estrus Records' Mono Men covered the Nomads instrumental in 1989 and shortened the title to simply "Rat Fink." In the mid–1980s, Prehensile Records released the album *Parts Unknown* by Dementia Precox. This industrial-noise project hails from Dayton, Ohio, and recorded a track called "The Incredibly Strange Creatures Who Stopped Living and Became Mixed-Up Zombies."

Pushing things into the 1990s, John

Waters prominently placed the Camp Video release of *Incredibly Strange Creatures* on a video store shelf in his 1994 film *Serial Mom*. In 1995, the Canadian garage rock band Forbidden Dimension released their album *Somebody Down There Likes Me* for Cargo records with the little ditty "Bloodshack."

Then two years later, Indiana's industrial metal act Sutur sampled the *Thrill Killers* line "One of the many caught in the web of non-reality ... non-reality." To great effect they punctuated and concluded their song "Interior Dishonor" with, "Unfortunately, Joe has refused to accept the world of reality and has found himself trapped." Sutur also sampled numerous lines from *The World's Greatest Sinner* for their 1999 CD *Cured by Porno*. Sutur guitarist and keyboardist Chris Chambers never missed an opportunity to wear an H.G. Lewis, Ted V. Mikels or Ray Dennis Steckler t-shirt during sound checks and/or encores.

In 1999, Inner Psyche Productions released an electronic-experimental compilation of various artists titled Hallucinogenic Hypnovision. A year later, surf rockers Zorros Petardos Salvajes from Buenos Aires, Argentina, covered the Nomads' "Rat Fink a Boo Boo" instrumental for their 1999 live *Pool Once* album.

Hi-wattage horror-punks The Creeping Cruds unleashed their debut album on SPAT! Records in 2004. The title: *The Incredibly Strange People Who Stopped Living and Became ... the Creeping Cruds*. Cruds guitarist Jeano Roid Coffinberry has stated that their upcoming studio release would contain an aural ode to Steckler in the form of a tune entitled "Cash Flagg." Cincinnati is host to an indie rock band calling themselves Cash Flagg; their debut album was released in 2008.

In 2009, actor-stuntman extraordinaire Gary Kent released his autobiography *Shadows & Light* which features a *Thrill Killers* photo of Steckler leveling a gun at Kent. Under the Westerbergs

Album art for Forbidden Dimension's *I Kiss Your Shadow* (1998) E.P. with a Ron Haydock/The Chooper depicted on the back cover. For a Steckler double-dip, the last track is entitled "Blood Valley Days," which was lifted from an article that Ron Haydock wrote on Steckler for *The Monster Times* #30 (1974) (courtesy Tom Bagley).

Album art for The Creeping Cruds' *The Incredibly Strange People Who Stopped Living and Became ... the Creeping Cruds* (2004) (courtesy Jeano Coffinberry).

Serve Hospital Food moniker, Soundscape artists Ken Van Roose and Couverts created an interesting picture utilizing frames from *Sinthia: The Devil's Doll*. This 15-minute movie was shown in a series of short films at the Cult! Live film festival in Entrepot (Bruges) on February 29, 2010. Apparently, the goal was to apply existing psychedelic and/or erotic images from vintage films and re-score them.

Hard rock group Dirty Rockers from Florence, Italy, have a noisy segue between tracks one and three on their 2010 album *Rock'N'Roll Monsters* entitled "The Incredibly Strange Creatures Who Stopped Living and Became Mixed-Up Zombies?!?" There is an industrial-noise unit from Jefferson, Ohio, called the Incredibly Strange Creatures Who Stopped Living and Became Mixed Up Zombies; members, Max Adams, James Horn and Cody Miksell uploaded an incredibly interesting *and strange* demo to bandcamp.com in 2011.

Horror punk performer Haunted George released his number "The Chooper" in 2012 on the GRGPNK label. Punk rockers Invisible Ghost Men from Dauphin, Pennsylvania, released their tribute to Steckler as "The Incredibly Strange Creatures Who Stopped Living and Became Mixed-Up Zombies" on their 2013 single *They Live. They Strike.* And in that same year, hardcore metal act Second-Hand Hero from Berlin, Germany, titled the eighth track on their album *Pictures* "The Incredibly Strange Creatures Who Stopped Living and Became Mixed-Up Zombies."

Spanish horror dub-step artists Max Powa calls their 2014 E.P. *Max Powa Encounters: The Incredibly Strange Creatures Who Stopped Living and Became Mind Controlled Monsters*. In 2015, Toronto, Ontario, punks War Balm entitled their six-song release *The Incredibly Strange Creatures Who Stopped Living and Became Mixed-Up Apocalyptic Warriors*. Also in 2015, singer-songwriter Chris Void released a series of tracks as Chris Void & the Incredibly Strange Creatures Who Stopped Living and Became Mixed-Up Zombies!?

The year 2015 also gave us the album *The Electric Ballroom* by horror-themed glam rockers Devilish Elvis and their song "Incredibly Strange Creatures" replete with plenty of text samples from the film. In 2016, lo-fi garage rockers The Animal Mothers from Glasgow released a tune entitled "Mixed Up Zombie." The album upon which it appeared was appropriately christened *The Incredibly Strange Animal Mothers Who Stopped Living and Became Mixed Up Zombies*. Then in 2019, Canadian artist Jackson Phibes released his version of *Rat Pfink a Boo Boo*'s "Eafin' and Surfin'" as "Rat Pfinky."

There is a National Dust Records

punk artist called the Lemon Grove Kids. Numerous punk and/or rockabilly groups have rocked under the Rat Fink a Boo Boo banner. Currently, Above Ground Records represents a San Diego heavy metal–punk band called The Thrill Killers. Syracuse, New York, is home to punk-style band Born Again Savages who bang out the tune "Skid Row Slasher." In years past and years to come, there is likely to be more Creatures, Thrill Killers, Rat Finks, Lemon Grovers and Slashers.

Poison Ivy of the Cramps fame has released (with the aid of Righteous Records) four compilation compact discs loaded with obscure surf and rockabilly tracks. What is curious is that only one Ron Haydock number, "99 Chicks," appears over the seven-disc set that came out between the years 2014 and 2016. It is curious because the titles of the series are as follows: *The Incredibly Strange Record Club, The Incredibly Strange Music Box, Deeper Into the Incredibly Strange Music Box* and *Magnificent: Long Gone in the World of Incredibly Strange Music*. Then in 2015, Memento Mori Records put out *Hollywood Strangler Meets the Crippled Masters of Kung Fu* that promised "Legendary recordings salvaged from the mists of time."

Editors Andrea Juno and V. Vale compiled what is arguably the first serious exploitation film compendium of interviews with filmmakers and articles on noteworthy genres. RE/Search published it in 1986 under the title *Incredibly Strange Films*. The ambitious editors expanded upon the theme by also publishing two volumes of *Incredibly Strange Music* with corresponding compact discs in 1993 and '94.

In 1988, host Jonathan Ross' *The Incredibly Strange Film Show* contained six episodes; Steckler's was the second. The show then morphed into *Son of the Incredibly Strange Film Show* and ran for one more season and six episodes in 1989. Four years later, Ross penned *The Incredibly Strange Film Book* as a companion piece to his successful series. Oddly, Ross resigned Steckler's only inclusion in his book to his Hallucinogenic Hypnovision gimmick.

Many other tributes could (and likely do) exist and hopefully more will come along with theaters to host Steckler retrospectives. Steckler's films will continue to capture the imagination of artists on a global level. It is a special honor that few filmmakers have garnered, but Steckler has struck a chord with the people, and the people have accordingly reacted, responded and rocked.

Collect 'Em All! An Overview of Ray Dennis Steckler Memorabilia

1. One-sheets, half-sheets, pressbooks, lobby cards and publicity stills for numerous but not all of Steckler's features including his adult titles.
2. Feature film and trailer prints for many but not all of Steckler's features including his adult titles.
3. Cash Flagg latex mask. (Note: Either an original Don Post cast or the recast by special effects technician Rob Tharp.)
4. *Wild Guitar!* promotional seven-inch single with picture sleeve by Arch Hall, Jr., by Fairway International.
5. Forty-five rpm seven-inch records containing radio ads.
6. Norton Records' seven-inch Ron Haydock single with picture sleeve.

A collage of three Steckler pressbooks: *Wild Guitar* (1961), *Incredibly Strange Creatures* (1963) and *The Thrill Killers* (1964). These booklets contain written promotional copy and newspaper ad mats of various sizes (author's collection).

7. The *Golden Turkey Awards* record that contains six Steckler-related songs.
8. *Wild Guitar! Arch Hall, Jr., and the Archers* CD by Norton Records.
9. *Ron Haydock and the Boppers: 99 Chicks* CD by Norton Records.
10. *The Wild Wild World of Mondo Movies Music* CD Big Beat Records that features a dozen Steckler-related tracks.
11. REL seven-inch singles for Billy Gholston's "Zombie Stomp" B/W "Monster 'A Go-Go," Danny Ware's "Mixed-Up Zombie Stomp" B/W "It's Incredible" and Carol Kaye and the Stone Tones' "Shook Out of Shape" B/W "Keep Talkin'."
12. Cap Records seven-inch single for "Rat Pfink" B/W "I Stand Alone" (released in 1964).
13. RE/Search's *Incredibly Strange Films* book (1986) contains a 20-

A collage of three Steckler-related compact discs: *Mondo Movies Music* (1990), *Ron Haydock and the Boppers* (1996) and *Wild Guitar!* (2004) (author's collection).

plus–page, heavily illustrated interview with Steckler and Carolyn Brandt by Boyd Rice.
14. *Shadows & Light* book by Gary Kent (2009) contains five pages on Steckler.
15. Andrew J. Rausch's *Gods of Grindhouse* book (2013) features a 13-page interview with Steckler.
16. *Grindhouse Purgatory* Vol. 1, #14 (2019) sports a six-page article, written by Aaron AuBuchon, outlining the differences between *The Chooper* and *Blood Shack*.
17. *Cult Movies* magazine (1993) #8 features a four-page interview with Steckler by James Elliot Singer.
18. *Cult Movies* magazine (1994) #10 features a two-page article written by Steckler on his old friend and colleague John Andrews.
19. *Cult Movies* magazine (1995) #15 has a four-page continuation of the Steckler interview conducted by James Elliot Singer.
20. *Flipside* magazine (1995) #94 contains the first part of a Steckler interview.
21. *Flipside* magazine (1995) #95

contains the second part of the Steckler interview.

22. *Glass Eye* magazine (1995) #8, Volume 2, features reviews of eight of Steckler's films by writer Edward Shimborske, Jr.
23. *Filmfax* magazine (1991) #28 houses a complete *Thrill Killers* pressbook reproduction as well as an article entitled "Eight Exploitation Experts Expound on Ethics of Excess" which features Steckler, H.G. Lewis, Ted V. Mikels *et al.*
24. *Fangoria* magazine (1983) #28 features Johnny Legend's four-page interview with Steckler.
25. *King of the Monsters* magazine (1977), edited by Ron Haydock, contains a four-page article by Bob Burns on *The Lemon Grove Kids Meet the Monsters.*
26. *The Monster Times* magazine (1974)

A collage of three vintage Steckler-related magazines (author's collection).

#30 contains a heavily illustrated four-page article on Steckler by Ron Haydock.

27. *Creem* magazine March 1973 includes a Lester Bangs essay on *The Incredibly Strange Creatures.* It runs eight pages with a two-page reproduction of the *Creatures* one-sheet as a centerfold.

28. *Mad Monsters* magazine #10 from 1965 features *The Incredibly Strange Creatures* on the cover as well as a six-page spread.

29. *Movies Illustrated: Picture Stories of New Films* magazine from May 1964 features a three-page spread on *Incredibly Strange Creatures*. This is the magazine that Joe Saxon falls asleep reading in *The Thrill Killers*.

30. Camp Video released four promotional ads slicks for *The Incredibly Strange Creatures*, *The Thrill Killers*, *Rat Pfink a Boo Boo* and *Las Vegas Serial Killer*.

31. VHS cassette tapes from Active Home Video, Arrow Films, Camp Video, Cinema Land, Facing All Death, Intervid, Liberty Video, Magnum Entertainment, Mascot Video, Medien Pool, Mondo Movies, MPV, Neon Video, Nightmare

A collage of the Media Blasters/Guilty Pleasures special edition DVD release of *Rat Pfink a Boo Boo* (1966) (author's collection).

Video, Premier Entertainment Group, Program Releasing, Regal Video, Rhino Video, Sinister Cinema, Something Weird Video, VEC, Vegas Video, VHE, Video Treasures and VMP Video.

32. DVD from Absolute Films, AFA Entertainment, Alpha New Cinema, Alternative Cinema, American Grindhouse TV, Bargain Bin Media, Desert Island Films, Diabolik, Digiview, Film Detective, Mascot Video, Media Blasters (under their Shriek Show and Guilty Pleasures banners), Media Collectibles, Reel Classic Films, Rocket, Scream House, Shout! Factory, Something Weird Video, Starry Night Video, Village and Vinegar Syndrome.

33. *Rat Pfink a Boo Boo* special edition DVD release by Media Blasters under their Guilty Pleasures banner. It features a replica of the pressbook and a vinyl sticker.

34. Cash Flagg/Mort "Mad Dog" Click trading card. (Note: This was part of the *Creep Skin and Vampire Blood* series created by artist Tom Bagley in 2013 and limited to 100 sets. Bagley planned to release a second series containing a card depicting an Incredibly Strange Creature and also one with Arch Hall, Jr.).

35. The 46-page *Ray Dennis Steckler Misfit a Boo Boo* scrapbook. (Note: These were compiled, photocopied and sold at Mascot Video.)

36. Mascot Video giveaway promotional ball caps.

37. Numerous unauthorized items exist such as one-sheet reproductions, t-shirts, embroidered and silk-screened patches, buttons, key chains, stickers and postcards.

38. A five-page salute to Steckler, written by Arch Hall, Jr., just days after Steckler's death, is included in Tom Weaver's book *A Sci-Fi Swarm and Horror Horde* (McFarland & Co., 2010). It includes a photo of Steckler at his last public appearance, a November 2008 screening of the documentary *No Subtitles Necessary: Laszlo & Vilmos* at the Los Angeles County Museum of Art.

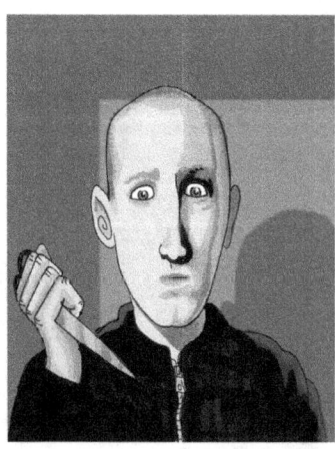  

Limited edition trading cards from artist-musician Tom Bagley of the Forbidden Dimension band (courtesy Tom Bagley).

Part Five

The Interviews

High Hopes to Hard Knocks: Carolyn Brandt on Living and Working with Ray Dennis Steckler

Curry: *How did you come to use Brandt as your last name?*

Brandt: My Danish great-grandmother was Caroline Brandt. My mother insisted that she was a countess but I take everything she said with a grain of salt. Also, at the time Ray was fabricating an international cast for *Creatures*. I was supposedly from Denmark, Atlas King was from Greece, Sharon Walsh was from Scotland, I think, and James Bowie was from Africa. Oh, and Cash Flagg was the only main actor from the United States. This was all just silly promotional gimmicks but it's what he told the trade papers.

Ray has gone on record stating that he spotted you on the set of a television series. Can you recall the title of that show? Ray claimed it was called The Magic of Sinbad *or something similar.*

That was a TV pilot we shot with Tommy Rettig at a studio on Santa Monica across from the old Sears building.

Now, what was Ray doing when he spotted you on this set?

He was there with his friend Rick from Reading, Pennsylvania. I'm not sure what they were actually doing at the studio, but I believe Rick was shacked up with someone and Ray was staying in his car.

Oh, that had to be the Nash Rambler. Backing up a bit. Did The Magic of Sinbad *go anywhere?*

No, there's so many pilots that go and just never get any place.

Was this your first television pilot?

Yes, let's see—I'd been doing Shakespeare and I was doing some kind of event in the park and then I wound up on *The Magic of Sinbad*.

Steckler legend has it that once he spotted you on set, he simply had to have you.

Yeah, that's pretty much it. The funny thing is that when he saw me, I was on a magic carpet with Tommy Rettig.

Oh, so that story is true.

Yes, that one is true. So, many of the things I see and read have been embellished but that one is true.

Previous to meeting you, Ray had worked on Timothy Carey's film Frenzy *which eventually became* The World's Greatest

Sinner. *Did you ever meet Carey or see the film?*

Tim was living down in El Monte, that's where his home was, and he was doing all the work in his garage. I was only down there once so I can't tell you a whole lot about Tim other than that he was kind of a wild guy.

Yes, Tim was quite the character. Your next film appearance was in 1962 on Secret File: Hollywood. *I describe you in the book as, "a gal getting her groove on to some beatniks with bongos." This appears to be where Ray met Arch Hall, Sr. Any particular recollections of their meeting?*

That film was for Ralph Cushman and it also had Francine York, who just passed a couple of years back. I think I still have a few pictures from that shoot. As far as the Arch Halls go, I don't recall their meeting specifically but I know *Secret File: Hollywood* led into *Eegah*.

Right, Eegah *was also from 1962 and you have a small role as the girlfriend to Mr. Fishman who was played by Ray. Any interesting memories of this shoot with Arch Hall, Jr., and Richard Kiel?*

Yeah, I was there by the pool when Eegah comes by and throws Fishman into the pool and then I bring him a cocktail. Only certain things really stick out in my mind, but Richard Kiel was truly a gentle giant. I remember one day bumping into him on Hollywood Boulevard when he was with another tall guy and they were busy passing out fliers for something. I waved and walked over and we shook hands and my hand just disappeared in his.

And Arch Hall, Jr. What did you think of him?

Ah, Junior, he was a good worker. He would show up when he was supposed to and he did his job. I wasn't

Carolyn Brandt circa 1967 (courtesy Carolyn Brandt).

actively involved. Ray would be busy on the set and I would only come in when I was needed and then I would go back home.

Lastly in 1962, you had another dancing role in Wild Guitar.

Right, we went from *Eegah* to *Wild Guitar*, but also in 1962 we were shooting *The Incredibly Strange Creatures*. Some of the dates that are out there are release dates and not when we were actually shooting them.

In the book, I describe your Wild Guitar *dance as "floating, almost ethereal."*

Oh, I love that word "ethereal," and I've always loved being linked to it. It was based upon another dance routine of mine called "Blue Violin" where I ran around floating with scarves.

It's a fantastic sequence and the set is even more so.

That was shot at the Ivar Theater at 1605 Ivar Avenue in Hollywood and the set was from *The Blacks* by the French dramatist Jean Genet.

Was this the same Ivar Theater that you and Ray worked at as ushers? If so, what were some or types of films that they were playing at that point in time?

Yes, that is the same theater. At that time, it was strictly a stage venue. I remember one show [*Only in America*, 1961] that had Herschel Bernardi and Maura McGiveney. Unfortunately, I can't remember the title of the play.

Any recollection as to when Goof on the Loose *was shot?*

That was probably the first thing Ray shot around 1958 and '59.

Ahh, okay. The film's title card states that it is a Morgan-Steckler production but he didn't meet George until later.

Right, we connected with George on *Creatures* and it was so funny because originally George was almost ready to commit and we were ready to start shooting and then George held back. So we went to my grandmother and got $500 to start shooting that weekend because Ray figured if we got going, George would come in. And thank God he did.

In the Incredibly Strange Creatures, *you play dancer Marge Neilson. This was quite the production for Ray. Surely you have some stories about the making of this film that hasn't been put out there time and again. On this film, you worked with the notable cinematographers Laszlo Kovacs, Joseph V. Mascelli and Vilmos Zsigmond.*

Let me say this, Billy and Leslie, that's Vilmos and Laszlo, always said that Ray was a cameraman's cameraman. Of course, that was before they were both Academy Award winners, but I know they always thought the world of Ray and his abilities with the camera. You know they were both just out of Hungary where they had been Freedom Fighters. They were living up on Cahuenga Boulevard and we used to go over there and hang out at their place a bit. Also, Joe Mascelli was around and he wrote *the* cinematographers handbook and I think we picked him up on *Secret File: Hollywood*. Oh, and one more thing about Billy [Vilmos] and *Wild Guitar*. Ray put Billy on skates and put him on the ice rink with a camera to spin around. Billy insisted it would never work and that there would be flares in the lens, to which Ray assured him that he would thank him one day.

[*Note: Kovacs and Zsigmond were fellow students at the Film and Drama Academy in Communist-controlled Budapest in the 1950s. The two covertly filmed the fighting between the Russian soldiers and Hungary's citizens. Then they made their way to the Austrian border where they posed as peasants. They hid their film cans in bales of hay and traveled by night. Once in Austria, the duo edited their footage and sold it to a producer who titled the 1956 documentary* Ungarn in Flammen *which translates to* Hungary in Flames. *It took the film five more years to make it stateside, where CBS aired it in 1961.*]

Let's stick with Creatures *a bit longer. How do you feel about your character Marge Neilson?*

She's a mixed-up and confused alcoholic looking for answers and not finding them and not at all happy. But I was thrilled because I got to dance with Bill Turner.

There's a story that Ray accidentally knocked one of his front teeth out and didn't have the time to see a dentist. As the story goes, he placed a piece of Styrofoam in the gap and continued shooting.

That's some story. The only problem I knew of was his appendix, which ruptured at Thanksgiving one year. We were at my mother's with Par Curry and James Bowie. That would've definitely been around the time of *Creatures*.

The Thrill Killers is up next and it is my personal favorite of Ray's films. What was it like working with Liz Renay, Gary Kent, Titus Moede and Herb Robins—or anyone else for that matter?

I didn't have any scenes with Liz Renay but whenever I bumped into her on set she was very pleasant. Oh, and Gary Kent, I'm so happy about *Danger God* [a documentary about Kent]. I haven't seen it yet but I have seen *Once Upon a Time in ... Hollywood*. I really have a lot of respect for him.

In 1966, you portrayed Cee Bee Beaumont, girlfriend of rock star Lonnie Lord, played by Ron Haydock, in the fan favorite Rat Pfink a Boo Boo. *Any particularly interesting memories from this shoot?*

Carolyn Brandt circa 1967 (courtesy Carolyn Brandt).

Ray had an idea where he wanted to do a costume type character and he was trying to sell it to the studios and he was having no luck. I remember him being very bitter when they decided to go ahead with *Batman*. There was something nice that came of it, though. At the time, we were involved with Earl Barton, Ray was doing some Scopitones with him, and Earl had worked with Julie Newmar on *Seven Brides for Seven Brothers* and he brought Julie over to our house. So, Linda (Steckler) got to meet Catwoman.

That's the Catwoman to meet, in my opinion. I'd almost forgotten to ask about Keith Wester.

I loved Keith. He and Ray were partners for a long time and whatever needed to be done, he just got it done. He was a very sweet man and he was very supportive of me when I had difficult times. Ray had a lot of girlfriends, let's just put it that way.

This sounds like a dicey situation that I would like to delve into more later but—let's jump back to Earl Barton and the Scopitones. If I'm correct, these things were the precursor to music videos. Can you recall any artists, in particular, that Ray had worked with in this capacity?

I know he did "Light My Fire" with Trini Lopez, not sure if that was still a Scopitone. About this time, "White Rabbit," by Jefferson Airplane. He was also responsible for "Winchester Cathedral" being used at the opening of an *ABC Wide World of Sports* while shooting for Andy Sidaris. Then he was responsible for Janis Joplin's coverage at a bar where she was performing during one of the surfing contests. That's all I can recall off the top of my head.

I think this is a good place to ask this question. Ray had been able to surround himself with some incredibly talented people and some of them went on to much bigger and better things. Why do you think they were willing to stick around and do these tiny projects with Ray?

Probably the fact that they could have a lot more freedom with Ray than they would have had with the studios. Jack Cooperman was also working with us as a cameraman on *The Lemon Grove Kids* and I think he was a gaffer on *The Thrill Killers*. Ray and I had a gang of people around us like Pat Kirkwood, and James Bowie practically lived at our place for a long time. Later on, it was Ron Haydock who was always around.

Around this time, you worked in the makeup department on Incubus *with William Shatner. How did you get involved in this project?*

Yes, I came in to do some makeup and I wound up being the stand-in that gets raped by the goat. So, those are my legs underneath the skirt. That's all I really remember from that one.

That's quite the harrowing scene that punctuates the ending of that bizarre film quite effectively. You played Cee Bee Beaumont two more times in The Lemon Grove Kids Meet the Monsters *and you also played a Vampire Lady. Ray claims that this film was the most fun he had ever shot. Are your recollections similar?*

In a sense, yes, and it really was fun. It brought out Coleman Francis, who we really liked, he was just a dear sweet guy. Also, we had this green grasshopper from outer space because my favorite book as a little girl was *Old King Grasshopper*. So when I was doing my tests to get into NABET as a makeup artist, I had to do some fantasy stuff. Marvin Hanks went with me and I made him up to be the green grasshopper and with his help, I passed the test. I'm also always reminded of my friend Cindy when I think of the *Lemon Grove Kids* movies. She was the girl that the mummy, played by Bob Burns, carried away. Unfortunately Cindy is no longer with us. She was always self-conscious about her nose, so she had some plastic surgery done on it and shortly thereafter she was diagnosed with cancer and then she passed away.

That's sad to hear. You may not know this but Media Blasters, the company that released The Lemon Grove Kids *on DVD, made your friend Cindy one of the focal points of the front cover.*

Oh, that's nice. She would've loved that. She was such a sweet and dear

A four-year-old Carolyn Brandt with a gorilla at an arcade on Market Street in San Francisco, around 1944 (courtesy Carolyn Brandt).

friend. I've been lucky to have good friends over the years.

One can never have too many friends, especially good ones. So, let's move forward one episode to my favorite where you played the Vampire Lady from Outer Space. *Any recollection as to who prompted you into that role? You make a very convincing Vampira-type.*

Oh, I don't recall exactly. Maybe it was Tom Scherman or maybe it was Ray. I just know that I have pretty fair skin and it lent itself well to *that* look.

I particularly love the second installment of the trilogy.

That was fun. Okay, we moved into this house, up on Spring Oak, which was in a lovely five-home cul-de-sac that was on a hillside. The weekend that we moved in, we drove up with our flying saucer and a few cast members from *The Lemon Grove Kids*. Oh, what the neighbors must've thought that first weekend. We must've scared the hell out of them.

That must've been quite amusing. Now, this film was primarily shot at this [Spring Oak] location, correct?

Yes. It was wonderful that we got that facility because we had the big backyard, the hillside and that unfinished dirt cellar that we used in several films. We used it in *Lemon Grove Kids* and we also used it in *Body Fever*.

It was also used in Sinthia: The Devil's Doll. *It appears as though you weren't involved in this film at all.*

Let me tell you this about my situation with Ray. *Rat Pfink a Boo Boo* started out as a straight horror-type movie. Ron Haydock and I went out on a date and he kissed me and then all of a sudden the movie became a comedy.

Am I to read into that what I think I'm supposed to read into that?

I think so. Ray always tells the story that he got bored with how the film was going along but from my perspective that wasn't the case at all.

Okay, we're going to dig further into this situation as this conversation continues. However, this seems like a good place to bring up Joe Karston, who took three of Ray's films out as roadshows and by all accounts was successful with them. Is this true and if so, did Ray see any of the monetary residuals?

I didn't know Joe. I wasn't involved in any of that stuff. As far as the money goes, my mother always insisted that Ray had money on the side that he never told me about, but I'm not aware of it. I just know we had a basket full of bills and he would reach in and pay one when he could.

These roadshows sound like a blast. Did you attend any of the screenings and if so, what was the audience like?

I assume you mean the shows with the monsters and stuff. No, I never attended those because we had two girls and I was the babysitter. But I did hear about them, just like the fan club that I was supposed to have. But I have gotten some fan letters in these last few years. I also made one appearance, in the early 2000s, up in Sacramento for a screening of one of our films and it was fun.

Backing up a bit, would you mind telling me about the Jefferson Airplane "White Rabbit" video shoot?

We shot that down at Zuma Beach and I ran all day long on that beach. We used to shoot up there quite a bit as Ray had a favorite spot. I remember one time we were shooting some sort of commercial and another shoot was going on using the Teamsters Union. This unit had like eight vans and this huge crew and here we come with one camera and four people. That's what I remember most about Zuma Beach. Oh, and we also shot some footage for *Incubus* there as well.

Also in 1967, you were credited as a dancer in Stephanie Rothman's feature It's a Bikini World.

I don't know, maybe. All I can remember is wearing a little purple outfit doing a go-go number.

The film had the working title The Girl in Daddy's Bikini. *Perhaps that's what it was called when you were involved.*

That could be, but I wasn't busty enough to be a bikini girl.

In 1969, Ray put you front and center in the film Body Fever *as Carrie Erskine. I really like this movie. What are your thoughts?*

I think I was getting better as I was going along. I was getting more comfortable in front of the camera. I was also the script girl and during the scenes in the office, I kept it in the drawer but pulled it out in between takes. That was as interesting shoot. We had Bernard Fein as Big Mack and he was great, but the scene that I like the best in *Body Fever*, that I thought was the most real and touching, was the scene with Ray and Coleman.

Bernard Fein was fantastic and yes, the scenes with Francis were very genuine and heartfelt.

Oh, there's a scene when Laura opens the door and says, "Mommy, there's a man on the floor." Well, Ray was the man on the floor. So the full take was, "Mommy, there's a man on the floor. It's Daddy!"

Next up is Sinthia: The Devil's Doll. *As mentioned earlier, you are conspicuously absent here, even while a large portion of the film was shot in your basement. Any recollection as to why you were unable or unwilling to participate?*

Oh, I was involved in it to some degree. I think maybe I helped with costuming or the script. I know I was on the set at least one time and that was for the masturbation scene and that's about all I remember from that one.

I thought you would've been great as Lucifer's wife in this movie.

Well, she did wear one of my wigs and I made her costume.

Okay, Blood Shack *is next.*

Right, that was 1971 but we moved to Las Vegas in 1970. We moved there because Ray was supposed to have a deal to shoot a TV pilot called *The Wig and I*. It was supposed to be a *Charlie's Angels*–type thing but with a Las Vegas showgirl who has a wig shop.

So I take it this was the primary reason for the move from Hollywood to Vegas.

Right, but also Ray had no place to go, at that point, in Hollywood. Nothing was happening and this was an opportunity, as he saw it, that he could parlay into something. I was really reluctant to move as I was getting a lot of work through NABET, at that time, for makeup, wardrobe, script, and for the first time in a long time I was seeing some cash come in.

Was this around the time that you finally realized that Ray's movie career wasn't going to work out the way that you had hoped? Was there a certain situation or series of events that prompted you to move on?

Oh, I knew that a long time ago. In fact, I told my mother, who wanted me to do the Hollywood thing, "Listen, if I'm gonna have to sleep with someone, at least it's going to be my husband." You either have someone with some push behind you or you sleep your way through and hope you get lucky and I just wasn't into that. We were committed and we kept hoping and trying but by the move to Vegas I was feeling defeated.

Wow, that is definitely your character in Blood Shack. *Many directors put reflections of their real lives onto the screen but if one were to analyze* Blood Shack *in that capacity, Ray's world was coming apart at the seams.*

Uh, yes.

This was the last film you would make with Ron Haydock. Ray has more than suggested that Ron's death was suicide. Was this ever brought to your attention?

That is what Ray told me at the time. That he took a walk on the freeway and got in front of a truck. Ron was despondent. I think he still carried a torch for Mary Demos.

That's too bad. Also in 1971, you appear briefly in Corey Allen's Pinocchio *as "girl with opera glasses." Was that the extent of your involvement with that picture?*

Actually, we shot that earlier at a studio over on Sunset. Oh, one day John Carradine was on the lot looking for someone and Ray misdirected him to our set so we could meet him.

Fan favorite Dyanne Thorn was also in the picture. Did you have any encounters with her?

Okay … um, she has nipples that invert when they get heated. So, I had to stand by with ice cubes so that Dyanne could properly—project.

Seriously? That's a visual image Carolyn Brandt and Dyanne Thorns fans will likely find difficult to shake—should we be foolish enough to want to.

Honest. It's just one of those crazy things, but she was very nice and professional on set. I liked her quite a lot.

Here's another one. I was working on a pilot for *Turn Off* which was a *Laugh-In*-type show that was a George Schlatter and Ed Friendly production. Joey Heatherton was on the set and she was on this big, huge white cyclorama with her black costume. So, as she's rolling around on this thing they have to keep brushing paint on it so it stays white. She's dancing on this thing and she's getting white paint on her black slacks. I'm then sent over to dust her off and upon my return, one of the assistants looks and says to me, "Now that she's had her ass brushed, does she feel like a star?"

Around this time, you worked with Ray on the unfinished film Bloody Jack the Ripper. *What can you tell the readers about this lost film?*

We shot five sequences down in Santa Fe walking around the fair. I was in hot pants, and I looked pretty good. Then we did another sequence on the bar in our kitchen where Laurel Spring was stripped down and they were stabbing her.

Hot pants, naked girls and stabbings—sounds like a good start to a slasher film. Recently, I've been made aware that Ray owned and operated a movie theater in Vegas during the '70s. Could you elaborate?

That was in was in North Las Vegas and he played a lot of Westerns, serials and the Bowery Boys stuff but he did catch a lot of flak from the city because they thought he was going to come in and start showing porn.

Now, what on Earth would give them that idea?

Because they knew he was shooting some porn.

Was this the straw that finally broke your camel's back as far as your relationship with Ray was concerned?

It probably contributed, but it really was that Ray couldn't be faithful if he wanted to. Also, he was pretty cocky when he was involved with someone and every single film he made, there was always someone else on the side. You know that story he tells about Roxy from *The Lemon Grove Kids*? Well, there was a lot more going on there than he ever wanted anyone else to know. I was pregnant at the time that he moved her in with us.

I'll give you an example of what he could be like. Did you ever see that film *The Bad and the Beautiful*? Well, Kirk Douglas plays a movie producer who coerces Lana Turner's character into falling in love with him in order to get the best performance out of her that he can. Along the way, she wins some award and goes to him and finds that he's in bed with another woman. He tells her something to the effect, "Sometimes I like a little 'dirt' on the side." Ray seemed to really identify with Kirk Douglas' character and things. Also, the caliber of women that he was bringing around only got worse once we moved to Vegas.

I just couldn't seem to find myself in a position to leave. In another instance, I bounced out of the house on Lemon Grove and Joe Mascelli said, "I don't think I've ever seen you happy before." This *did* happen from time to time, but you know that rash I got while making *Body Fever*? Well, that was a result of me dealing with Ray and his latest female acquisition. It's like that old saying, "In for a penny, in for a pound." I made a bad decision.

This is an awful and unfortunate series of events.

It is what it is, Chris. I look at it this way: I am currently with the love of my life and if I hadn't gone through what I'd gone through, I wouldn't have met the person that I am sharing the best part of my life with.

That is wonderful and you've come out on the better side of that chaos. Let's switch gears to some less heavy fare. In 1979, you acted on-screen one final time for Ray as the Skid Row Slasher in The Hollywood Strangler Meets the Skid Row Slasher.

Right, but also around that time I went back to the university to get my diploma. I just kept taking jobs and only getting so far, so I thought it would be best if I got my diploma. Anyhow, I couldn't afford to spend four years at college so I crammed a four-year curriculum in two and a half years and I graduated at the top of my class in the College of Business and Economics and I majored in financial administration.

That had to have taken a lot of ambition and drive. There's a 1983 film called Funny Money *for which the IMDb credits you as cinematographer. This seems odd.*

That's because I was never the

Carolyn Brandt as the title character Laura in the play *Laura,* **staged at the PAC Theater in Laguna Woods Village, California, in 2018 (courtesy Carolyn Brandt).**

cinematographer on any film. I would do wardrobe, costuming, makeup and scripts but never any camerawork. Plus, I've never even heard of that movie.

What role and performance do you feel best represents your acting abilities?

Well, probably the straightest and cleanest one would have been *The Thrill Killers*. That was just a straight, simple part. The Vampire Lady was fun. I love to do characters. With *Body Fever,* I was just never that satisfied with that performance even though it was probably my showiest one. It's okay. I'm very fussy. I've been doing plays. I've done *Laura and Laura, Agnes of God, Eleanor Roosevelt* and it turns out that I've become, what I believe to be, a good actress. I've done some good work. It's all on stage but I've been very pleased with it.

Not a thing wrong with stage productions. What's your favorite film of Ray's?

Body Fever probably came the closest to actually doing a full-on real movie kind of thing, so in a sense I like that. The *Lemon Grove Kids* movies were sweet.

What's your least favorite film of Ray's?

Oh, the first *Lemon Grove Kids* because of Roxy and besides I'm not really in it. I think Ray cut some stuff in at the end where I appear with a group of people but otherwise I'm not in it.

At this point, I'm also curious to know if Ray ever had a day job where he punched a clock. Did he always work for himself in one capacity or another?

Oh, he got close to working at Universal Studios, but then that whole thing happened with Hitchcock and that was the end of that. Ray tried different things over the years other than making movies. He had the furniture store for a while. Then he had the movie theater and the video stores much later. One time I found a stash of questionable pharmaceuticals in the closet.

Questionable pharmaceuticals?

Quaaludes.

Wow. This conversation just took another unexpected turn.

Well, Ray knew people who could "move" things.

Seems so. While speaking of dubious or questionable acts, let's move on to Ray's adult films. Did he approach you about making these types of things?

Yeah, it was just a matter of survival. We had the opportunity to do them and we did them and I do remember the cops coming around looking for stuff.

With so many nefarious things going on in Vegas, why would the cops care about Ray making pornography?

Well, if you have "cover," you can do it and if you don't, you'll be one of the ones they hit on in an effort to show that they are doing their jobs.

In 1971, you acted under the alias Jane Bond as Dracula's wife Elaina in The Mad Love Life of a Hot Vampire. *Were your scenes for this film possibly shot for some other project entirely?*

Possibly, Ray was always doing things like that. I'll tell you, for those pornos he bought a lot of footage from other people to cut those things together and those things are just awful.

Jim Parker the Vegas Vampire: *It's my understanding that he was a personal friend of the family.*

Yes, he was. Once he even came to one of Linda's birthday parties dressed as the Vegas Vampire.

In 1974, you played Janice Lightning in The Sexorcist. *You have a fairly large role in this curious film about sex and satanism. Any thoughts on this one?*

That sounds like something he cut together out of one of the other ones. What am I wearing?

Blue jeans and a blue top as I recall.

Okay, that's the one where I just ran around with a camera taking pictures and at one point I was taken around back where the guys were, and there they were with everything just hanging out. I wasn't used to that but I had a job to do.

In 1976, you played Helga Swartz in Teenage Massage Parlor. *How do you feel about your role in the film?*

I have no recollection of that one at all. Gosh, I may have blocked some of this stuff out. Oh, wait! Was that the one where I wore a blonde wig and spoke in a high-pitched, squeaky voice?

That's the one. You were really funny and cute in that role.

Awe, thanks. Well, that was another character role and as I said before, I do enjoy playing characters. By the way, I want to make it clear to the readers that while I *did* appear in and work on those porn films, I never participated in any of the sex acts.

Let's talk some about Cindy Lou Sutters.

Oh, that sounds familiar.

Right, Ray made about a dozen films under that name and you were his voice in the narration.

Yeah, I did do a whole lot of that, again, just so we could put food on the table. These were just voiceovers. Ray would just give me a script to read into

Time off from the 2010 production of *Cuckoo's Nest* which was staged at the PAC Theater in Laguna Woods Village, California. Left to right, Carolyn Brandt who played Candy Star, the director David Dearing and Alan Brevin, who played McMurphy (courtesy Carolyn Brandt).

a recorder and then he would place them into whatever movies. As we've already discussed, once or twice I was involved in a walk-on character roles but what I mainly did was cut the darn negatives.

Carolyn, your willingness to speak with me on this topic leads me to believe that you're nowhere near as sensitive about this subject as Ray was. Why do you think this is the case?

For me, it was simply a matter of having a job to do and doing it in order to help keep the household up and running. For Ray, I think it would be that he wanted to be remembered a certain way. I guess he just didn't want his legacy tarnished but, Hell, he *did* make the things.

And he made a lot of them.
Yes he did.

Carolyn, you've graciously answered some very difficult questions. This interview needs to be taken out on a high note. Please tell the readers a story or an anecdote that best sums up your feelings about working in the film industry and being, arguably, one of cult cinema's most beloved performers.

One of the most enjoyable films was *The Lemon Grove Kids Meet the Green Grasshopper and the Vampire Lady from Outer Space*. Most of the crew had kids and it was easier to put them in that movie than to arrange babysitting. As I mentioned earlier in the conversation, the grasshopper harkens back to one of my favorite children's books growing up and was my inspiration for my makeup tests for NABET. Then I got to be a slinky, silly vampire and discover how much fun it is going in for the comedy.

Growing Up Steckler: A Conversation with Laura H. Steckler

Curry: *Are you a fan of this type of cinema or does your interest begin and end with your father's films as far as low-budget movies go?*

Steckler: I can appreciate any filmmaker being able to complete their projects. However, my preference is psychological thrillers. I think stories are best served when things are left to one's imagination. I love Stephen King novels, and I think *The Dead Zone* and *Misery* are some of the best screen adaptations. Then I really enjoy classic films like *What Ever Happened to Baby Jane?* and more recently *Parasite* and *Get Out*.

Ah, all solid choices. I read somewhere that your sister Linda was born in 1961.

I'm guessing you came along four or five years later?

Yes, Linda was born in 1961 and I was born in 1965.

Your first appearance, as far as I can tell, in one of your father's movies was in the second installation of The Lemon Grove Kids. The Lemon Grove Kids Meet the Green Grasshopper and the Vampire Lady from Outer Space *in 1969.*

Yes, that sounds right. As I've told people before, my first actual gig was at six months of age. I was an Ivory Snow baby.

I'm sure you were a natural. Later in 1969, you had an even bigger part in The Lemon Grove Kids...Go Hollywood! *In this one, you acted alongside one of my favorites, Herb Robins.*

Herbie, or *Uncle* Herbie as we called him, was always around. Herbie was a nice guy. I don't have much more to add about him. However, somewhere in my house I have an autographed poster from *The Worm Eaters*.

Very nice. Here's something I picked up on while perusing the credits of this film. You're credited as Jeannie Rae. Do you have any idea why as you were credited properly in the previous film and not this one?

I was baptized Jeanie Rae after my father's favorite aunt, and the Rae is a feminine version of his name. The H. is for Hardy as in Laurel and Hardy. My father named me after his mother and added the Hardy in tribute to the comedy legends. My mother and her side of the family were not amused as Dad had run off and signed the birth certificate without my mother's consent.

Well, I hope they warmed up to it. I find it very cute and clever. In the 1969 film Body Fever, *you had a very small role as the "Girl in the Hallway" with your one line, "Mommy, there's a man on the floor." Obviously, Ron Haydock was not the man on the floor but he must've been around during this time as he does have a supporting role.*

Ron was a frequent visitor to our house. I would often wake up and go out to the living room to find him asleep on the couch wrapped in a green blanket. So I christened him "The Green Monster."

Knowing Ron's love of horror films, I can only imagine him loving his new nickname. In 1971, your father shot Blood Shack *and you, your sister and your mother returned as cast members. Still,*

Laura Steckler in 2015 (courtesy Laura H. Steckler).

this was also the year that your father would dive headfirst into the adult film industry. Do you have any knowledge as to why he felt the need to go in this direction? Personally, I never really felt that

Laura Steckler and Bob Burns as Kogar in 1966. This picture was titled "Beauty and the Beast" by Burns and hung in the front window of a photography studio on Sunset Boulevard (courtesy Carolyn Brandt).

your father was happy doing these things and that it was merely a means to an end.

No, I don't believe making adult films was my father's dream. More a means to an end by providing us with food and shelter. Still, from that period I do own a pair of prop roller skates. I also have the drug satchel from *Body Fever*, rubber prop axes from the *Thrill Killers* roadshow days and a mummy costume from *The Lemon Grove Kids*. Oh, and my father originally shot *Blood Shack* as *The Chooper*.

Right, and I actually prefer that version for various reasons. One, being that it contains what is possibly Ron Haydock's last recording, "The Chooper." I am also quite fond of the fantastically grisly artwork used during the credit sequence. In 1979, you were credited as a makeup artist on The Hollywood Strangler Meets the Skid Row Slasher. *At this point, you were only 14 or 15 years old, so what exactly did you do on this picture?*

Just as the credits state, I was responsible for makeup, but just basic stuff, not prosthetics or any of the gore effects. I'm not really a fan of that stuff anyway.

An old family friend, Jim Parker, made an appearance in this one as Slasher Victim 2. What do you remember about his and his wife P.J. Parker?

Jim was a family friend who once made an appearance at my sister's birthday party. My mother and I made an appearance on *The Vegas Vampire* promoting the Hollywood Theater, my father's movie theater in North Las Vegas.

Sitting on the left is birthday girl Linda Steckler with little sister Laura beside her eating pizza. The other three children are unidentified. Jim Parker as the Vegas Vampire looms over the festivities (circa 1973–1974) (courtesy Laura H. Steckler).

Oh, I did not know about this theater. Please fill us in on some of the particulars.

Well, I'm not sure what years he had it, but would have to guess late '70s. Mom can probably give you a more accurate timeline on that. I remember Dad screening his own films, H.R. Pufnstuf movies, and his favorites such as old cowboy serials and that sort of thing.

That sounds like great fun. In 1986, you're credited as "caterer" on Las Vegas Serial Killer, *and you also have a bit part as a rodeo goer.*

That is correct. I also worked craft services on a film called *Las Vegas Weekend* written and directed by Dale Trevillion. My father played the part of the college professor in this film.

That title rings a bell. I believe it gets a mention in Las Vegas Serial Killer chapter. At this point in time, the video tape market was in full swing and several of your father's films were on video shelves all over the country and even the world. You were in your early 20s during this period of time. Do you recall your father's attitude about his films being virtually resurrected with the home video boom?

I suspect that Dad was thrilled to have his movies out and available on video. I know I got a kick out of spying them in other movies and television shows. Like, I spotted *Creatures* in John Waters' *Serial Mom* and an episode of *The Ghost Whisperer* starring Jennifer Love Hewitt and directed by James Chressanthis. I've read that *Creatures* was thought to be a myth, and people were shocked to learn that it existed.

Oh that's great. I definitely should have caught The Creatures *in* Serial Mom. *I love that movie and I can guarantee that John hand-picked those videos for that scene. He loves these types of movies. On a similar note, I've gotten a charge out of catching one-sheets, pressbooks and lobby cards of your father's films in his films. There's something of his past in almost every one of his movies.*

Always shamelessly self-promoting [laughs].

Agreed, but for me it's just another part of the Ray Dennis Steckler brand. Plus, they're just fun to look for, kinda like an Easter egg hunt.

I also get a kick out of catching Andre Brummer's music in TV commercials and other random settings.

Andre was an incredible talent who stuck by your father's side for many years and worked with him tirelessly for probably very little money.

Linda, Ray and Laura Steckler visiting San Diego, California around 1985 (courtesy Laura H. Steckler).

I believe the casts and crews from Dad's films worked for low or no pay for the thrill and passion of making movies, and being exposed to his genius. We always believed that one day Dad would walk across a stage to receive his Academy Award. Of course, some of them did, like Vilmos Zsigmond and Joseph Mascelli. By the way, we called Andre "Boom Boom."

Did you by chance give him that nickname like you did "The Green Monster" to Ron Haydock?

No, I am not responsible for Andre's nickname. Not really sure who gets that credit.

Through it all, it appears as though Ray was a loving and caring father who doted on his children and never quite fell out of love with Carolyn. Was this the case?

Yes, he would be the first one to tell you that he would always love my mother. Speaking for myself, my father and I had a very special relationship which has been acknowledged by the family, but I am not necessarily comfortable saying I was his favorite. Even though we all knew it was true.

Do you still live up to your nickname "Tickles"?

I'm not sure what you mean.

Your dad always said that you were bestowed with that nickname because you were always laughing and smiling at everything.

While that was true, and still is, that's not the story I've always been told and I think Mom can back me up on this. The year I was born, Linda wanted a Tickles doll for Christmas. They couldn't afford one so I was her Tickles doll. And yes, I am extremely ticklish to this day not just physically but mentally as well, I suppose you could say. Uncle Bill was one of the last people who still called me that. He was Mom's dance partner in *The Creatures* who was murdered at the beginning of the movie. Oh, and I still have my "Tickles" Christmas stocking that I hang up every year. I grant a few people permission to call me that when asked [*laughs*].

[Note: Deluxe Reading manufactured the original "Tickles" doll in 1963. She is approximately 20 inches long and, with the aid of a single D battery: "Spank her—she cries! Tickle her—she laughs!"]

After all those years of dodging inquiries about his adult film career, how do you think he would feel about this book?

I think that depends how much you intend to focus on his adult film career. As you yourself mentioned, he has gotten up and walked out on interviews when it is brought up. I understand if you wish to truly paint a full picture of his career, but

Laura, Ray and Linda Steckler at the entrance of Busch Gardens in Los Angeles, 1968 (courtesy Laura H. Steckler).

The Deluxe Reading "Tickles" doll, Laura's "nicknamesake" (author's collection).

I sincerely hope you don't dwell on that part of it too much.

As I point out in the book's preface, those films are discussed though not at great length. Case in point: There's far more attention and detail given to your father's eight-minute short movie Goof on the Loose *than five or six of his adult features combined. In a previous conversation, you mentioned that* Rat Pfink a Boo Boo *was your favorite of your father's. Which is your least favorite and why?*

Summer Fun is probably my least favorite, mostly I find it unwatchable. I think Dad set out to make a modern-day Lemon Grove Kids but missed the mark.

You also brought up that The Incredibly Strange Creatures *was a difficult watch for you.*

Personally, I don't mind watching Creatures. I love the dancing, the costumes and seeing Uncle Bill, who played Mom's dance partner and was murdered first. When I have trouble watching, it is if I try to show it to someone else. I think it moves at a pace that most people don't have the patience for. The finale where Dad is shot and killed and falls into the ocean is classic. I also get a kick out of the footage of the Long Beach Pike which isn't there any more. However, I have spent many days in the area where it used to be. Long Beach Grand Prix. Scuba Show, Aquarium of the Pacific and so on. I think of him whenever I'm in the area.

Some people just don't have the patience for any of these types of films. Do your other siblings carry the torch for your father's film work like you seem to?

I do recall Morgan and Bailey attending some of the later screenings and helping to set up the merchandise table. I don't want to come off as harsh here but I just think that they are all busy with their children and their lives.

Do you think any of them will even have a passing interest in this book?

Linda might read your book. I think Morgan and Bailey would be less likely to do so.

In my estimation, that is totally understandable. Morgan and Bailey weren't really around for your father's prolific moviemaking years like you and Linda were. If you don't mind me asking, what do you miss the most about your father?

Well, I miss hugging him and then there are times when I have to suppress the urge to pick up the phone to share some news with him. I fondly remember our Sunday dates where we would go to lunch and then catch a movie matinee. I also enjoyed when we would go to the old MGM Hotel which stood where the Paris Hotel now stands. They had a great movie theater that would play the classics like *The Maltese Falcon*, *The Wizard of Oz* and a host of other classics. The theater had blue leather love seats with cocktail tables. The cocktail tables had call buttons to order drinks. My favorite was having a Shirley Temple delivered to me while watching a movie.

Sounds wonderful and not too unlike a Sunday outing with my father, who passed in 2010.

Here's something I just thought of: I wasn't allowed to see *Creatures* until I was a tween because Dad kills Mom in the film.

Richard Kiel and Laura Steckler around 1977 (courtesy Laura H. Steckler).

Laura Steckler in 2012 (courtesy Laura H. Steckler).

I guess that would be a cause for concern. What format would you have watched it on? I don't think it was out on VHS yet?

Oh, I probably saw it on 16mm. We used to watch a lot of movies projected on the living room wall. There was another movie I was not allowed to watch too, *The Exorcist*. We had the first VCR in the neighborhood and it was ¾" tape and we had *American Graffiti*, *Blazing Saddles*, *Jaws* and *The Exorcist* to name a few. One day I came down the hall and Linda was watching *The Exorcist* with some friends. Bad timing on my part. I walked in as Linda's head started spinning. Blair's head not my sister's [*laughs*].

Thanks for the clarification on which Linda head was spinning. Tell me about the time you met Richard Kiel.

Dad took me to a celebrity softball game at UNLV and Richard was playing. Afterwards I approached him for an autograph. I said that he had worked with my father in the past. Curiosity piqued, he inquired, "Who's your father?" I said, "Ray Steckler." He looked me square in the eye and corrected me, "That's Ray *Dennis* Steckler!" [*Laughs*]

You've graciously answered some difficult questions and I very much appreciate your candor and willingness to address some of these tough subjects. So, let's take this thing out on a fun note about you. Are you ever recognized out in public?

Actually, yes. Once I was checking into a comedy club called the Ice House in Pasadena. When I gave my name at check-in, the guy joked, "Do you spell that like Ray Dennis Steckler?" My reply was, "I spell it exactly the same way my father does." The guy flipped out. I was promoted to instant celebrity status and given the best seat in the house. He then asked if he could introduce his writing partner to me when he arrived.

Perfect.

Gary Kent: The Danger God Speaks

Curry: *How did you meet Ray and how long was it after this that you signed on to work with him on* The Thrill Killers?

Kent: Ray had a house across the street from my house and I was out mowing my yard one day and I waved to him to say hello. He came over and we started talking and he asked me if I wanted to be in a movie because he had found out that I was an actor. I said, "Sure. What's going on?" And he was making this movie and he didn't have a script. He just had a bunch of notes. Ray never did really ever have a script. At least he didn't on any of the films I worked on, anyway. He had pages and notes and he would say to you, "Okay, you enter the room and you're pissed off and you get angry." Then it was up to you to figure out the dialogue and what you were going to say and why you were angry and pissed off.

Yeah, that sounds about right. Your then-wife Laura Benedict was in this one and she performed quite well. It's my understanding that this was her first and last time in front of a movie camera.

That is correct. Well, she did a lot of stage work back in Texas, but as far as movies go, I think that was her only one. She now lives just over the hill from Hollywood in the Valley and she's still acting; in fact, she just joined another theater group. She's one of those people who just loves to act and it wouldn't matter if she was doing it on the sidewalk in front of a fire hydrant.

Too bad she didn't do more film work. She's quite striking to look at. You wrote quite a

Gary Warner Kent swinging into action in 2020 (courtesy Gary Warner Kent).

lot on how you felt about Liz Renay in your autobiography Shadows & Light, *which is a delightful read by the way. But how did you feel about Carolyn Brandt?*

Glad you enjoyed the book and, as far as Carolyn goes, I really admired her. Ray put her through the chops, man. She had to do a lot of stuff on his movies plus be a mother and pursue her own career as a dancer. She was always very polite and she was always driven. Whatever the part was, she threw herself into it 100 percent.

And that shows on the screen. Body Fever *was next on your Steckler résumé. You wrote fondly of this experience in your book but would you like to add anything to that here?*

You know, again, there was no script. I just had to improvise whatever I did. But I really enjoyed playing the bad guy. Come to think of it, I was always a bad guy in a Steckler movie, but in *Body Fever* I enjoyed that part a lot. I just immersed myself in the part and it was a lot of fun.

Liz Renay has a brief part in the film but I always felt Ray wasted her. I don't even think she has a line.

I didn't really know Liz all that well but I had to chase her all over that canyon in *The Thrill Killers*. I just thought she was a great lady. She was dedicated and serious about what she was doing. She wasn't the greatest actress but she was ... um ... pliable, so she could do what Ray would ask her to do. I chased her up and down that canyon and she had on high heels and she did it without any complaints at all.

Yeah, she really helped carry that film. Ray shot quite a bit of this one in his basement. Was that a really big basement?

It was a big basement and he went down there and made it into a soundstage. It was a big basement but a small soundstage and he did a lot of work down there. I have to hand it to him, he had his soundstage right in his house. What can I say?

I've always found it remarkable what he could achieve down there. Ray claimed Body Fever *had only one theatrical screening and it was with Richard Rush's* Getting Straight. *Did you happen to attend this viewing?*

I wasn't at that screening but I did see it once and I don't remember much about it. But I did see it.

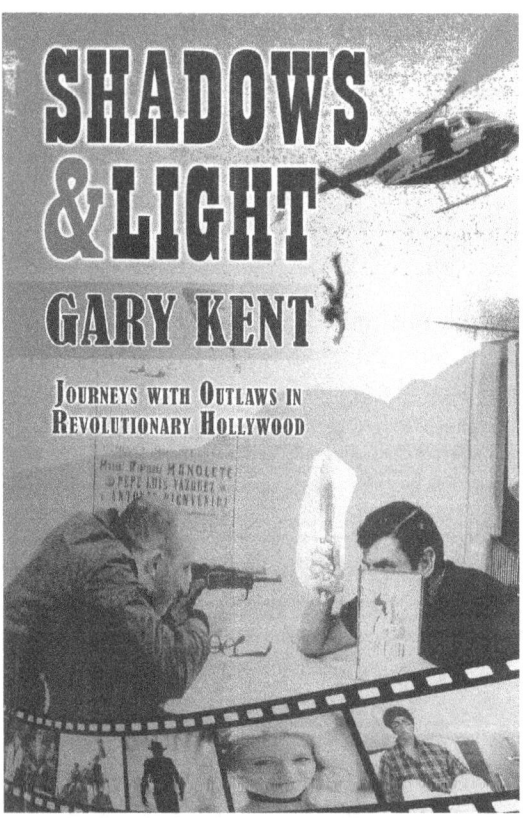

The cover of Gary Kent's autobiography *Shadows and Light: Journeys with Outlaws in Revolutionary Hollywood* (2009). The picture is an outtake from *The Thrill Killers* (1964). Notice that Steckler is leveling two guns at Kent with his (Steckler's) eyeglasses lying to his left (courtesy Gary Warner Kent).

Body Fever has a lot going for it but it does seem to kinda sputter and stall at times, making it a bit underwhelming. Sinthia: The Devil's Doll was your last film for Ray. In your autobiography you described it as "a seriously flawed art piece." Obviously, you weren't impressed with the outcome. What are your recollections of that production?

You know, it was one of Ray's attempts at being a really serious filmmaker and there were parts of it that I remember being excellent. I always enjoyed working for Ray. He was fun to be around. He was driven. Again, he never had a script that I saw but he was always by the camera and he always acted like he knew what he was doing even though he left so much up to the actors. As an actor, Ray would expect you to come up with your own dialogue and motivations but he would get you to do it with his own enthusiasm. He was very infectious. His own energy and belief in what he was doing, and you would get caught up in all of that and you really wanted to give him what he was after.

I've always felt that this was Ray's best-looking film. You may or may not be aware of this but Sinthia *ran on a double-bill, in England, with* One Million AC/DC *for a while, making it a Gary Kent double feature of sorts.*

Wow! That's interesting. I did not know that.

It was certainly a nice little piece of history to uncover. You were in three of Ray's movies from 1964 to 1970. Was there any difference between the Ray Steckler of the early '60s compared to the latter-day Ray?

No, Ray was the same old Ray. Whenever I talked with Ray, he was the same guy. He never changed. He

Gary Warner Kent (circa 2018) wearing a promotional t-shirt for the Joe O'Connell documentary *Danger God: The Lives and Love of a Hollywood Stuntman* (2019) with the original title *Love and Other Stunts* (courtesy Gary Warner Kent).

never got a big head that I knew of. I just remember him as this very driven and energetic guy who would catch you up in his enthusiasm and you were off to make a movie.

Did you ever see any of Ray's movies that you did not work on?
  No, I did not.

You mentioned in your book being paid for your involvement in The Thrill Killers, *but what about* Body Fever *and* Sinthia? *It always seemed like Ray never had money for anything.*
  No, there was never much pay at all. Lunch would be a bologna sandwich, if that. You were working mainly because you wanted to be in a movie and all the actors in Hollywood were dying to get in a movie. It's funny, L.A. is a movie town and yet it is so hard to get in a movie and it's so easy to do stage plays. It's not really a stage play town either. So, there's all these actors working on stage just dying to get into a movie. So Ray brought his enthusiasm and that big camera and I just loved the sight of it. I love cameras and sets and hearing A.D.s running around giving directions and Ray always had that kind of thing going on.

Any last thoughts on Ray and your relationship with him? When was the last time that you saw him?
  I don't remember the last time I saw him, but I do remember the last time I talked to him, which was close to when he died. He was telling me about standing in line at the post office and that this beautiful girl was in front of him. He said to her, "I think that you're probably an actress." To which she said, "Yes I am." Then he told her that he was a director and they hit it off really well. He was all excited because he thought he might even get to date her. Ray was always a little horny. So, yeah, that was the last time I talked with him but he did say that he was gonna send me some pages for a movie he was making. But that never happened. I guess this was around the time that he got sick.

In your autobiography, you wrote of being in a bar where writer Charles Bukowski was drunk and arguing with one of your friends. Did you ever meet the guy?
  Charles Bukowski? [*Laughs*] I knocked him down one night because he pissed on my shoe.

Oh my God! Why didn't you put that in your book?
  I don't know. It's just that so many people love Charles Bukowski and he was a drunk. I guess he was a nice guy to a lot of people. I didn't know him well but he used to hang out in this alley between the Raincheck Room and Barney's Beanery and I just thought he lived in that alley. He was always in there drunk and people would stop by and talk to him. Well, he came out and started talking to me and all of a sudden I felt this trickle and he was pissing on my shoe and out of reflex I just hit him and down he went. I was with some other people and they helped him up and said, "That's Charles Bukowski and he's a great writer." So I just walked away and went on up to Barney's.

That is hilarious! In 2018, Joe O'Connell directed a wonderful documentary on you called Danger God: The Lives and Love of a Hollywood Stuntman. *This thing is fantastic. Please talk as much as you like about it.*
  Joe is a writer, a very good writer, and he's gotten into doing documentaries. I met him at the Writer's Week here in Austin [Texas] and we kinda bonded and wrote a script together that never went anywhere but I got to know Joe and

Cover art for *Danger God: The Lives and Love of a Hollywood Stuntman*, Joe O'Connell's 2018 documentary on Gary Warner Kent (courtesy Joe O'Connell).

he said, "Gary, someone ought to do a documentary on you." And then about an hour later, he called me on the phone and said, "I've decided it should be me." I helped him out in any way that I could and he got the thing made.

Again, it's a wonderful documentary. This brings us to Quentin Tarantino's Once Upon a Time … in Hollywood. *Do you feel that Tarantino captured the spirit of that era?*

Oh, yeah, he totally captured Hollywood in that era. I know Quentin and we had a long talk while he was here in Austin making a movie. I was out looking for a gallery that was exhibiting some artwork by a friend of mine and pulled into the Sante Fe Hotel parking lot to ask for directions. The guys working the parking lot didn't know where it was but said for me to leave my car there and ask inside. So, I went inside to ask and I heard, "Gary!" And it's Quentin sitting alone at a table eating a sandwich. He asked me to sit down with him but I told him my car was out there and he said, "Don't worry about that. I'll take care of your car." So, I sat down and we started talking about Jack Nicholson and those two Westerns I did with him up in Utah. All of a sudden, Quentin adopted Jack's voice and started reciting every single line Jack had in that movie. I was amazed. He was spot on. He had everything down perfectly. Oh, and that's when I told Quentin my Charles Manson story.

You must've spoken with him around the time he was making Death Proof. *How did you feel about Bruce Dern's portrayal of George Spahn?*

You know, Bruce doesn't look anything like George Spahn but that's okay. I knew George Spahn not as a person lying in bed but as a person sitting at a table all the time with cats everywhere. He would sit at that table in that ramshackle house drinking coffee with these cats all over the table. He seemed like a jolly person and I would have to go to him all the time (because we were shooting a lot on the Spahn Ranch) and ask how much it was gonna cost to shoot another day. He was always very affable and seemed glad to have the company. He did have those Manson girls hanging around but they were hanging around the set anyway.

They were always hanging around saying, "Can I have your lunch?" They were just these ragamuffin girls who would invite us up to Charlie's place, but I didn't want to go because I had other things to do. A couple of our crew members went up there and regretted it, because they said the girls smelled bad and Charlie was crazy.

Too funny. Could you have seen yourself in the role of George Spahn?

Gee, no, I'm nothing like George. I remember him being really overweight, balding with white hair.

It's known that, while a portion of Brad Pitt's character Cliff Booth was partially based on you, he was also based off of Burt Reynolds' stunt double Hal Needham. Did you know him at all?

I never worked with Hal and I never met him. The stunt community, at that time, was small and we all seemed to know one another but somehow I never met Needham but I do know a lot of people that did know him and worked with him.

As mentioned before, another Tarantino film featuring a Hollywood stuntman was Death Proof. *Here, Kurt Russell plays Stuntman Mike. When asked how he got into this line of work, he said something to the effect of, "Well, in Hollywood, anyone fool enough to throw himself down a flight of stairs can usually find someone to pay him for it." Was that pretty accurate as far as you're concerned?*

Yes [*laughs*], and stair falls are a bitch. They're not as exciting as a car chase *per se* but they're a bitch because they hurt all the way down, even when you're wearing your pads. I've done two stair falls in the movies and both times I got pretty bruised up. That's a good line of Kurt's.

Did a director ever ask you to perform a stunt that you simply would not do?

I never had it happen to me but it did happen to my wife, who I was dating at the time, Tomi Barrett. The director was asking her to do a stunt that I knew was not safe, so I suggested something else. He wanted her to go down this river where there were all kinds of rapids and rocks that would just beat the hell out of her even if she was wearing pads. The river was just too swift and too dangerous so I talked the director into having her do a high fall off of a cliff into a deep pool which was a great shot and worked probably better than her going down the river. The stunt was totally safe. In fact, I went up and did it before her and said, "Just don't look down. If you look down, that water will just slap you in the face. Just go for it." Now, Don Jones, who was directing that movie, went up and did it but he looked down and wound up with a bloody nose. That water hit him in the face like a hammer.

Hey, Don, listen to the seasoned stuntman! Lastly, what's Boo saying right now?

[*Laughs*] He says, "Go for it. Relax. Have a good time."

Wonderful.

Have Talent, Will Travel: A Conversation with Cult Movie Star Ron Jason

Curry: *Ray Dennis Steckler always claimed that he met you while you were working on his air conditioner; is this accurate?*

Jason: No, that's not true.

Then why does he always say that?

Ray always made up stuff like that. He just thought these stories were more interesting. I met Ray through a gentleman named Ron Kerns. Ron had done a movie with Ray and Zalman King called *Trip with the Teacher*. I was working on a documentary about treasure-hunting and Ron told me to go see Ray. So that's how I met Ray. I never did finish that documentary but Ray started telling me about this movie he was doing with Pierre Agostino and asked me if I was interested.

Was this War Cat *or* Las Vegas Serial Killer? *The timelines of those two movies seem to overlap a bit.*

It was *Las Vegas Serial Killer,* but *War Cat* was around the exact same time too. Here's what Ray would do a lot of times: Say we had a girl working for free or whatever. Pierre would strangle her and I'd slash her throat and then he'd get a two-for-one.

That's probably in the low-budget filmmaking handbook somewhere. Las Vegas Serial Killer *really only has three central characters. There's Pierre as Johnathan Klick, Chris Cave as Jack and you as Clarence with the remaining cast being nameless victims being mugged or murdered. Tell me about your co-stars.*

Pierre knew Ray before I did. Pierre was born in São Paulo, Brazil, and he was a really good guy and died of a heart attack at like 66 years old. Chris Cave and I were actually best friends and I got him into the movie. Ray said I needed a sidekick and I said, "Hey, I have a sidekick in real life and he loves to work on movies." It's another one of Chris's passions. So I introduced Ray to Chris and we started filming.

Unfortunately, I came up empty-handed on any other information on Chris.

Okay, let's see … Chris is in a movie called *Ride Out of the Past* which is a biker film that we did and I'm not sure when that thing is going to be released.

About what year was that?

That one was made in the '90s and John Wayne Bobbitt had a guest appearance in it and we killed him with a shotgun in a shoot-out. Anyhow, Chris always wanted to be an actor, so we talked about it and that's how I got him hooked up with Ray.

Steckler claimed that Chris was a former police officer. Is this more Steckler lore?

No, that one is true. Chris had been an M.P. in the Army, a police officer in Oklahoma and on the Las Vegas Metropolitan police department for about three years. Then he became an electrical contractor through the Journeyman's Union.

After watching countless hours of Steckler interviews, you can catch him chasing his tail trying to recall which story he told before.

[Laughs] Absolutely!

One of the other Steckler stories that may be a myth as well since you weren't an air conditioning repair man…

I actually I owned an air conditioning construction company where I did mostly new construction.

Did Chris ever work with you?

Yes he did whenever he needed a little side work.

Okay, more accurate Steckler-lore. Linda and Laura worked on Las Vegas Serial Killer. *Do you have memories of them on that shoot?*

Well, let's say more Laura than Linda. Linda was in Hawaii most of the time and Laura had come back to Las Vegas for a while after living in Los Angeles. When we opened up the acting school, Laura was also working at the editing bay, but she wasn't editing *Las Vegas Serial Killer*. So I had a lot of interaction with Laura. I've had a lot of interaction with Linda and Morgan and Bailey as well as Katherine. As far as the movie goes, Laura was more involved.

When did you start shooting Las Vegas Serial Killer?

Early '80s, I think. If you look at the scene where Pierre is standing outside the barber shop, he looks much younger than when he's walking out of prison, and Laura had worked on the earlier stuff. I didn't come along until after all of that. Ray had started that film but hadn't finished it and when I came along, we got along so well that I think that I may have been the catalyst that helped get it finished. I'm not trying to brag on myself but I think my enthusiasm for the project helped Ray see it to the finish line.

Was War Cat *next? I'm guessing you knew it then as* Angel of Vengeance.

Yes, and it was released under both titles. Here's the interesting thing about *War Cat*: I was supposed to play the character Ron but then I ended up in the hospital with a kidney stone. So I didn't get to play my character and in the interim Ray backed out of the film and Ted finished it. Then Ted and Jeff Hogue, who produced it, both came to me and said, "Hey, Ron, you furnished the props, you furnished the sets and you were supposed to co-star in this film and we're not finished shooting yet so please be in the film." So I wound up with a much smaller role as a camp terrorist.

Do you know exactly what happened with the transitioning of the director's chair? Ray and Ted each had his own version.

Ray and Ted were shooting a scene at the city building downtown and they had a disagreement and Ray just left.

Wow, that's not at all the story Ted told me.

Really? What did Ted tell you?

Ted told me that Jeff Hogue and his money people were getting antsy with Ray shooting exterior shots for three solid days and they went back to Ted and asked if he could finish the picture. Ted told them that he would only step into that position if Ray was okay with it. According to Ted, Ray said, "Have fun with the movie. We'll be out of here by tomorrow."

Basically, there was a problem with what Ray was shooting, but Ray did find the locations and figured out what and where they were going to shoot. I wasn't actually there for the confrontation, as I was still in the hospital, but Jerry Carroll told me that Ted, Ray and Jeff butted heads and Ray just gracefully walked out. Ray was not at all upset. He gracefully walked out and he even left all his people there. He left Rick Ties there. He left Jerry Carroll there. He left Glenda Savage there. He left all his people there to help Ted finish the movie. There was no animosity when Ray pulled out.

I would like to know if the energy on the set differed from Ray to Ted, but I guess you wouldn't know since you weren't on set yet.

Well, yes and no. Since I've worked with both of them, and while they do things very differently, the energy is always very positive on both of their sets. I really liked both of them a lot.

You made a few more movies with Ted V. Mikels: Mission: Killfast, Dimension in Fear, Mark of the Astro Zombies *and*

Heart of a Boy. *Can you tell me something interesting that most people wouldn't know about one of them?*

You've seen *Mark of the Astro Zombies,* right? Do you remember the end where they freeze-frame on a boy that was chasing all the girls? Okay, this is very personal to me, and I'm probably gonna go to tears telling it, that's my son Randy and he died two years ago at 31 years old. I'm so thankful that Ted shot that footage when I brought Randy down to the location and Ted put him in that movie. There are probably very few people that know that.

Ron that's very touching. Thanks so much for sharing that story. If you don't mind me asking, how did Randy pass away?

He was robbed and killed in his apartment in Las Vegas. I brought him to Los Angeles and I buried him in Chatsworth in the Valley, where I live.

That's truly awful to hear and a terrible way to lose a loved one. Whenever you're ready, we can move on to something else.

Okay, what do you want to know next?

*All right, a lot of this stuff seems to be happening around the same time—*Las Vegas Serial Killer *and* War Cat *both are 1986 and it's my understanding that Ray opened Mascot Video during this period as well.*

Right, Ray opened up Mascot Video shortly after we finished *Las Vegas Serial Killer* but while we were still shooting *Las Vegas Thrill Killers.* We even shot some of *Las Vegas Thrill Killers* scenes in one of his Mascot Video stores. He eventually had three of those stores and I built him all of his shelving units just to help him out.

While digging around on YouTube, I ran across a short video where you and a woman give a tour of Mascot Video.

Yep, and that was shot by Joaquin Mantalvan, who I've been working with recently. The woman is Glenda Savage. She's in *Las Vegas Serial Killer* and she's in *War Cat.* In *Serial Killer* she's the one who gets strangled with her bathing suit top at the pool party. She still lives in Las Vegas and we still stay in touch. She's a real sweet person.

Here's something funny. I'm on my third movie with Joaquin and it's almost as though Ray is the catalyst for us to make this thing. That's why my character's name is Ray and Chris Cave plays a character named Dennis and we have Glenda in a bit part and there's just all kinds of innuendos and references to Ray and his work.

What's this film's title?

Rebel Drifters Ride Again. The first movie I made with Joaquin was *The Legend of Hillbilly Butcher* and next came *Cannibal Corpse Killers.* I had about 30 percent screen time on that one and I'm starring in this latest one.

These are great titles. I have to check them out. Backing up a bit, around 1986, Ray was featured on The Incredibly Strange Film Show *and you were also a participant. I was wondering what your recollection of that experience was. And how it was working with Jonathan Ross?*

Jonathan Ross was a very nice fellow and they interviewed me on that show and that's where we told that phony story about the air conditioning stuff. So, that's where that rumor started.

Did Jonathan Ross know that it was a fabricated tale?

Oh no, we never told him that we made all that stuff up. Also, we got the police called on us that night because we were using a location, that naturally we didn't rent, in a warehouse district and we were firing a gun with blanks. So somebody called the cops on us.

That's classic guerrilla-style filmmaking. I was actually going to ask about that film that was being shot during the documentary which was under the working title Dark Alleys in a Well-Lit City. *Which I think is a really good title.*

It's a great title.

Whatever happened with that one? Did it ever get much further along than what was shot for the show?

It was never finished and no, not a lot more was done on it but I was the guy firing the gun. That was me and Chris Cave in the black biker jackets that say The Thrill Killers on the backs.

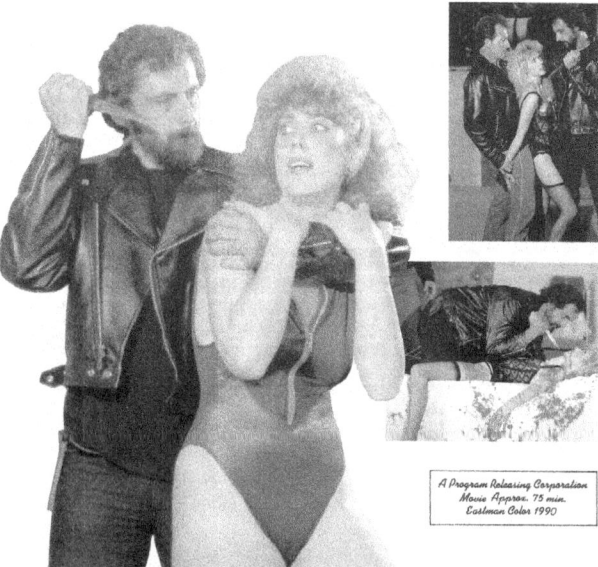

Promotional ad slick for the unfinished and thought-to-be-lost *Las Vegas Thrill Killers* (1990) (courtesy Ron Jason).

Okay, here's the big question: Tell me about this lost film called Las Vegas Thrill Killers.

That's the one that I sent you the ad slick for as well as a couple of production stills. That girl that I slashed the throat of, in the production stills, had been in *Playboy* at one time. Of course, in our movie she was considerably older but Ray told me she had been in *Playboy*. I think her name was Corinne Broskette. Ray and I had her coming over to kill her in that scene. I painted the walls. We dragged the set pieces in and created that room and I killed her as the paint was drying on the wall.

[Note: Ms. Broskette was in a touring production of the musical *Hair* in 1968. She appeared in the December 1969 *Playboy* in a spread called "The Girls of *Hair*."]

I understand that there is a possibility of obtaining this film, or at least some footage from it.

My understanding is that some of the footage got lost at a place called United Color Lab. Another bunch of footage got bought in Las Vegas by a guy named Adam and I've been in contact with him. He supposedly wants to digitize that footage and finish that movie. Now, I'm not sure what sort of situation that is for him to do that or not. You know, that film belongs to me and Ray but we are in communication and I'm just waiting to see what the guy does. Supposedly he bought a storage unit and that's how he got the footage.

So anyway, back to the actual movie: We filmed 90 percent of *Las Vegas Serial Killer* and 90 percent of *Las Vegas Thrill Killers*

Behind-the-scenes photo from *Las Vegas Thrill Killers* (1990). As Corinne Broskette watches, Steckler aims his 16mm Bolex directly at Ron Jason (courtesy Ron Jason).

in Las Vegas and the remaining ten percent in Los Angeles. Let's say Pierre strangles a girl in a parking lot in Hollywood and then I take the same girl and I slit her throat in the same parking lot. Because Ray was trying to do a two-fer. The girl was there and you're paying her so we basically shot the two films at the same time and then put the pieces together later. At least that was the theory. Somewhere I have a preview trailer for *Las Vegas Thrill Killers*.

Now, circling back to *Las Vegas Serial Killer*: There was a scene where Pierre kills some girls and stacks their bodies in the living room of a very fancy house. That scene was shot up in the Hollywood Hills and that house belonged to someone who owed Ray a favor. That was the only part of the movie that was shot with sync sound. Everything else was looped and dubbed and I know this because I operated the boom mic for the Nagra on that scene. We shot two or three different scenes on that trip where Pierre and I would murder the girls in our respective fashions.

Okay, I want to step back a bit and ask if you knew Carolyn Brandt.

I met Ray around 1980 or '81, just as they had gotten divorced so I didn't know Carolyn, but I was there before he met Katherine. He met Katherine while he was teaching film at UNLV. She was one of his students.

She acted as producer on some of his later movies. When you knew Ray in the early '80s, did he ever ask you to be involved in his adult features?

No, because by the time I was in the picture, he was winding that part of his life down. He was constantly editing his legit films and teaching at UNLV and he

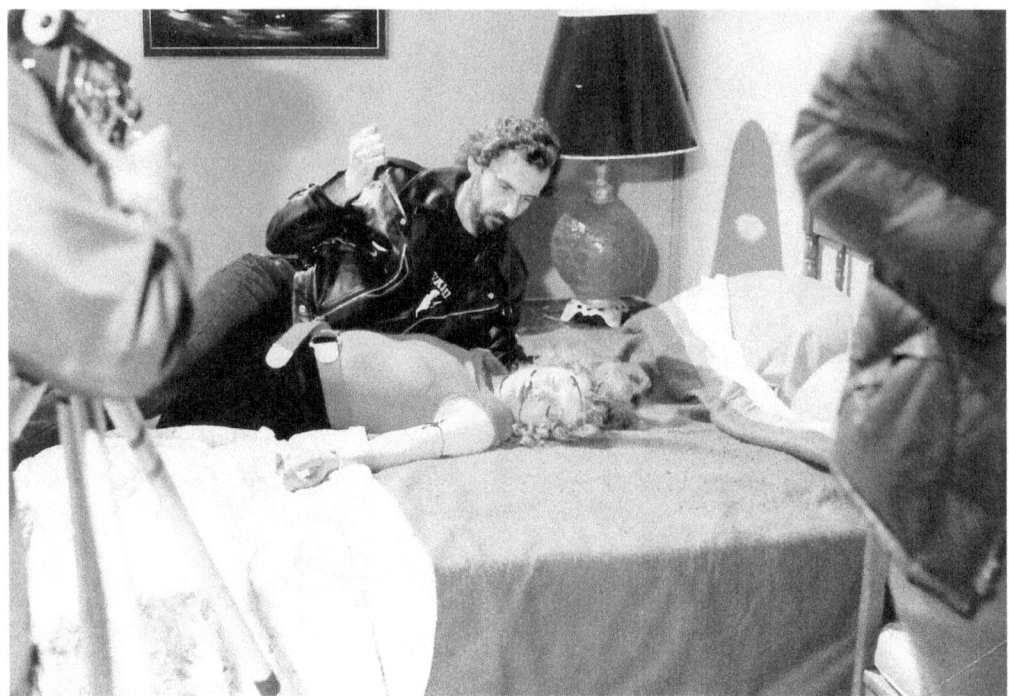

Another behind-the-scenes photo from 1990's *Las Vegas Thrill Killers*. Ron Jason has just sliced up Corinne Broskette (courtesy Ron Jason).

lost his job there because of some politics. Apparently, some board members had a hard-on for Ray and his porn past and they didn't feel that he was suitable teaching material, so they fired him. And Ray loved teaching and he was broken-hearted when they let him go.

I know Ray spent decades trying to hide from those films but with the Internet it became impossible for him to continue doing so. These days the attitude towards pornography is totally different anyway. It really shouldn't have bothered him that much. Let's talk about your 1993 movie High Desert.

Okay, that one was directed by Charles Lang. A couple of years earlier, he done a movie called *Soul of the Demon*. Anyhow, *High Desert* is a biker movie about a gang that terrorizes unsuspecting campers. By the way, it was Pierre Agostino's final movie and he took the screen name Peter Gold because he was also one of the producers as Pierre Agostino.

Let's spend some time on your latest projects for director Joaquin Montalvan.

Joaquin was just about finished shooting *Hillbilly Butcher* and he got a-hold of me because he needed someone to play Papa Jessup and he also needed someone to do the ending of the movie for him. So we did the part of Papa Jessup, and when the son of Papa Jessup goes to Hell, Joaquin just said, "Ron, you do what you want to do." So, I ad-libbed the whole end of that movie for him and I actually won Best Actor for the Pollygrind Film Festival for that ad lib.

Oh, that's fantastic. You know, both of his films are getting really good reviews.

That's good to know. Now, when he did *The Cannibal Corpse Killers,* Joaquin came to me and said, "Ron, I think you're perfect to play the Evil Magistrate." So I played that part, and as I mentioned before, I got about 30 percent screen time. Then he came out to my house and interviewed me and put some stuff up on YouTube and we got to talking about *High Desert* which led to me mentioning my unfinished movie *Ride Out of the Past*. So Joaquin took that footage and edited it together. We don't have a release date yet but he got so excited about these two biker movies, he said, "Ron, let's make a third biker movie." That's how *Rebel Drifters Ride Again* came about and I'm starring in that picture.

That's very cool. The Ron Jason biker trilogy. Okay, let's wrap this thing up with one final question. Tell me your feelings about Ray as a person and Ray as a moviemaker.

As a person, Ray was a dedicated family man and he was very protective of his children. I always respected that about him. When I was making the transition to move to L.A., there were a lot of nights that Ray and Katherine let me sleep at their home. And I got to meet Ray's mother, she always called him Dennis, and sit with them and watch home movies that Ray made in junior high school. So, again, Ray was good to his family and he was also good to his friends and we were very close friends.

As a filmmaker, I think in his own way, he was a genius. With Ray, we never shot with a script; with Ted, we always shot with a script. For some reason, Ray was able to edit pieces of nothing into something. Also, me and my dad would go around to Ray's garage where he was editing *Serial Killer* and we would loop sound. Like, that's my Dad's voice that introduces Toni Alessandrini. And something else that a lot of people don't know is that Ray shot that film on 35mm and 16mm. I think if Ray had stayed in Hollywood, he would've become a very successful filmmaker.

Conclusion

Work on this book began in earnest around 2017 and wrapped up in the late winter months of 2021. RE/Search's *Incredibly Strange Films* book was immediately consulted for a filmography. (This book of indispensable exploitation film information contained Boyd Rice's 20-plus-page interview with Steckler.) Eleven titles in all with one being unreleased (*Bloody Jack the Ripper*) and *Sinthia: The Devil's Doll* being repeated. With only nine films to cover and the knowledge of a tenth (*Las Vegas Serial Killer*), the assumption was that this book would be easy, breezy and fun to concoct.

The search for the films was on and eBay was perused first. This dig yielded two Steckler box sets containing four films each. The DVD company Media Blasters released these eight films between 2003 and 2005 under their Shriek Show and Guilty Pleasures banners. In 2007, they repackaged these titles in two separate boxes as *Midnight Movies Collection* and *Midnight Movies Collection II*. These discs were jam-packed with extras including trailers, short films, still galleries, interviews and, most importantly, audio commentaries by Steckler himself.

Eight of the ten titles were easy enough to procure and the balance was not much more difficult. *Wild Guitar* has been in the public domain for decades so drumming up a copy of that at the local Dollar Tree was swift. Then Something Weird Video had paired *Sinthia: The Devil's Doll* with the Anton LaVey–First Church of Satan documentary *Satanis: The Devil's Mass*. What now remained were the features leading up to Steckler's directorial debut.

Before *Wild Guitar*, Steckler, had been cinematographer on a handful of films starting with *The World's Greatest Sinner*. This particular DVD had been in the collection for years—check. The remainder, as with *Wild Guitar*, were property of the public so *Secret File: Hollywood*, *Wild Ones on Wheels* and *Eegah* were a snap to track down.

Another eBay search revealed three Steckler-related CDs: one from England's Big Beat label entitled *The Wild Wild World of Mondo Movies* and two from Norton Records, *Ron Haydock and the Boppers: 99 Chicks* and *Wild Guitar! Arch Hall, Jr., and the Archers*. The latter two CDs came complete with a wealth of information contained within their booklets penned by Norton Records founder (and *Kicks* magazine editor) Miriam Linna.

As these items began to trickle into the mailbox, daily eBay and Amazon searches were the norm. Here comes *Cult Movies* magazine #8, #10 and #15 with several interviews and reviews regarding Steckler by James Elliot Singer. That magazine, published by Buddy Barnett and edited by Michael Copner, also had an interview-based tie-in television program called *Cult Movies TV*. One episode featured Titus Moede (or Moody as he is credited on the box). Hopefully, Boo Boo would tell all.

West Indianapolis' R.D. Steckler Research Library (2021) (author's collection).

Armed with the above along with Michael Weldon's *Psychotronic* guides, Video Hound's *Cult Flicks and Trash Pics*, Andrew J. Rausch's *Gods of Grindhouse* and a copy of *The Incredibly Strange Film Show*, this thing seemed a go. It would just be a quaint little salute to one of the unsung underdogs of underground cinema. However, that crystal ball can sometimes get cloudy as a quick peek at IMDb confirmed. This project would neither be quick, quaint or breezy. Ray Dennis Steckler, director of 50 movies—40 more than bargained for.

Sure, the balance of these films were Steckler's adult titles but how in God's green hell could they all be located? The original decision made was to simply ignore them. Enter Patrick M. Leer as initial editor to help keep this project on track, cohesive and correct. Pat felt that there was no need to even pursue this endeavor if the adult titles were not discussed. It was agreed that each of those flicks would be given its day in court if only very briefly.

Now, the hunt was on for three dozen (or more) obscure, cheaper-than-cheap pornographic films. Something Weird Video afforded three and Vinegar Syndrome, arguably one of the most popular boutique video company (as of this writing), offered up five. Still, this was a long way from 36 movies. The basic thought was to simply get a grip on how Steckler handled this type of material and move on.

More video companies, releasing other Steckler adult movies, started popping up on eBay and Amazon; this was going to get expensive. An inquiry to an old friend, Rob Spay, rendered a remedy: xhamster.com. This free streaming site featured about 30 of the films that were needed. Yet, with this deluge of material at the fingertips and at the ready, the self-imposed one-year deadline was slipping far into the distance.

So the writing and editorial sessions began without one single solitary publisher contacted to find out if anyone would even be interested in the subject of Ray Dennis Steckler. This routine went on for years as my (mostly) patient and largely uninterested wife, Julie Marie, listened to the low-budget cinematic yammerings of her husband.

As the work wound down, it appeared obvious that Steckler's ex-wife, Carolyn Brandt, should be contacted, along with daughter Laura H. Steckler, who seemed to carry the torch for her father's cinema. Through Facebook she was made aware of the project but no mention of the adult titles was forthcoming. For years Steckler hid from these films. It was a very touchy subject but in the end Carolyn and Laura felt it was okay to confront these things that Steckler would rather have had erased from film history. They candidly answered every question asked of them whether by telephone or email in the most cordial of manners. No inquiry seemed too tough for them. Furthermore, they all seemed to be sincerely interested in the project.

But would a publisher? Then a 2019 edition of the bi-yearly magazine *Grindhouse Purgatory*, Volume 1, Issue 14, slid across my desk. Inside was an article by Aaron AuBuchon outlining the differences between *The Chooper* and *Blood Shack*. Not only was it great to see interest in Steckler's movies in the year 2019 but to also know that there was a shared belief that *The Chooper* was the superior of the two.

The sheer amount of cooperation received on this project had to be unprecedented in these types of circles. Nearly everyone contacted was excited by the prospect of the work and were pleased to lend a hand. Fast friends and/or acquaintances were made of family members and actors (Carolyn Brandt, Laura Steckler, Gary Kent, Ron Jason), artists and musicians (Boyd Rice, Tom Bagley, Jean Coffinberry) and fellow writers (David Dent, Raleigh Bronkowski, Michael Weldon, Jim Morton and again Boyd Rice).

Eventually, one query letter was sent out and one positive reply was received. A query package with three sample chapters was sent and a contract was offered. A few details were hammered out, a contract with a proposed word count and deadline was signed, and that aching question was finally answered: There *was* interest in this stuff.

Then, while digging through the archives, an interview from 2005 surfaced. The Q&A was conducted by author Mark Seiber for his website–message board The Horror Drive-In. Here is an excerpt proving that this project had been a possibility for over a decade. "Mark Seiber: So, after the [Ted V.] Mikels book is sold, what's next? Christopher Curry: Filmmaker-wise, we'll have to see. Hmmm, Ray Dennis Steckler might be in the running."

Bibliography

AuBuchon, Aaron. "The Chooper Vs. Blood Shack." Grindhouse Purgatory Vol. 1, Issue 14 2019, pp. 44–49.

"Audio Commentary." *Blood Shack,* produced by Media Blasters, Inc under the Shriek Show banner, 2004. DVD.

"Audio Commentary." *Body Fever,* produced by Media Blasters, Inc under the Guilty Pleasures banner, 2004. DVD.

"Audio Commentary." *The Hollywood Strangler Meets the Skid Row Slasher,* produced by Media Blasters, Inc under the Guilty Pleasures banner, 2004. DVD.

"Audio Commentary." *The Incredibly Strange Creatures Who Stopped Living and Became Mixed-Up Zombies!!?,* produced by Media Blasters, Inc under the Guilty Pleasures banner, 2004. DVD.

"Audio Commentary." *The Las Vegas Serial Killer,* produced by Media Blasters, Inc under the Guilty Pleasures banner, 2005. DVD.

"Audio Commentary." *The Lemon Grove Kids Meet the Monsters,* produced by Media Blasters, Inc under the Guilty Pleasures banner, 2003. DVD.

"Audio Commentary." *Rat Pfink A Boo Boo,* produced by Media Blasters, Inc under the Guilty Pleasures banner, 2003. DVD.

"Audio Commentary." *The Thrill Killers,* produced by Media Blasters, Inc under the Shriek Show banner, 2003. DVD.

Bangs, Lester. *Psychotic Reactions and Carburetor Dung.* New York: Vintage Books, 1988.

Brandt, Carolyn. "Personal Interview." June 06, 2021.

Bronkowski, Raleigh. *The Scene of Screen 13.* Facebook group.

Burns, Bob. "Lemon Grove Kids Meet the Monsters." *King of the Monsters* no. 1, 1977, pp. 63–65.

Carey, Romeo. *The Romeo Carey Podcast:* "Legendary B-Movie Director, Ray Dennis Steckler." Podcast originally aired November 15, 2020.

Curry, Christopher Wayne. *Film Alchemy: The Independent Cinema of Ted V. Mikels.* Jefferson, North Carolina: McFarland, 2008.

Curry, Christopher Wayne with John Curry. W. *A Taste of Blood: The Films of Herschell Gordon Lewis.* London: Creation Books International, 1999.

Daley, Astrid B., and Adam Parfrey. (essay by Miriam Linna). *Sin-A-Rama: Sleaze Sex Paperbacks of the Sixties.* Port Townsend, Washington: Feral House, 2016.

Dent, David. "Goof on the Loose: The Films of Ray Dennis Steckler—Part—1—The Hollywood Years." Dark Eyes of London. Published by David Dent November 30, 2018 http://darkeyesoflondon.blogspot.com/2018/11/goof-on-loose-films-of-ray-dennis.html.

Dent, David. "Goof on the Loose: The Films of Ray Dennis Steckler—Part 2—The Las Vegas Years." Dark Eyes of London. Published by David Dent April 21, 2019. https://darkeyesoflondon.blogspot.com/2019/04/goof-on-loose-films-of-ray-dennis.html.

Farquad, Abernathy. "Mad Monsters Proudly Presents the First Monster Musical for Your De-Frightful Pleasure!" Mad Monster no. 10, 1965, pp. 25–30.

The 50 Worst Movies of All Time. Produced by Dante J. Pugliese, performances by Carlos Larkin. Passport Video, 2004. DVD.

Friedman, David F. *A Youth in Babylon: Confessions of A Trash-Film King.* Buffalo, New York: Prometheus Books, 1990.

Grey, Rudolph. *Nightmare of Ecstasy: The Life and Art of Edward D. Wood Jr.* Los Angeles, California: Feral House Publishing, 1992.

Haydock, Ron. "Blood Valley Days." *The Monster Times* Feb. 1974 No. 30. pp.19–21 & 29.

Helman, Sheldon M. "The Incredibly Strange Creatures." *Movies Illustrated: Picture Stories of New Films* May 1964, pp. 68–70.

The Incredibly Strange Film Show. Hosted by Jonathan Ross. Season 1—episode 2. Produced by the British public service television broadcast Channel 4 August 12, 1988.

Juno, Andrea, and V. Vale. *Incredibly Strange Films.* California: Re/Search, 1986.

Juno, Andrea, and V. Vale. *Incredibly Strange Music Volume 1.* California: Re/Search, 1993.

Kent, Gary. *Shadows and Light: Journey's with Outlaws in Revolutionary Hollywood.* Austin, Texas: Dalton Publishing, 2009.

Kerswell, J.A. *The Slasher Movie Book.* Chicago, Illinois: Chicago Review Press, 2012.

Konow, David. *Schlock-o-Rama: The Films of Al Adamson.* Los Angeles, California: Lone Eagle Publishing Company, 1998.

Legend, Johnny. "The Incredibly Strange Ray

Dennis Steckler." *Fangoria* magazine Issue 28 1983, pp. 24–27.

Linna, Miriam. *Ron Haydock and the Boppers: 99 Chicks.* New York: Norton Records, 1996.

Linna, Miriam. *Wild Guitar: Arch Hall, Jr., and the Archers.* New York: Norton Records, 2005.

MacGillivray. "The Lemon Grove Kids Meet the Monsters (1966–1969)." *Filmfax* magazine, August/September 1996 issue no. 57. pp. 53–54.

Medved, Harry, and Michael Medved. *The Golden Turkey Awards: The Worst Achievements in Hollywood History.* New York: Berkley edition, 1981.

Moede, Titus. "Interview." *Cult Movies TV,* produced by Alpha Home Entertainment, Inc under the Alpha New Cinema banner, 2011. DVD.

Muller, Eddie, with Daniel Faris. *Grindhouse: The Forbidden World of Adults Only Cinema.* New York: St. Martin's Griffin, 1996.

O'Connell, Joe. *Danger God: The Lives and Love of a Hollywood Stuntman,* documentary produced by Nickel Pickle Films and distributed by Wild Eye Releasing 2018.

Oswalt, Patton. *Zombie Spaceship Wasteland: A Book by Patton Oswalt.* New York: Scribner's, 2011.

Rausch, Andrew J. *Gods of Grindhouse: Interviews with Exploitation Filmmakers.* Duncan, Oklahoma: Bear Manor Media, 2013.

Roberts, Chris. *I Saw It on Linden Street: Cult Films, Exploitation Oddities & Cinema Classics*: "Rat Pfink A Boo Boo (1966)." Podcast originally aired on May 10, 2021.

Ross, Jonathan. *The Incredibly Strange Film Book: An Alternative History of Cinema.* London, England: Simon & Schuster Ltd, 1993.

Rutherford, Scott *Roller Coasters.* Ann Arbor, Michigan: Lowe and B. Hould Publishers, 2003.

Schwartz, Carol with Olenski, Jim. *Cult Flicks and Trash Pics.* Canton, Michigan: Visible Ink Press, 2002.

Singer, James Elliot. "Cult Movies Interview: Ray Dennis Steckler." *Cult Movies* no. 8, 1993, pp. 30–33.

Singer, James Elliot. "Ray Dennis Steckler: Take Two." *Cult Movies* no. 15, 1995, pp. 70–73.

Sounes, Howard. *Charles Bukowski: Locked in the Arms of a Crazy Life.* New York, NY: Grove Press, 1998.

Steckler, Laura. "Personal Interview." March 30, 2021.

Steckler, Ray Dennis. "John Andrews: Through My Eyes." *Cult Movies* no. 10, 1994, pp. 34–35.

Steckler, Ray Dennis. *Steckler Interviews Volume #1,* produced by Steckler Enterprises, Inc and distributed by Program Releasing Corporation, 1993. VHS.

Thompson, Dave. *Smoke on the Water: The Deep Purple Story.* Canada: ECW Press, 2004.

Thompson, John Jr. "Las Vegas Filmmakers Dabble in the Odd and Offbeat." *Las Vegas Sun* Wednesday, August 12, 1998.

Walker, Mark. *Ghostmasters: A Look Back At America's Midnight Spook Shows.* Boca Raton, Florida: Cool Hand Communications, Inc. A Publishing Company, 1994.

Weldon, Michael. *The Psychotronic Encyclopedia of Film.* New York: Ballantine Books, 1983.

Weldon, Michael J. *The Psychotronic Video Guide.* New York: St. Martin's Griffin, 1996.

Index

Numbers in **_bold italics_** refer to pages with illustrations

A-Bones (musical artist) 196
Abbott and Costello Meet Frankenstein 92
ABC Studios 210
Ackerman, Forrest J 69, 75
Adams, Max (musical artist) 200
Adamson, Al 1, 19–20, 32, 54, 112, 119
The Addams Family 35
The Adult Version of Jekyll and Hyde 153
Agnes of God 216
Agostino, Leigh 148
Agostino, Pierre (aka Peter Gold) 134, 136, 139, 141, 144–145, 147, 152, 194, 231–232, 235–236
Air Force One 73
Alcoa Corporation 56
Alessandrini, Toni (Reenee, Toni) 147, 183, 185, 187, 237
Alexander, Victor (Delony, Jerry) 155
Alford, Chuck 138, 140, 147
Alford, Denise 140, 146
Alice in Wonderland: An X-Rated Musical Fantasy 49
Allen, Corey 132–133, 214
The Amazing Mrs. Holiday 29
The Amazing Ormond 62–63
Amazon.com 239, 241
American Cinematographer Manual 20
American Graffiti 224
The Andrea True Connection (musical artist) 177
Andrews, John 111–112
Andrews, "Slim" Arkansas 112
Angel's Flight 36
Anger, Kenneth 35
The Animal Mothers (musical artist) 200
Anne, Rox (Roxy) 84, 86
Anthony, Charles 183
Anthony, Franklin 186
Ape Rape (book) 69

Apostolof, Stephen C. 54, 112
Arch Hall, Jr., and the Archers (musical artist) 21–22
Armageddon 73
Arness, James 69
Arnold, Maria 154, 158–159, 170
The Astronauts (musical artist) 67
Atasaya 122
AuBuchon, Aaron 241

Babb, Kroger 7, 60, 115, 153
Baby Bubbles 159, 170, 173–174, 184, 192
Bach, Eddie 162–167
Bachelor Party 147
The Bad and Beautiful 215
Bagley, Tom 242
Bangs, Lester 43
Barbary Coast (Las Vegas, Nevada) 147
Bardo, Joe (aka Brick Bardo) 45, 48–49, 53, 57, 88, 101, 104, 112
Barnett, Buddy 240
Barney's Beanery (Hollywood, California) 228
Barrett, Tomi 230
Barron, Bebe 29
Barron, Louis 29
Bartel, Paul 142
Barton, Earl 210
Basket Case 2
Bates, John 126, 129, 154
Batman 66–67, 72, 74, 210
Batman and Robin 1, 67, 78
Baty y Roby contra el Crimen 78; see also *The Degenerate*; *The Insane*; *Rat Pfink a Boo Boo*; *Rock and Roll Superheros*
Baxter, Les 113
Baykok 122
"Bazooki" (musical recording) 66–67
Beast from 20,000 Fathoms 31
The Beast of Yucca Flats 38, 85, 103
The Beatles (musical group) 47

Bechard, Gorman 142
Behind the Green Door 138
Benedict, Laura (aka Gallegly, Rose Mary) 45, 53, 225
Bernardi, Herschel 209
The Best Little Cathouse in Las Vegas 185
The Best Little Whorehouse in Texas 185
Beyond the Valley of the Dolls 43, 103
"Big Boss A Go-Go Party" (musical recording) 66, 75, 197
"Big Red Balloon" (musical recording) 194
The Big Snatch 153
Bigfoot 85
Black Dynamite 159
Black Garters 180–183
Black Rain 73
Black Silk Stockings 188
Blackmore, Ritchie 52
The Blacks 208
Blazing Saddles 224
Blood Feast 48
Blood of Dracula's Castle 32
Blood Monster 122; see also *Blood Shack*; *The Chooper*; *Curse of the Evil Spirit*
Blood Shack 120–135, 146, 154, 160, 179, 185, 191, 194, 213–214, 219–220, 241; see also *Blood Monster*; *The Chooper*; *Curse of the Evil Spirit*
"Blood Shack" (musical recording) 199
"Blood Valley Days" (musical recording) 199
Bloody Jack the Ripper 3, 132, 192, 214, 239
Bloody Vision 40–41
Bobbitt, John Wayne 231
Body Double 108–109
Body Fever **_9_**, 96–109, 111–112, 114, 123, 128, 132, 191–192, 194, 212–213, 215–216, 219–220,

245

226–227; see also *Cheat for Life*; *Deadlocked*; *The Last Original "B" Movie*; *Snowjob*; *Super Cool*
The Bog People 192
Bogart, Humphrey 99
Bond, David 9
Bond, Jane 156, 216; see also Brandt, Carolyn
Bond, Rene 11, 158–159
The Boo Boos (baseball team) 72
Boone, Buddy 155
Boorman, John 19–20
Born Again Savages (musical artist) 201
"Born to Be Wild" (musical recording) 52
The Bowery Boys 23, 82, 92, 107, 214
The Bowery Boys Meet the Monsters 83
Bowie, James 22, 24, 29, 59, 67, 207, 211
Boyd, Sunny 173, 192
Boys in Chains 162
Brady, Jack 24
Brain Damage 2
Brandt, Carolyn 2, 9–11, 19, 24–25, 29–30, 45, 52–53, 55, 65, 68–71, 73, 75, 76–79, 84, 87, 90, 93, 96–98, 101, 103, 105, 107, 120, 124, 127–128, 130–131, 132, 134–135, 138, 146, 150, 155–159, 162–164, 166–167, 169–175, 179–181, 184–185, 187, 190, 192, 196, 207–219, 222, 226, 235, 241–242; see also Bond, Jane
Breedlove, Craig 102
Brennan, Colleen 188
Brevin, Alan 217
Briggs, Joe Bob 30, 133
Bronkowski, Raleigh 8, 11–12, 18, 40, 62, 77, 86, 95, 116, 158, 164, 228, 242
Broskette, Corinne 234–236
Broulard, Gerard 157
Bryan, Dina 100
Bubba Ho-Tep 54
"Bud and Steak Square Off "(musical recording) 14
Bukowski, Charles 36
Bundy, Ted 143
Buñuel, Luis 96
Burns, Bob 74–75, 87, 211, 219
Burr, Ron 45, 53
Burton, Richard 52
Burton, Tim 100
The Busy "B" Theater 156

Caesar's Palace (Las Vegas, Nevada) 187
Caged Lust (book) 69
Caldwell, George (aka McCall, Force) 65, 67, 70

California Girls (aka *The Champ*) 177–179
Camel, Toni 25, 33
Camp Video 44, 145, 152
Cannes Film Festival 7
Cannibal Corpse Killers 233, 236
Capital Records 15, 68–69, 172
Capone, Al 49
Cardoza, Anthony 85
Carey, Romeo 190
Carey, Timothy 7–8, 70, 190, 207
Carlson, Michelle 146
Carol Kaye and the Stone Tones (musical artist) 36
Carolyn Brandt: Queen of Cult 145, 195–196
"Carolyn Brandt's Theme" (musical recording) 121, 127
Carpenter, John 124
Carradine, John 214
Carrol, Jerry 147, 232
Carsell, Bart 79, 84
Carson, Jill 23
Cash Flagg (musical artist) 199
"Cash Flagg" (musical recording) 199
Cassavetes, John 7
Cassidy, Rick 189
Castle, William 64
Cat on a Hot Tin Roof 10
Cathouse Fever 188–190
The Cauldron: Baptism in Blood 147
The Cave (movie theater) 141
Cave, Chris 144, 151, 194, 231, 234
CBS Studios 209
Cecil B. Demented 4
Center Drive-In Theater (Raleigh, North Carolina) 77
Cha Cha Records 51, 69
Chadwick, Onrita De
Chain Gang Women 112
Chambers, Chris 199
Chambers, Marilyn 138
Chandler, Larry 102
Chaplin, Charlie 23, 94
"Charlie Smith and Carrie Erskine Theme" (musical recording) 97
Charlie's Angels 213
Charlottetown Mall Charlotte, North Carolina 95
Cheat for Life 108; see also *Body Fever*, *Deadlocked*; *The Last Original "B" Movie*; *Snowjob*; *Super Cool*
"Choo Choo Cha-Bootchie" (musical recording) 26, 36
The Chooper 121–123, 132–134, 149–150, 194, 220, 241; see also *Blood Monster*; *Blood Shack*; *Curse of the Evil Spirit*
"The Chooper" (musical recording) 121, 124, 220

"The Chooper" (musical recording by Haunted Garage) 200
The Choppers 11–12, 15
Chressanthis, James 221
Chris Void & The Incredibly Strange Creatures Who Stopped Living and Became Mixed-Up Zombies!? (musical artist) 200
Church of the Subgenius 65
Cimino, Michael 19–20
The Cincinnati Kid 99
Clark, Tiffany 178
Clarke, James Kenelm 186
Clarke, Madison (aka Kirkwood, Pat) 25, 31
The Class Reunion 153
Cleopatra 94
Clive Barker's A-Z of Horror 195
Close Encounters of the Third Kind 19
Coe, Frank A. 124
Coffinberry, Jeano Roid 199–200, 242
Cohen, Mickey 49
Colt, John 169, 189
Columbia Pictures 27
Conners, Julie 96, 103
Conrad, Judy 197
Convent of the Sacred Heart 9
Cooperman, Jack 104, 211
Copner, Michael 240
Corman, Roger 195
The Corpse Grinders 12
Coscarelli, Don 119
Country Cuzzins 154
Couverts (musical artist) 200
Cox, Ronny 145
The Cramps (musical artist) 201
Craven, Wes 195
Creem (magazine) 43
The Creeping Cruds (musical artist) 199
The Crest Theater 196
Croft, Douglas 67
Cuckoo's Nest 217
Cult Flicks and Trash Pics (book) 143, 241
Cult Movies (magazine) 100, 109–110, 112, 119, 143, 152, 194, 239
Cult Movies TV 240
Cummings, Rita 162, 167
Cured by Porno (musical recording) 199
Curry, Julie Marie 241
Curry, Par 210
Curse of the Evil Spirit 121–134; see also *Blood Monster*; *Blood Shack*; *The Chooper*
Cushman, Ralph 208
The Cyclone Racer (roller coaster) 28, 31, 38, 196
Czar, Nancy (aka Czarnecki, Nancy Jean) 13, 15–16, 19, 21

"Daisy Dance" (musical recording) 14
Daisy Lay: Ozark Virgin? (aka *Daisy Lay and the 52 Pick-Ups*; *Daisy May: Ozark Virgin*; *Hillbilly Sex Clan*; *Inside Daisy Lay*; *Ozark Virgin*) 125–126, 154–155, 158–159, 170–171, 186
Dale, Syd 158–159
Danger God: The Lives and Love of a Hollywood Stuntman 119, 210, 227–229
Dante, Joe 195
Dark Alleys in a Well-Lit City 194, 234
Dark Eyes of London (internet blog and fanzine) 118
Darla, Darling 185, 187
Darush, Doug 159
Davis, Jerry 176, 183, 187, 189
Dead End Kids 82
The Dead Zone 218
Deadlocked 194; see also *Body Fever*; *Cheat for Life*; *The Last Original "B" Movie*; *Snowjob*; *Super Cool*
Deadly Weapons 165–166
Dearing, David 217
Death Proof 229–230
Debbie Does Dallas 183
Debbie Does Las Vegas 182–183, 187
DeChadwick, Orita 171–172
The Deep 84
Deep Purple (musical artist) 52
Deep Throat 116, 138, 190
Deeper Into the Incredibly Strange Music Box (musical recording) 201
The Deer Hunter 20
The Degenerate 67; see also *Baty y Roby contra el Crimen*; *The Insane*; *Rat Pfink a Boo Boo*; *Rock and Roll Super Heros*
The Del-Aires (musical artist) 43
Deliverance 19
Dementia Precox (musical artist) 198
Demos, Mary (Curtis, Mary Jo) 67, 214
Dennis, Rick 8, 22–23, 207
Dent, David 242
DePalma, Brian 108
Dern, Bruce 229
DeSalvo, Albert (The Boston Strangler) 139–140
Desert Maniacs 194; see also *Drivers to Hell*; *Wild Ones on Wheels*
Destroyer (musical recording) 139
Deviates in Love (aka *Fade to Red*) 175, 184, 187

The Devil In Miss Jones 138
Devilish Elvis (musical artist) 200
Devil's Little Acre (aka *Devil's Acre*; *Oakie Maid*) 159
The Devil's Sisters 33
DeVito, Danny 69
Diabolical Dr. Voodoo 40; see also *Face of Evil*; *Incredibly Mixed-Up Zombies*; *The Incredibly Strange Creatures Who Stopped Living and Became Mixed-Up Zombies!!?*; *Infernales Extranas Criaturas*; *The Teenage Psycho Meets Bloody Mary*
Dimension in Fear 147, 232
Dino's Lounge 15
The Dirtiest Game 70, 103
Dirty Rockers (musical artist) 200
Disney, Walt 48
Do You Wanna Be Loved? 49
Dobbs, Bob 65
Dobie, Pat 100
Dr. Jekyll and His Weird Show 64
Dr. Macabre's Frightmare of Movie Monsters 64
Dr. Satan's Shrieks in the Night 64
Dr. Strangelove Or: How I Learned to Stop Worrying and Love the Bomb 27, 52
Dr. Zomb 63
Dr. Zomb's Seance of Wonders 63
Dog Day Afternoon 84
The Doll Squad 54, 98, 109
Don Post Studios 40, 61
Don't Just Lay There 112
"Dope Doll Jungle" (music video) 198
Double Agent 73 166
Douglas, Kirk 215
Downey, Kathryn 149
The Downtown Cinema (Tampa, Florida) 116
Dozier, William 74
"Dream Your Dreams" (musical recording) 121, 124
Driller Killer 143
Drivers to Hell 8, 14–15; see also *Desert Maniacs*; *Wild Ones on Wheels*
Duke, Forrest 141
The Dunes (Las Vegas, Nevada) 147
Dvorak, Joe 149

"Eaffin' and Surfin'" (musical recording) 66–67, 200
East Side Kids 82
Easy Rider 32
Eating Raoul 142

Ebay.com 239, 241
Echo Park Lake 24
The Ecstasies of Women 172
The Ed Sullivan Show 47
Eddy, Nelson 49
Edgar, William 97
Edward Scissorhands 84, 100
Edwards, Steve 129
Eegah 11–12, 15, 19, 73, 208, 239
Eleanor Roosevelt 216
The Electric Ballroom (musical recording) 200
Elfman, Richard 89
Elizabeth Holloway School for the Theater 9
Elms, Desiré 169, 172, 188
E.M. Loews Center Theater (Boston, Massachusetts) 39
Emery, Geoff 52
Endless Lust 112
Enyo, Erina (Graham, Caroline) 24, 30, 34, 45, 51
Eraserhead 100
The Erotic Adventures of Hercules 162
The Erotic Adventures of Pinocchio 132–133, 214
Esper, Dwain 7
Evans, Rod 52
Everybody Loves It 64–65, 111
The Exorcist 224
The Exotic Dreams of Casanova 119

Face of Evil 192; see also *Diabolical Dr. Voodoo*; *Incredibly Mixed-Up Zombies*; *The Incredibly Strange Creatures Who Stopped Living and Became Mixed-Up Zombies*; *Infernales Extranas Criaturas*; *The Teenage Psycho Meets Bloody Mary*
Face of Evil (film short) 192
Fairway International Films 11, 17, 23–24, 38
Famous Monsters of Filmland (magazine) 69
Fangoria (magazine) 63, 77, 123, 192
Fantastic Monsters of the Films (magazine) 44, 69, 84
Farrell, Sharon 145
Fause, Nina 170, 186
Fawcett, Farrah 169
Fein, Bernard 96, 98, 213
Fellini, Federico 115
Female Trouble 126
Ferrara, Abel 143
The Fickle Finger of Fate 77
The 50 Worst Movies Ever Made 45
Film Alchemy: The Independent Cinema of Ted V. Mikels (book) 193

Filmfax (magazine) 96
Findlay, Michael 67
Findlay, Roberta 67
Finger Licking Good 162
First Church of Satan 239
Fisher, Larry 124
The Five Cs of Cinematography (booklet) 20
The Flamingo (Las Vegas, Nevada) 147, 187
Flesh (trilogy) 67
Flesh Gordon 155
The Flick Theater 138, 143
Flipper 33
Flothow, Rudolph C. 67
Flying Saucers Over Hollywood 8
Flynn, Tony 52–53, 75, 79, 92
Footloose 185
Forbes, Elliot 60
Forbidden Dimension (musical artist) 199
Forbidden Planet 29
Forbidden Zone 89
Forester, Robert 109
Frances, Coleman 38, 49, 79, 85, 88, 102–103, 213
Fraze, Ermal 56–57
Freeman, Hal 185
French Fantasies 139, 166–167, 180
French Heat 166–167, 171, 180
French Throat 166–167, 171, 180
Friedman, David F. 32, 89, 103, 153–154, 171
Friendly, Ed 214
Fulci, Lucio 143
The Fun House 54
Funny Money 187, 215

Gardner, Marla Lee 189
Garters and Lace 188
Genet, Jean 208
Get Out 218
Getting Straight 108
Ghost Men (musical artist) 200
The Ghost Whisperer 221
Ghoulston, Billy (aka Gholston, Billy) 43
Giant Claw Records 196
Giant Dipper (roller coaster) 196
Girard, Bernard
Girl in Gold Boots 141
The Girls from Thunder Strip 124
Glow, Bernard 110–111
God's Little Acre 159
Gods of Grindhouse (book) 241
The Golden Turkey Awards (book) 64, 68
Goldmine, Lovie 167, 192
Goof on the Loose 22–24, 73, 83, 94, 154, 158, 209, 223
Gorcey, Leo 82, 84
Göring, Hermann 50

Gourmet Zombie Chef from Hell 152
Grand Guignol Theater 60
Grant, April 141, 146
Grauman's Chinese Theater (Hollywood, California) 15, 48
Grauman's Egyptian Theater (Hollywood, California) 15
"Graveyard Stomp" (musical recording) 43; see also "Mixed-Up Zombie Stomp"; "Zombie Stomp"
Greenwood, Vaughn 139
The Greenwood Drive-In (Greenwood, Indiana) 62
Grier, Pam 109
Griffith, Charles B. 89
Griffith, Griffith J. 69
Griffith, Melanie 4
Griffith Park 69, 105–106
Grindhouse Purgatory (magazine) 241
Groundhog Day 129
Guilty Pleasures (video company) 239
Guthrie, Kelly 164, 170, 177, 186

Hair (stage production) 234
Hall, Arch, Jr. 2, 11, 16, 19, 21, 29, 38, 48, 110, 197, 208
Hall, Arch, Sr. 10–11, 13–14, 17, 22, 27, 38, 42, 51, 110, 114, 208; see also Merriweather, Nicholas; Watters, William
Hall, Huntz 82, 84, 91–92, 107
Halloween 61, 124, 143
Hallucinogenic Hypnosis 63
Hallucinogenic Hypnovision 3, 38–40, 62–64, 201
Hallucinogenic Hypnovision (musical recording) 199
Hammet, Dashiell 99
Hanks, Marvin 211
Hanks, Tom 147
Harlow 86
Harlow, Jean 86
Harmon, Jim 84
Harout, Yegishe 10
Hart, Marsha 160, 174
Hart, Veronica 112
Hartford, J. Jay 79
Haunted George (musical artist) 200
Haunted House (movie theater) 141
Haydock, Ron (Lord, Lonnie; Saxon, Vin) 24, 55, 59, 68, 71–72, 74, 75–76, 77, 84, 87, 96, 101–102, 120, 122, 124–125, 127, 131–133, 175, 192, 197, 199, 201, 211–212, 219–220
Hayward, Susan 28
Hazelwood, Lee 194
Heart of a Boy 147, 233

Heatherton, Joey 214
Heinrich, Rock 156–157
"The Hell Raisers" (musical recording) 158–159
The Hellcats 85
Hell's Angels on Wheels 54
Hell's Bloody Devils 32
Hell's Chosen Few 124
Help Me... I'm Possessed 136
Henenlotter, Frank 2–3
Hernandez, George 124, 127
Hetherington, Laura A. 150
Hewitt, David L. 54
Hewitt, Jennifer Love 221
Hiatt, Joanne 139
High Desert 236–237
Hillyer, Lambert 67
Hitchcock, Alfred 10, 47, 216
Hodgson, Joel 44
Hogan's Heros 98
Hogue, Jeffery C. 193, 232
Hollyweird 192
Hollywood International Stars Pictures 47
Hollywood She-Wolves 112
The Hollywood Strangler 143; see also *The Hollywood Strangler Meets the Skid Row Slasher*; *The Model Killer*
The Hollywood Strangler in Las Vegas 194; see also *The Las Vegas Serial Killer*
Hollywood Strangler Meets the Crippled Masters of Kung Fu (musical recording) 201
The Hollywood Strangler Meets the Skid Row Slasher 134–147, 149, 175, 177, 192, 194, 215, 220; see also *The Hollywood Strangler*; *The Model Killer*
The Hollywood Theater (Las Vegas, Nevada) 220
Holmes, John C. 178
The Holy Mountain 96
Hooper, Toby 123
Hopper, Dennis 32
Horn, James (musical artist) 200
The Horny Vampire (aka *Count Al-Cum*) 155, 157
Horror Castle 39
The Horror Drive-In (website/message board) 242
The Horror of Party Beach 42
Horror of the Blood Monsters 112
"How Do I Stand with Your Heart" (musical recording) 26, 35, 93
How to Make a Sex Movie!! 155–156, 160–161, 171
Howard, Joan 23
H.R. Pufnstuf 220
Hudson, Rock 28
Hungary in Flames 209; see also *Ungarn in Flammen*

Hunter, Tab **77**
Hypno-Disc 63
Hypno-Wheel 34, 36, 63

I Dismember Mama 68
I Kiss Your Shadow (musical recording) **199**
"I Stand Alone" (musical recording) 66, 72
I Was a Teenage Beatnik 196
The Ice House Comedy Club (Pasadena, California) 225
Ilsa, Harem Keeper of the Oil Shieks 155
Ilsa: She Wolf of the SS 173
"I'm Growing Taller" (musical recording) 14
IMDB.com 241
Immaculate Heart in Hollywood 9
Imperial Palace (Las Vegas, Nevada) 147, 187
The Incredible Two-Headed Transplant 54
Incredibly Mixed-Up Zombies 40; see also *Diabolical Dr. Voodoo*; *Face of Evil*; *The Incredibly Strange Creatures Who Stopped Living and Became Mixed-Up Zombies!!?*; *Infernales Extranas Criaturas*; *The Teenage Psycho Meets Bloody Mary*
The Incredibly Strange Animal Mothers Who Stopped Living and Became Mixed Up Zombies (musical recording) 200
"Incredibly Strange Creatures" (musical recording) 200
The Incredibly Strange Creatures Who Stopped Living and Became Apocalyptic Warriors (musical recording) 200
The Incredibly Strange Creatures Who Stopped Living and Became Mixed-Up Zombies!!? 19–20, 24–45, 47, 51, 53, 60, 62–63, 65, 68, 70–71, 73, 78, 82, 90, 93, 100–101, 104–105, 111, 114–116, 120–121, 123, 128, 137, 141, 149, 152, 190, 192, 197–199, 207–210, 221–224; see also *Diabolical Dr. Voodoo*; *Face of Evil*; *Incredibly Mixed-Up Zombies*; *Infernales Extranas Criaturas*; *The Teenage Psycho Meets Bloody Mary*
The Incredibly Strange Creatures Who Stopped Living and Became Mixed-Up Zombies (musical artist) 200
"The Incredibly Strange Creatures Who Stopped Living and Became Mixed-Up Zombies" (musical recording by Dementia Precox) 198
"The Incredibly Strange Creatures Who Stopped Living and Became Mixed-Up Zombies?!!?" (musical recording by Dirty Rockers) 200
"The Incredibly Strange Creatures Who Stopped Living and Became Mixed-Up Zombies" (musical recording by Invisible Ghost Men) 200
"The Incredibly Strange Creatures Who Stopped Living and Became Mixed-Up Zombies" (musical recording by Second-Hand Hero) 200
The Incredibly Strange Film Book 34, 201
The Incredibly Strange Film Show 34, 40, 61, 73, 194, 201, 233–234, 241
Incredibly Strange Films (book) 1–2, 6, 8, 11–12, 16, 20, 28, 63, 68, 72, 99, 114, 122, 133, 143, 192, 201, 239
Incredibly Strange Music volumes 1 and 2 (books) 201
The Incredibly Strange Music Box (musical recording) 201
The Incredibly Strange People Who Stopped Living and Became...The Creeping Cruds (musical recording) 199–200
The Incredibly Strange Ray Dennis Steckler 145, 195
The Incredibly Strange Record Club (musical recording) 201
The Incubus 81, 211
Indian Lady 183–185
The Indiana Theater (Indianapolis, Indiana) 62
Infernales Extranas Criaturas 41–42; see also *Diabolical Dr. Voodoo*; *Face of Evil*; *Incredibly Mixed-Up Zombies*; *The Incredibly Strange Creatures Who Stopped Living and Became Mixed-Up Zombies!!?*; *The Teenage Psycho Meets Bloody Mary*
The Insane 67; see also *Baty y Roby contra el Crimen*; *The Degenerates*; *Rat Pfink a Boo Boo*; *Rock and Roll Super Heros*
Insatiable 169
Inside Baby Sister 174
"Interior Dishonor" (musical recording) 199
Invisible Ghost Men (musical artist) 200
It's a Bikini World (aka *The Girl in Daddy's Bikini*) 213
"It's Not You" (musical recording) 26, 33
Ivar Theater (Hollywood, California) 10–11, 208–209
Ivory Snow 218

Jack the Ripper 139
Jackie Brown 109
Jackson, Pat (aka Romero, Patty) 96, 103
Jackson, Samuel L. 109
Jason, Ron 144, 146, 151, 194, 230–237
Jaws 224
Jaye, Bonita 30–31
Jefferson Airplane (musical artist) 82, 210, 212
Jeremy, Ron 112
The Jerk 84
Jesse James Meets Frankenstein's Daughter 68
The Jet Drive-In (Montgomery, Alabama) 12, 18
Jewels of the Sea (muscial recording) 113
Jodorowsky, Alejandro 96
Johnson, Lyndon B. 22
Johnson, Tor 61
Jones, Carolyn 35
Jones, Don 230
Joplin, Janis 82, 210
"Judy Poody" (musical recording) 14
Juno, Andrea 2, 201

Kannon, Mike 28, 33, 65, 67, 79, 83, 84, 88
Karson, Joe 41
Karston, Joe (aka Price, Joseph) 40–41, 63–64, 82, 212
Kaufman Astoria Studios 6
Kaye, Carol 26, 33
Kaye, John 52
Keaton, Buster 23, 94
Keitel, Harvey 7
Keller, Craig T. 193
Kennedy, Ken 78
Kent, Gary 7, 17, 46, 57–58, 64, 96, 98, 100, 103, 105, 111, 113, 117–119, 124, 199, 210, 225–230
Kerns, Ron 231
Kerswell, J.A. 143
Kevke, E.M. (aka Miles, David) 79, 90–91, 111, 117
The Keystone Cops 23, 94
"The Kidnappers" (musical recording) 14
Kiel, Richard 17, 208, 224–225
Kill Bill 2 109
Kim, Kim 156
King, Atlas (aka Kesdakian, Dennis) 2, 30, 33, 36, 45, 49–50, 207
King, Fritz 156
King, Stephen 218

King, Zalman 231
Kirksey, Kirk 83
KISS (musical artist) 139, 177
Kogar the Swinging Ape 65, 74, 78, 87
Kovács, László 5, 23, 32, 35, 209
Krskova, Leona 149
Kubrick, Stanley 7, 27–28, 52
Kulick, Bruce 177

Lamarr, Lilly 164
Landis, James 48
Lang, Charles 236
Lanza, Anthony M. 119
Las Vegas Erotica 186–187
The Las Vegas Serial Killer 144–152, 192, 194, 220, 231–233–235, 237, 239; see also *The Hollywood Strangler in Las Vegas*
The Las Vegas Thrill Killers 194, 233–236
Las Vegas Weekend 145, 220
Las Vegas Wives 176
The Last Movie 32
The Last Original "B" Movie 108; see also *Body Fever*; *Cheat for Life*; *Deadlocked*; *Snowjob*
The Last Time I Saw Archie 12
Laugh-In 214
Laugh-O-Color 82
Laura 215–216
Laurel, Stan 86
LaVey, Anton 239
Lease, Maria 117
Leave It to Beaver 31, 83
Lee, Bruce 162
Lee, Christopher 39
Leeds, Anna 162, 167
Leeman, John 142
Leer, Patrick M. 241
Legend, Johnny 63, 123, 192, 197
Legend of Hillbilly Butcher 233, 236
Lemoine, Michel 3
The Lemon Grove Kids (musical artist) 201
"The Lemon Grove Kids" (musical recording) 93–94
The Lemon Grove Kids and the Not-So Great Race 85; see also *The Lemon Grove Kids*; *The Lemon Grove Kids at the Great Race*; *The Lemon Grove Kids...Go Hollywood!*; *The Lemon Grove Kids Meet the Green Grasshopper and the Vampire Lady from Outer Space*; *The Lemon Grove Kids Meet the Monsters*
The Lemon Grove Kids at the Great Race 79, 81–88, 95; see also *The Lemon Grove Kids*; *The Lemon Grove Kids and the Not-So Great Race*; *The Lemon Grove Kids...Go Hollywood!*; *The Lemon Grove Kids Meet the Green Grasshopper and the Vampire Lady from Outer Space*; *The Lemon Grove Kids Meet the Monsters*
The Lemon Grove Kids...Go Hollywood! 92–95, 218; see also *The Lemon Grove Kids*; *The Lemon Grove Kids and the Not-So Great Race*; *The Lemon Grove Kids at the Great Race*; *The Lemon Grove Kids Meet the Green Grasshopper and the Vampire Lady from Outer Space*; *The Lemon Grove Kids Meet the Monsters*
The Lemon Grove Kids Meet the Green Grasshopper and the Vampire Lady from Outer Space 88–92, 95, 212, 218; see also *The Lemon Grove Kids*; *The Lemon Grove Kids and the Not-So Great Race*; *The Lemon Grove Kids at the Great Race*; *The Lemon Grove Kids...Go Hollywood!*; *The Lemon Grove Kids Meet the Monsters*
The Lemon Grove Kids Meet the Monsters 20, 24, 79–96, 103, 105, 108, 111, 114, 121–124, 128, 157, 191, 211–212, 215–216, 220, 223; see also *The Lemon Grove Kids*; *The Lemon Grove Kids and the Not-So Great Race*; *The Lemon Grove Kids at the Great Race*; *The Lemon Grove Kids...Go Hollywood!*; *The Lemon Grove Kids Meet the Green Grasshopper and the Vampire Lady from Outer Space*
Lemondrop the bassett hound 84
Leonard, Elmore 109
Levin, Lynn 115
Lewis, Herschell Gordon 1, 48, 54, 68, 103, 172, 194, 196, 198–199
Lieberman, Art 124
"Light My Fire" (musical recording) 210
Linda and Abilene 54
The Lindsey Theater (Lubbock, Texas) 40
Linna, Miriam 17, 133, 239
The Little County Jail 156
Little Miss Innocence 161–162
Little Orphan Dusty 141
Little Red Riding Hood 55
Lobato, Eber 77
Locked in the Arms of a Crazy Life (book) 36
Loew's Cinema 70 Theater (West Palm Beach, Florida) 86
London Hypnotic Seance 63

Long, Will 156, 162
Lopes, Trish 141–142
Lopez, Trini 210
Lord, John 52
Lott, Ruthann 157
Lovelace, Linda 138, 186
Lussler, Deke 21
Lust Vegas Joyride (aka *Heavenly Desires*) 177
Lustig, William 143
Lynch, David 50, 100
Lynch, Richard 145
Lyon International Distributors 7

MacGillivray, Scott 96
The Mack 84
Mad Dog Click 63, 194; see also *The Maniacs Are Loose*; *The Monsters Are Loose*; *The Thrill Killers*
The Mad Ghoul 38
The Mad Love Life of a Hot Vampire (aka *Hot Vampire* and *Love Life of a Red Hot Vampire*) 138, 156, 160–161, 174, 216
Madigan, Helen 182
The Magic of Sinbad 9, 207
Magnificent: Long Gone In the World of Incredibly Strange Music (musical recording) 201
Magnum P.I. 172
Mailer, Richard 159
Majors, Lee 169
The Making of The Incredibly Strange Creatures Who Stopped Living and Became Mixed-Up Zombies 195
Mallet's Bay Drive-In (Burlington, Vermont)
The Maltese Falcon 99, 102, 224
Man-Trap 98
Maniac 7, 143
The Maniacs Are Loose 46, 62–63; also *Mad Dog Click*; *The Monsters Are Loose*; *The Thrill Killers*
Mann, Groovy 198
Manson, Charles 54, 229–230
Mantalvan, Joaquin 233, 236–237
Margello, Franklin 162, 167
Mariel, Caylene 169
Marins, José Mojica (aka Coffin Joe) 35
Mark, Phillip 111
Mark of the Astro Zombies 147, 232–233
Markham, Pigmeat 88, 182
Martino, Rick 160
Marx, Groucho 174
Mary Poppins 48
Mascelli, Joseph V. 20, 32, 50, 59, 209
Mascot Video 145, 151, 195, 233

Mason, James 49
Matango, the Fungus of Terror 68
Matchi Manitou 122
Matuszak, John 145
Mawra, Joseph P. 67
Max Powa (musical artist) 200
Max Powa Encounters: The Incredibly Strange Creatures Who Stopped Living and Became Mind Controlled Monsters (musical recording) 200
Mayer, Devon 176
Mayer, Jim 176
Maynard, Antoinette 172
McCoy, Buzz 198
McDonald, John D. 99
McDowell, Rose 194
McGarter, Lane 164–165
McGill, Ormond 63; see also The Amazing Ormond
McGivney, Maura 209
McGowen, Tara 149–150
McQueen, Steve 99
McWatters, Ed 79, 85–86
Media Blasters (video company) 4, 27, 30, 38, 53, 67, 95, 108, 123, 132, 211, 239
Medium Cool 108
Medved, Harry 64, 68
Medved, Michael 64, 68
The Mel Theater (Detroit, Michigan) 164
Mermaids of Tiburon 113
Merriweather, Nicholas 42; see also Hall, Arch, Sr.; Watters, William
Meyer, Russ 1, 29, 113, 194, 198
Michael Shayne (television series) 98
Midnight Movies Collections 1 and 2 239
Midnite Plowboy 154
Mikels, Ted V. 1–2, 12, 54, 68, 98, 109, 141, 147, 193–194, 196, 198–199, 232–233, 237, 242
Miksell, Cody (musical artist) 200
Milland, Ray 49
Miller, Gene 170, 172, 188
Miller, Gordon (aka Drake, Tommy) 189
Mills, Barbara 112
Misery 218
Misfits (musical artist) 198
Miss Nymphet's Zap-In 103
Miss Stardust of Arizona 49
Miss World Burlesque 147–149, 185
Mission: Killfast 147, 232
"Mixed Up Zombie" (musical recording by Animal Mothers) 200
"The Mixed-Up Zombie Stomp" (musical recording) 26,
38, 43; see also "Graveyard Stomp"; "Zombie Stomp"
The Model Killer 143; see also *The Hollywood Strangler*; *The Hollywood Strangler Meets the Skidrow Slasher*
Moede, Titus (aka Moody, Titus) 46, 51–52, 59, 65, 70, 76, 103, 112, 124, 210, 240
Mom and Dad 7, 60
Mondo Macabro (video company) 3
Mondo Steckler 2
"Money and Records" (musical recording) 14
Mono Men (musical artist) 198
Monogram Studios 59
Monroe, Mary 173
The Monster Times (magazine) 24, 44, 192, 199
Monster World (magazine) 73
The Monsters Are Loose 62; see also *Mad Dog Click*; *The Maniacs Are Loose*; *The Thrill Killers*
Monsters Crash the Pajama Party 41
Monstrosity (aka *The Atomic Brain*) 20
Moon, Millie 170, 172, 188
Moore, Ken 156
Moran, Henry 162, 162
"More More More" (musical recording) 177
Morgan, Chesty 166
Morgan, George J. 23–24, 27–28, 30–31, 38, 40, 44–45, 47, 49, 51–53, 56, 60, 69, 84–85, 94, 110, 145, 209
Morgan, Mary 52, 84, 94
Morgan, Read 49
Morgan-Steckler Productions 24, 45, 49, 65–66, 87, 209
Morris, Eric 79, 93
Morris, Lori 136
Morton, Jim 99, 133, 143, 242
Motorpsycho 103
Mousetrap (board game) 23
Movies Illustrated (magazine) 52
MTV (music television) 20, 44
Mudhoney 29
The Munsters 73
Murray, Bill 129
The Music Box Kid 98
Mute Records 194–195
My First 2,000 Men (book) 49
My Life with the Thrill Kill Kult (musical artist) 198
Mystery Science Theater 3000 (MST3K) 44

N A B E T (National Association of Broadcast Employees and Technicians) 211, 213, 218

Nabors, Jim 177
Napier, Charles 145
Nash Rambler 10, 36, 147, 150–151, 207
The Nazz (musical artist) 82
Necromania: A Tale of Weird Love (aka *Necromania*; *Necromania: A Tale of Weird Love!*) 112, 153–154, 159
Needham, Hal 230
New Steppenwolf (musical artist) 52 see also Steppenwolf
New York City Physicians Hospital 9
New York, New York 32, 143
New York Ripper 143
Newmar, Julie 210
A Night at the Follies 7
Night of the Ghouls 85
"Night of the Sadist" (musical recording) 197
Night Train to Mundo Fine 85
"99 Chicks" (musical recording) 69, 201
Nizet, Charles 136
The Nomads (musical artist) 198
Non (musical artist) 194
Norton Records 17, 133, 239
The Notorious Daughter of Fanny Hill 32
Novak, Harry 154

The Oasis (Las Vegas, Nevada) 147, 187
O'Brien, Keith (Pierce, Keith) 46, 54–55
O'Connell, Joe 119, 227–229
O'Day, Alan 21
O'Farrell, Barbara 173
O'Hara, Brett 24, 28, 34
Okeus 122
Old King Grasshopper (book) 211
Olga series 67
Olivera, Carmen 159
One Man Force 145
One Million AC/DC 118, 227
One More Time 196–197
Once Upon a Time... in Hollywood 119, 159, 210, 229–230
Only in America 209
"Open My Eyes" (music video) 82
"Organ Twist" (musical recording) 14
Orgy of the Dead 112, 153
Orlando (British television series) 159
Orlando, Charles 160, 170, 186, 192
Oswalt, Patton 77
Ouspenskaya, Maria 38

P A C Theater (Laguna Woods Village, California) 215, 216

Pantages Theater 15
Paranoia (aka *The Seduction of Monica*) 139, 167, 177
Parasite 218
The Paris Theater (Los Angeles, California) 158
Parker, Art 189
Parker, Ben 48
Parker, Jim 138–139, 156, 216, 220
Parker, P.J. 138, 140–141, 156, 220
Parts Unknown (musical recording) 198
Pasadena Playhouse 54
Passport Video 45
Peanuts the Pony 129–130
Pearson, Brett 99, 107, 110
Peck, Gregory 70
Peeping Tom (aka *The Creeper*) 125, 160–162
Pepper, Jeannie 150
Percepto 64
The Perfect Storm 73
Perkowski, Andre 196
Perverted Passion (aka *Fire Down Below*) 125, 162–163, 167–168, 176, 179, 192
Peters, George 154, 170, 186
Petty, Rhonda Jo 169, 178, 185, 189
Phibes, Jackson (musical artist) 200
The Picture of Dorian Gray 29
Pictures (musical recording) 200
"The Pied Piper of Love" (musical recording) 34
The Pike (Long Beach, California) 28, 196, 223
Pillow Talk 139
Pit Stop 70
Pitt, Brad 230
Plato's Retreat 141
Plato's Retreat 2 141
Plato's Retreat West 140–141, 172, 181, 186
Plato's Retreat West 188
Playboy (magazine) 234
Pleasure Motel 161–163
Plunkett, Jim 86
Poison Ivy (musical artist) 201
Pollack, Gene 30, 59
Pollygrind Film Festival 236
Pool Once (musical recording) 14
Pop Tab 56–57
Pork Chop Hill 70
Post, Don 61–62
Presley, Elvis 11–12
Price, Henri (aka Brummer, André) 29, 114, 124, 151, 221–222
Prison Babies 112
Producers Releasing Corporation (PRC) 10, 59

Psycho 24, 47–48
Psycho a Go-Go 19
Psychos IN Love 142
Psychotic Reactions and Carburetor Dung (book) 43
The Psychotronic Encyclopedia of Film (book) 241
Psychotronic Video Guide (book) 10, 108, 119, 152, 241

Quinn, Libby 26, 29, 43

Rabinowitz, Mort 54
Raincheck Room (Hollywood, California) 228
The Rammrodder 89, 153
Randal, Teri 26, 36
Randall, Anne 97
Ranger, Mike 169, 172, 179, 181, 188
Rat Fink 68
"Rat Fink" (musical recording by Allan Sherman) 198
"Rat Fink" (musical recording by Mono Men) 198
"Rat Fink" (musical recording by Ron Haydock) 66, 71–72, 197
"Rat Fink a Boo Boo" (musical recording by The Nomads) 198
"Rat Fink a Boo Boo" (musical recording by Zorros Petardos Salvajes) 199
"Rat Finks, Suicide Tanks and Cannibal Girls" (musical recording) 198
Rat Pfink a Boo Boo 1, 40, 65–79, 82, 85–86, 91–92, 105, 114–115, 121, 123, 131, 136, 152, 158, 194–196, 200–201, 210, 212, 223; see also *Baty y Roby contra el Crimen*; *The Degenerate*; *The Insane* and *Rock and Roll Super Heros*
"Rat Pfinky" (musical recording) 200
Rausch, Andrew J. 241
The Ravager 136
Ray Dennis Steckler Is "The Teenage Psycho": The Steckler Collection 195
Ray Dennis Steckler Presents a Tribute to Carolyn Brandt 196
Rebel Drifters Ride Again 233, 237
Red Heat 136, 141, 159, 167–168, 176, 180, 192
RegularScope 66
R E L records 43
The Ren and Stimpy Show 159
Renay, Brenda 49, 51
Renay, Liz 45, 49, 51, 58, 98, 104, 158, 210, 226
Republic Studios 59

Reservoir Dogs 7
The Resurrection of Eve 138
Rettig, Tommy 207
The Return of the Hollywood Strangler 152
Revenge of the Ripper 192
Revue Studios 15
Reynolds, Burt 230
Reynolds, R.J. 170, 172, 178, 188
Rice, Boyd 1, 6, 8, 11, 16, 20, 28, 61, 63, 68, 72, 114, 122, 192, 194–195, 239, 242
Ride Out of the Past 231, 237
Ring of Desire 112
Ripple, Jeremy Von 174
Ritter, Tex 112
Roan, Shula (aka Allison, Bonnie) 110–112
Roberts, Jean 140, 149
Roberts, John 2, 20
Robins, Herb (Rabinowitz, Herb) 46, 53–55, 57, 79, 84, 91, 93, 96, 98, 102, 110–111, 115, 122, 192, 195–196, 210, 218–219
The Rock 73
Rock and Roll Monsters (musical recording) 200
Rock and Roll Super Heros 68, 194; see also *Baty y Roby contra el Crimen*; *The Degenerate*; *The Insane*; *Rat Pfink a Boo Boo*
Rogers, Bill 33
Roller Coasters (book) 31
The Rolling Stones (musical artist) 47
Romeo Carey Podcast 190
Ron Haydock and the Boppers (musical artist) 51, 69, 239
Ron Haydock and the Boppers 99 Chicks (musical recording) 133
Roose, Ken Van (musical artist) 200
Ross, Jonathan 34, 40, 73, 194, 201, 233
Roter, Ted (Balocoff, Boris) 88, 92–93, 110–113
Roth, Ed "Big Daddy" 67–68, 198
Rothman, Stephanie 213
Rowan, Eddie (or Roland) 17
Roxy, Rox Anne 84, 215–216
Rufus Potter's Hooker Scam 172, 192
Rum Punch (book) 109
Rush, Richard 54, 108, 119
Russell, Kurt 230
Rutherford, Scott 31

Sacrilege 157–158
The Sadist 48
The Sahara (Las Vegas, Nevada) 187
Samples, Candy 158

Santa Cruz Beach Boardwalk 196
Santo and Johnny (musical artist) 67
Sarno, Alberto 142
Satanis: The Devil's Mass 239
Satan's Sadists 19, 38, 54
Satryicon 115
Savage, Becky 188, 189
Savage, Glenda 148, 232–233
Savage, Herschel 189
Scherman, Tom 28, 37, 48, 67–68, 212
Schlatter, George 214
Schlitz Brewing Company 56
Schneider, Don 23
Scopitones 210
Scorcese, Martin 32
Scream of the Butterfly 77, 81
Seasons in the Sun (musical recording) 194
Second-Hand Hero (musical artist) 200
Secret File: Hollywood 10, 208–209, 239
Seiber, Mark 242
Seka 177
Semple, Lorenzo, Jr. 74
The Sentinels (musical artist) 67
Serial Mom 199, 221
Seven Brides for Seven Brothers 210
Seven Women for Satan 3
77 Sunset Park 195
Sex-a-Reenos (book) 69
Sex Rink 140–141, 169–172, 176, 179–180, 188, 192
The Sex Shuffle (aka *The Love Shuffle*; *The Shuffle*) 110
Sexloose (aka *Las Vegas Hustle*) 185
The Sexorcist (aka *The Sexorcist Devil*; *The Sexorcist's Devil*; *Undressed to Kill*) 163–167, 176, 216
Shades of Grey (review website) 77
Shadows 7
Shadows & Light: Journey's with Outlaws in Revolutionary Hollywood (book) 7, 17, 54, 64, 100, 103, 199, 226
"Shaft" (musical recording) 178
Shakespeare, William 207
"Shanty Tramp" (musical recording) 196
Shatner, William 61, 81, 211
Shea, Cindy 87, 211
Sheer Panties 188
Sherman, Allan 198
The Sherman Theater (Indianapolis, Indiana) 62
Shields, Laverne 189
Shock Theater (television show) 138

"Shook Out of Shape" (musical recording) 26, 36
Shriek Show (video company) 239
Sidaris, Andy 210
Siegel, Bugsy 49
Simone, Starlyn 154, 170, 186
Sinatra, Nancy 194
Sinclair, Snowy 137
Simon of the Desert 96
Sin-O-Ram (movie theater) 141
Singer, James Elliot 100, 109–110, 112, 119, 143, 152, 194, 240
Sinthia: The Devil's Doll 98, 110–120, 123, 125, 127–128, 154, 190, 194, 200, 212–213, 227, 239; see also *Teenage She Devil*; *Where the Devil Toils*
Siodmak, Curt 122
Ski Fever 81, 122
"Skid Row Slasher" (musical recording) 201
Skin Deep 184–185
The Skydivers 85
Slashed 192
The Slasher Movie Book (book) 143
Slatzer, Robert F. 85
A Smell of Honey, a Swallow of Brine 32
Smith Brother's Studios 53
Smith, Bonnie 139
Smith, C. (Charles) Davis 157
Smith, Greta 156
Smith, Alan 30, 33–34, 101
Smoke on the Water: The Deep Purple Story (book) 52
Snowjob 108; see also *Body Fever*; *Cheat for Life*; *Deadlocked*; *The Last Original "B" Movie*
Snyder, Don 26, 35, 74, 79, 93–94, 97
Snyder, Patty 160–161
Somebody Down There Likes Me (musical recording) 199
Something Weird Video 239, 241
Son of a Rat Pfink 195
Son of Incredibly Strange Film Show 194, 201
The Son of the Hollywood Strangler 152, 194
Sonney, Dan 7
Sonney, Dorothy K. 110–111
Soul of the Demon 236
The Sounds of Syd Dale (musical recording) 159
Sounes, Howard 36
South of the Border 125, 170–171, 176, 184
"The South's Gonna Rise Again" (musical recording) 197
Spahn, George 230
Spahn Ranch 54, 119

Spay, Rob 241
Specimen: Female 159
Spell (musical artist) 194
Spelling, Aaron 35
Spelvin, Georgina 112
Spiderman (animated series) 159
Spielberg, Steven 31
Spiritual Psychic Science Church 64
Spook Busters 92
Spooks Run Wild 82
Spring, Laurel 126, 214
Stacey 97
"Stairfall" (musical recording) 14
"Steak's Theme" (musical recording) 14
Steckler, Bailey 194–196–197, 223, 232
Steckler, Katherine 145, 148–150, 195, 197, 232, 235, 237
Steckler, Laura H. (Jeannie; Rae; Tickles) 44, 79, 92, 107, 113, 124, 130, 141, 146, 150, 194, 196, 213, 218–225, 231–232, 241–242
Steckler, Linda (Christina) 30, 75, 79, 92, 113, 124, 130, 146, 150, 194, 197, 219–220–221, 223–224, 231–232
Steckler, Morgan 145, 148–150, 194, 196, 223, 232
The Steckler Collection 195
Steckler Interviews Volume #1 2, 20, 145, 195
Steckler Mania 145, 195
Steppenwolf (musical artist) 52; see also New Steppenwolf
Stillman, Neil 33
Strawberry Switchblade (musical artist) 194
Suburban Confidential 112
Suburbia Confidential 112
Sugarplum the puppy 130
Sullivan, Dave 21
Summer Fun 195, 223
Sun Art Enterprises 110–111
Sunset Boulevard 69
Sunshine, Sandy 169–171, 187, 188
Super Cool 108; see also *Body Fever*; *Cheat for Life*; *Deadlocked*; *The Last Original "B" Movie*; *Snowjob*
Sutur (musical artist) 198
Swanson, Liz 162, 167
Swenson, Denise 170, 172, 188
Swink, Lenore 162, 167

Taboo 169
Take It Out in Trade 153
Tarantino, Quentin 7–8, 109, 119, 229–230
A Taste of Blood 33
Taziner, Rick 174

Teenage Dessert 171, 179
Teenage Hustler (aka *Young Hustle*) 139, 172, 174, 184, 192
Teenage Innocence 188
Teenage Massage Parlor (aka *Massage Parlour*) 139, 217
The Teenage Psycho Meets Bloody Mary 39–41, 156; see also *Diabolical Dr. Voodoo*; *Face of Evil*; *Incredibly Mixed-Up Zombies*; *The Incredibly Strange Creatures Who Stopped Living and Became Mixed-Up Zombies!!?*; *Infernales Extranas Criaturas*
Teenage Seductress 49, 188
Teenage She Devil 118, 194 see also *Sinthia: The Devil's Doll* and *Where the Devil Toils*
Teenage Strangler 48
Tenney, Del 42–43
Terrorama 26
The Texas Chainsaw Massacre 123
Tharp, Cathy 61
Tharp, Rob 61–62
"Theme from Wild Guitar" (musical recording) 14
They Live. They Strike. (musical recording) 200
This Island Earth 103
Thompson, Dave 52
Thorn, Dyanne 214
The Three Stooges 20, 92
The Thrill Killers 4, 20, 45–66, 70, 75, 82, 92, 100, 111, 114, 121, 126, 128, 133, 136, 152, 194, 198–199, 210–211, 220, 225–226, 228; see also *Mad Dog Click*; *The Maniacs Are Loose*; *The Monsters Are Loose*
The Thrill Killers (musical artist) 201
Throw Mama from the Train 69
Tibbs Drive-In (Indianapolis, Indiana) 62
"Tickles" (the toy doll) 222–223
Tierney, Lawrence 8
Ties, Rick 232
The Tingler 64
Tobacco Roody 154
A Touch of Love 179–180, 183–184
Trader Hornee 103
Tranum, Charles B. 67
Trevillion, Dale 145, 220
A Tribute to Ron Haydock 195
Trip with the Teacher 166, 231
Triple Play 158–159
True, Andrea 170, 177, 182, 186
Truelove, Debbie (aka Moreno, Chica) 169–170, 177, 182–183, 185–187, 189
Tsentas, Jane 157
Tulip, Jenny 160, 174

Turn Off 214
Turner, Bill (aka Ward, Bill) 29, 33–34, 222–223
Turner, Glenda 173
Turner, Lana 215
The Twin Drive-In Theater 22
"Twist Fever" (musical recording) 14, 20
Two Lost Films by Ray Dennis Steckler 195

Undergraduate 155
Ungarn in Flammen 209; see also *Hungary in Flames*
Universal Studios 10, 38, 40, 216
University of Nevada, Las Vegas (UNLV) 138, 235–236
Uno Mas (magazine) 8
Up from the Depths 89
Up Your Alley 124

Vale, V. 201
Van, Bert Leu 22–23
Variety (magazine) 76–77
The Vegas Vampire 138, 156, 216, 220
The Velvet Trap 77–78, 81
Venus Movie Arcade 141
"Vickie" (musical recording) 14, 19
"Vickie, Run" (musical recording) 14
Video Archives (Manhattan Beach, California) 109
Video Hound 241
Viet, Howard 77
Vincent, Gene 51
Vinegar Syndrome (video company) 241
The Virgin Cowboy 98
The Vista Continental Theater (Hollywood, California) 8
Void, Chris (musical artist) 200

Wagner, Edward C. 87
Walsh, Sharon 31, 207
Wanda: The Sadistic Hypnotist 158
War Balm (musical artist) 200
War Cat (aka *Angel of Vengeance*) 147, 193, 231–233
Ware, Danny 43
Warfield, Chris (aka Thornburg, Billy) 161–162, 188
Warning: No Tresspassing 192
Wasmund, Gerd 185
Waters, John 4, 126, 198–199, 221
Waterworld 73
Watson, Wade "Doc" 96, 103
Watters, William 17, 42; see also Hall, Arch, Sr.; Merriweather, Nicholas
Wayne, Jason 120, 125, 154, 160, 170, 173, 174
We Want Our Mummy 92

Webber, Diane 110, 113
Weekend Cowgirls 184–186,
Weldon, Michael 10, 108, 119, 152, 197, 241
Wersterbergs Serve Hospital Food (musical artist) 199–200
West, Mae 53
Wester, Keith (aka Danger, Dean) 68, 73, 87–88, 93, 97, 104, 107, 110, 210
Wexler, Haskell 108
Wham Bam Thank You Spaceman 141
What Ever Happened to Baby Jane? 218
What's Up Front? 23
Where the Devil Toils 118; see also *Sinthia: The Devil's Doll*; *Teenage She-Devil*
WHHY (radio station) 18
Whisky a Go Go 68
"White Rabbit" (music video) 82, 210, 212
White Zombie (musical artist) 198
Wide World of Sports 159, 210
Wieternik, Nora 155
The Wig and I 213
Wild, Free and Hungry 112
Wild Guitar 12–23, 32, 45, 47–48, 51, 68, 72, 83, 85, 108, 115, 208–209, 239
Wild Guitar (song) 18
Wild Guitar: Arch Hall Jr. and the Archers (musical recording) 17, 239
Wild Ones on Wheels 8–9, 23, 28–30, 90, 100, 194, 239; see also *Desert Maniacs*; *Drivers to Hell*
The Wild Wild World of Mondo Movies Music (musical recording) 239
Wilde, Oscar 29
Wilder, Billy 69
Wilkerson, Joe 148
Williams, Dick Anthony 84
Williams, Maggie 173
Williams, Wayne 164
Wilson, Lewis 67
Wilson, Liz 173
Wine, Women and Horses 68
Wishman, Doris 157, 165–166
The Wizard of Oz 224
The Wolf Man 38
Wolfe, Kedric 79, 89
Wolfschmidt Vodka 123
The Wonderland Murders 178
Wood, Ed 1, 8, 112, 118, 153–155, 159, 198
Woodman, Joan 162, 167
Woods, Bambi 183
The World's Greatest Sinner (aka *Frenzy*) 7–8, 23, 54, 70, 190, 199, 207–208, 239

"The World's Greatest Sinner" (musical recording) 196
The Worm Eaters 54, 219

xhamster.com 241

"Yes, I Will" (musical recording) 14, 17–18
Yocum Brother Cigars 6, 146
York, Francine 208
York Theater (Los Angeles, California) 44

"You're My Love" (musical recording) 142
"You're Running Wild" (musical recording) 51, 66, 69

Zappa, Frank 8, 196
Zeller, Brett 98, 111–112, 115
Zenker, Veronica 148
Zombie, Rob 198
Zombie Spaceship Wasteland (book) 77
"Zombie Stomp" (musical recording by the Del-Aires) 43
"Zombie Stomp" (musical recording) 25, 43; *see also* "Graveyard Stomp"; "Mixed-Up Zombie Stomp"
Zorros Petardos Salvajes (musical artist) 199
Zsigmond, Vilmos 19–20, 23, 31–32, 35, 37, 59, 209, 222
Zutger, Richard 164

www.ingramcontent.com/pod-product-compliance
Lightning Source LLC
Chambersburg PA
CBHW060339010526
44117CB00017B/2885